CLASS
OF
2000

THE MAKING OF A CHAMPION TEAM

SUDEEPT

Copyright © Sudeept 2024
All Rights Reserved.

ISBN 979-8-89519-599-4

This book has been published with all efforts taken to make the material error-free after the consent of the author. However, the author and the publisher do not assume and hereby disclaim any liability to any party for any loss, damage, or disruption caused by errors or omissions, whether such errors or omissions result from negligence, accident, or any other cause.

While every effort has been made to avoid any mistake or omission, this publication is being sold on the condition and understanding that neither the author nor the publishers or printers would be liable in any manner to any person by reason of any mistake or omission in this publication or for any action taken or omitted to be taken or advice rendered or accepted on the basis of this work. For any defect in printing or binding the publishers will be liable only to replace the defective copy by another copy of this work then available.

Contents

SECTION 3: THE TRANSITION

SECTION 4: THE CLIMAX

Author's Note

My earliest cricket memory is of a sleepy December afternoon in 1989, watching a 16-year-old in a classic white helmet dancing down the pitch and smashing the legendary Abdul Qadir for four sixes in a single over. This incredible performance announced his arrival on the world stage in spectacular fashion. (No prizes for guessing who I am talking about). That moment etched itself in my subconscious as a 'core memory' that otherwise, I doubt a 7-year-old could have preserved so vividly.

It also sparked my lifelong love affair with the wonderful game of cricket, a love that remains strong even after 35 years. If anything, it's only grown stronger, maturing like a fine wine, just as all true loves do.

From adolescent dreams of winning the World Cup for India by hitting a last-ball six off Imran Khan, to skipping classes and tuitions—and even, in one memorable instance, a 'date' with my first teenage crush (which might explain my current relationship status)—cricket has always been my top priority. I remember those days fondly, losing track of time while playing in rustic tennis-ball cricket tournaments in the mofussil town of Sitapur, my beloved hometown near Lucknow. The years from 1996 to 2000 were the best days of my life, filled with the unbridled joy and boundless passion of a true cricket aficionado.

After cricket, my greatest passion has always been books. From as far back as I can remember, I've been a voracious reader. I devoured everything from comic books of *Super Commando Dhruv*, *Doga*, and *Phantom* to Enid Blyton's *The Famous Five* and *The Secret Seven*, and even magazines like

Filmfare and *India Today*. Whatever I could get my hands on, I read it all (as long as it wasn't part of my school syllabus).

Around 1996, during one of my many reading sessions, I stumbled upon *Azhar - A Definitive Biography* by the eminent Harsha Bhogle. To my delight, I discovered that reading about cricket could be just as thrilling as playing it or watching it on television. From that moment on, reading about cricket was added to my growing list of interests. *The Sportstar* and *Cricket Samrat* soon joined *Filmfare* and *India Today* on my monthly reading list.

The second cricket book I read and loved was *Sunny Days* by the great Sunil Gavaskar. From there, cricket books became a staple of my reading diet. Some books that left a lasting impression on my young mind included the classic *Beyond a Boundary* by the legendary C.L.R. James, *Fifty Years of West Indian Cricket* by the great Tony Cozier, and more recently, *The Unquiet Ones* by the wonderful Osman Samiuddin.

But never in my wildest dreams could I have imagined that one day I would be writing one myself!

Then social media came along, and I jumped on the bandwagon like everyone else. I started expressing myself on Orkut, the top platform at the time, and later transitioned to Facebook around 2012-2013. To my pleasant surprise, my posts resonated with many, who encouraged me to write more and even consider it professionally. By then, I had joined the IT industry and wasn't doing badly enough to think about alternative careers. Besides, my top priority during those years was looking after my ailing father, who had recently been diagnosed with stage 3 Hepatitis C. As a result, I could never devote enough time to writing, aside from some casual blogging.

In 2020, my father passed away after a heroic last stand of 24 days in the ICU. It took us a couple of years to come to *some semblance of* terms with our grief. Then, spurred on by the constant encouragement of my mother and younger brother, I decided to write a book. However, for months, I struggled to zero down on a subject or genre. That's when my dear Maa again came to my rescue, suggesting I should write about cricket, my passion and comfort zone. It was a Eureka moment for me, and I conceived an ambitious dream project: a story about the rise and rise of Indian cricket in the 21st century, from the year 2000 to the present day.

As I began writing, I soon realized that covering such a vast span of time in just one book was too ambitious. So, the idea evolved into a trilogy: Book 1 would chronicle events from 2000-2007, Book 2 from 2008-2015, and Book 3 from 2016-2025.

I began working on Book 1 on the auspicious day of Hindu New Year, April 2, 2022 (as the pinned post on my Instagram can attest) and completed the first draft on my Maa's birthday, October 5, 2023, after almost 18 months. Writing this book has been a journey of passion, dedication, and self-discovery. As I immersed myself in the period from 2000-2007, drawing heavily from ESPNcricinfo's extensive archives and old YouTube footage, I found myself learning and growing alongside the stories I uncovered.

So, dear reader, I'm pleased to present to you, Book 1 of 'The Century of India' Trilogy: **Class of 2000 - The Making of a Champion Team**

This book chronicles the phoenix-like rise of Indian cricket, from the ashes of the match-fixing scandal to the crowning glory of the inaugural T20 World Cup; and the key figures and architects behind this epic resurrection. The USP of this book—if I may say so myself—is its riveting account of every single match ever played by the Indian cricket team between the year 2000 and the T20 World Cup final in 2007. Be it a Test match, a one-day international, or a T20 international, and even the first-class practice matches that serve as warm-ups on international tours.

As my first book, this work represents a true labour of love, born from countless hours of research, writing, revision, and re-revision. I've poured my heart and soul into it, and I sincerely hope you find it enjoyable.

Happy reading!

Prologue

The new millennium couldn't have begun on a more eventful note for the sport of Cricket. South Africa had just concluded a two months tour to India, comprised of 2 Tests and 5 ODIs. South Africa clean-swept India to take the Test series 2-0; in the process becoming the first team to beat India in India in 13 years. Before this, the last team to manage this feat was Pakistan in 1987.

This comprehensive debacle, following close on the heels of similar heart-breaking drubbing down under a few months earlier, not to mention some unconfirmed reports of a rift with some board officials, prompted Sachin Tendulkar to resign from captaincy just before the start of the ODI leg. Sourav Ganguly, who had been in the form of his life for the past couple of years, especially in ODIs, was appointed the captain for the upcoming assignment ahead of frontrunners Anil Kumble and Ajay Jadeja, perhaps owing to the fact that he was a certainty in both formats. To his credit, he took to this elevation at such a short notice with elan, leading from the front with some inspired batting and captaincy to take the ODI series against a formidable team like South Africa, 3-2.

After the five-match series, both teams headed to UAE for the Coca-Cola Cup, where India's fortunes took a turn for the worse. They failed to reach the final, losing twice to South Africa and once to Pakistan. They managed to beat Pakistan only once, and that too unconvincingly, thus ending a most stormy season on a low note.

It was around this time that the Delhi police happened to accidentally intercept a call between a bookie and the then South African captain Hansie Cronje. Delhi police was tapping some phone numbers in the hope of catching Underworld but stumbled upon a conversation about fixing cricket matches for money purely by chance.

Murmurs about match-fixing in cricket had been around since as early as late 1800s when the game was still in its infancy. So, it would not be wrong to claim that match fixing, in some form or the other, is as old as Cricket itself. However, it became institutional in the late 1980s only when Sharjah began hosting Cricket matches. Since then, the rumours have been steadily gaining in strength but nothing had been substantiated as yet.

But all that was to change now.

On April 7 2000, Delhi police charge-sheeted South African captain Hansie Cronje for match fixing and by April 11, after initially refuting the charges, a distressed Cronje had confessed of his role to the Chairman of South Africa cricket board, Dr Ali Bacher in a 3am phone call, in light of which Cronje was sacked as the captain and King's Commission was set to conduct a thorough enquiry into the whole affair and bring out the whole truth.

The commission got to work in earnest. Players like Jacques Kallis, Pat Symcox, Herschelle Gibbs and Nicky Boje testified before the commission, more or less confirming the allegations and by the end of August, the commission wrapped up the enquiry, submitted its findings and pressed charges.

Hansie Cronje was found guilty of match fixing and banned for life. Gibbs and Boje were banned for six months each.

Now, Hansie Cronje was not just the captain of South Africa's cricket team but arguably the most respected personality after 'Madiba' Nelson Mandela himself. His involvement in such a sordid act as throwing away matches for money came out as a terrible shock to the sport loving nation of South Africa.

But South Africa by no means was going to be the only cricket playing nation shook to its core as a result of this disclosure. The ripples were to reach Indian shores soon.

Cronje, very early on in the investigation before King's commission in South Africa, named the then Indian captain Mohammad Azharuddin as the one who introduced him to Mukesh Gupta, another blacklisted bookie kingpin who ran a syndicate of sorts who eventually offered him to fix matches for money as early as in 1996.

Azhar, on his part, rubbished the charges but the cat was out of the bag by now.

Since the crime took place in India and the bookies were of Indian origin, Government of India initiated a CBI probe into the whole thing on April 28.

In May 2000, *Tehelka* - an upcoming Indian digital media house headed by a maverick Tarun Tejpal - smelled blood in the story and decided to give it the investigative journalism treatment. For this, they collaborated with former Delhi and India all-rounder Manoj Prabhakar, who had already made headlines by making a sensational claim that an unnamed player had offered him money to underperform in a Singer cup match against Pakistan in 1994. BCCI constituted a one-man committee composed of Justice Y.V.Chandrachud to look into the allegations but not much had come out of it.

These sensational exposes and sting operations may not hold up in a court of law, but they do in the court of public opinion. They shattered the trust of the average fan in the integrity of not just the players they idolized so passionately, but also the game they followed so religiously.

The match-fixing scandal kept haunting Indian cricket, even as they took a long break of nearly 2 months. A leading news channel aired an explosive interview with a former BCCI President, IS Bindra, who dropped a bombshell alleging that the player Prabhakar accused was none other than the current coach of the Indian team, Kapil Dev himself. Kapil, on his part, broke down and shed tears on national television as he rubbished the allegations but the die had been cast. The team had to leave for Dhaka for their only assignment of the season 2000, the Asia Cup shrouded in a storm of controversies. To their credit, they managed to start the series well, beating the hosts Bangladesh riding on a captain's knock by Ganguly, who scored his 13th ODI hundred. But they faltered in the next match against Sri Lanka due to another insipid batting performance by the middle order.

On June 3, 2000, a spot in the final was up for grabs as arch-rivals India and Pakistan faced off in a huge encounter. Pakistan batted first and posted a formidable score of 295, thanks to a brilliant century by Yousuf Youhana. India's chase never got going and they fell short by 45 runs, ending their hopes of going further in the tournament.

Even though their names had been under the scanner for months, yet no one - not even Azhar and Jadeja themselves - expected this match to be their swansong for India. Mohammad Azharuddin and Ajay Jadeja, two of the most stylish and successful batsmen of their era, made their last appearance in Indian colours in this match. Azhar did not have a memorable last ODI innings, unlike his final Test where he hit a hundred. He was dismissed early and could not contribute much. Jaddu, however, managed to sign off with a valiant 93, smashing 4 sixes in a losing cause. Wicket keeper Nayan Mongia was to play one more Test in a few months' time but as far as cricket in coloured clothing went, this turned out to be his last outing as well.

India's campaign ended in disappointment as they failed to make it to the final in their second consecutive tournament. But amid all the gloom and doom, there was a glimpse of hope in the way Ganguly spoke his mind and held his senior players accountable. He did not shy away from criticizing the batsmen, especially the middle order for their lack of intent, nor did he hesitate to bench Srinath, who had a poor outing against Bangladesh.

The next season was far away, but a disillusioned Kapil Dev had had enough. He was tired of facing the constant heat from fans and politicians and resigned as India's coach. This put the BCCI in a dilemma and they brought in the no-nonsense Anshuman Gaekwad as the interim coach for the next two assignments. They hoped to find a new permanent coach by then.

India had a fresh start with a new team, leaving behind the tainted players. They dazzled everyone in the ICC Knockouts, but crumbled miserably in the Coca Cola cup final against Sri Lanka, as we'll see in more detail in the first chapter.

On 01st November, CBI finally submitted its report indicting Azhar and Ajay Lamba of match-fixing and Ajay Jadeja and Dr. Ali Irani of having ties with bookies. In an ironical twist of fate, it also found the whistleblower of the *Tehelka* sting, Manoj Prabhakar himself guilty of match-fixing! Nayan Mongia was found not guilty[1].

Trust is the foundation on which the paying public throngs to the stadiums in thousands and makes the matches a spectacle. What this expose did was to erode that very foundation which is the basis on which a sport grows into a religion.

The team had betrayed the trust of the fans and the nation by their off-field actions. Their performance on the field was also dismal and didn't inspire any hope of a turnaround in the foreseeable future.

All in all, the reputation of Indian Cricket had hit rock bottom and it seemed like there was no way out of this crisis.

---

[1] **Disclaimer** - As of 2024, the bans on most of the players accused in the scandal have been overturned by due process of law. For instance, Mohammad Azharuddin's life ban was overturned in 2012 after a successful appeal in Andhra high court, allowing him to stage a remarkable return to the cricket fold as the president of the Hyderabad cricket association in 2019. Similarly, Ajay Jadeja's 5 years ban was overturned by the Delhi high court in 2003, leading to his successful comeback in domestic cricket, even going on to feature in the great Sachin Tendulkar's final appearance in first-class cricket in 2013 at Lahli. More recently, Jadeja earned a lot of praise as a mentor for the Afghanistan team during their impressive 2023 ODI World Cup performance.

Section 1

THE ASCENT

01

System Reboot

To be honest, to any keen observer of Indian cricket, the storm had been brewing for a long time and was bound to explode sooner or later. There had been rumours of corruption and match-fixing since the late 80s and they had grown stronger in the recent years, especially after 1996. India's performance was inconsistent and unpredictable. They were unbeatable at home but hopeless abroad, especially against West Indies and SENA countries. The captaincy was a hot potato that was tossed between Azhar and Sachin, the two senior-most players, for four years. The team was divided by regionalism and favouritism and the politics was rampant in every aspect of the game. It was no surprise that the results were disappointing and frustrating.

The crisis was looming and it exploded when Cronje's match-fixing affair was exposed.

Now, the need of the hour to pull Indian cricket out of this absolute nadir was two-folds:

1. Giving the harshest punishments to the culprits and sending a strong message of zero tolerance for any such activities in the future

&

2. Fixing the problems in the team and restoring the winning mentality.

Credit where it's due, the board, led by the stern A.C Muttiah, passed on both counts with flying colours.

Those found guilty were given the severest of punishments, ranging from life bans to Azhar and Ajay Sharma, 5 years ban to Ajay Jadeja and bans to Manoj Prabhakar and Dr. Ali Irani.

On the team front, the selection committee chaired by the revered Chandu Borde, reposed their faith in Sourav Ganguly as the captain to lead Indian cricket out of this dark phase. It could be rightly argued that Anil Kumble had an equally strong claim, but history vindicated the selectors' choice. Kumble would have his moment later, but for now it was the Prince of Kolkata's turn to step up to the challenge. And step up he did.

Having already begun on a promising note in his earliest assignments as captain: a 2-1 victory over a Brian Lara-led West Indies in Toronto in 1999 followed by a hard fought 3-2 triumph over S. Africa earlier in the year, Sourav set about the task of getting Indian cricket back on track with a real gusto. The fact that he was also in top form with the bat, scoring runs even in the losses only made his task easier.

First order of business was the appointment of a new permanent coach in the aftermath of Kapil Dev's resignation from the post.

Sourav Ganguly and Rahul Dravid had a long history of rising through the ranks together, ever since their days of age-group cricket. They debuted together at the hallowed ground of Lords, etching their names in history with memorable knocks and went on to excel in their respective domains - Dravid, the wall of Test cricket, and Ganguly, the prince of ODIs - while also performing admirably in the other. But beyond their individual feats, they shared a camaraderie that was based on mutual respect and forged a bond that transcended the boundaries of the game, despite their contrasting temperaments as players and as people.

Unbeknownst to even themselves at this point in time, this unlikely partnership would become the catalyst for the revival of Indian cricket, in the here and now, and in the years to come[2].

---

[2] **Update-** The glorious scenes of Team India's epic victory in the final of the T20I World cup on June 29th, 2024 are still fresh in our collective memory. This much-awaited grand triumph is another testament to the enduring influence of the Ganguly-Dravid partnership on Indian cricket. As BCCI Chairman, it was Ganguly who first convinced a reluctant Dravid to take up the mantle of the head coach and then facilitated the rather tricky transition of captaincy from Virat Kohli to Rohit Sharma. Dravid and Rohit then went on to forge one of the most successful captain-coach associations in the history of Indian cricket, taking the team to the finals of both the world test championship as well as the ODI world cup 2023, before finally ending the 13-year long wait for a world cup by lifting the 2024 T20World cup.

As soon as the 1999-2000 season ended, Ganguly, Kumble and Dravid headed to England to play county cricket for different teams - Lancashire, Glamorgan and Kent. Ganguly and Dravid kept in touch through phone calls and visits, whenever they got a chance. Dravid was impressed by the coaching style of John Wright, a former Kiwi cricketer who was in charge of Kent. He was modest but meticulous, and Dravid thought he would be a good fit for India.

He arranged a meeting between Wright and Ganguly, who was also looking for a change. Both Ganguly and Dravid sensed that the match-fixing scandal was going to explode soon, and that they would have to take charge of the team. Sachin Tendulkar had already given up on captaincy, and they knew it was up to them to prepare for the future. They started planning ahead, months before the crisis hit.

The board on its part paid heed to these inputs from the captain and vice-captain - (team for Asia Cup had been announced and Dravid was named vice-captain) - and gave indications that they were willing to reconsider their previous stance of not hiring a foreign coach.

But for the next two assignments, the new 'power couple' had to make do with the interim coach, Anshuman Gaekwad, a quiet and unassuming former Indian cricketer who had lent yeoman services to Indian cricket in various capacities such as a gutsy opener, selector and two-time coach etc.

Though the CBI verdict was yet to be made public yet the selectors left out the tainted trio for the ICC knock outs, which meant replacements needed to be found to fill the mighty shoes of Azhar and Jadeja, the two mainstays of Indian middle-order. Vinod Kambli, who was already on a comeback trail in the ODIs for the past year or so, was given one more opportunity to come good. Three young batsmen were selected to fill the remaining spots, number 5 and number 6, Sridharan Sriram and Hemang Badani from Tamilnadu and the uber talented Yuvraj Singh from Punjab. Robin Singh, thankfully, was still there and primed to take up the mantle of the finisher at number 6 in the absence of Jadeja. Vijay Dahiya, known for his gritty batting, was brought in for Mongia in a like-for-like swap (although to be fair Mongia's glovework was far superior). A young and lanky left-arm fast bowler from Mumbai by the name of Zaheer Khan was also selected for the first time as a replacement for Srinath who was out due to injury.

India faced the hosts Kenya in the first match of the tournament on October 3, 2000. It was a special day for three young players - Zaheer Khan, Yuvraj Singh, and Vijay Dahiya - who received their maiden caps. India chose to bowl first and dismissed Kenya for a modest score of 208. Zaheer impressed with his pace and accuracy, and finished off the innings with some lethal yorkers, a sight that delighted the Indian fans. India chased down the target with ease in 42.3 overs, thanks to another solid partnership between the captain and vice-captain.

Young Blood Steps Up

Second game was when the world really sat up and took notice of these two young talents in this new look Indian team. It was the quarter-final against the reigning world champions Australia, who had beaten India seven times in a row prior to this match. They were the clear favourites, but India had other plans. Steve Waugh won the toss and asked India to bat first. Sachin, in an especially belligerent mood on the day, launched an attack on his arch nemesis Glenn Mcgrath, coming down the track and hitting him straight past twice in the same over. Sourav Ganguly was also in fine touch, and the two gave India a terrific start, reaching 75 for no loss in 12 overs. Then disaster struck, as both fell in quick succession, and Rahul Dravid followed soon after. India were 90 for 3 in 19 overs, and in big trouble. Enter Yuvraj Singh, the 18-year-old left-hander from Punjab, who joined Vinod Kambli in the middle. Kambli was struggling for form, but he hung around long enough to give Yuvraj some time to settle in. Yuvraj grew in confidence with every stroke, and the two added 40 runs to steady the ship, before Kambli departed. It turned out to be a blessing in disguise, as it brought Robin Singh to the crease, who was a seasoned campaigner in such situations. Yuvraj was well set by now, and was playing some exquisite shots, especially the drives and the pulls. Under Robin's guidance, the two played smartly, rotating the strike and attacking the weaker bowlers, while respecting the more experienced ones. They put on 65 runs, before Robin fell. Yuvraj continued his onslaught, with the help of the tail-enders, and was finally dismissed in the 47th over, after scoring a brilliant 84 off 80 balls, with 12 glorious boundaries. It was his maiden innings, against the best team in the world, at the age of 18. Let that sink in!

Chasing 266 to win, Australia got off to a decent start with Adam Gilchrist blazing away in typical fashion, but Agarkar broke through in the eighth over, dismissing Mark Waugh. Zaheer Khan, who was celebrating his 22nd birthday, followed up with the big wicket of Gilchrist in the ninth over, and India were on top. Then came a moment of magic from Yuvraj Singh, the 18-year-old sensation, who leapt in the air and plucked a stunning catch to send Ian Harvey back. Yuvraj was not done yet. He also ran out Michael Bevan, who was a master of chases, with a direct hit, breaking a dangerous partnership with Ricky Ponting. Sachin Tendulkar, who was back to bowling regularly under Ganguly's captaincy, got rid of Ponting, but there was still the not-so-small matter of a certain Steven Waugh to contend with. That's when the birthday boy Zaheer returned to bowl a perfect yorker, shattering Waugh's stumps with a 145 kmph missile right in the blockhole. Brett Lee hit a couple of sixes, but Agarkar and Venkatesh Prasad wrapped up the tail, and just like that…the underdogs had stunned the champions. Yuvraj Singh was rightly named the Man of the Match, for he had shown his class and courage. And it was only his second international match.

It had been more than a year since the Indian fans had experienced that exhilarating feeling of watching their team perform heroically against a stronger opponent in a crucial match.

Buoyed by this terrific performance, the Indian team turned up in the semi-final against South Africa brimming with new-found self-belief. This was evident in them winning the toss and electing to bat first. The prolific opening pair of Tendulkar and Ganguly gave India another fine start, before the marvellous Alan Donald removed Tendulkar, who was looking in good touch. Ganguly, in contrast, had started off a bit iffishly but in the able company of his deputy, gradually found his groove and by the halfway mark of the inning, was timing the ball beautifully. Ganguly unleashed his fury on Nicky Boje, the left-arm spinner, hitting him for 3 huge sixes in 2 overs. Dravid also completed a half-century, but fell soon after. Yuvraj, fresh from his match-winning knock the other day, joined Ganguly and the two left-handers dominated the South African bowlers, except for Donald and Pollock. Ganguly reached his 14th ODI century, and was hitting boundaries at will. India seemed to be heading for a score above 300, when Yuvraj's wicket triggered a collapse. Vinod Kambli and Robin Singh both got out for ducks, the latter run out, and India ended up with 295.

Sensing another victory, Indian bowlers again bowled with fire with Zaheer Khan again claiming 2 top order wickets. South Africa, in the absence of their most experienced batsman Cronje, seemed lost and kept losing wickets at regular intervals. Ganguly's judicious use of his non-regular bowlers, including himself ensured South Africa were bundled out for 200 in 41 overs. India's brave new captain deservedly won the man of the match award.

Who could have guessed that within the space of a week India would knock out the top two favourites and qualify to the finals where they'd meet New Zealand.

The New Zealand team of the late 90s, under the astute leadership of Stephen Fleming, had been developing beautifully and playing some very attractive cricket lately, especially in the ODIs. Unlike most international sides, the NZ team was composed mostly of many bits-and-pieces utility cricketers who combined together beautifully to form a formidable opposition in at least the ODIs. They had a strong showing in the previous world cup and were eyeing their first big ICC trophy after beating Pakistan in the semis to make it to the final.

Fleming decided to bowl first after winning the toss. India's openers continued their splendid form and put on 140 runs in 26 overs before Sachin was run out for 69. Ganguly then joined Dravid and added another 50 runs to take India past 200 in the 37th over. India seemed poised for a big total with nine wickets in hand, but another run out cost them Dravid's wicket. Ganguly reached his second consecutive hundred and his 15th overall, but fell soon after with the score at 220/3 in the 43rd over. Kambli failed to impress once more, indicating that his time was up. New Zealand's bowlers bowled tightly in the final overs and restricted India to 265, with Yuvi and Robin unable to cut loose.

New Zealand's chase began cautiously, but they soon found themselves in trouble as the Indian bowlers picked up wickets at regular intervals. However, Chris Cairns played an inspired innings and turned the tide in

New Zealand's favour. He found a reliable partner in Chris Harris, who scored 46, and together the two Chrises took New Zealand closer to the target. Cairns remained unbeaten on 102 and guided New Zealand to a historic victory with four balls to spare. It was their first ICC trophy and a fitting reward for Cairns' brilliance.

This was the third instance in the last 8 months when Ganguly's India had failed to cross the final hurdle which marked the beginnings of a worrying trend. For now though, the loss in the final notwithstanding, there was more cause to cheer than despair as Indian cricket had taken its first steps on the long road to redemption.

Little did they know that everything would change in a week.

India travelled to Sharjah for the second time that year to participate in a triangular series with Sri Lanka and Zimbabwe. Each team had to play two matches against the others in the league stage, and the top two teams would qualify for the final. India started well with a win over Zimbabwe, but lost Dravid to an injury. He missed the rest of the tournament. India still managed to reach the final by beating Zimbabwe again, but faced a formidable challenge from Sri Lanka, who defeated them twice in the league stage.

Sri Lanka had rebuilt their team after the retirement of their legends Ranatunga & Mahanama and sidelining of Aravinda de Silva; and had rediscovered the magic that had made them world champions four years ago. Jayasuriya, who had taken over the captaincy, was in sublime form, Atapattu had become a reliable opener in both formats, and two young talents Jayawardene and Sangakkara had shown their potential to fill the middle-order void left by de Silva and Ranatunga. Their bowling was led by the lethal duo of Vaas and Muralitharan, with the rest of the bowlers providing good support. All in all, it was a potent mix, at least in the subcontinent.

Granted Lanka were playing better cricket at the moment, yet there is no way to wrap one's head around what transpired in the Final.

Sri Lanka chose to bat first after winning the toss and scored 265 runs, thanks to a brilliant 189 by their captain, the Matara mauler Jayasuriya. He was lucky to be dropped by Sunil Joshi when he was on 93 and then went on to add another 96 runs in a total rampage.

India had to chase 266 to win, which was not an impossible target even in those days, but they were so demoralized by Jayasuriya's onslaught that they crumbled to 54 all out, their lowest score ever. Only Robin Singh reached double digits, with 11 runs. They lost the final by a massive 210 runs, the biggest margin in ODI history.

It was as abject a surrender as ever witnessed in India's one-day history.

The fans back home, who had just begun to regain their faith in the team after the ICC knockouts, had their hopes dashed again and that too, in such humiliating fashion.

Clearly, redemption was still a long way away as far as Indian cricket was concerned.

Such a crushing loss called for some heads to be rolled, and that's precisely what followed. That final marked the end of Vinod Kambli's India career. He was an Anglo-Indian prodigy who burst on the scene with that record-breaking 664-run stand with his childhood buddy Sachin in the Harris Shield tournament in Mumbai's school cricket circuit. He hit a six off the first ball he faced in Ranji trophy, but still had to wait for 3 years for a national call-up. He then made a stunning debut in Test cricket, scoring 4 centuries, including 2 doubles, in his first 8 innings. He was the fastest Indian to 1000 Test runs and drew frequent comparisons in those early days to Brian Lara, another left-handed wizard from West Indies. Kambli had a twinkling footwork that made him especially deadly against spinners, and he once took Warne to the cleaners with 22 runs in an over. He had a weakness for the short ball, but looking back, he seemed more suited for Tests than ODIs. However, he never got a chance to play Tests after 1995, while he was given 9 opportunities to return to ODIs.

It makes one wonder if things could have been different for Kambli and other talented but temperamental players like Sreesanth, if the BCCI had a system in place to mentor and guide them.

Why did the team fall so flat so soon, right after the highs of the ICC Knockouts? It could be attributed to two factors:

1. Losing Dravid to an injury in the first game itself.

&

2. Yuvraj, who had dazzled everyone with his debut, could not repeat his heroics.

This created a gap in the middle-order, which the Sri Lankan bowlers, particularly Vaas and Murali exploited to the hilt.

The team faced a lot of flak when they returned home. The coach, Anshuman Gaekwad, termed it as the worst debacle in his two stints. The captain, however, took the loss in his stride and called for patience and faith in the youngsters.

India's next destination was Dhaka, where they played a one-off Test against Bangladesh. It was a historic occasion, as Bangladesh had just become a Test-playing nation and India had agreed to be their first opponents. It was also the final assignment for Anshuman Gaekwad as the coach of India, as the board had already decided on his successor and the next full-time coach of the team.

Bengalis are an excitable and passionate lot when it comes to their two favourite sports football and Cricket. This is true for the Bengalis on both sides of the border. Cricket had become very popular in Bangladesh, thanks to the recent achievements under the visionary leadership of BCB President Saber. He had helped Bangladesh gain Test status and challenge the established teams. The first Test match for Bangladesh was a momentous occasion and the fans in Dhaka were eager to witness it. They packed the Bangabandhu stadium to support their team, who faced India in their debut. The two captains walked out for the toss amid a roaring crowd.

Bangladesh won the toss and chose to bat first, but lost their openers quickly. However, their star batsman Habibul Bashar and former captain Aminul Islam steadied the innings and batted through the first session. They continued their partnership in the second session, and Islam reached his hundred on the second day. He became only the second batsman in history to score a century in his country's first Test. The rest of the batsmen chipped in with some useful runs, and Bangladesh surprised everyone by scoring 400 in their first innings. India's bowling was lacklustre, with Srinath looking rusty after his comeback. The only bright spot was Sunil Joshi, who took 5 wickets with his left-arm spin.

India's reply was steady, but not spectacular. They had a new opener in Shivsundar Das, who joined Ramesh at the top. Ramesh scored another fifty, but none of the other batsmen could convert their starts into big scores. India managed to take a narrow lead of 29 runs, thanks to Joshi's fighting 92. He made up for the catch he had dropped in the final against Sri Lanka. Bangladesh's captain Naimur Rahman took 6 wickets, including the prized scalp of Tendulkar. He joined Islam in the honours board by becoming the first Bangladeshi bowler to take a five-wicket haul in a Test match.

Bangladesh had put up an admirable fight for three days, but their inexperience showed on the fourth day. They were bowled out for just 91 in less than 4 hours, as Srinath shook up the rust to pick up 3 wickets and so did Joshi. India had no trouble in chasing the small target of 63, losing only one wicket. They won the match by 9 wickets on the fourth day, giving their coach Anshuman Gaekwad a winning farewell. Sunil Joshi was the Man of the Match for his all-round performance.

BCB did a great job of organizing the historic match, and their team too gave a good account of themselves barring the collapse on day4 which was understandable given their lack of experience.

Before this most eventful of years in the history of Indian cricket drew to an end, there was one more little piece of business to be taken care of: the home series against Zimbabwe, with 2 Tests and 5 ODIs. The board had listened to the captain and his deputy, and hired John Wright as the full-time coach, the first foreigner to be appointed to this position. Although his official designation was that of the coach, he was entrusted with the additional charge of the Manager as well. The series against Zimbabwe was to be his first assignment in charge as coach-cum-manager.

Zimbabwe played two practice games, drawing one and winning the other chiefly on the back of good showing by their batsmen.

The first Test was a comfortable win for India. Zimbabwe batted first after winning the toss, but lost their openers early to the wily Srinath.

However, Zimbabwe recovered thanks to their middle order, especially Andy Flower, who scored a big hundred. They made 422 in their first innings, with Srinath taking 4 wickets.

India replied with a strong batting performance, declaring at 458/4. Dravid scored a double hundred, with 27 fours. Tendulkar also scored a hundred, and Das made his first fifty in Tests. Srinath was again the star with the ball, claiming a fifer in the second innings. He ran through the Zimbabwean batting, with only Andy Flower putting up some fight with 70 runs. Zimbabwe were all out for 225, setting India a target of 190. India chased it down easily on the fifth day, with Ganguly and Dravid scoring unbeaten fifties. Srinath was the Man of the Match for his match tally of 9 wickets.

The second Test at Nagpur was a run-fest, that ended in a high-scoring draw. India batted first and piled up 609/6, with Das scoring his first hundred, Dravid making another 150-plus score and Tendulkar blasting a double hundred. Zimbabwe fought back with Grant Flower scoring a hundred at number 6, after being bowled for a duck in the first Test. His brother Andy also scored a fifty but the rest of the batsmen failed to support them. Zimbabwe were bowled out for 382 and India enforced the follow-on. Zimbabwe showed more resistance in the second innings with their captain Campbell scoring a hundred and Andy Flower scoring an unbeaten double hundred. He played the reverse sweep with remarkable skill and frequency, neutralizing the Indian spinners. Zimbabwe saved the match finishing at 503/6.

Sarandeep Singh, the debutant off-spinner, took 6 wickets in the match, including 4 in the second innings. He was the only Indian bowler to trouble the Zimbabwean batsmen.

For his defiant batting throughout the tour, Andy Flower was deservedly adjudged the Player of the match as well as series. His batting was a masterclass in playing on Indian pitches and the Indian players, past and present, agreed that he was one of the best foreign batsmen they had ever seen in India, along with the West Indian Jimmy Adams in 1994. The way he negated Indian spinners by unfurling the reverse sweep with amazing regularity and precision - unlike Adams who employed padding for the same - came in for special praise by all and sundry.

Apparently, he was just warming up, for over the course of the next 13 months he was to embark on one of the greatest purple patches ever witnessed in the history of cricket, with a tally of 1466 runs in 15 Tests at a Bradmanesque average of 133 with 6 centuries and 7 half centuries, thereby cementing his legacy as Zimbabwe's greatest ever cricketer.

The one-day series between India and Zimbabwe was expected to be more competitive, as Zimbabwe had a better record in the shorter format. However, India dominated the series and won it 4-1.

In the first ODI at Cuttack, Zimbabwe scored 252/9 but India chased it down with 10 balls to spare. Hemang Badani anchored the chase with a steady 58 and won the Man of the Match.

In the second ODI at Ahmedabad, India batted first and posted 306/5, with captain Ganguly scoring his 17th ODI hundred. He also took 2 wickets as India restricted Zimbabwe to 245/8, winning by 61 runs. Ganguly was the Man of the Match for his all-round performance.

In the third ODI at Jodhpur, India seemed to have the match in their grasp as Tendulkar scored a brilliant hundred and took India to 282/8. However, Zimbabwe fought back with Grant Flower scoring 84 and taking 2 wickets. The match went down to the wire, and Zimbabwe's last pair scraped through with 1 ball to spare, chasing down 283. Grant Flower was the Man of the Match for his heroics.

In the fourth ODI at Kanpur, India sealed the series with a comprehensive win. They bowled out Zimbabwe for 165, with Ganguly taking 5 wickets. He then scored an unbeaten 71 as India cruised to the target in 25 overs, losing only one wicket. Ganguly was the Man of the Match again for his superb display.

The fifth ODI was a dead rubber, and Ganguly rested himself giving Dravid the opportunity to captain India for the first time. India's top order faltered but Badani steadied the ship with the lower middle-order. Then, Agarkar unleashed a stunning assault slamming the fastest fifty by an Indian in just 21 balls. He broke Kapil Dev's record and took India past 300. He also took 3 wickets, as India bowled out Zimbabwe for 262, winning by 40 runs. Agarkar was the Man of the Match for his all-round brilliance. His record of 21-ball fifty still stands today.

This match also marked the comeback of Virender Sehwag, a hard-hitting batsman and a handy off-spinner from Delhi. He had made his debut in 1999 but failed to impress and was dropped. He earned his recall after performing well against Zimbabwe in the tour games. He had a decent outing, scoring 19 off 24 with a six and taking 2 wickets.

India won the series 4-1 with Ganguly being the Man of the Series for his 264 runs and 7 wickets in 4 matches. The only concern was Yuvraj's loss of form. He had not scored much since his brilliant 84 against Australia in the ICC knockouts and needed to regain his touch.

For now though, Indian cricket had somehow managed to end its most tumultuous year yet on a winning note.

02

The Turning Point

2001

After the final ODI at Rajkot, the players enjoyed a well-deserved 2 months break. They needed to recharge their batteries, for they were about to face a formidable challenge on their home turf. Awaiting them was none other than Steve Waugh's Australia - a team that had etched its name in the annals of history as perhaps the greatest cricket team ever assembled.

From 1877, when they featured in the first ever official Test match against England, Australia had been the pre-eminent cricket playing nation in the world for more than a hundred years till the early eighties. Then, the twin blows of the Kerry Packer World Series of Cricket fiasco and the simultaneous retirement of three of their pillars - Greg Chappell, Dennis Lillee and Rodney Marsh - after the last Test in the series against Pakistan in 1984, created a huge vacuum and threw the team into a prolonged transition phase. Australia were lucky to find in Allan Border just the kind of man to oversee such a phase and the tenacious pug from New South Wales ensured Australia stayed competitive even in the midst of a transition. Heck, he even managed to galvanize a bunch of young and inexperienced rookies all the way to a World Cup crown in 1987. Border passed on the baton to Mark "Tubby" Taylor who proved to be a worthy successor and took the team further than where he found it, before handing over the reign to Steve Waugh, one of the heroes of that famous 1987 World Cup win.

Taylor had built a strong team, but Waugh made it invincible. He was not as shrewd a captain as Taylor, but with John Buchanan as their coach he led his team to unprecedented glory in both formats. They had won the World Cup in 1999 and were on a record-breaking streak of 15 consecutive Test wins. But there was one challenge that Waugh had not yet overcome - a series win against India in India. He termed it the 'Final Frontier' and was determined to conquer it.

Just how serious the Aussies were in their pursuit can be gauged by the fact that they had asked for as many as three 3-day practice matches to start off the tour and get acclimatized to the conditions before the first Test. They got only two, and one more before the second Test. The tour started with a match against a decent India A side led by VVS Laxman in Nagpur. Australia scored 291 in the first innings, but the star of the day was a 19-year-old off-spinner named Harbhajan Singh. He bamboozled the Aussies with his drift and spin and took the wickets of Ponting and Martyn. Laxman, the India A captain, got a call from Ganguly during Tea. Ganguly told him to limit Harbhajan's bowling so that Australia would not get familiar with him. Laxman agreed, and Harbhajan was unhappy. He did not know that Ganguly had a plan for him.

India A replied with 368, thanks to Ramesh's century, Laxman's 94 and Mongia's 70. The Aussie pacers struggled on the flat pitch. In the second innings, Australia did better with Langer's hundred and fifties from Ponting and Martyn. Hayden also got some runs. Harbhajan, who was allowed to bowl only after chief of selectors Chandu Borde's intervention, took three more wickets. The match ended in a draw. Laxman said that they had achieved their goal of not letting Australia dominate.

Australia faced the Ranji champions Mumbai in their second practice match. Sachin Tendulkar, who had led the West Zone in the Duleep Trophy, opted out of this game as part of the mind games before the first Test. He had earlier fired the first salvo by saying that the Aussies had not faced much pressure in their 15-Test winning streak.

McGrath and Warne, who had missed the first game, played this one and troubled the Mumbai batsmen. Mumbai were 82/5 when captain Dighe, along with Bahutule and Powar, revived the innings and declared at 328/9.

Australia fared worse than Mumbai and were saved by a gritty hundred from Steve Waugh. Mhambrey and Kulkarni shared 8 wickets between them and restricted Australia to 306.

Mumbai started well in the second innings but then Warne spun his magic and took 7 wickets. Dighe declared again at 192/8, denying Australia the chance to bowl them out.

Chasing a target of 317, Australia found themselves in trouble again, this time against the big turn of Bahutule and once again it was their skipper, the redoubtable Waugh Sr. who managed to eke out a draw with another face-saving innings in the company of the tail; Mumbai had given the world's best team a scare, which meant that the upcoming series wasn't going to be a cakewalk by any means, even for a team riding high on a 15 Test winning streak. It was for a reason Waugh had named it 'The Final Frontier'.

The warm-ups were done and the real battle was about to begin. The Australians had an advantage of staying in Mumbai for the first Test, even though it was at a different venue, the Wankhede. They did not have to travel and adjust to a new place like Chennai or Kolkata.

But on the eve of the Test match, a sad news shook the cricket world. The greatest batsman of all time, the legendary Sir Don Bradman had passed away. Both teams paid their tribute to the G.O.A.T. with a minute of silence.

Australia gambled on bowling first on a Wankhede pitch that was known to crumble after the third day, but also to help the seamers on the first two mornings. Their gamble paid off as they reduced India to 55/4 before lunch. Only Tendulkar resisted their attack with a masterful 76 with 13 boundaries. He added some valuable runs with VVS but McGrath broke their partnership and dismissed both of them in quick succession. Sachin has always had a great sense of the occasion and this knock was a fitting homage to Sir Don who had once remarked that Sachin's batting reminded him of his own. It was one of the most sublime 70s ever seen in Test Cricket.

A returning Nayan Mongia fought hard but Warne weaved his magic around the tail and ended India's innings for 176. Warne and McGrath were the heroes with 7 wickets between them. India got a consolation wicket before the end of the day when Agarkar finally bowled Slater, after several near misses. But the first day of the series clearly belonged to the Aussies.

That was to change dramatically the next morning as Ganguly unleashed his secret weapon, the lanky 19-year-old off-spinner from Punjab, Harbhajan Singh. He struck twice in his first over, snaring Langer and Mark Waugh with edges to the slip cordon. Steve Waugh avoided the hat-trick, but soon fell to a sharp turner from the debutant left-arm spinner Rahul Sanghvi. In the next over Harbhajan bamboozled Ponting and left Australia in tatters at 99/5. In just half an hour, the game had turned on its head.

In walks Adam Gilchrist - the Australian wicketkeeper who had succeeded the great Ian Healy behind the stumps - to join Matthew Hayden, who had been holding on at one end. Gilchrist had decided to attack the Indian spinners on the tricky pitch and he unleashed a barrage of shots from the start. He drove, cut, pulled and slogged his way to the boundary, forcing Ganguly to spread the field. This gave Hayden some breathing space and he also started sweeping the spinners effectively. The Indian spinners lost their rhythm and Ganguly had to replace them with the seamers. But by then, both batsmen had settled in and there was not much help for the seamers from the pitch. They continued to plunder runs and in the next hour and a half, added 197 runs for the sixth wicket.

Both batsmen reached their second Test centuries in contrasting styles. Hayden's 119 was a gritty knock that lasted six hours and included 18 fours and a six. Gilchrist's 122 was a dazzling display of aggression that took only an hour and a half and featured 15 fours and four sixes.

Fittingly it was Harbhajan who had the honour of dismissing Gilchrist but not before he had played one of the great counter-attacking innings in history. Warne also chipped in with a few lusty blows and Australia ended their innings with a lead of 173 runs. Harbhajan was the best bowler for India with 4 wickets.

In reply, India lost their opener SS Das early while his partner S Ramesh rode his luck to score 44 before falling to McGrath. With the day coming to an end, India sent Mongia as a night watchman to shield Tendulkar. But Mongia hurt his finger while fending off a bouncer and had to retire hurt. Tendulkar had to come out and join Dravid in the middle. They survived the remaining overs without any more damage.

The next morning was crucial for India. They had lost one wicket and were still trailing by 119 runs. Dravid and Tendulkar had to bat well to keep India in the game.

The first session on Day 3 was a thrilling contest between two great batsmen and a formidable bowling attack. Dravid and Tendulkar had different approaches to the same goal - reducing the deficit while preserving their wickets. Dravid was solid and defensive, blocking everything that the Aussie pacers threw at him. Tendulkar was cautious but aggressive, punishing the rare bad balls with his stroke play. It was a contrast of styles but a display of class. It was Test cricket at its riveting best.

The runs flowed more freely after lunch as Tendulkar decided to take on McGrath. Dravid also played a few shots instead of just ducking and leaving. But he was so focused on his task that he scolded himself for chasing a wide ball and hitting a boundary. He was not going to give his wicket away easily.

But sometimes, luck plays a part in cricket. And India's luck ran out when Tendulkar pulled a short ball from Mark Waugh, only to see it hit Langer at short-leg and pop up in the air. Ponting dived and took a stunning catch to end Tendulkar's innings. It was a freakish dismissal for Tendulkar, who was looking set for a big score.

Another piece of brilliant fielding resulted in the run-out of Ganguly a few overs later. The pitch by now was turning square. This was what had prompted Australian captain's decision to have Mark Waugh bowl his off-spin to go with Warne's leg-spin from the other end and the move bore fruit again when Waugh Jr had VVS caught behind by the keeper. The very next over Warne flummoxed Dravid in flight and bowled him round his legs, thereby ending any hope of setting Australia a sizeable target to chase. Mongia hit a few blows but the tail didn't last long and India were bowled out for 219, leaving Australia a target of 47 runs. Australia chased it down without losing any wickets and won the match by 10 wickets. Gilchrist was the man of the match for his sensational century and six dismissals behind the stumps.

Australia had won the first Test with two days and 10 wickets to spare, extending their winning streak to 16 matches. The scorecard might suggest a one-sided affair, but the match had many twists and turns. India had their moments, but failed to capitalize on them. Australia showed their resilience and skill, and Gilchrist played a match-winning knock. It was a memorable Test match, and one that is still remembered by the players and the fans who witnessed it.

Australia had taken the first step towards conquering the final frontier. India were disappointed but not dejected. They knew they had the ability to bounce back.

Before the second Test at the Eden Gardens in Kolkata, the Australians played another practice match against the Indian Board President's XI. The Australians used this game to give their batsmen more practice and rested their main bowlers. They scored over 450 runs in both innings and dominated the match. The Indian Board President's XI could only manage 208 runs in their only innings. The only bright spots for them were Sarandeep Singh and Narendra Hirwani, who took five wickets each in the first and second innings respectively.

An Epic Unfolds at Eden

The stage was set for the second Test at the Eden Gardens in Kolkata, the most iconic and grandiose cricket stadium in India. It was also the home ground of the Indian captain, Sourav Ganguly. But India had some problems to deal with before the match. Their pace spearhead, Srinath, was ruled out with an ankle injury. Many players also suffered from viral fever after arriving in Kolkata. Dravid recovered in time but Agarkar could not. India had to play with Prasad and Zaheer Khan as their seamers. They also chose the experienced Raju over the impressive Sarandeep as their third spinner.

Australia chose to bat first after winning the toss. They began strongly as the openers added 100 runs before Zaheer got Slater caught behind. But India could not celebrate for long as Langer and Hayden continued the onslaught and put on another 95 runs. Harbhajan finally broke the stand by trapping Hayden lbw for 97. Mark Waugh came in and saw Langer reach his fifty, but then Langer edged Zaheer to Mongia and departed for 58. Mark Waugh tried to build a partnership with his brother Steve, but Harbhajan struck again with his extra bounce and had him caught behind for 39. Steve Waugh and Ponting tried to steady the innings, but then came a spellbinding passage of play in the last hour of the day, which was the first of many that made this Test one of the most iconic in the history of the game.

On the second ball of his 16th and day's 72nd over, Harbhajan castled his old bête noire from his debut series in 1998, Ricky Ponting plumb in front of the wicket off a ball that turned and rose too sharply for Ponting's estimation. The next ball, Harbhajan pitched it fuller and lower and trapped Gilchrist lbw for a golden duck. The replay showed that the ball 'might' have kissed the bat before the pad, but there was no DRS in those days and

Gilchrist had to walk back. Harbhajan was on a hat-trick and the crowd was ecstatic. They cheered him on as he prepared to bowl the next ball. The batsman facing him was the legendary Shane Warne, the king of spin himself. He looked nervous as he saw eight close-in fielders around him. Steve Waugh tried to calm him down, but he was feeling the pressure too.

Harbhajan kissed the *Khanda* (a sacred Sikh amulet) he wore around his neck, touched it to his forehead and tucked it back under his shirt collar. He looked up at the sky and then ran in to bowl. He delivered the ball faster and fuller than he wanted to, and Warne tried to flick it to the leg side. But the ball hit his pad and popped up in the air. Ramesh at short leg dived and took a brilliant catch. The umpire was not sure, so he referred it to the third umpire. The replay was inconclusive, but the third umpire gave it out.

And just like that, at just 20 years and 272 days old, Harbhajan Singh from Punjab became the first ever bowler in the history of Indian cricket to claim a hat-trick in Test cricket. He was also the second youngest to achieve this feat overall, just a few days older than Pakistan's Abdul Razzaq.

Some turnaround this was, for a guy who, just 14 months ago, had been thinking of quitting the game for good and moving to Canada to work as a truck driver after the death of his father. Talk about fairy tales!

Steve Waugh was joined by Kasprowicz, who replaced Damien Fleming in the playing eleven. They hoped to survive the remaining overs of the day but Ganguly had other plans. He brought himself on to bowl and struck with an off-cutter that trapped Kasprowicz lbw. The Eden crowd cheered for their favourite son.

Gillespie came in and managed to hang on till the end of the day. Australia were 291/8 and India were confident of wrapping up the innings quickly. But they were in for a rude shock the next day. Steve Waugh batted brilliantly with the tail, keeping most of the strike and protecting Gillespie, who also showed great temperament. They frustrated the Indian bowlers and added 133 runs for the ninth wicket. Steve Waugh reached his 25th Test hundred, a superb innings under pressure. Harbhajan finally broke the stand by getting Gillespie caught at short leg. He also dismissed Steve Waugh lbw to end the innings with 7 wickets. But Australia had scored 445 runs, much more than India had expected.

In response, India lost their opener S Ramesh in the second over itself. Das and Dravid steadied the ship till Tea, but then the Australian bowlers ran through the Indian batting line-up in the final session. India collapsed to 128/8, with only Laxman showing some resistance with 26 not out. By the close of play on Day 2, it looked like Australia had virtually sealed the game and with it, the series.

VVS Laxman had been longing for a chance to bat in the middle order for a couple of years. He finally got his wish after Azharuddin's exit and a prolific domestic season. This series was a crucial one for Laxman, but he was in sublime form and touch, both in the nets and on the field. He resumed the third day with some elegant drives off the fast bowlers, while also protecting the tail-enders. He reached his fifty in just 69 balls, with 11 graceful boundaries. He added one more before falling to Warne for 59 off 83 balls. India were bowled out for 171 and Steve Waugh enforced the follow-on.

Indian openers showed more fight in the second innings and added 50 runs before Warne had Ramesh caught by Mark Waugh for 30. Then came a crucial decision by the Indian team management. They sent Laxman at number three instead of Dravid, who was going through a lean patch. They did not know then that this decision would have a huge bearing on the match and the series.

Laxman picked up from where he had left and played some exquisite shots. He and Das took the team to 97 when Das was out in a bizarre manner, hit wicket to Gillespie.

Tendulkar walked in to join Laxman. He had batted superbly in both innings in Mumbai and India needed him to score big here. He was also involved in some fascinating duels with McGrath and Warne, the best bowlers of his era. He had a chance to assert his dominance as the best batsman of his generation. But he missed the opportunity, as he edged a Gillespie inswinger to Gilchrist and was out for 10. The Eden crowd was stunned and silent.

Ganguly, the local hero, joined Laxman, who was nearing his century. They added 100 runs and revived some hope in the crowd. But just when they looked set to bat till the end of the day, Ganguly was caught behind off McGrath for 48.

Dravid, coming in at 6, saw off the ten odd overs left in the day's play in the company of VVS, who completed a magnificent hundred laced with 17 impeccably timed boundaries before stumps. It was the lone highlight in what was another dispiriting day at the office for Sourav Ganguly's men.

Day3 ended with India 254/4, still trailing behind Australia by 20 runs with their last recognised pair at the crease. Clearly it was just a matter of when rather than if.

Or so everyone thought.

Miracle!

The fourth day began with Dravid and Laxman resuming their innings. They had different styles but the same goal: to save the match for India. Dravid was calm and composed while Laxman was fluent and graceful. Steve Waugh took the new ball, hoping to finish off the Indian innings. But Dravid and Laxman survived the hostile spell and took India past the follow-on mark of 274. They scored more freely after that and reached 376 by lunch, with Laxman on 171 and Dravid on 80.

But batting was not the only challenge they faced that day. They also had to battle the heat and humidity of Kolkata and their own physical ailments. Dravid was still recovering from a viral fever and was prone to cramps. Laxman had a chronic back problem that had almost ruled him out of the match. The team physio, Andrew Leipus, worked hard to keep them fit and fresh. He used ice towels, ice baths and massages to cool them down and ease their pain.

They did not let their efforts go in vain and came out after lunch with more positive intent. Dravid played some glorious shots and matched Laxman's elegance. Laxman was in a zone of his own, playing some breathtaking strokes. He tormented Warne, who tried to bowl in the rough outside leg. Laxman danced down the track and hit him over or through the off side. He also cut him late and fine. He flicked him through the leg side. He was unstoppable. Dravid also punished Warne, rocking back and hitting him through the off side. None of the Australian bowlers, except McGrath, could contain them. Gillespie and Kasprowicz were hit all over the park.

Steve Waugh tried to break the partnership by using his brother Mark as a part-timer, a ploy that had worked like a charm in Mumbai test but to no avail here. The duo soldiered on and on, hurting the Aussies not just in body but in spirit too, to the extent that they stopped chasing the ball to the boundary and let the ball boys throw it back. Laxman reached his maiden double hundred in Test cricket, a sublime innings. Dravid also completed his century, his 12th in Tests, and uncharacteristically gestured to the press box, who had criticized him lately, as if to say "Take that!"

They scored more runs after lunch and took India to 491/4 by tea, leading by 217 runs. Laxman was on 227 and Dravid on 106. They had one more session to bat till stumps.

They had to take ice baths and massages during the break to recover from the heat and exhaustion. They had batted brilliantly, but they also had to battle the elements and their own physical ailments.

Meanwhile, the word had spread about their amazing fightback and fans thronged to the Eden Gardens. The crowd swelled from 40,000 to 80,000 by the time they came out after tea. The Australians looked dejected and exhausted. They tried everything, even using Gilchrist and Steve Waugh as bowlers, but nothing worked. Dravid and Laxman were now dealing mostly in boundaries. The famed Aussie bowling attack had been well and truly tamed.

But their heroics had taken a toll on their bodies. Laxman's back started to give way and Dravid began experiencing severe cramps. They had to dig deep and fight their pain. How much more could their tired and dehydrated bodies take?

In such a situation, reaching a milestone like surpassing 236 - the record for the highest individual score by an Indian, held by the legendary Sunil Gavaskar - would have surely given Laxman a surge of adrenaline to keep going.

But as the day neared its end, Laxman's back pain worsened, while Dravid seemed to have regained his energy. They decided to let Dravid face most of the deliveries, so that Laxman could rest his weary body. He had been batting for much longer than anyone else. The plan worked brilliantly and Dravid reached his 150 just before the close of play.

The two heroes walked off the field, leaving behind a stunned Australian team. The scoreboard showed: India 2nd innings 589/4 VVS Laxman 275*, Rahul Dravid 155*, 165 overs, leading Australia by 315 runs with a day to go. All four of Australia's main bowlers had bowled more than 30 overs each, and given away more than 100 runs each. They had no clue how to stop the onslaught.

Dravid needed an IV drip as soon as he reached the dressing room. He had given his all for his team.

What happened on the field that day was beyond belief for both sides. But as the night fell, the verdict was clear and unanimous: two of the most gentlemanly cricketers had scripted one of, if not *the* greatest, fightback in the history of the sport!

The stage was set for a thrilling finale. Had it been against any other team, India would have declared overnight or early on the fifth day. But this was Steve Waugh's Invincibles, who had won 16 Tests in a row. Some of them, like Gilchrist, had never tasted defeat in their Test careers. They had the firepower to chase down any target. Slater, Hayden, and Gilchrist himself were capable of scoring at a brisk rate, as they had shown in the previous Test.

So, Ganguly decided to let the overnight pair continue their partnership in front of a packed Eden Gardens crowd. Laxman had the opportunity to become the first Indian to score a triple century in Tests, but nicked a McGrath outswinger to second slip, drawing curtains to what was arguably the greatest knock ever played in Test cricket all things considered and inarguably the greatest ever played by an Indian. It was not just the quantity, but the quality of his runs that made his 281 stand out. He had scored them with grace and elegance, using his wrists to create magic, carrying forward the tradition of the great Hyderabad batsmen, like Pataudi, Jaisimha, and Azhar. 80000 plus strong Eden crowd rose as one to give a very very special send-off to a player who had now proved, beyond a shadow of any doubts whatsoever, that he was going to be Very Very Special for this Indian side for many years to come.

Dravid was unfazed by the loss of his partner. He was eyeing a double century of his own, but a misunderstanding led to his run-out. That was the only way the Australians could get rid of him, because he was impregnable otherwise. He had batted for almost 8 hours, facing 353 balls and hitting 20 fours in his 181. His place was called into question going into this inning but this daddy hundred had answered all those questions in an emphatic manner once and for all. Never again would anyone dare question the utility of The Wall in the Indian batting order in Tests for as long as he played. Way to silence the critics!

Zaheer Khan swung his bat with gusto, adding another 40 vital runs in a hurry. Ganguly declared at 657/7, an hour before lunch, setting Australia a daunting target of 383 in a little over two sessions on a crumbling fifth day pitch. Most teams would have settled for a draw, but not the Invincibles. This was the most dominant Test team ever, and they lived up to their reputation. Steve Waugh's men chose to chase the impossible. And that's what made this Test a timeless classic, not just another great one.

Australian openers survived the tricky period before lunch, and returned with a positive mindset. They reached 50 in just 15 overs, but then Harbhajan Singh struck. The off-spinner had Slater caught by Ganguly in the slips. Langer came out with uncharacteristic aggression, smashing Raju for two sixes. But he too fell to Harbhajan, caught by Ramesh at short leg. Venkatapathy Raju, who had played a key role in many home victories under the Azhar-Wadekar regime in the early-to-mid 90s, had a disappointing comeback match until he got the vital wicket of Mark Waugh, Australia's best batsman, lbw. Hayden was solid as ever, and joined forces with his captain Steve Waugh. They denied India any more success in the session. Hayden completed another half-century in the series, and took Australia to 161/3 at tea. They needed 222 more in the final session. It was a tough task, but not impossible for this formidable team. They still had two set batsmen, and Ponting and Gilchrist to follow. They still had a slim chance to extend their winning streak to 17-0. And even if they couldn't, they had enough wickets in hand to avoid a loss.

But the young turbaned spinner had other ideas. He struck twice in the third over after tea, removing the Australian captain with a sharp catch by Badani. Then, he snared his nemesis and now his bunny Ponting, who was caught brilliantly by Das at short leg for a duck. It was a pair of golden ducks for the future legend in this Test.

The game had turned on its head in a matter of minutes, as two quick wickets brought the crowd to their feet. They were ecstatic at the possibility of witnessing a historic win. The Indian players were also pumped up and showed their intensity. Captain Ganguly sensed the opportunity and surrounded the new batsmen with eight close-in fielders, who were breathing down their necks. He also made a bold move, bringing on Sachin Tendulkar to bowl from the other end.

Now, Tendulkar was a natural-born cricketer, who belonged to the elite group of players like Grace, Bradman, Sobers, and India's own Kapil Dev. He was India's undisputed match-winner with the bat, but he also had a knack of taking crucial wickets, especially in ODIs. He had not yet shown the same magic with the ball in Tests, but Ganguly had faith in his bowling. He had used him regularly as captain, but his decision to bowl him at a critical stage in the previous Test in Mumbai had backfired and drawn flak from the experts.

Sachin had a quiet series by his standards, despite the two promising knocks in the first Test. He scored only 10 in each innings here, and must have been eager to contribute in some way to this historic moment for the team. What sets the all-time greats apart from the other greats is their sense of the occasion. And few among the all-time greats had a sense of the occasion as keen as Sachin Tendulkar.

Just three balls after Ponting's dismissal, Sachin trapped the danger man Gilchrist plumb before the wicket for a duck, and in the next over, he did the same to Hayden, the last recognised batsman. In the following over, Shane Warne got a taste of his own medicine as he was outfoxed by a Sachin googly to become his third plumb victim. In the span of three overs, Sachin Ramesh Tendulkar ensured that his name too would be among the main architects of this era-defining win.

The tail-enders - Gillespie, Kasprowicz and even McGrath tried bravely to hang on and delay the inevitable, but a rampaging Harbhajan took the final two wickets to seal an epoch-making win in the history of not just Indian cricket, but world cricket (as we will see by the end of this book). He bagged 6 in the second innings, taking his match-tally to 13. In any other match, such figures would have surely won him the Man of the Match, but here VVS Laxman pipped him to the award, and deservedly so, for that second innings haul could not have been possible without that once-in-a-lifetime knock of 281. Harbhajan may have missed out on the Man of the Match, but his exploits here earned him a more special title, a title that he would carry throughout his illustrious career – 'The Turbanator'.

As soon as the umpire raised his finger to signal the end of the last Australian wicket, both the Indian team on the field and the 80,000 plus crowd in the stadium erupted in delirious joy. There was a scramble among the players to secure the stumps as souvenirs from a memorable victory, followed by hugs and high fives. Players were finding it hard to control their emotions, none more so than their captain, who personified passion and wore his heart on his sleeve.

There were epic scenes of jubilation in the crowd.

And not for the first time in history, yet another world-conquering streak lay broken at the feet of the land of the brave yet gentle, India.

The Final Act

The streak was over. The series was tied 1-1 and the stage was set for the grand finale in Chennai, at the historic Chepauk stadium. It was a fitting venue for the climax of this epic series.

The players had little time to rest or celebrate, as they had to fly to Chennai the same evening. The third and final Test was only two days away.

The Indian team had a small celebration at their hotel in Chennai. The stunning win in Kolkata had boosted their morale and confidence. The underdogs had gone from hoping to put up a fight to aiming for a series win.

Going against traditional wisdom, India made two bold changes to their playing XI for the decider, handing debuts to two Mumbai players - leg-spinner Sairaj Bahutule and wicketkeeper Samir Dighe. They replaced Raju and Mongia, who was injured and out of form. He had played his last Test for India, though he did not know it then. One of these changes would prove to be crucial in the outcome of the match and the series. This also meant that the captain himself had to share the new ball with Zaheer Khan in this all-important match.

The Chepauk, or the M.A.Chidambaram stadium, is a historic venue for cricket in India. It is the second oldest cricket stadium in the country, dating back to 1916. It was here that India achieved their first ever Test victory in 1952. The Chepauk is also known for producing sporting pitches that offer a fair contest between bat and ball. The Chennai crowd is widely respected as the most knowledgeable and sporting in India.

Australia chose to bat first on a typical Chepauk pitch that offered good batting conditions for the first three days and assistance to spinners for the last two days. Slater started with a boundary, but was soon caught in the slips. Hayden was joined by Langer, who had been getting starts but not converting them. He fell into the same trap again, as he edged Harbhajan to Dravid at slip after looking set for a big score. Mark Waugh came in at 67/2, and looked determined to make up for his poor form in the series. He and Hayden took Australia to lunch at 140/2, with Hayden completing another solid fifty in the series.

The pair continued to dominate after lunch, taking Australia past 200. Hayden reached a superb hundred off just 153 balls, with 8 fours and 5 sixes. Mark Waugh also scored his first substantial score of the series, a fluent 70 with 7 fours and a six. He fell before tea, giving debutant Bahutule his maiden Test wicket. Steve Waugh joined Hayden, and they took Australia to tea at 248/3.

The final session saw a slowdown in the scoring rate, as India tightened their grip and the batsmen became cautious. Only 78 runs were added in the session, as Hayden and Steve Waugh denied India any further breakthroughs. They took Australia to stumps at 323/3, with Hayden nearing 150 and Steve Waugh just 7 short of a gritty fifty. It was a tough day for the Indian bowlers, especially Harbhajan, who bowled 45 overs for one wicket.

Cricket showed its unpredictable nature the next day, and rewarded the hard-working turbaned spinner of the Indian team for his tireless effort the previous day. Steve Waugh, a veteran of over 100 Tests, was out in a rare manner, handling the ball, off a delivery from Harbhajan that bounced sharply. The very next ball, Harbhajan deceived Ponting with a straighter one that lured him out of his crease, and Dighe - who had been struggling behind the stumps - pulled off a smart stumping to send Ponting back for another duck. It was a horror run of form for a batsman of Punter's class.

In the next over, Harbhajan, bowling round the wicket to the left-hander, trapped Gilchrist, who had just got off the mark, lbw. It was like a replay of the Kolkata collapse. Gilchrist, like Ponting, had been out of sorts after his match-winning knock in the first Test in Mumbai. Hayden tried to farm the strike, and managed to keep Warne with him for eight overs, before Harbhajan foxed him with a slower one that he popped to Das at short leg. India's close-in catching had been excellent throughout the series. Gillespie tried to hit out but mistimed a lofted shot and was caught by Ganguly. He also failed to score, as did Colin Miller in the next over. Hayden, running out of partners, switched gears and completed a well-deserved double hundred, before becoming the last wicket to fall to Harbhajan. His 203 came off just 320 balls, with 15 fours and 6 sixes, and was a masterclass of sweeping on a subcontinent turner.

Australia were all out for 391 at lunch on day2, from 323/3. Harbhajan was the star of the show again, with another 7-wicket haul. The Turbanator had arrived and how!

The Indian openers resumed after lunch with a solid display, leaving and blocking the good deliveries and punishing the bad ones. Das was batting with more intent than usual and reached a well-compiled fifty before tea. The pair continued their good work after tea, posting their first century stand in the series. Ramesh also completed a fifty, with some typically elegant shots on the leg-side. They looked set for a big partnership, but Warne broke through, getting Ramesh caught by Ponting. He made 61.

Laxman, who had been promoted to one down after his epic 281 in the previous Test, got going quickly, maintaining the momentum. He played some glorious cover drives off McGrath and Gillespie, and some trademark inside-out drives off Warne. Das also grew in confidence, and even hit a rare six off a spinner. Laxman reached another stylish half-century, and the pair ensured that India ended the day on 211/1, leading by 20 runs with 9 wickets in hand.

The third day began with a wicket on the first ball, as McGrath bowled Das with a swinging delivery for a well-crafted 84. This set the stage for another battle between India's best batsman, Sachin Tendulkar, and Australia's best bowler, Glenn McGrath. The two had a personal rivalry since

India's tour of Australia in 1999, and McGrath had dismissed Tendulkar twice in the series.

Tendulkar was determined to make amends, and played cautiously against McGrath while scoring freely against the other bowlers. He got off to a good start but lost his partner Laxman, who was caught in the slips by Mark Waugh off McGrath for 65. Ganguly joined Tendulkar, and they took India to lunch at 266/3.

Steve Waugh brought back McGrath for a short spell after lunch, and he delivered by getting Ganguly caught behind for 22. It was another wasted start for the Indian captain, who had failed to convert four out of five starts in the series.

Dravid came in at number 6 and looked confident after his marathon innings in Kolkata. He and Tendulkar scored at a brisk rate for the rest of the session. Tendulkar reached his fifty, his second in the series, and shifted gears. He played some glorious cover drives against the pacers, and a variety of sweeps against the spinners Warne and Miller. One of his sweeps off Miller cleared the boundary for a six.

Steve Waugh brought back his ace bowler, McGrath, to break the partnership. McGrath peppered Tendulkar with short-pitched bouncers, challenging him to pull or hook. Tendulkar sensed the importance of this phase of play and refused to take the bait. He ducked and swayed away from the most menacing bouncer in the game at that time, and waited for his chance against McGrath. In an earlier interview, Tendulkar had said that you don't always need to hit a bowler out of the attack to win a personal battle, sometimes you can achieve the same by playing out his spell. He demonstrated that to perfection in Chepauk, taking India to tea with 378/4 on the board, himself on 77* and his partner two short of a fifty. India were just 13 behind Australia's first innings total.

Dravid reached his fifty, and India went past 391 and then 400 soon after tea. Tendulkar was in his element, and raced to the nineties. He completed his hundred with a towering six off Miller. It was a delayed but masterful innings by the world's best batsman, and he stamped his authority on the series in the decider. Chepauk had always been a happy hunting ground for the little master. He had scored a brilliant 137 against Pakistan here, which had ended in heartbreak. Today, he treated the knowledgeable Chennai crowd to another masterclass in Test batting against a top-quality attack, and the entire stadium rose to give him a prolonged ovation.

India's most dependable pair added another 150 runs, before Gillespie broke the stand getting Dravid caught behind for a fluent 81. Tendulkar hit another six, this time off Warne, but fell soon after to Gillespie in the same manner as Dravid. The two Australian spinners then took three quick wickets, and India ended the day on 480/9.

McGrath was the best bowler for Australia, with three wickets for his lion-hearted effort, but the day belonged to Tendulkar, who had played a superlative innings.

Miller finished off the Indian innings early on the fourth day, dismissing them for 501, a lead of 110 runs. The Australian openers came out all guns blazing, hitting three sixes and several fours off the spinners. They reached lunch at 69/0 in just 16 overs. They were nearing a century stand, when Hayden got carried away and holed out to the boundary, trying to hit another six off Kulkarni.

Australia tried a gamble by sending Gilchrist at number 3, with a license to attack the bowling. But it backfired, as he fell lbw to Harbhajan for the third time in a row. Slater should have been more cautious after that, but he played a loose shot and edged Harbhajan to Laxman in the slips, just two runs short of a fifty. India smelled another collapse, but Mark Waugh and Langer steadied the ship with a fifty-run stand, before Bahutule got Langer caught by Laxman for 30. Australia were 141/4, and needed the Waugh brothers to bail them out. They took Australia to tea at 159/4.

Mark Waugh reached his fifty, his second in the series, but could not go on. He was caught at slip by Dravid off Harbhajan for 55. Harbhajan then tormented his bunny Ponting, who tried to slog his way out of trouble, but only managed to hit one six before falling to Harbhajan's trap yet again. Warne hung around for a while, but was trapped lbw by Harbhajan for 11. Steve Waugh found some support from Gillespie, who blocked everything. They took Australia to stumps at 241/7, with Steve Waugh on 43 and Gillespie on 10. Australia were 131 ahead of India.

The series was on the line on the fifth and final day. The fate of the match depended on Steve Waugh's wicket. If he could add another 70 runs or so with the tail, India would have a tough chase of over 200 on a turning Chepauk pitch, against an attack that had Warne in it. If India could get him out early, they could fancy their chances of pulling off a historic win, and a remarkable comeback in the series, against the most successful Test team ever.

But Steve Waugh could not last long, and it was Harbhajan who got him, caught by Dighe for 47. The Turbanator once again ran through the tail, ending the Australian innings for 264, leaving India a target of 154 to win the match and the series.

Chasing 155 on the final day may not seem too difficult, but on a fifth-day Chepauk pitch against the best bowling attack in the world, it was a daunting task. India had suffered a heart-breaking loss against Pakistan here in 1999, when they failed to chase 137. They had to overcome that memory and the Australian spirit, which never gave up.

McGrath struck early, catching Das off his own bowl. Laxman continued his sublime form, batting as if in a trance. He and Ramesh added 50, calming the nerves in the dressing room. But then Ramesh was run out in a horrible mix-up with Laxman. Tendulkar joined Laxman and took India past 100. Only 55 more runs were needed for a historic series win. But the drama was not over yet. At 101, Gillespie got Tendulkar to edge one to Mark Waugh at slips, and Chepauk went silent. The ghost of 1999 came back to haunt them.

Laxman creamed two beautifully timed boundaries to let off some steam. Ganguly also started with a four, but soon fell prey to his old weakness, driving away from his body on a well-pitched outswinger, this time nicking one to Mark Waugh at slips off Gillespie. He made just 4.

The match was hanging in the balance when Ganguly departed, leaving India at 118/4. But the real shock came ten balls later, when Dravid edged one to the keeper and walked back with only 4 runs to his name. India were reeling at 122/5, and the Australians sensed blood. They unleashed their ruthless aggression, tightening the screws on every batsman who came to the crease. Laxman, who had been playing with sublime grace, felt the pressure mounting on him. He knew he was the last hope for his team, and had to carry them across the line.

With as many as 9 men breathing down their neck, Laxman and the debutant wicket-keeper Sameer Dighe took the score to 135 but then Laxman succumbed to the pressure. He tried to break free from the shackles of Miller's off-spin, but only managed to find a fielder. He departed for a brilliant 66, with 12 glorious fours in his 82-ball knock.

The match was on a knife-edge, as India lost their last recognised batsman at 135/6, needing 20 more runs. The tail was green and shaky, with two debutants and two rookies. The inexperience showed when Bahutule, who had a solid domestic record and had remained unbeaten in the first innings, holed out to Miller for a duck, just three balls after Laxman's dismissal. India were staring at defeat at 135/7.

But Sameer Dighe, the other debutant, was a battle-hardened veteran for Mumbai. He had the grit and the temperament to handle the pressure. He needed someone to back him up from the other end, and he found a willing partner in Zaheer Khan. The left-arm pacer defended his wicket for half-an hour like his life depended on it, giving Dighe the chance to whittle down the target. They added 16 vital runs, bringing India within a whisker of victory, when McGrath finally ended Zaheer's stubborn resistance and had him caught at slip by Mark Waugh. India were 151/8, with 4 runs to win and two wickets in hand.

It was a moment of destiny, as the man who had tormented the Australians with the ball throughout the series, walked out to bat. Harbhajan Singh, the Turbanator, had the chance to seal the deal with the bat. And he did not disappoint, smashing the ball to the boundary and sparking wild celebrations. He had completed the unthinkable.

Yes. The unbelievable had happened. This hastily put-together Indian team had forced the mighty Australian juggernaut to surrender. Sourav Ganguly's men had first snapped the longest winning streak in Test history and then, as if to show that the win at Kolkata was no fluke, inflicted another stunning defeat on the formidable Australians, handing them their first series loss in the process.

03

Surging Forward with Momentum

The test series victory was a historic feat, but to make it count, it was crucial to display the same courage and flair in the ODI series as well, regardless of the outcome.

Both India and Australia made some changes to their squads for the 5-match ODI series. Australia brought back some of their ODI specialists, such as Michael Bevan, Darren Lehmann, Ian Harvey and Nathan Bracken. India, on the other hand, decided to give more opportunities to their promising young talents, such as Virender Sehwag, Yuvraj Singh, Hemang Badani and Dinesh Mongia, while veterans Srinath and Robin Singh returned from their injuries.

The day after the third test ended, a practice game was arranged for these ODI players from both sides as preparation for the upcoming series. India won the game comfortably, thanks to the contributions from Tendulkar and Robin Singh.

The first ODI at Bangalore was a one-sided affair, as India piled up 315 runs thanks to half-centuries from Dravid, Sehwag and keeper Vijay Dahia. Australia were never in the chase and folded for 255, with only Bevan showing some fight apart from Haydos, who carried on from his exploits in the Test series, missing out on a century by just 1 run. Sehwag was the star of the show, with a gritty fifty and 3 vital wickets, earning him the man of the match.

Australia staged a strong comeback in the second ODI at Pune, by bowling out India for 248 and then chasing it down with nine wickets and five overs to spare. Badani scored his maiden hundred for India and Laxman added another stylish fifty, but they were overshadowed by a vintage Mark Waugh innings of 133 not out. Australia's best batsman had been out of form in the tests, and it was high time he delivered. He did just that, winning the man of the match.

Not one to be left behind by his one-time rival, it was the turn of world's foremost ODI batsman Sachin Tendulkar to light up the stadium at Indore with a sparkling century of his own, his 28th in this format, with Laxman once again playing the perfect anchor. India posted 299, a formidable total on any ground. The bowlers - except for Zaheer who was taken apart by Gilchrist at the start - then worked together to dismiss an Australia without Hayden for a paltry 181, with Harbhajan finally getting among wickets in ODIs too, after drawing a blank in the first two games.

The series was levelled at 2-2, after Australia dominated the fourth ODI at Vizag. They batted first and amassed 338, with two contrasting centuries from Hayden, who was in sublime form, and Ponting, who was struggling for runs. India had no answer to the Australian onslaught, and were bowled out for 245, with McGrath and Warne leading the attack.

Little did anyone know, including the man himself, that this was the final time that one of the unsung heroes of Indian cricket, Robin Singh, would don the Indian colours. Making his comeback to the national side at the age of 33 in 1996, he went on to play one test and 136 ODIs for India and never gave less than 120% in any of those appearances.

The stage was set for a thrilling finale in Goa, after a seven-week showdown between a champion team and a spirited underdog. The series was tied at 2-2, and both teams were eager to clinch the trophy.

India had been troubled by the gradual loss of form and confidence of their captain Sourav Ganguly. What started as a run of middling scores in the tests had now grown into a full-blown crisis with Ganguly managing only 19 runs in the 4 innings thus far. He even tried demoting himself to middle order in the third match but without success. So, he returned as opener for this decider, and finally found some of his mojo, scoring a fluent 74 off 83 balls, with 2 trademark sixes. This had been a career defining tour for VVS Laxman and he ended it with a bang by posting another silken hundred, his first in ODIs, helping his team post a total of 265/6 in 50 overs.

In response, the new Aussie opening pair of Hayden and Gilchrist went hammer and tongs against the Indian seamers posting a 100-run stand - the first of the 16 century partnerships they would share over the years, making them one of the most fearsome opening pairs of all time. Then Michael Bevan, the best finisher in the game, showed his class and skill and guided Australia to a comfortable win and a series triumph.

Australia clinched the series 3-2, ending one of the most intense and captivating cricket tours in the history of sports, a tour that breathed a fresh lease of life into test cricket.

The test series win against the invincibles was a landmark achievement and had far-reaching consequences. First and foremost, it cemented Ganguly's position as the undisputed leader of the Indian team for the foreseeable future. He had the most supportive and dependable coach and deputy in John Wright and Rahul Dravid, who shared his vision and passion. Tendulkar took on the role of the mentor/locker-room leader, a role that suited him perfectly. The other senior pro Anil Kumble, though sidelined by a serious shoulder injury, was also his usual cooperative self, having taken the young offie Harbhajan under his wings right from the time of the preparatory camp prior to the series.

On the batting front VVS Laxman had finally arrived, filling the huge shoes of Azharuddin.

But the real shot in the arm was the emergence of the Turbanator, which meant India now had not one but two world class spinners in their ranks and both very different from each other in bowling styles as well as personalities.

Coming to the pace department, Srinath had blossomed into a world class seamer and had taken on the mantle of the veteran fast bowler of the side very well. Agarkar too seemed to be maturing well and Zaheer looked a very promising prospect for the future.

In comparison, India's ODI unit was still a work in progress, as they were looking for suitable replacements for the big shoes of Azhar and Jadeja, who had been ODI stalwarts for India. Robin Singh too wasn't getting any younger, which meant that the whole middle-order needed to be rebuilt. The silver lining was that Laxman had carried his form from the test series to the one-dayers, filling the huge void left by Azhar, at least temporarily. Young guns Yuvraj and Sehwag had also shown promise, but they still had a long way to go before they could become a finisher of the calibre of Ajay Jadeja.

On the bowling front, Agarkar's knack of taking wickets had him challenging for the mantle of India's main strike bowler though Srinath was still going strong. Team management seemed to have made up its mind to move on from Venkatesh Prasad, and started grooming Zaheer Khan as India's third-choice seamer.

As far as spin was concerned, it took a few games but Harbhajan had begun to adapt to the demands of the shorter format as well, a sign that augured well for the future.

But what the ODI unit desperately needed was a quality wicket-keeper batsman, which most of the good one-day sides had. Australia had the explosive Gilchrist, Pakistan had the gritty Moin, Sri Lanka had Kaluwitharana and his talented understudy Kumar Sangakkara.

After the exhilarating home series against Australia, India was scheduled to play in the Sharjah Cup with Australia and Pakistan in April. But the Indian government intervened and barred the Indian team from participating in that tournament. The government's reasons were more political than cricketing, but the decision turned out to be a blessing in disguise for the players, who needed a break after the exhausting series against the best in the world. They got a good two months of rest before their next assignment, which was a 2-match test series and a ODI tri-series, both in Zimbabwe, in June-July.

Before embarking on the tour, coach John Wright organised a preparatory camp for the team, just like he had done before the series against Australia. Ashish Nehra, a tall and lanky rookie left-arm seamer from Delhi, who had made his test debut two years ago in 1999 but had fallen out of favour, earned a comeback on the basis of his good performance in domestic cricket.

The team played two 3-day practice matches before the first Test. The first one ended in a draw, with Dravid scoring a big hundred and the bowlers, including Nehra and the lone spinner Harbhajan, impressing with their skills. India won the second 3-day game easily, with three batsmen - opener Das, VVS and Badani - hitting hundreds and the others also scoring some easy runs.

Zimbabwe batted first on a lively pitch, and were soon in trouble against India's bowlers on the first day of the first test. Nehra, the rookie left-arm seamer, bowled with pace and swing, and took 3 wickets, including Andy Flower, who scored 83. Zimbabwe were all out for 173 in less than 60 overs.

India's reply started shakily, as they lost 5 wickets for 98. Tendulkar and Dravid then steadied the ship, with a solid 80-run partnership. Tendulkar scored 74, and Harbhajan slammed a quick 66, taking India to a lead of 145.

Zimbabwe fought back in the second innings, with the Flower brothers scoring 83 and 71 respectively. They set India a target of 184, which India chased down easily, losing only 2 wickets, just after tea on day 4. Opener Das played another good innings, remaining unbeaten on 84. He was adjudged the man of the match for his batting and sharp close-in catching.

Though it came against Zimbabwe, the win was still significant, as it marked India's first test victory outside the subcontinent in 15 years. It also showed that the dream run that began in Kolkata was still alive, as India followed up their historic series win against Australia with another impressive performance.

It was to come to a scratching halt in most unpredictable fashion in the second and final test in the series.

04

From Triumphs to Tribulations

India won the toss and batted first, but were soon in trouble against Zimbabwe's bowlers. Badani, the makeshift opener, was out in the third over, and VVS and Tendulkar also failed to convert their starts. Das scored a fifty, but fell soon after, and Ganguly continued his poor run. Dravid was the only one who resisted, scoring an unbeaten 68 and taking India to 237. Streak and Blignaut shared 7 wickets for Zimbabwe.

Zimbabwe started their innings poorly, losing 3 wickets for 31, before Andy Flower and Ebrahim steadied the ship with a 90-run stand. Harbhajan broke the partnership, and took 4 wickets, but Grant Flower played a gritty knock of 71, and took Zimbabwe to 315, a lead of 78. Nehra also took 4 wickets for India.

India's second innings was a disaster, as they lost wickets at regular intervals. Dighe, the new opener, was out for 4, and VVS and Ganguly also failed. Tendulkar and Das added 100 runs, but both fell to Streak, who took 4 wickets. Dravid was out just before stumps, leaving India at 197/4. Blignaut took a crucial 5-wicket haul and wrapped up the tail, dismissing India for 234.

Chasing 157, Zimbabwean openers survived the initial onslaught from the Indian seamers, but Srinath and Harbhajan soon removed them. Carlisle played a steady innings, but the other batsmen struggled to score. Campbell, Grant Flower and Streak all fell cheaply, and Blignaut, who had a terrific game, was bowled by Nehra. It was up to the injured Andy Flower, Zimbabwe's best batsman, to join Carlisle and take them home. He did just that, with two exquisite boundaries, and sealed one of Zimbabwe's greatest wins in test history. Carlisle remained unbeaten on 69, but Blignaut was the man of the match for his all-round performance.

This result was a shocker of epic proportions. It left the Indian team shell-shocked and their fans speechless. Just when Indian cricket seemed to be on the rise and the fans were starting to hope again, this unforeseen defeat came as a rude awakening.

The only positive was the form of ShivSundar Das, who bagged the Man of the Series award for his series total of 202 runs, the highest among both teams; and the emergence of Ashish Nehra as the series' top bowler with 11 wickets.

The ODI tri-series with West Indies as the third team was next on the agenda. India warmed up with a convincing win in a practice match. Eager to avenge the shock defeat in the second test, they dominated the tournament from the start and reached the final undefeated, thrashing both Zimbabwe and West Indies with ease thanks to some splendid batting by their openers, especially Tendulkar who won three Man of the Match awards in four games, and a collective effort by the bowlers who coped well without the injured Srinath. Now the final beckoned and as expected it was against West Indies.

Going by the recent form, as well as the fact that the West Indies were without the services of their best batsman Brian Lara who had to sit out this tournament due to an injury, India were the favourites in the final. A win here would somewhat make-up for the disappointment of losing the second test.

As it turned out, it wasn't to be as Ganguly's men once again failed to cross the final hurdle and a spirited Windies edged them out in a well contested final.

Ganguly opted to bowl first under cloudy skies and hoped to exploit the conditions. But Gayle and Darren Ganga had other ideas, as they launched a blistering attack on the Indian bowlers and put on 86 in just 13 overs. Harbhajan finally broke through, dismissing Gayle for 43, but Ganga carried on with his aggressive batting and reached his fifty in quick time. He fell for 71 off 62, caught by Laxman off a slower delivery from young Reetinder Singh Sodhi. Sodhi also removed the sluggish Hinds, leaving Hooper and Chanderpaul to rebuild the innings. The experienced duo did a fine job, adding 108 runs in a fluent partnership, with both of them scoring brisk fifties. They rotated the strike well and punished the loose balls from the inexperienced Indian attack. Zaheer and Nehra managed to get rid of them in the end, but not before they had taken West Indies to a formidable 290.

India's chase got off to a disastrous start, as Sachin, who was suffering from a stomach upset, perished for a duck, caught off a mistimed pull from Collimore. Ganguly, Laxman and Dravid all showed glimpses of their class, but none of them could convert their starts into a big score. Sehwag, batting at number five, also failed, scoring just two. India were in deep trouble at 80/5 in 18 overs, facing a humiliating defeat. Sodhi - the 19-year-old prodigy who had led India to the Under-15 World Cup title in 1996 and was the Man of the Final in the Under-19 World Cup final in January 2000 - and Dighe then staged a remarkable fightback, putting on 101 runs for the sixth wicket and keeping India in the hunt. Sodhi smashed 67 off 74 with 3 sixes, while Dighe played a gritty knock of 94 not out. But their efforts were not enough, as India fell short by 16 runs in the end.

Collimore was the Man of the Match for his splendid 4-wicket haul. Sachin won the Man of the Series for his 282 runs, but that was a small consolation for the team that returned home empty-handed.

The team's next assignment was a trip to Sri Lanka for a tri-series and a test series. Sachin Tendulkar, for the first time since his debut in 1989, had to withdraw from the tour due to an injury. This meant that the team would miss the services of three of its senior players - Sachin, Srinath and Anil Kumble, who needed two more months of recovery.

In the absence of these stalwarts, the team began the tournament on a dismal note, losing its first 3 matches - once to hosts Sri Lanka and twice to New Zealand, who was fast becoming a thorn in the side of Ganguly's team since the ICC Knock-outs final. The team also experimented too much with the batting order, especially the opening pair. To make matters worse, Ganguly injured his back and had to miss the crucial game against Sri Lanka. Dravid took charge and led the team to a convincing win, restricting the hosts to 183 despite their century opening stand, thanks to some smart bowling changes. He then partnered with Laxman to chase down the target with ease. Laxman was the Man of the Match for his unbeaten 87.

Ganguly returned and guided the team to another win over Sri Lanka, powered by a splendid knock of 98 not out by Yuvraj Singh, who was well supported by the consistent Dravid. The bowlers also did a fine job, with Nehra being the standout performer with 3 wickets. It was an important innings for Yuvraj, who had been doing well with his left-arm spin, but had not been able to contribute much with the bat. This knock boosted his confidence and proved that he was not a one-hit wonder.

The last league game against New Zealand was a virtual semi-final, with the winner advancing to the final against Sri Lanka, who had already qualified. Astle, who was in sublime form, scored his second hundred of the tournament and helped New Zealand post 264, with some help from Fleming and Lou Vincent. Nehra was again the best bowler for India, taking another 3 wickets.

India's reply was a masterclass from makeshift opener Sehwag, who smashed a hundred in just 68 balls, the sixth fastest in ODI history, studded with 19 fours and a six. It was coach John Wright's idea to try Sehwag as an opener and it turned out to be a total game changer. Ganguly played a mature knock of 64 and added 143 for the first wicket with Sehwag. Dravid, who was becoming Mr. Dependable at number 4, scored a fluent 57 off 57 balls and helped India overhaul the target with more than 4 overs to spare. Sehwag was the obvious choice for the Man of the Match.

Riding on this remarkable turn-around, India stormed into another final with momentum on their side having beaten the other finalist Sri Lanka twice in three games in the league phase. All that came to a naught as the hosts posted an imposing target of 295 on the back of a blistering 99 by Jayasuriya who had rediscovered his form after becoming the captain, and a couple of contrasting fifties by the young guns Jayawardene and Arnold. India had no answer to the crafty Sri Lankan bowling and were bundled out for 174 in 48 overs, losing by a massive margin of 121 runs. Russel Arnold was the Man of the Match for his all-round performance and Jayasuriya was the Man of the Series for his 300-plus runs. Once again, this young Indian team had shown glimpses of potential, but had failed to deliver in the final.

The Finals curse carried on.

The team was bolstered by the return of Srinath and Prasad, who added some experience to the bowling attack, for the three-match Test series against the hosts. But the batting line-up was still weakened by the absence of Tendulkar and Laxman, who was ruled out of the first test due to his recurring back problem. Dravid was promoted to bat at number 4, while the very promising Mohammad Kaif, the Under-19 World Cup winning captain, was slotted at number 3.

Jayasuriya, who had an uncanny knack of winning tosses, chose to bowl first and unleashed his fast bowler Dilhara Fernando on the Indian batsmen. Fernando bowled with pace and venom, and rattled the Indian innings with a fiery spell on the first and second day. India were bowled out for 187, their lowest first innings total in Sri Lanka. The hosts replied with 365, thanks to contrasting centuries by their flamboyant captain Jayasuriya and their young and talented wicket-keeper batsman Sangakkara, who scored his maiden test hundred. Srinath, who had to retire hurt after being hit on the finger by a Fernando bouncer, showed great courage and bowled 25 overs, taking 5 wickets. Zaheer also chipped in with 3.

India were 178 behind and needed to bat well in the second innings to save the test. But they were undone by the spin wizardry of Muralitharan, who claimed his 25th five-wicket haul in tests. Only Dravid resisted with a defiant 61 not out, and helped India avoid an innings defeat. But the match was over on the fourth day, when the Sri Lankan openers knocked off the 14 runs required to win. It was Sri Lanka's first win over India in almost 16 years. Jayasuriya won the Man of the Match.

To compound India's problems further, Srinath was ruled out of the remainder of the series. Yet, the team bounced back with a strong showing in the second test. They won the toss and chose to bowl first, and managed to bowl out Sri Lanka for 274, with a collective effort from the bowlers. Zaheer was the leader of the pack with 3 key wickets, while Ganguly also contributed with a couple of vital wickets. India's reply was not very convincing, as they could only muster 232, thanks to a gutsy 44 from Harbhajan.

India were 44 behind and needed to bowl well in the second innings to stay in the game. Venkatesh Prasad and Zaheer did just that, as they ran through the Sri Lankan batting line-up and dismissed them for 221.

Veteran Prasad took a 5-wicket haul, while Zaheer claimed 4, including the top-order batsmen.

India had to chase 264 in the fourth innings, which was not an easy task against Muralitharan. But the captain and the vice-captain rose to the occasion and forged a crucial 91-run partnership, playing Murali with skill and confidence. Dravid scored 75 with 12 boundaries, while Ganguly remained unbeaten on 98, hitting 15 boundaries. Ganguly was the Man of the Match for his all-round performance and leading from the front. He couldn't have chosen a better time to signal his return to form.

The series was level at 1-1 and the final test was a decider. Ganguly won the toss and chose to bat first, hoping to put up a big score. Das and Ramesh gave India a solid start, adding 97 for the first wicket. But then Muralitharan unleashed his magic and ran through the Indian batting line-up, bagging 8 wickets, bowling India out for 234 on the first day. Sri Lanka then batted with authority and piled up 610/6, with four of their batsmen - Atapattu, Jayawardene, Tillakaratne and Samaraweera - scoring hundreds. They batted for the whole of the second day and most of the third day, before declaring and giving India a few overs to survive.

India were exhausted and demoralized after chasing the leather for almost two days, but still put on a semblance of some fight, with the openers putting on 100 runs. But Muralitharan broke their partnership and took three more wickets, completing an 11-wicket haul in the match. India collapsed and lost by an innings and 77 runs. Muralitharan was the Man of the Match and the Man of the Series for his 23 wickets in 3 matches.

The sole consolation was that some of the youngsters like Harbhajan, Zaheer, Nehra, Sehwag and Yuvraj had started to justify the faith shown in them by the team management, which meant that a tentative core of a team for the next decade or so had begun to emerge.

However, the team was still struggling with consistency and seemed to be caught in a cycle of one-step forward, two-steps back loop.

05

African Safari

India's next challenge was a tour to South Africa for a tri-series and a three-match test series. It was only after the home series against South Africa that the match-fixing scandal had first erupted, having a devastating impact on the cricket in both countries. In the aftermath of the scandal, the cricket boards of both countries had to overhaul their domestic structures and bring in wholesale changes in their national teams, the repercussions of which were still felt by both sides in transition. Now, a year and a half after that life-changing event, the two teams were set to face each other in a full tour.

The tour began with a tri-series that also featured Kenya as the third team. India entered the opening match against the hosts South Africa with confidence, having won both their practice games comfortably before the start of the tri-series.

First match saw India's openers giving them an excellent start, scoring a century each and putting on 193 runs in 35 overs. But the middle order failed to capitalize on their platform and were restricted to 280. South Africa chased down the target with ease, thanks to a superb opening stand of 114 in 17 overs with Gary Kirsten carrying his bat for a typical workman like 133 and the rest providing able support.

India bounced back in the next match, despite scoring only 233. Their bowlers did the job, as the seamers removed the openers and then Harbhajan and a returning Anil Kumble spun a web around the South African middle order. They bowled them out for 192 in the 46th over, with Harbhajan taking 3 wickets for 27 runs and claiming the Man of the Match honour. The Turbanator had announced his arrival in South Africa with a bang.

Bowlers continued their good form against Kenya, bowling them out for 90. Agarkar was the Man of the Match for his 4-wicket haul, while Kumble claimed 3. It was good to see the great Jumbo back among the wickets after a long and arduous lay-off. The experimental opening pair of Sehwag and the new wicket-keeper Deepdas Gupta chased down the target without losing a wicket and gave India a 10-wicket win.

Kenya showed great character in coming back from such an absolute drubbing and pulled off a stunning upset in the next match, winning by 70 runs and injecting some excitement into the otherwise predictable tournament. They batted as a unit and posted 246, and then bowled and fielded with passion and skill to dismiss India for 176. Joseph Angara was the the Man of the Match, taking 3 wickets for 30 runs. The famed Indian batting line-up had no answers for Kenyan brand of dibbly-dobbly medium pace, especially in the middle overs. This was Kenya's second greatest win, only behind their 1996 World Cup victory over West Indies, and the fact that it came in absence of their captain and MVP Maurice Odumbe made it all the more special.

Shook from this unexpected loss, India went on to lose their next game as well, this time against the hosts. South Africa won the toss and chose to bat first, scoring 282/4 with good contributions from most of their top six. Gibbs was the top scorer, making a quick 47. India started the chase well, with their regular openers Tendulkar and Ganguly adding 100 runs in the first 15 overs. But Kallis broke the partnership, bowling Tendulkar for 36. Ganguly continued to bat with flair and aggression, and looked set for a hundred, when he holed out to Kallis off Boje for 97. His dismissal triggered a collapse, as the inexperienced middle order succumbed to some brilliant South African fielding, resulting in 3 run-outs. Dravid fought hard, but ran out of partners, as India fell short by 41 runs. Ganguly was declared the Man of the Match, despite being on the losing side.

India faced a must-win situation in their last league game against Kenya, and they rose to the occasion with a dominant performance. Both openers scored magnificent centuries and set the tone for a huge total of 351. Sehwag, who was sent in at one down, added more firepower with a blazing fifty. Kenya had no chance of chasing down the target, and they could manage just 165/5 in 50 overs. Sachin, who was the highest scorer with 146, was awarded the Man of the Match.

Thus, Team India reached another final, hoping to break their jinx of losing in the summit clashes.

But South Africa's captain Shaun Pollock had other plans, as he won the toss and decided to bowl first. He bowled a superb spell of seam bowling, and dismissed the in-form Indian captain early. His partner Nantie Hayward also bowled with pace and got rid of Sachin for 17. Pollock had gambled with an all-seam attack, leaving out Boje, and his gamble paid off. All the 5 bowlers bowled with discipline and accuracy, and did not allow any Indian batsman to settle. Dravid was the only one to cross 50, but he did not get any support. India were bowled out for 183, failing to bat out their 50 overs.

South Africa chased down the target with ease, with Kirsten and Kallis leading the way. Kirsten continued his sublime form and scored 87, while Kallis played another solid knock. South Africa won by 7 wickets and 7 overs to spare. Shaun Pollock was the Man of the Match for his brilliant spell, and Kirsten was the Man of the Series for his 387 runs, that included 2 hundreds.

It was India's ninth consecutive loss in a final, and fifth under Ganguly's captaincy. The finals curse remained unbroken.

The dejected team was dealt another blow when their 3-day practice game preceding the start of first test got washed out without a single ball being bowled. To make matters worse, they lost Harbhajan to a groin infection and Dighe to back spasms on the morning of the first day. Ganguly also lost the toss and was put in to bat on a pitch that looked favourable for the bowlers.

Pollock made the most of his decision, as he dismissed makeshift opener Dravid for just 2 in the fifth over, caught by Kallis in the slips. The other bowlers also bowled well, and India were reduced to 68/4 after 20 overs. Tendulkar was joined by debutant Sehwag, who was under pressure. But Tendulkar decided to take the attack to the bowlers, and played a stunning innings. He drove, cut, pulled and hooked with authority, and punished every bowler, including Pollock. He scored at a rapid pace, hitting 8 boundaries in 18 balls at one stage. He allowed Sehwag to settle in, and soon Sehwag also joined the fun with some elegant drives. Tendulkar reached his 26th Test hundred off just 114 balls, and Sehwag got his fifty on debut. They added 220 runs for the fifth wicket at five runs per over, and took India to a position of strength. Tendulkar finally fell for 155 off 184 balls, with 23 fours and a six. It was a sensational counter-attacking knock, reaffirming his status as the best batsman of his generation.

Sehwag, who was well set by then, shifted gears and raced to his maiden hundred, also on debut, with a flurry of boundaries. But he got carried away and was bowled by Pollock soon after. He made 105 off 173 balls, with 19 fours. Deepdas Gupta hung on, but Kallis removed Kumble in the last over of the day, leaving India at 372/7. It ended quickly on the second morning, as India could add only 7 more runs to the overnight total. Pollock was the best bowler for South Africa, taking 4 wickets.

In response, South Africa's openers continued from where they left in the one-dayers and put on a mammoth partnership of 189 for the first wicket, with Gibbs being especially harsh on the young Indian left-arm pacers Nehra and Zaheer, whom he smashed over long-on for a gigantic six to reach his century in style. He made 107 off 145 balls, with 16 fours and 2 sixes. It was the returning Anil Kumble who got India their first breakthrough, dismissing a well-set Kirsten for 79. Srinath also got Gibbs in the next over, giving India some hope. But McKenzie and Kallis dashed their hopes, as they added another 130 runs for the third wicket. McKenzie fell to Kumble on the last ball of the day for 68. South Africa ended day2 at 327/3, just 45 runs behind and Kallis just one short of another fifty.

A lot had been written and said about the two young left-arm pacers of India, Zaheer Khan and Ashish Nehra in the build-up to the series but the duo failed to live up to the buzz, with Nehra in particular coming in for special thrashing at the hands of Gibbs.

Nehra redeemed himself on the third morning, by getting rid of Kallis for 68. Srinath also bowled well, and took two wickets in two balls, dismissing Boeta Dippenaar and Pollock. South Africa were 377/6, still trailing by 2 runs. India needed a couple more wickets to gain the upper hand. But Lance Klusener had other ideas, as he played a typically aggressive innings and smashed 121 runs for the seventh wicket with Boucher, who made 47. Klusener ended his poor run of form with a well-deserved hundred, before falling to Kumble. Srinath and Nehra wrapped up the tail, but South Africa had scored 563, taking a lead of 189 runs.

Srinath was the standout bowler for India with a 5-wicket haul to show for his toil. Kumble chipped in with 3 prized wickets making it a decent comeback to test cricket.

India faced a daunting task of saving the Test, as they trailed by 189 runs in the second innings. They started well, with Das and Dravid scoring at a brisk rate. But Pollock struck in the fifth over, removing Dravid for 2, caught by Kirsten in the slips. Das and Laxman then added 80 runs, but Pollock broke their partnership, as Laxman edged one to Kallis at first slip for 29. Two balls later, Das also departed, nicking a Hayward delivery to the keeper for a fluent 62, with 13 boundaries.

India once again needed their designated saviour Tendulkar to rescue them, but he failed to deliver on this occasion. He fell for 15, caught by Gibbs at point off a Kallis outswinger. Kallis achieved a milestone with this wicket, as he became only the eighth player in history to complete the double of 100 wickets and 3000 runs in tests. Ganguly and Sehwag tried to hang on, but Ganguly was undone by a bouncer from Hayward, while Sehwag was bowled by an inswinger from Pollock. Pollock then ran through the tail, and bowled India out for 237, taking 6 wickets for 56 runs. He finished with 10 wickets in the match, the first time he had done so in tests. None of the Indian batsmen could convert their starts into a big score.

South Africa had to chase only 54 runs to win, and they did so with ease, losing only Gibbs' wicket. They won by 9 wickets and a day to spare. Pollock was the deserved Man of the Match for his 10-wicket haul. India put up a good fight for better part of three days, but collapsed meekly on the fourth day. Looking back, it was Klusener's onslaught on the third evening that broke their morale and snatched the game away from them.

The series was now 0-1 in favour of South Africa, with two more tests to go.

No one could've anticipated what was to follow in the coming days.

India's chances of making a comeback in the series were further hampered by the weather, as their second three-day tour match against South Africa A was cancelled due to rain.

Ganguly won the toss and put South Africa in to bat first. India went in with two changes, Harbhajan and Agarkar replacing Zaheer and Nehra. A rejuvenated Srinath continued from where he left off in the previous test and got India an early breakthrough again by dismissing the in-form Kirsten caught in the slips. However, Gibbs was again looking in ominous touch and added 70 runs with Kallis, before Srinath came back and bowled Kallis with a beautiful inswinger for 24. Harbhajan also got into the act, and bowled McKenzie to reduce South Africa to 117/3. Gibbs then took charge, and scored at a brisk rate, while Dippenaar played a supporting role. They added 105 runs, before Dippenaar edged Agarkar to the keeper for 29. Gibbs carried on, and reached his hundred with a huge six over long-on off Zaheer. He made 107 off 145 balls, with 16 fours and 2 sixes. Srinath also got rid of him, and then dismissed Klusener cheaply. South Africa ended the day at 237/5.

Gibbs resumed his innings on the second day, but lost his captain Pollock soon, caught by Harbhajan off a slower ball from Srinath. Gibbs then found an ally in Boucher, and they added 80 runs in quick time. Gibbs fell for 196, caught by Sehwag off Tendulkar. Kumble also got a wicket in the next over, dismissing Boje. Srinath and Nehra finished off the tail, but South Africa had scored 362, with Boucher making 68 off 69 balls. Srinath was the best bowler for India, taking another 5-for - his second in two tests.

India's reply was dismal, as they were blown away by Pollock & co. Only Laxman and Ganguly showed some fight, scoring 89 and 49 respectively. India were bowled out for 201, giving South Africa a lead of 161 runs. Pollock took 5 wickets, while Kallis took 2.

South Africa batted aggressively in their second innings, and scored 211/5 by the end of the third day, with Kallis and Pollock at the crease. Kallis remained unbeaten on 89, and declared early on the fourth day, setting India a target of 394.

Rain washed out most of the fourth day, giving India some hope of saving the Test. They batted with determination on the fifth day, with opener Deepdas Gupta and Dravid putting on a solid partnership. Gupta made 63 off 281 balls, while Dravid made 87 off 241 balls. Their partnership was broken just before tea, and then rain intervened again. South Africa could not take the remaining eight wickets in the shortened final session, and had to settle for a draw. Gibbs was the Man of the Match for his splendid ton.

But more than the actual cricket, what this test is remembered for is the huge controversy that erupted at the end of the second day, when the match referee Mike Denness accused Sachin Tendulkar of ball tampering. It was a shocking allegation, as Tendulkar was widely regarded as a gentleman and a role model. To make matters worse, Denness also imposed harsh bans on four other Indian players for excessive appealing, and on the Indian captain for failing to control them.

The verdicts were outrageous and unfair, and they sparked a huge uproar. The team was outraged and the team management - which included the coach, captain, vice-captain and senior players Sachin and Anil Kumble - expressed their displeasure to the newly elected BCCI President Mr. Jagmohan Dalmia, who threw his weight behind his players in an unprecedented manner, demanding the bans be revoked and Denness be sacked. ICC refused to do either. But they had underestimated Dalmia's tenacity. Rather than backing down, the diminutive Bengali further escalated the assault, accusing Denness and ICC of racism. This serious allegation turned the controversy from a sporting issue to a national issue, with former Indian cricketer and member of parliament Kirti Azad raising the issue in the Indian parliament, urging the government to intervene and cancel the tour if ICC did not revoke the bans and take action against Denness.

By now the general public too had got sufficiently incensed. In a country where cricket is a religion and Sachin Tendulkar its sole deity, such actions were bound to provoke a strong reaction. Thousands of fans took to the streets in major cricketing centres like Delhi, Mumbai, Kolkata and Hyderabad, burning effigies of Denness and the ICC chief and calling them racists.

The Master Puppeteer

Born in 1940 into a wealthy Kolkata business family that had a legacy of building landmarks like the Birla Planetorium, Jagmohan Dalmia had a passion for cricket since his childhood and excelled as a wicketkeeper-batsman, scoring a double century at the college level. He graduated in commerce from the prestigious Scottish Church college and joined his father's construction and real-estate business as an apprentice.

However, his love for cricket never faded and he found his true calling in cricket administration. He became a member of the Cricket Association of Bengal and rose rapidly under the guidance of B.N Dutta. He joined the BCCI as treasurer in early 1983, just before India's historic World Cup victory. He teamed up with Inderjeet Singh Bindra of Punjab and convinced the then board president N.K.P Salve to bid for the hosting rights of the next World Cup in the subcontinent. This was a masterstroke that not only brought the cricket boards of Pakistan and Sri Lanka closer to India, but also shifted the balance of power in the cricketing world from England and Australia to Asia.

The Reliance World Cup 1987 was a huge success and cemented the position of Dalmia and Bindra within the board. They played a key role in electing MadhavRao Scindhia as the board president, who in turn appointed Dalmia as the secretary. It was in this role that Dalmia executed his first major coup - the auction for the TV broadcast rights. He realized the potential of cable television, which had just entered the Indian market in the early 90s, and challenged the monopoly of *Doordarshan*, the state-owned broadcaster. He won the legal battle and sold the rights of the upcoming England series to WorldTel, a broadcast agency headed by Marc Mascarenhas (another visionary who had also revolutionized celebrity management in India when he signed a then-22 years old Sachin Tendulkar for a whopping 5 year-45 crore contract in 1995). This was the beginning of the era of BCCI becoming the richest board in world cricket.

Dalmia's success at home propelled him to the top of the ICC, where he became the president in 1997. He repeated his magic there and turned the fortunes of the parent body around. When he took charge, ICC had only 16000 pounds in its account. By the time he left, it had 15 million dollars. He also backed his players strongly when they faced allegations of match-fixing and racism. He stood by them and refused to allow Mike Denness to officiate the third test between India and South Africa. ICC did not grant official status to the game, but Dalmia did not budge. He had already made his mark as the most influential and powerful man in cricket.

South Africa batted first in the unofficial third test and amassed 566 for 8, with Gibbs, Kirsten and Pollock scoring tons. Pollock also shone with the ball, reducing India to 232. Srinath was the lone Indian bowler to trouble Proteas, taking 4 wickets but he had to retire hurt after a Ntini bouncer. India followed on and did better in the second innings, with Tendulkar and Das hitting fifties, but still lost by an innings and 73 runs. Ntini and Pollock shared 7 wickets. Pollock was the man of the match for his brilliant all-round show.

The match was a forgettable one for the visitors, who failed to put up a fight against a dominant South African side. But regardless of the defeat, this episode cemented India as the undisputed power centre in the cricketing world.

06

An English Challenge

India faced England at home after the disappointing tour of South Africa. The lacklustre performance in South Africa prompted selectors to drop some players like Ashish Nehra and Zaheer Khan, thus India fielded a brand-new pace attack of Tinu Yohanan, Iqbal Siddique and Sanjay Bangar at Mohali, a fast bowler's paradise. England's captain Nasser Hussain lost his 13th toss in a row but scored a gritty 85 after coming in at one down. However, he was undone by the spin duo of Harbhajan and Kumble, who shared 9 wickets and bundled out England for 238. India ended the day at 24/1, with Kumble as the nightwatchman.

On day 2, Kumble and Deepdas Gupta, the makeshift opener, blunted the English seamers in the morning session. They added 53 runs before debutant spinner Dawson broke the partnership. Dravid joined Deepdas Gupta and the pair batted with patience and poise, like they had done to save the second test in South Africa. Deepdas Gupta took over 5 hours to score his maiden hundred, before falling for exactly 100. Tendulkar came in next and delighted the crowd with his elegant drives. Dravid also reached his fifty and the pair took India to 262/3 at stumps.

Dravid fell early on day 3, adding just eight to his overnight 78. Tendulkar and Ganguly added 80 for the fifth wicket, taking India past 300. Tendulkar missed his hundred by 12 runs, edging a late swinger from Hoggard to the keeper. Ganguly also fell soon after, 3 short of his fifty. Laxman and Bangar took India past 400, but Dawson struck again with a late spell, taking 3 wickets and ending India's innings at 469.

England were 231 behind and had to bat out the remaining overs on day 3. They did well to reach 34 without loss. But on day 4, they had no answer to Kumble, who ripped through their batting with 6 wickets. Only Thorpe showed some fight, scoring 62. England were all out for 235, leaving India to chase just 5 runs. The openers did that easily after tea, giving India a 10-wicket win. Kumble was the man of the match for his match-winning spell. 'The Silent Sniper' was well and truly back.

In the post-match press conference, Nasser Hussain dubbed Indian spinning duo of Kumble and Harbhajan as "the best bowling pair in the world". This was high praise, coming from the captain of an English team that had successfully negotiated spinners of the calibre of Muralitharan and Saqlain Mushtaq in their respective dens.

Both sides went in with a couple of changes for the next test at Ahmedabad. For India, a fit-again Srinath came in for Iqbal Siddique and Sehwag returned to the playing XI after serving his ban replacing Sanjay Bangar. England replaced Ormond with Giles and Vaughan stepped in for Thorpe who had to fly back home owing to familial reasons on the very morning of the test.

Nasser Hussain's toss losing streak came to an end after 13 tests and the English openers celebrated with a hundred plus runs opening stand that came to an end when Kumble got Mark Butcher caught behind for 51 and then proceeded to run through the rest of the English top order, claiming the wickets of Hussain, Vaughan, Trescothick and Flintoff who had no answer to his googly and top-spinner.

Just as it seemed England had made a mess of a great start, their number 7 Craig White stepped up and stitched together a couple of crucial partnerships for the 6th and 7th wicket to take his side to a respectable first innings total in excess of 400, registering his own maiden century in the process. He was the last man out for 121 out of a total of 407.

In reply, Indian top order ran into an inspired English bowling attack led by the crafty Hoggard and the fiery Flintoff and the lower order succumbed to the guile of the veteran spinner Ashley Giles who bowled tirelessly and was rewarded with a fifer for his efforts. Only bright spot for the Ahmedabad crowd being the masterly knock from Tendulkar who posted his 27th test hundred in the company of VVS who was last out for 75.

Trailing by over a hundred runs, the Indian spinners managed to restrict England's second innings to 257 with Harbhajan getting the 5fer this time round and Kumble bagging 3 to make it 10 for the match.

This meant India needed 374 to win, a tantalizing target raising expectations of an exciting final day. But all those expectations came to a naught as India opted for a safety-first approach with the openers bringing up 100 in the 42nd over. And even though both fell in succession after completing their respective fifties, by then the fate of the match was more or less sealed as a tame draw.

This result meant that India wouldn't lose the series but the much-improved showing by England here gave them a realistic hope of squaring the series, thus setting up a fitting third and final test of the series to be played at Bangalore.

After a lot of deliberation, Indian selectors decided to go in with 3 spinners meaning Ganguly would have to share the new ball duties with Srinath. This turned out to be a fatal mistake given the weather which had more in common with Headingley than Bangalore. This selection fiasco coupled with Hussain again calling correctly at the toss meant India was on the back foot right from the start.

England batted as a unit to post 336 in the first innings with contrasting fifties from Vaughan - who looked in pristine touch but got out handling the ball, becoming only the seventh batsman in history to be dismissed in this fashion - and Ramprakash, and plucky contributions from White and Foster lower down the order.

For India, Srinath was the pick of the bowlers with a 4fer while Sarandeep Singh justified his inclusion with 3 wickets. With the wicket of Hoggard, Bangalore's own Kumble became the second Indian and only the fourth spinner to bag 300 test wickets. He achieved this feat in just 66 tests.

In reply, Indian batsmen found the going tough against the spirited bowling by Flintoff and Hoggard who made the most of home-like conditions to wreck the Indian top-order. Only Tendulkar and Sehwag - batting at number 7 - could manage to stand up to the English bowling attack and they did so in contrasting fashion, with Tendulkar having to find ways to score against 'negative bowling' from Giles and Flintoff, while Sehwag choosing to counter-attack his way out of the leg-side trap. Giles' relentlessness bore fruit when he finally got his man Tendulkar stumped just 10 short of his hundred.

Hoggard got rid of Sehwag for 66 with his trademark outswinger and the rest couldn't last much signalling the end of Indian innings at 238, 88 runs in deficit. Flintoff and Hoggard bagged 4 apiece while Giles snared the prize wicket of Tendulkar.

Thus, in spite of losing a significant amount of time and overs on day2, the test was still poised for a thrilling finale with England fancying their chances for a series-levelling win. Unfortunately for them, that was not to be as the last two days got washed out with hardly any overs bowled. This meant that the test ended as a draw and India 'escaped' with a series win by the margin of 1-0, to end a promising year on a satisfactory note.

The way England staged a comeback in the test series after losing the first test was a testament to Nasser Hussain's leadership acumen and promised for an even more hard fought ODI series that was to follow.

2002

India suffered a minor setback before the start of the ODI leg when the vice-captain Dravid had to pull out of the first 3 matches due to a shoulder injury.

First match at Eden Gardens delivered on that promise with an exciting finish that saw India post a healthy 281, thanks chiefly to brisk knocks from the top order with Dinesh Mongia - who was drafted in as Dravid's replacement - being the top-scorer with almost a run-a-ball 71. In reply, Marcus Trescothick single-handedly kept England in the hunt with a record-breaking hundred which came of just 80 balls making it the fastest ODI hundred by an English player. But his dismissal - to a questionable lbw decision - in the 36th over triggered such a collapse in the English ranks that they lost their last 5 wickets for just 25 runs and ended up losing by a margin of 22 runs. The adjudicators did well to still award the Man of the match to Trescothick.

Ganguly again called correctly at the toss but chose to field first in the second match. Indian bowlers once again bowled well as a unit but England still managed to post a decent total of 250 thanks to healthy contributions from their middle-order comprised of Hussain, Vaughan and one of their ODI specialists Paul Collingwood who top-scored with an unbeaten 71.

India, in reply, looked on course despite losing Ganguly early but absolutely shambolic running between the wickets resulting in 3 back-to-back run-outs derailed the chase and they fell short by 16 runs in the end. Paul Collingwood was adjudged the Man of the match for his all-round performance.

Venue for the 3rd ODI was the Chepauk at Chennai. India were without the services of their captain Sourav Ganguly who had to sit this one out due to a slight niggle. As Rahul Dravid was already not available, this gave Anil Kumble the chance to lead the Indian side for the very first time in his career.

This match shall also be remembered in history books for being the first outing of Tendulkar and Sehwag as openers in an ODI.

Hussain won the toss and elected to bat first. Another fine collective effort from the bowling unit saw the English team all-out for just 217 in 48 overs. Agarkar with a 4fer was the pick of the Indian bowlers.

India chased down the target, albeit with a few hiccups, with 3 overs to spare thanks to an enthralling century platform laid by the Sachin-Viru pair in their first outing together as opening partners. Sachin Tendulkar's 68 which came off 79 balls was the highest score on either side and won him the Man of the match.

The teams travelled to Green Park at Kanpur for the fourth match of the series with Hussain winning the toss and electing to bat first. The match got curtailed to 39 overs a side due to wet outfield. India were bolstered by the return of their captain Sourav Ganguly and he immediately underlined his value by chipping in with 2 wickets in another decent outing overall for the bowling unit, barring the early assault from Nick Knight, who was especially severe on Agarkar. If England could still manage to post 218 on the scoreboard it was largely due to the composed knock by a returning Graham Thorpe.

In response, the brand-new opening pair of Sachin and Sehwag put on a masterclass on stroke play that rendered the English bowling attack stunned into submission, in the process registering their second century partnership in two appearances, and this one came at a run-rate of almost 8 runs an over. It doesn't happen too often that the mighty Tendulkar is outscored but that's exactly what happened on this day as Sehwag raced away to 82 while Sachin was still 3 shy of his 50. The result, India gunned down the target with almost 10 overs to spare even in the stipulated 39. To no one's surprise, Sehwag was named the Man of the match.

The experiment to open with Sehwag had proved to be an unqualified success, adding a new dimension to India's batting approach in the ODIs.

Thus, India went into Kotla at Delhi for the 5th match leading the series 3-1. Ganguly won the toss and chose to field first. Nick Knight capitalized on his return to form with a typically stroke-filled century, his 4th in ODIs, employing the sweep, both conventional and reverse, with great success against Indian spinners. His 100+ runs partnership with Hussain, plus a late assault by Flintoff helped England post a respectable 271 on the scoreboard.

India, in reply, stayed in the hunt courtesy decent contributions from Sehwag, Ganguly, the newcomer Kaif and a late flurry by Agarkar who blasted 36 off just 24 balls to bring the equation to 8 needed in the final over. Darren Gough bowled a great last over but fittingly it was a terrific diving save at the boundary by Giles - who had earlier bagged a 5fer too - that sealed the match in England's favour by just 2 runs. Giles was rightly declared the Man of the match.

With the series scoreline reading 3-2, the two teams converged at Wankhede stadium for the sixth and the final match of the series. Hussain won the toss and decided to bat first. His decision proved correct as their top order set them on course for a 300 plus total, with Trescothick once again leading the way with another free flowing 95 off just 80 balls. But a mid-innings collapse inflicted by Bhajji who spun his way to 4 wickets in a space of just 7 balls, derailed the English inning and it took another responsible knock from Flintoff down the order to take them to a respectable 255.

Needing 256 to win, India's top order came good once again and a win looked a mere formality before Ganguly's dismissal, just like it did in the previous match at Delhi, triggered a panicky collapse and an inspired Flintoff polished off the Indian tail, winning the match for England by just 5 runs. The result also meant that England had managed to square the series 3-3 after being down by 3-1 at one stage. This prompted some wild celebrations from the English camp, particularly the overjoyed Freddie Flintoff who had played a major role in this comeback. Trescothick was named the Man of the match while Tendulkar was adjudged the Man of the series.

It was a fitting end to what had been a very exciting and highly competitive couple of months of top-flight cricket between two young but rapidly improving sides led by two very ambitious captains.

Indian team's last assignment for season 2001-2002 was at home against Zimbabwe where they were to play a 2 Test series followed by 5 ODIs.

The lone 3-day practice game preceding the first test saw a very promising young Delhi opener Gautam Gambhir serving notice to the selectors with a fabulous double-hundred against the visitors.

First test of the series was played at Vidarbha Cricket Stadium at Nagpur. It also happened to be the first ever match that the writer of these lines watched live from the stadium. Zimbabwe were led by newly appointed captain Stuart Carlisle who won the toss, elected to bat first and justified his decision by adding 106 runs for the second wicket in the company of his predecessor Alastair Campbell. Campbell's wicket in the second session triggered a mini collapse of sorts and Zimbabwe went from 117/1 to 194/7 at one stage, before their tail wagged vigorously to take the visitors to a respectable 287 in the first innings. Evergreen Kumble was once again the pick of the Indian bowlers with a 4-wicket haul while Zaheer bagged 3. Harbhajan too bowled well albeit without luck.

In reply Indian batsmen made merry against an inexperienced bowling attack on a good batting wicket for two days before declaring at 570/7, studded with three centuries, each one of a different quality - a typical test opener's 105 by SS Das, a quickfire 100 by the very promising Sanjay Bangar coming in at number 7 in what was only his second test appearance, and the most glorious of them all, a 176 by the master blaster Sachin Tendulkar, his 28th Test hundred - which took him past Alan Border and Steve Waugh on career test centuries list, just 1 behind the legendary Sir Donald Bradman and 6 behind the all-time leader, the original little master, Sunny Gavaskar who had 34. Sachin also went past 7500 test runs during the course of this inning.

Zimbabwe needed 283 runs or to survive close to 5 sessions which was always going to be a daunting prospect against the spin duo of

Kumble & Harbhajan on a 4th and 5th day pitch and that's exactly what happened as the brothers of destruction combined to bowl Zimbabwe out for 181 to make it a win by an innings and 101 runs. Kumble added 5 more to his 4 in the first innings while Harbhajan too made up for the lack of wickets in the first innings with a very handsome 4-fer of his own. Kumble also won the Man of the match for his match haul of 9 wickets.

The teams travelled to Feroz Shah Kotla stadium in the national capital for the second test. Zimbabwean skipper called correctly at the toss and elected to bat first but got clean bowled for a duck by a Srinath inswinger on the 4th ball of the match. Zaheer Khan soon made it 11/2, but Dion Ebrahim stitched a couple of crucial partnerships in the middle order with the Flower brothers to rescue the team from that poor start and take them to stumps on the opening day at 260/6

Ebrahim didn't last long the next morning but a handy knock down the order by Travis Friend took Zimbabwe's first innings to a very decent 329. Kumble was again the pick of the bowlers for India with 3 wickets while Srinath, Zaheer and Harbhajan all took a couple each.

Zimbabwean bowlers led by Heath Streak and Ray Price then put in a very disciplined performance to restrict the mighty Indian batting line-up to 354, conceding a lead of just 25 runs. Indian captain Sourav Ganguly was the top scorer of the inning with a fabulous 136, which was his first test hundred in 28 months. Sehwag played the supporting hand with a fine 74 studded with as many as 16 boundaries.

After playing terrific cricket for the first three days, the Zimbabwean batsmen then let their team down by failing to capitalize on their good showing and got bundled out for just 146 courtesy Harbhajan Singh, who claimed 6, including the wicket of the great Andy Flower for a duck. He was ably supported from the other end by Kumble who claimed the remaining 4.

But there was still some drama left for the fifth and final day. Needing just 125 to win, the Indian team managed to get there after a lot of huffing and puffing in the face of some inspired bowling and fielding by the Zimbabweans with Raymond Price once again being the star of the show causing headaches to the likes of Dravid and Tendulkar, no less. In the final analysis though, the skilful 42 by Tendulkar on that final day Kotla wicket proved invaluable. But fittingly, it was Harbhajan who sealed the match with some audacious blows at the end. He was named the Man of the match while his partner-in-crime Anil Kumble won the Man of the series for his series haul of 16 wickets in 2 tests. Their *jugalbandi* proved to be the decisive factor in the series as they managed to keep the great Andy Flower relatively quiet, unlike the previous occasion fifteen months ago when he ran amok on the hapless Indian bowling in the absence of Kumble & Harbhajan.

Another huge positive for India was the return to form of their captain Sourav Ganguly. While he had been his usual prolific self in the one-dayers since taking over the captaincy, the same wasn't true when it came to Tests where he hadn't had a three-figure score in over two years. So, him finally succeeding in getting that huge monkey off his back with that handsome 136 in the first innings of the second test augured well for his as well as the team's future.

The standout performer of the series, though, was Zimbabwe's Ray Price who bowled with such skill and guile throughout the series that he even had batsmen of the stature of Dravid and Tendulkar in all sorts of troubles and to his immense credit, he did it without having to resort to 'negative bowling' like Ashley Giles did a month or so back.

The future of spin bowling looked very bright what with the likes of Kumble and Harbhajan and Ray Price all putting up such performances in the same series.

On to the ODI leg of the tour. Indian selectors decided to give some much-needed rest to the two most experienced players, Tendulkar and Srinath while Sehwag had to miss out due to an injury. What these omissions did was level the playing field somewhat, giving Zimbabwe a fighting chance to make something of the series.

The Zimbabweans too were cognizant of this opportunity and grabbed it in the very first encounter and that too, in unforgettable fashion.

Winning the toss and electing to bat first at Faridabad, the Indian captain and his new opening partner Dinesh Mongia gave their team a decent start by adding 46 in 8 overs, before Streak got Mongia caught behind for 25. Ganguly carried on unfettered and added 74 in the company of VVS before falling to a brilliant stumping by the diminutive Zimbabwean wicket-keeper Tatenda Taibu. He made 57 off 70 balls. VVS showed signs of a return to form with a decent 75 before falling once again to poor running. Grant Flower, in the middle of a miserly spell, trapped Dravid in front of the wicket to put further brakes on the scoring, and it was only thanks to a couple of contrasting 40s by the newcomer Kaif and the enigmatic Agarkar that took India to 274/6 by the end of the innings. Kaif ran hard for his 39 off 45 balls while Agarkar smote 40 off just 19 balls.

Zaheer Khan had reduced Zimbabe to 21 for 2 before the old firm of Campbell and Andy Flower added 111 for the third wicket to bring the chase back on track. Kumble, who was having a rare off-day at the office, still managed to break the stand clean bowling Flower when he was on 71. A couple of nagging spells in the middle overs by Harbhajan and Bangar reduced Zimbabwe to 210/8 in the 45th over, when in-walked Douglas Marillier and proceeded to play a knock straight off every tail-enders' wildest dreams.

With the equation reading 66 runs required off 34 balls, Marillier blasted 56 runs off just 24 balls with the help of a sixer and ten boundaries, most of which came off a brand-new shot that he unveiled during the course of that whirlwind knock, wherein he would repeatedly step across and hit, or rather scoop the ball over the wicket-keeper's head. Interestingly, it was the best bowler of the day Zaheer Khan, who had to bear the brunt of Douglas' pyrotechnics as he went for 34 runs in his last two overs. By the time the final over arrived, Marillier had batted himself in such a zone that even the experienced Anil Kumble couldn't prevent him from taking his side home with 2 balls to spare.

It was, and remains one of the most remarkable come-from-behind victory made possible by one of the most unforgettable knocks ever played in this format of the game! Of-course Marillier was named the Man of the match.

From Faridabad the teams moved to nearby Mohali for the second game. Ganguly won the toss again and the Indian top order batted brilliantly to post a mammoth 319/6 in the allotted 50 overs, with Ganguly and Laxman scoring their second successive fifties and Dravid too contributing a fluent 66 off just 59.

Zimbabwe began poorly losing their first wicket to Agarkar in the second over itself but the gamble to send Travis Friend as a pinch hitter at one down paid off as he went on to score a brisk fifty while adding 134 runs for the second wicket with the in-form Alistair Campbell, to bring the chase back on track. But Harbhajan struck twice in two overs and then ran-out Grant Flower a little later to turn Zimbabwe from 137/1 to 166/4 by the end of the 28th over. Part-time spinner Dinesh Mongia then turned in a very fine spell which basically sealed the game in India's favour. He should have been the Man of the match but the adjudicators named Sourav Ganguly for his tone-setting 86 off 83 balls.

With the series levelled at 1-1, the two teams then travelled down south to Kochi for the 3rd game of the series. Having won the third toss in a row, Ganguly once again chose to bat first but this time the decision backfired as the Indian top order succumbed to an inspired spell of fast bowling by Douglas Hondo. It took a 86 run partnership for the 5th wicket between Bangar and Kaif, who played with the maturity belying his age and experience, to take India from 51/4 in 13 overs to 137. Some deft middle-over bowling by the duo of Marillier and Grant Flower meant India could only manage 191.

Zimbabwe chased it down with 5 overs to spare courtesy a hundred plus run stand for the 3rd wicket between the in-form Campbell and Grant Flower, who missed out on a much awaited fifty by just 1 run. Douglas Hondo was awarded the Man of the match for his devastating 4fer. Thus, the unfancied Zimbabwe once again found themselves leading the series 2-1. What made this win even more remarkable for Zimbabwe was the fact that they did it without their number one match-winner Andy Flower, who had to sit this one out due to an injury.

Trailing the series 1-2 forced the Indian selectors to ring in some changes. Out went S.S Das, Sarandeep Singh and the injured Anil Kumble. In came Yuvraj Singh, Murali Kartik and Vijay Bharadwaj. While Yuvraj and Kartik had earned their inclusions, Bharadwaj's selection to the national side after a gap of 28 months came as a bit of a surprise.

It was refreshing to see Zimbabwe batting first for the first time in the series in the fourth game at Hyderabad, but they failed to get a good start losing 2 wickets at a score of just 13 within the first 4 overs. It was once again left to the great Andy Flower to salvage the situation and he did so with able support from his brother Grant and his skipper Carlisle to take Zimbabwe to a respectable 240/8. Andy Flower made a well-compiled 89. Agarkar with 4 wickets was the pick of the Indian bowlers.

In reply, India were 56 for 3 at one stage but a couple of valuable partnerships, first between the vice-captain Dravid and young Kaif and then between Kaif and the returning Yuvraj sealed the match in India's favour comfortably towards the end. The prodigal son Yuvraj made a triumphant return to the side with a typically stroke-filled 80 off just 60 balls, studded with 8 boundaries and a six and that won him the Man of the match. The 94-run stand between Kaif and Yuvraj was their first match-winning partnership and the way their styles complimented each other, augured well for the future of the team.

With the series squared at 2-2, the fifth and final game at Guwahati turned into the rubber match. Electing to bat first, the Indian openers added 50 odd before Ganguly nicked one to Taibu for 28. Laxman was run out, not for the first time in the series. Dravid was clean bowled by a beauty from Hondo. Kaif had a rare failure and suddenly India found themselves at 157/4 in the decider with 19 overs to go, when the in-form Dinesh Mongia was joined at the crease by the hero of the previous game, Yuvraj. The dasher from Punjab started off from where he left in the previous inning, thrashing the Zimbabwean bowling to all parts of the ground. His Punjab teammate, Mongia too came into his own, finding boundaries more regularly and together the two lefties put the pressure back on Zimbabwe bowlers, particularly the hapless Gary Brent who had to be taken out of attack. Mongia became even more adventurous after completing his maiden century and the two lefties added 158 in 18 overs with the final 10 overs yielding an astounding 121 runs, to take India to a mammoth 333/6 in 50 overs. Mongia carried his bat with a very impressive 159 while Yuvraj's 75 came off just 52 balls studded with 6 boundaries and 3 glorious sixes.

To add to Zimbabwe's woes, they were docked 2 overs for slow over rate. Still their top order tried to make a contest of it but were no match to the pace of Zaheer and the guile of Harbhajan, and folded for 232 in the 43rd over itself, losing the match by 101 runs. Dinesh Mongia expectedly walked away with the Man of the match as well as the Man of the series honours.

The relief of avoiding the ignominy of losing a series to Zimbabwe at home was writ large on the faces of the entire team. This hard-fought series win in the absence of stalwarts like Tendulkar, Srinath, Kumble (for the last 2 games) and Sehwag augured well for the World cup that was due in less than a year's time. The kind of skill, and more importantly, the level of maturity some youngsters like Mongia, Kaif and Yuvraj had shown in this series promised of a very bright future for this Indian team in the not-so-distant future.

But first up right away was a three-month away tour to the Caribbean.

07

The Caribbean Quest

Next, Ganguly & co. were slated to visit the West Indies for a gruelling 3-month tour to take part in a 5-test series followed by a 5 match ODI series between April and June 2002. Having been the most feared and dominant force in world cricket during the 70s and 80s, the West Indies cricket had been in a continuous state of decline since the mid-90s, to the extent that a visiting Indian side started off as the favourites for the first time in 30 years.

On their previous visit to these shores, under the captaincy of Sachin Tendulkar, the Indians had come within sniffing distance of a historic victory only to end up losing the series-deciding match by a mere 38 runs. Tendulkar has been on record terming it as "*the* lowest point in his 23 years long career", to the extent that he even contemplated quitting the game altogether.

Five years on, this new look team India seemed determined to exorcise the demons of not just the last tour but the many preceding it. The last time an Indian team managed to beat Windies in West Indies was way back in 1971 when the OG Sunny Gavaskar burst on the scene with a record-breaking debut series where he amassed 774 runs at an average of 154 with 4 hundreds. Since that momentous series, no Indian team had ever managed to win a single test, let alone a series on West Indian soil. The entire Indian cricket establishment, from the BCCI to the team, seemed determined to change that and the selectors did a fairly decent job with the squad selection. The only surprising decision was to continue with Deepdas Gupta as the first-choice wicket-keeper for tests, despite his horrible showing behind the wicket in the last two series. The fact that he could open the innings might have saved him. Ajay Ratra who had shown great promise, both in front as well as behind the wicket in red ball cricket was selected as his back-up.

The tour started off on promising note as the team won its first 3-day practice match before the first test with ease, with the bowlers in particular looking prime and ready.

The enigmatic Carl Hooper, who had been persuaded to come out of an early retirement and entrusted with the responsibility of leading the Windies through this challenging phase, won the toss and elected to bat first in the first test on his home ground in Guyana. On a wicket that looked tailor-made for batting, an inspired opening spell from Srinath reduced West Indies to 44/3 within the first 10 overs, including the prize wickets of Lara for a duck. Hooper too began nervously but settled down gradually to salvage the situation, first by adding 123 with fellow Guyanese Ramnaresh Sarwan and then a massive 293 with another fellow Guyanese Shivnarine Chanderpaul, to take the team past 500 for only the second time in 39 tests, stretching back to over 4 years. Sarwan scored 53, Chanderpaul 140 with 23 boundaries while Hooper converted his first ton on his home ground into his maiden double century. He was finally dislodged by Kumble for 233, studded with 29 exquisitely hit boundaries and 3 huge sixes. It was another reminder of the fact that there were few sights prettier in cricket than watching Carl Hooper in full flight.

Srinath was the pick of the bowlers with those 3 wickets in the first session, Zaheer and Kumble managed 2 apiece, while the gamble to pick Sarandeep over Harbhajan backfired big time.

In response, India had to fight to avoid follow-on as their top three fell cheaply. It was once again left to the middle order trio of Tendulkar, Dravid and Laxman to bail the team out of a precarious situation and they did so in their own respective styles; Tendulkar with an authoritative 79, Laxman with a stylish 69 and Dravid with a defiant knock of 144, his 10th test hundred, staying unbeaten till the rains arrived to wash away the final day and a half of play, ensuring India escaped with a draw. Hooper won the Man of the match.

Second test was to be played at Port of Spain which had historically been a happy hunting ground for Indian teams. The team think-tank made two changes going in - Deepdas Gupta was out making way for Ajay Ratra and Harbhajan Singh was drafted in as the lone spinner replacing Kumble and Sarandeep as the team management decided to go with Nehra as the third seamer.

Hooper won the toss and invited India to bat first. Bangar was promoted to opening but the new opening pair failed to give a decent start and were both back in the hut by the 15th over with the score being just 38. The old firm of Tendulkar and Dravid, back to his favourite one-down position, then put together another century partnership to make up for the poor start, before Dravid got cleaned up by a beauty from Marlon Black for a neat 67. Tendulkar carried on unperturbed, putting together a couple of decent partnerships each with Ganguly and Laxman, who looked in fine nick. In the course of those partnerships, Tendulkar also completed his hundred before being lbw by a Cameroon Cuffy inswinger for 117.

This was test century number 29 for Tendulkar, taking him level with the greatest of them all, Sir Don Bradman and it took his test batting average to 59.17, the highest it ever reached in his entire career.

Cuffy also ruined Ratra's test debut by getting him caught behind for a duck and when Harbhajan and Zaheer too followed soon, 300 began looking difficult. Thankfully, VVS found an able partner in the experienced Srinath and the two added very crucial 41 runs to take the team to a decent 339. VVS remained unbeaten on 69 with the help of 11 silken boundaries.

West Indies began well with an opening stand of 50 which was broken by Srinath when he got Gayle caught at third slip by Das. The rest of the Windies top order all got starts but failed to convert them into something substantial and the last 6 could only manage 66 between them to finish on 245. Srinath once again was the most successful bowler with 3 wickets to his name while Zak, Nehra and Harbhajan shared 2 apiece.

Trailing by 94 runs, Windies quicks had India reeling at 56/4 with both Dravid as well as Tendulkar back in the hut. That's when the captain and VVS stepped up. Their 150-run partnership not only rescued the situation but also pushed India's lead beyond 300. But just when things seemed rosy, Laxman's wicket triggered a collapse. Ganguly could only watch in dismay as the last 5 wickets fell like dominoes, adding a mere 13 runs to the scoreboard to finish on 218. Ganguly stayed unbeaten on 75 off 227 balls, a very responsible captain's knock.

Needing 318 to get in just over four sessions, the Windies lost the wicket of Stuart Williams early while Gayle had to retire hurt due to a forearm pull. Sarwan and Lara took the team past 100 when Sarwan lost his wicket against the run of the play just before stumps on day4. The score read West Indies 131/2

All this set up the fifth and the final day of the test beautifully, with the hosts needing 187 to win with 8 wickets in hand and their two best batsmen at the crease. A full house had turned up in anticipation of watching one of Trinidad's own, Brian Lara do his thing and guide Windies to a famous win. Queen's Park Oval happened to be Lara's home ground but he was yet to score a test hundred here. The pressure showed in the way Lara began uncharacteristically nervously on the morning of day5. He had added only 7 to his overnight score when a tentative poke at a perfectly pitched away swinging delivery from Nehra ended up in the safe pair of hands of Dravid at first slip. In the very next over, Nehra removed Hooper too, mistiming a pull straight to Das at square leg and just like that, the game was on. Gayle who had to retire hurt the previous returned to the crease to partner Chanderpaul and the two lefties joined hands to undo the damage in their own contrasting ways; Gayle looking for boundaries and Chanderpaul dead batting anything and everything that came his way. The pair had succeeded in adding invaluable 73 runs for the fifth wicket, when a momentary lapse in concentration after reaching his fifty gifted Zaheer and India the breakthrough that they had been so desperately looking for. Part of the credit for his dismissal must also go to Harbhajan who took a very difficult catch in the outfield to send Gayle packing for 52. This opened the floodgates as the Windies went from 236/4 to 238/7 in no time. The tailenders tried their best but could only manage to delay the inevitable for another 20 overs or so, leaving Chanderpaul stranded on 67 after 4 and a half hour and 162 balls of solid resistance, as India registered another momentous win at their happy hunting ground at Port of Spain.

It was India's first win in West Indies in 26 years and only their third overall, all three coming at this very venue. But unlike the first two occasions, the hero of this win were not the spinners but the pace trio of Srinath, Zaheer and Nehra - with a combined match haul of 17 wickets out of the total 20. Man of the match was awarded to Laxman for his twin fifties but it could well have gone to Srinath, who led the young Indian bowling lineup from the front picking 3 in each innings.

In many regards it was a very special win.

Proving the pre-tour predictions correct, India were now leading the series 0-1 after the first two tests with three more to go. A historic series win seemed well on cards.

Before the third test, the visiting Indians were scheduled to play another 3-day practice game against the Busta Cup XI comprised of many current internationals and hopefuls. This is where things started going south for Ganguly's men inexplicably, as the Busta Cup XI batsmen like Wavell Hinds, Devon Smith and Ridley Jacobs feasted on Indian bowlers to post 437 in the first innings and then subjected Indians to the embarrassment of having to follow-on in a tour game.

From there the teams flew to Barbados for the third test. The Kensington Oval in Bridgetown, Barbados had historically been a dreaded venue for Indian cricket teams, as evident from the record - 7 defeats in 8 matches, including the infamous one suffered during the previous tour in 1997 when the team, needing just 120 for what would have been a memorable win, got all-out for 81, giving a heartbreak of a lifetime to the then captain Tendulkar.

Hooper won the toss and elected to field first again, a brave decision given that the same call had resulted in a defeat at Trinidad. His decision though was proven right this time when his bowlers bowled India out for just 102 barely fifteen minutes into the second session. Dillon led the way with 4 wickets followed by Sanford who bagged 3. Ganguly's 48 was the top score for India.

From there on, it was always going to be an uphill battle for the visitors to save the test. Zaheer Khan sent both Windies openers back cheaply but fifties from Sarwan and Lara and hundreds from Hooper and Chanderpaul took Windies to 394.

Trailing by 292 runs, the new opening pair of Das and Wasim Jaffer gave India their best start in a long time by adding 80 for the first wicket, before Jaffer got run-out for an uncharacteristically fluent 51. But this start was wasted as Das, Dravid and Tendulkar fell in quick succession adding only 38 runs to the total. Ganguly cobbled together two mini-partnerships of 65 and 74 with Laxman and Zaheer respectively but was left stranded again on 60 off 146 balls, as Dillon & co. polished off the tail to restrict India's second innings to 296, leaving WI just 4 to get which they overtook with ease without losing any wicket. India lost by 10 wickets with a day to spare. Mervyn Dillon with another 4-wicket haul was adjudged the Man of the match.

True to its reputation, the Kensington Oval had once again turned out to be a graveyard for Indian dreams. From 0-1 down, the hosts had rallied to level the series and with Antigua and Jamaica being the venues for the remaining two tests, Indian team had its task cut out to try and save the series, since a win seemed like a distant possibility now.

Windies skipper won his fourth toss on trot and chose to field first for the third time in a row. This time, however, the pitch turned out to be so lifeless that it yielded 1142 runs for just 18 wickets with as many as five batsmen on either side - Laxman and Ajay Ratra for India and Hooper, Chanderpaul and Ridley Jacobs for the Windies - helping themselves to test hundreds that were there for the taking. Ironically, the only two batsmen to miss out on this run feast were the two best batsmen of this generation- Tendulkar and Lara.

The test meandered to a boring draw with Chanderpaul still there on an unbeaten 136 off 510 balls over 675 minutes, enroute to breaking Jacques Kallis' record of 1241 minutes between dismissals in tests set earlier in the same season.

One positive for India was Ajay Ratra putting his horror run with the bat behind him with a very fine hundred coming in at number 8, in the process, also becoming the youngest wicket-keeper in history to achieve this feat and the first Indian wicketkeeper to score a test hundred overseas. When his opposite number, Ridley Jacobs too got himself a hundred it was the first occasion in the nearly 125 years history of wicketkeepers of both sides scoring a hundred in the same match.

But the enduring image of this otherwise forgettable test match shall always be the sight of a heavily bandaged Anil Kumble emerging from the pavilion to have a go at the two best Windies batsmen despite nursing a broken jaw. This raw saga of courage and commitment soon turned into stuff of legend as he managed to trap the great Lara plumb in front with one that pitched on off-and-middle and straightened just enough. He almost had Hooper too, twice but it was given a no-ball. In all, he sent down 14 overs straight till stumps, ending up with figures of 14-5-29-1. Next day he flew back to India to undergo a surgery to fix his fractured jaw.

It remains an unforgettable memory for anyone who witnessed it live, whether the ones in attendance that day in the stadium or the millions who watched it in disbelief on their television sets. Even the legendary Sir Viv Richards termed it as "one of the bravest sights he had ever seen on a cricket field"

A lion-hearted effort from one of Indian cricket's most committed and self-less soldiers. Take a bow, Jumbo!

With the series levelled at 1-1, both teams went into the fifth and final test at Sabina Park in Kingston, Jamaica with everything to play for. After 4 tests, the coin finally fell in Ganguly's favour and he elected to field first on the grassiest Sabina wicket in memory but the Indian bowlers failed to exploit the conditions, allowing the Windies openers to put together a hundred plus runs opening stand, laying a strong foundation for the batsmen to follow. After Gayle's departure, Sarwan added another hundred odd runs for the second wicket with Hinds, who made his return to the test side memorable by scoring a brilliant century, only the second of his career. India came back in contention briefly with three quick wickets late in the day, starting with Hinds, followed with one more, that of the in-form Hooper early next morning, but again ran into their old nemesis Chanderpaul who stitched together an invaluable 109 run partnership with the in-form Ridley Jacobs to dash the Indian hopes once again. Chanders had completed yet another fifty when he was finally dislodged by Srinath, a world record 1513 minutes after his previous dismissal spread over 4 tests. Windies' last 5 fell for just 21 allowing Harbhajan to claim his first five-for of the series, but not before WI had posted 422 on the scoreboard.

In reply, India lost Jaffer and Dravid cheaply before Das and Tendulkar stabilized the innings with a 70-run stand. After they departed in quick succession, Ganguly and Laxman put together another 82 runs but Dillon returned and removed Ganguly, Ratra and Harbhajan in an inspired spell.

The rest of the tail too failed to put up any fight leaving Laxman high and dry, not for the first time in the series. He made 65 not-out. Dillon was rewarded for another brilliant effort with 5 for 71.

Trailing by 210, the Indian bowlers made amends for their poor showing on the first day by bundling the hosts' second innings for under 200. Zaheer took 4 while Bhajji picked 3. Only Chanderpaul who was in the form of his life managed to go past 50.

Needing 408 to win, which was 2 more than their own record 4th innings total to win at Port of Spain in 1975-76 series, Indian openers were back in the hut with only 25 runs on the scoreboard. Tendulkar then took centre stage and released the pressure somewhat with a flurry of boundaries. Him and Dravid had added 52 for the 3rd wicket when Sanford trapped Dravid in front for the third time in the series to make it 77/3. This prompted Tendulkar to go on counter attack mode and he drove, cut, pulled and hooked his way to score 93 runs off the next 20 odd overs with Ganguly playing the perfect foil.

Just when the target started seeming a little less daunting, Collins coming round the wicket succeeded in breaching Tendulkar's defence and sent his middle stump flying. He made 86 off 139 deliveries with 13 pristine boundaries. His dismissal signalled the end of any real chance of India overtaking the target but it were the twin soft dismissals of Ganguly and Laxman towards the end of the 4th day that really sealed the fate of the match and the series in WI favour. Despite overnight rains delaying the start of the play on the final morning, the result was a foregone conclusion. All it took Hooper's men was just 8 overs to pick the remaining three wickets to beat India by 155 runs and take the series 2-1. Wavell Hinds was declared the Man of the match for his tone-setting first innings hundred and some sharp catches.

Hooper ended up as the leading run-scorer of the series with an aggregate of 579 runs while the marvellous Mervyn Dillon led the bowling charts with 23 wickets in the series, but the jury correctly chose Chanderpaul for the Man of the series for his 562 runs at an average of 140. This was his second successive Man of the series award in a home series against India, the one-of-a-kind southpaw was the Man of the series in 1997 as well.

From India's point of view, while Sachin had a quite series by his standards, Dravid enhanced his reputation as India's second-best batsman in test cricket with over 400 runs in the series. Laxman's return to form was a relief and Ganguly too showed signs of the same.

On the bowling front, spinners, especially Kumble, had a rather forgettable tour with Harbhajan's 5-for in the last test being the only notable performance. Fast bowling unit fared much better in comparison, with the two left-arm quicks Zaheer and Nehra in particular showing a lot of promise.

Over all though, it was the same old story of so near yet so far once again. An overseas tour that began with so much hope and excitement ended up on the same note of disappointment as all such tours did in the last decade and a half, ever since England '86.

Biggest cause of concern were the positions of openers and wicketkeeper. Deepdas Gupta's abject failure both in front as well as behind the wickets in the first half of the series meant that his international career was as good as over. While Jaffer and Ratra had shown some early promise as the second opener and wicketkeeper respectively, they needed to be a bit more consistent if they were to make those positions their own.

For now though, the team needed to focus all its attention on the 5 match ODI series that was to follow.

The selectors rested Srinath replacing him with Agarkar. Other ODI specialists like Sehwag, Yuvraj and Kaif were back too while left arm spinner Murali Karthik was brought in as the replacement for injured Kumble.

The 5-match series soon turned into a 3 match affair as the first 2 games got washed away without a ball being bowled.

Coach John Wright and captain Ganguly wanted to go into this truncated series with a couple of major tactical changes, first one being playing Sachin at number 4 to add some gravitas to the relatively inexperienced middle order, specially while chasing and using Dravid as a wicketkeeper so as to accommodate all three of Dinesh Mongia, Yuvraj and Kaif in the playing XI. While both Tendulkar as well as Dravid weren't really convinced of the rationale behind the experiments, being the consummate team players, they agreed to it.

So, after two washed out matches at Sabina Park, it was with the third ODI at Kensington Oval that the series actually got underway. Indian captain won the toss and asked the hosts to bat first. Windies got complacent after the test series win and it showed in the way they batted here. Most batsmen, including the mighty Lara, threw their wicket away with rash shots. Once again it was just Hooper, probably in the form of his life, who batted with any degree of responsibility. He looked capable of single-handedly taking his side to a respectable total but was left stranded at a ran-a-ball 76 as the Indian bowlers, aided by some very sharp fielding, bundled out the rest of the side for just 186 in 45th over itself. Tinu Yohannan bowled well for his 3 wickets and Agarkar polished off the tail with 3 wickets of his own. Sehwag too chipped in with 2 important wickets in the middle.

India chased down the total in clinical fashion with a solid 74 from Dinesh Mongia, who came in at one-down and a couple of decent contributions from Ganguly and Sachin, who did a good job of finishing the game at number 4.

What made this win special was the fact that it was the first time an Indian team had tasted victory in any format here at the Kensington Oval, in Bridgetown, Barbados. These milestones may seem small in hindsight but have a major impact on the journey of a team that is still evolving.

The joy proved short lived though as the Windies came back hard at the Indians in the 4th match at Queen's Park Oval, one of India's favourite hunting grounds in the Caribbean. Winning the toss and electing to bat first in the rain truncated 25 overs a side game, the Indian batsmen, in the absence of Sachin who was out nursing a sore shoulder, batted without any plan or direction in the face of some tight, disciplined bowling from the opposition bowlers, specially Collymore and Collins to get bundled out for just 123 in their stipulated 25 overs.

WI chased it down with plenty to spare thanks to a 117 runs opening partnership between Gayle and Hinds. This was the match that the world got its first real glimpse of the devastating power of one Christopher Henry Gayle. His 84 came off just 67 balls and were studded with nine sweetly timed boundaries and three thundering sixes. He was especially severe on India's bowling hero from the previous game, Tinnu Yohannan, plundering him for 25 runs in a single over at one point during the chase.

This stunning assault was enough for Gayle to win the Man of the match over Collymore who had an equally strong case.

With the series tied at 1-1, the fifth and final match to be played at the same venue became the decider. India had never won an ODI series in the Caribbean. Sensing the opportunity and gravity of the occasion and being the great team man that he had always been, Sachin Tendulkar decided to play this one despite the pain in his injured shoulder.

Ganguly won third toss in a row and elected to bat first in the decider. He then proceeded to give a good start to India in the company of the more enterprising Sehwag, who was looking in prime touch as he crunched as many as 6 boundaries in his run-a-ball 32 before getting out to Gayle off Dillon. India's new one-down batsmen Dinesh Mongia then added 60 odd at a healthy rate with his captain but failed to make the start count falling to the crafty Collymore. His dismissal brought to the crease the master blaster in his new role as the team's number 4. Sachin proceeded to add 40 runs each with Ganguly and Dravid to take India close to 200 before the 40th over. 280 looked on cards but Yuvraj and Kaif failed to deliver and the onus to get the maximum out of the final 5 overs fell upon the great one's injured shoulders. He tried gamely but the shoulder injury meant he had to cut out several of his run-getting strokes from his arsenal, and he had to depart trying to pull a short-pitched ball from Dillon, but not before scoring 65 invaluable runs off just 70 balls with just three boundaries and a six. It was just the kind of inning that you expect from a number 4 batsman in the middle overs and proved that the coach and captain were right in asking him to don that role. It was thanks to his knock that India managed to put 260 on the board.

For Windies, Dillon took his maiden 5-for in ODIs while Gayle, revelling in the confidence gained from his performance in the previous game, chipped in with 3 wickets with the ball this time.

Needing to defend 260, India's fast bowlers were on the money from the get go, with the returning Nehra sending back Hinds in the third over itself, followed by Zaheer Khan yorking the danger man Gayle in the very next. Sarwan and Lara stabilized the ship with a 60 runs stand but just when the chase threatened to be back on track, two wickets fell in two overs to once again derail the chase. Now all came down to the two lefties Lara and Chanderpaul. But before they could begin the damage control, Ganguly, in an inspired move, lobbed the ball to Tendulkar and the 'Golden arm' of the great one yet again did the trick, as he got the all-important wicket of Lara holing out to Mongia at long on. The score at this point read 88/5 and it was game over for Windies for all intents and purposes. Chanderpaul and Jacobs tried their best but all they could manage to do was delay the inevitable, as Agarkar finished off the tail to bundle the hosts out for 191 in 37th over and India winning by 56 runs by Duckworth Lewis method.

With that, India sealed its first ever ODI series win in West Indies, a huge milestone on this team's journey to becoming a champion side.

Of course, the heartbreak from the test series still rankled but this historic ODI series win healed some of those wounds and bode well for the upcoming world cup which was now less than 8 months away.

08

An English Summer to Remember

Next up on the Indian cricket calendar was another even lengthier away assignment, the 90-days tour of England where the team was scheduled to participate in the Natwest tri-series followed by a 5-test series.

But the team received a big jolt even before it could depart for the tour, and that too from a least expected corner.

For close to a decade, Javagal Srinath, fondly known as 'The Karnataka Express', had been shouldering the responsibility of spearheading the Indian bowling attack with great aplomb sans any fanfare. With 13 wickets to his name, he can be said to have done reasonably well in the recently concluded test series in the Caribbean as well, still the selection committee headed by the great Chandu Borde decided to rest him for the ODI series which followed, without Srinath having requested for it. Peeved by this perceived snub, Srinath announced his retirement from test cricket soon after returning home. The announcement took even his teammates by surprise, none more so than his captain Ganguly who seemed keen to have the services of his pace spearhead on the upcoming England tour. Ganguly tried his best to convince Srinath to change his mind but Srinath refused to budge. So, the team had to embark on the challenging tour to England without their most experienced fast bowler.

In hindsight, even though he had his reasons to feel the way he did, still it was an impulsive call on the part of Srinath to give such an important tour a miss at that stage of his career.

First international assignment on the tour was the **Natwest trophy** which was a ODI tri-series to be contested between the hosts, Sri Lanka and India. Team India came into the tri-series well-acclimatized, having won 2 out of the 3 50 overs practice games against sides like Sussex, Kent and Leicestershire.

Their first match was against the hosts at Lords. Nasser Hussain won the toss and elected to bat first. Trescothick and Nick Knight had given England a very good start before a brilliant throw from Tendulkar found Knight short. Trescothick carried on undeterred and was looking all set for a hundred when he nicked a Ganguly outswinger to the keeper Dravid who was now the designated gloveman. Trescothick made 86 off 78 with 8 fours and a six. Hussain then added another fifty partnership with Flintoff but Yuvraj struck thrice in three overs to send back Flintoff, Thorpe and the set Hussain to restrict the English inning to 271.

One trait that had always stood out about Sourav Ganguly's captaincy since the beginning was that he placed a lot more faith in his non-regular bowlers than his predecessors and they more often than not delivered. This match was a great example of this. In an inning where 3 out of the 4 regular bowlers went wicketless, Ganguly still managed to get the breakthroughs through his judicious use of himself and the slow left arm spin of Yuvraj who picked up 3 for 39 off his 7 overs.

The still relatively new opening pair of Ganguly and Sehwag put together another century partnership in little over 15 overs. Sehwag was the more aggressive of the two, smashing 9 boundaries and a powerful six off Giles. However, an attempt to repeat that stroke led to his dismissal at 71 off 65 balls. Sehwag's wicket triggered a mini-collapse: India lost two more wickets in quick succession, including the crucial one of Sachin. When Ganguly also fell, caught brilliantly by Kirtley in the deep, India found themselves in trouble at 141/4.

It was then that the Indian vice-captain was joined at the crease by the young stallion from Punjab, Yuvraj Singh. Emboldened by the good outing with the ball earlier in the day, Yuvi didn't let the pressure of the situation get to him and snatched back the initiative from England bowlers with a couple of cracking fours. Once the pressure was off, the two began milking the bowling with singles, doubles and the occasional boundary to keep apace with the required run rate. If it was Yuvi who took the initiative early on in the partnership, it was the turn of Dravid to up the ante with a flurry of well-timed and placed boundaries towards the climax. In the end, their unbroken partnership of 131 runs off 118 balls proved to be match winning. Yuvi was declared the Man of the match for his unbeaten half century plus those three wickets.

It was a great way to start off the tour with two promising young stars of India announcing themselves to England in their first outing at the Mecca of Cricket, Lords.

Poor scheduling on the part of the organizers meant Indian team was required to play their second game the very next day against the third participant in the tourney, Sri Lanka.

Sri Lankan captain Jayasuriya won the toss and elected to bat first, but his team could only manage 202/8 in their 50 overs in the face of some purposeful bowling from India's three-pronged pace attack, who claimed 7 out of the 8 wickets to fall. Going in with three fast bowlers meant Harbhajan had to miss out, but the move to have Nehra share the new ball with Zaheer and using Agarkar as first change worked like a charm as he destroyed the Lankan top order with 3 wickets for 44 runs.

For their part, the Lankan pace battery tried hard to make a match of it, reducing India to 135/5 at one stage. But a target of just 202 was always going to be tough to defend, especially in the absence of Muralitharan. A mature partnership of 60 at a run a ball between Kaif and previous day's hero Yuvraj sealed the match in India's favour in the 46th over itself. Agarkar was declared the Man of the match for his brilliant spell.

Two things stood out in this match. First, the manner in which Rahul Dravid applied himself to his new role as the wicketkeeper, as evident from the three catches he held, including the brilliant one to get rid of Jayasuriya. Second was the amazing chemistry between India's new number 6 and 7, Yuvraj and Kaif. These two had played a lot of cricket together in the junior and U19 level and it showed in the way they stole their singles and doubles. It was reminiscent of Ajay Jadeja and Robin Singh at their pomp.

India again met their hosts for their third match at Chester Le Street. Ganguly won the toss and chose to bat first. The match got to a sensational start as he was given lbw off the first ball of the inning. Mongia and Sehwag didn't let that hamper the run rate, as they added 48 in as many balls before Sehwag lost his wicket to a sharp catch by Trescothick at point. Three overs later, Gough sent Mongia on his way. At 52/3, need of the hour was a partnership and that's what Dravid and Tendulkar set about doing. Dravid was in better touch initially than his partner who was not timing it as well as he usually does, especially against the wily medium pace of Ronnie Irani but slowly regained his touch after the introduction of the spinner Giles. The two had added 169 for the fourth wicket when Dravid got out trying to accelerate in the slog overs. He made 82 off 117 balls. Tendulkar meanwhile completed his 32nd century in ODIs but it was the blistering cameo from Yuvraj - 40 off just 19 balls with 4 fours and a six - that propelled India to an imposing total of 285.

In pursuit, England had lost their best bastman Trescothick and were trying to recover at 53/1 in the 13th over when rain interrupted the proceeding for the third time. As 25 overs had not been bowled for Duckworth Lewis to come into play, the match had to be called off. With India clearly in the driver's seat at that stage, it was a lucky escape for the hosts. Tendulkar won the Man of the match.

Two days later, India met Sri Lanka for their fourth match of the tourney at Birmingham. Ganguly called correctly at the toss and his bowlers justified his decision to field first by restricting Lankan innings to 187 all out in the 48th over, with only Atapattu and Jayawardene able to make some decent contribution.

Chasing 187, India found itself 0 for 1 for the second game running with Sehwag being the one to be dismissed for a duck this time. Mongia failed again and when Fernando dismissed Sachin for 19, India again found itself in a spot of bother at 4 down for 59. For the second time in the tournament, Dravid and Yuvraj bailed them out with an invaluable partnership of 91 runs, as India got home with 11 balls to spare. Dravid won the Man of the match for his clinical 64.

Their next match against the hosts at The Oval turned out to be a rain-truncated affair of 32 overs a side. England's allrounder Ronnie Irani single handedly handed India their first loss of the tournament by first scoring a free flowing 50 as a pinch-hitter, and then rocking the Indian middle order with a 5fer for just 26 runs. To be fair, Indian middle order was due a failure and it had to happen at some point.

Since India had already qualified for the final by virtue of topping the points table, their final league match against Sri Lanka was of academic interest only. Batting first after winning the toss, Sehwag started off in his by now customary fashion, picking at least one boundary per over, not letting the loss of Ganguly to a run-out affect the run rate, with Dinesh Mongia keeping him solid company. Sehwag was looking good for a half-century and plenty more when he too got run-out backing up too far. He made 39 off 40 balls with 6 boundaries. This brought to the crease Sachin Tendulkar, who started off with a flurry of boundaries against the hapless Zoysa who had to be taken off the attack. Mongia added 99 with Tendulkar before losing his stumps to Samaraveera, missing out on his 50 by just 2 runs. Dravid and Yuvraj had an off day with the bat but another 74 run stand off just 66 balls between Tendulkar and Kaif took India past 300. The maestro from Mumbai completed his 33rd ODI century before getting out trying to accelerate. Clearly the move to number 4 had done little to diminish his hunger and penchant of scoring hundreds. Especially against Sri Lanka against whom it was his 7th ton.

Sri Lanka lost their main man Jayasuriya early in the chase. The trio of Atapattu, Sangakkara and Jayawardene, however, kept their side in the hunt with some sensible batting but the introduction of Harbhajan Singh - playing his first match in the tournament - broke the back of their middle order, and all they could manage was 241 before getting bundled out in the 45th over, losing the match by 65 runs. Tendulkar was the unanimous choice for the Man of the match.

Now it was time for the final and fittingly it was to be contested at the Mecca of Cricket.

Vanquishing the Finals curse

Even though India were the side with the most wins in the tournament so far, yet heading into the final, hosts England were the clear favourites and not just for the bookies. The reason being, India had lost 9 consecutive tournament finals leading up to this one. One more loss and the tag of chokers was in real danger of changing hands from South Africans to Indians.

To make matters worse, toss too didn't go India's way. Nasser Hussain called correctly and elected to bat first on what promised to be a fantastic batting wicket. This meant the added pressure to chase in a final.

England's openers, specially Trescothick went after Indian bowlers from ball one. They were closing in on 50 when Zaheer cleaned up Nick Knight with a beauty. That did little to curb Trescothick who continued to punish Indian bowlers with strokes all across the ground en route another fabulous ODI century off just 86 balls. The pair of Trescothick and Hussain had added 178 runs for the second wicket at a pretty good clip when Trescothick dragged a Kumble topspinner onto his stumps to be dismissed. He made 109 with the help of 7 fours and 2 sixes. By now, the English captain Nasser Hussain had batted himself back into form by sheer force of will. He was joined at the crease by Freddie Flintoff who got going from the first ball and the pair added 80 runs in just 60 balls to take England past 300. Both got clean bowled in successive overs trying to force the pace; Flintoff made 40 off 32 with 2 fours and a huge six while Hussain compiled an impressive 115 off 128 balls with 10 boundaries. The English captain couldn't have chosen a better occasion to issue a resounding reply to all those who doubted his ability to bat at number three position. Zaheer Khan was the pick of the bowlers with 3 wickets on a day when every bowler had gone for runs as England finished with 325/5 in 50 overs.

At the innings break it seemed like a certainty that India was well on its way to losing its 10th straight final. These are the moments which serve as a true test of leadership. Ganguly is said to have given a rousing pep talk to his players at the innings break which ended with "They've scored, and so will we"

It was not every day that targets in the range of 325 were successfully hunted down in those days. Only a blazing start could have provided India with an outside chance of maybe hoping to make a match of it.

After seeing off a near perfect first over by the crafty Gough, both Sehwag as well as Ganguly warmed up with a boundary each off the second over of the inning bowled by the lesser experienced Alex Tudor.

In the few matches that these two had opened so far, usually it was Sehwag's role to be the aggressor, but on this occasion, Ganguly took it upon himself to take the attack to the opposition with a barrage of boundaries that left both the English players as well as fans stunned while reigniting hope among the Indian fans who had thronged the Lords that day. Sehwag too was his usual self at the other end and the two raised India's 50 in just 8 overs. A personal duel of sorts was going on between Flintoff and Ganguly since the beginning of the year when England was touring India. Now brimming with confidence, Ganguly welcomed Flintoff with a four and a six off his first and innings' 10th over. Not to be left behind, Sehwag too carted 4 boundaries off Ronnie Irani's over. A trademark Ganguly cover drive off the first ball of the 14th over bowled by Flintoff took India past 100 but that was to be the end of a rollicking knock by the Indian captain as he succumbed to the adrenalin rush in the very next over, clean bowled while trying to make room to hit Tudor over the infield in the last over of powerplay. He made 60 off just 43 balls studded with 10 fours and a six.

Ganguly's wicket against the run of the play triggered a collapse as England pulled things back with the wickets of the dangerous Sehwag, Mongia and Rahul Dravid in the next 6 overs and when Giles grabbed the prize wicket of Sachin Tendulkar for just 14, India found itself at 147/5 after 24 overs.

Although they had both done well in the tournament so far, this was unfamiliar territory for Yuvraj and Kaif, as the situation demanded a major reconstruction job, something they were not used to, coming in at number 6 and 7. But to everyone's surprise, the duo applied themselves to the need of the hour with a maturity that belied their experience and age, 20 and 21 respectively. They began by cutting down all risk and dealing in singles then gradually moved to converting singles to twos and twos to three runs relying on deft placement and unbelievable running between the wickets. Then as they approached the 35th over mark, Yuvraj shifted gears and unfurled his whole range of shots to bring the required run rate down to manageable level with a huge six off spinner Giles and a couple of sweetly timed boundaries off the dibbly-dobbly medium pace of Irani and Collingwood. When Hussain brought Flintoff back into the attack, Yuvraj welcomed him with three glorious boundaries in a row to take India to 235/5 in the 38th over.

With 90 more needed in 12 overs, Kaif too got in the act by hitting a six and a four off the 39th over bowled by Tudor. Yuvraj kept the momentum going with a boundary each in the next couple of overs. The youthful exuberance and sheer audacity that these two had shown had the crowd on their feet and Hussain & co. were officially in panic mode now.

Kaif had just completed his fifty when Yuvraj lost his wicket against the run of the play, caught at long-on trying to hit Collingwood out of the park. He made 69 off just 63 balls with the help of 9 stunning boundaries and a six.

The equation now read: 59 more runs needed off 50 balls with 4 wickets in hand as Harbhajan joined Kaif in the middle. Clearly, the pendulum had swung back in England's favour.

Kaif released some of the pressure with a much needed six over midwicket off Irani. The pugnacious Sardar followed suit in the next over tonking Collingwood for another invaluable six over long-on.

India were 295/6 at the end of the 45th over which meant 31 more to go in 30 balls with 4 wickets in hand. Mohammad Kaif was an U19 world cup winning captain and it showed in the way he was guiding the temperamental Harbhajan through this delicate phase. The duo batted sensibly to pick 6 off a good 46th over bowled by Flintoff to take the team's score past 300. Kaif then managed to carve out 2 deftly placed boundaries in the 47th over bowled by England's most experienced fast bowler, the wily Gough to make it 312/6.

With 14 more needed off the last 3 overs, it seemed India had it under control. But there was another twist remaining. Flintoff brought England right back into the match with a brilliant 48th over in which he sent back Harbhajan and Kumble giving away just 3 runs to make it 315/8.

With 11 needed off the final 12 balls, Darren Gough bowled a decent penultimate over but was unlucky as a total mishit from Kaif's bat managed to sneak through the third man boundary to make it 324/8 at the end of the 49th over.

The tension was palpable as India needed two runs off the last over to win the final at Lords. Zaheer Khan was on strike facing a fired-up Flintoff, who had dismissed Harbhajan Singh and Kumble in his previous over. He started the over brilliantly with two dot balls but in trying to fire in a yorker for the third, ended up bowling a low full toss on the off which Zaheer managed to nudge to mid-off and took off for the non-striker end. Stationed at mid-off was the world's best fielder, Paul Collingwood who picked up and threw the ball to Flintoff in one motion but the pressure of the moment got to Flintoff as he failed to gather resulting in an overthrow. That was it! India had won. The man of the moment Kaif let out a huge war cry and ran back to embrace his partner Zaheer as the whole Indian team erupted in joy. Leading the wild scenes of jubilation was none other than their captain, the Bengal Tiger Sourav Ganguly who, in an iconic moment, took off his shirt and waved it from the hallowed balcony of the Lords, in a gesture of defiance and triumph. Moments later the whole team was running onto the field embracing Kaif and Zaheer in the tightest of bear hugs ever witnessed on a cricket field.

After 9 unsuccessful attempts, India had finally managed to cross the final hurdle and emerge victorious in a tournament final. The Indian fans in the stadium and back home rejoiced wildly as India achieved one of the greatest run chases in ODI history. The Indian team went on a victory lap around the stadium with some players lifting young Kaif on their shoulders, who was named the Man of the final for his heroic unbeaten 87 off 75 balls adorned with 6 fours and 2 sixes.

If that epic win against the mighty Australians at Eden Gardens fourteen months ago was the first major turning point for this Indian team in red ball cricket, then *this* historic triumph at Cricket's headquarter was the second major turning point for this team, this time in white ball cricket. With the ODI World cup less than six months away, it couldn't have come at a better time and was a testament to the plans chalked out by the coach and the captain. Plans like opening with Sehwag and Ganguly, having Sachin bat at number 4 and playing Rahul Dravid as the wicketkeeper batsman, though far from ideal, had helped in getting the combination right and this showed in the results since this strategy was put in place - a first ever ODI series win in West Indies followed by this historic win in England. The selection committee led by the great Chandu Borde also deserved some credit for being on the same page and supporting the vision of the coach and captain. Now all that was needed was to persist with the same combo and iron out the minor chinks that still remained.

09

Soaring to New Heights

For now however, it was time for some good ol' test cricket. As expected, it was curtains for Deepdas Gupta; the selectors picked Ajay Ratra as the first-choice keeper and the 17 years old Parthiv Patel from Gujarat as his backup. Also back were other test specialists like SS Das, Wasim Jaffer and Sanjay Bangar.

The team got into test mode by playing out a couple of 3-day practice matches, drawing the one against a strong Windies A side while beating Hampshire comfortably by 66 runs.

It had been hardly two years since Zaheer Khan burst on the scene but even in such a short span of time, he had rapidly grown in stature to become the *de facto* leader of the Indian pace attack in the absence of the ageing Srinath. The reason for his steep rise in the ranks was the sharp cricketing brain he possessed and there is no greater proof of that than the fact that it was Zaheer's idea to try Sehwag as an opener in tests as well. To their immense credit, the team thinktank was receptive of such suggestions and thus it was decided that Sehwag would open with Jaffer in the first test.

England too had its fair share of headaches going into the test series. Injuries to key players like Trescothick, Gough and Caddick meant that Nasser Hussain would have to field a less than full strength eleven.

Thus, twelve days after that memorable final, the two teams congregated once again at Lords for the inaugural test. Nasser Hussain won the toss and elected to bat first on a wicket that looked conducive to batting. Zaheer gave India the perfect start when he trapped Michael Vaughan plumb in front for a duck with one that came in sharply. This brought the English captain to the crease. Together with Mark Butcher, he weathered an inspired opening spell from Zaheer and ensured there was no further damage in the first hour. England were 71 when Kumble had Butcher caught at short leg by Jaffer for 29. Thorpe, visibly distressed by marital problems, lasted a total of 8 balls before losing his middle stump to a jaffa from Zaheer Khan and England went to lunch struggling at 78/3.

Another quick wicket post lunch and it could well have been game over for England on day1 itself. Realizing this, the English captain dropped anchor. In Jack Crawley, in the midst of his second comeback this summer, he found an equally determined ally and together they bailed their team out of the precarious situation with an invaluable partnership of 145 run. It was Sehwag who got India the breakthrough when he had Crawley caught at slip for 64. Hussain responded with a flurry of boundaries to reach the coveted three figure mark, and in the company of the veteran Alec Stewart took his team to stumps at 257/4. This was his 3rd test hundred against India and 11th, overall and it was a proverbial captain's knock in every sense of the word.

Alec Stewart, who had overtaken Graham Gooch to become England's most capped test player the previous day, couldn't last long next morning falling lbw to a Zaheer inswinger for 19. Flintoff resumed his on-going rivalry with the Indian team, particularly their captain, with aggression as he stroked his way to a quickfire 59 off just 62 balls in a partnership of 93 with his captain, before nicking one to the keeper off an Agarkar delivery. Two overs later Agarkar struck again to dismiss the English captain much in the same manner as Flintoff ie caught behind. Hussain departed for 155, his highest test score in five years.

With England at 357/7, India had another chance to get back in the test but they messed it up as they let the English tail wag for another 130 odd runs before Kumble was able to bring the innings to a close with wickets of Craig White and Simon Jones, both of whom employed the long handle to good effect against the tired Indian bowlers. Zaheer was the pick of the bowlers with 3 big wickets. Kumble was also rewarded for his workhorse like toil with 3 wickets. The decision to go in with third seamer instead of Harbhajan had turned out to be a costly mistake.

India's reply began on a horrible note as Jaffer lost his stumps to Hoggard on the fifth ball itself. Sehwag, opening in tests for the first time, didn't let that affect his batting as he went after the English bowlers as if this was an

ODI. First Hoggard and then Giles were hit out of the attack. Rahul Dravid at the other end was reduced to a mere spectator as he watched Sehwag race off to a fifty in just 41 balls. With a half-century already under his belt, he became even more audacious in his stroke play and Simon Jones and Craig White were taken to the cleaners with cuts and pulls of the highest ferocity. The pair had added 126 runs for the second wicket, when Hussain's gamble to bring Giles on just before stumps paid off as Sehwag managed to drag one onto his stumps. He scored 84 off 90 balls with 10 fours and a six. Nehra was sent in as the night watchman but was dismissed off the last ball before stumps to make it 130/3 for India.

India began day3 with caution but just as the new pair seemed to be settling in, Dravid lost his wicket to a nasty lifter from Hoggard, just 4 short of his fifty. Three overs later White got lucky with the prized wicket of Tendulkar caught behind for 16 and India was in a big trouble at 168/5. Hussain brought Flintoff back into the attack to have a go at Ganguly and the big guy got the better of his nemesis in this round, dismissing him for just 5. Laxman tried to battle it out but was again left stranded for 43 as the English seamers polished off the tail to close India's first innings at 221.

Hussain decided to not impose follow-on to give his bowlers some rest. Kumble dismissed Butcher for the second time in the match and Agarkar had Hussain in the exact same manner as the first innings albeit for much cheaper this time. Thorpe's wretched run continued as he was caught at covers off Kumble for just 1. But Crawley once again proved to be difficult to dislodge for Indian bowlers and he and Vaughan took England from 76/3 to 184/3 at stumps on day3.

Vaughan raced to his hundred the next morning but was dismissed on the very next ball by Nehra. He joined a select group of English greats to have their name appear twice on the Lords honours board twice in the same summer, having scored a sublime 115 against Sri Lanka just a couple months back. This was his 3rd test century and contained 11 hits to the fence.

Hussain declared at 301/6 as soon as Crawley reached his 100, only the 4th of his start-stop career. Crawley's knock contained only 8 hits to the fence, still came off just 132 balls. A great example of exploiting the gaps to perfection. Kumble was India's best bowler again with 3 wickets to his name.

Set a humongous 568 to win, Indian openers began in earnest with even the usually restrained Jaffer not shy of punishing the loose balls. They had added 61 in little over 12 overs when Jones uprooted Sehwag's stumps with a peach of a delivery. Things settled down a bit with Dravid's arrival at the crease and he and Jaffer took the score past 100. Jaffer completed his half century but lost his wicket to the part-time spin of Vaughan soon after. Tendulkar began well but was undone by a beautifully set-up inswinger by Hoggard. He scored only 12. Very next ball, Hoggard trapped Ganguly in front for a duck. Dravid, closing in on a half century, was joined at the crease by Laxman but there was to be no repeat of Eden Gardens here as Giles succeeded in breaching Dravid's defence to dismiss him for a neat but insufficient 63. While he was doing a decent job behind the wicket, Ajay Ratra's batting didn't inspire much confidence, that hundred at West Indies notwithstanding. Here too he could last just 11 balls before being bounced out by Hoggard. Laxman and Agarkar took India to stumps on 232/6 ensuring the match would go on till the fifth day.

They added another 64 runs on the morning of day5 when Jones ended Laxman's resistance for 74 with the team's score at 296. For a change, the tail hung on, just enough for the maverick Ajit Agarkar to complete a most astonishing of test hundred, and that too, at Lords of all places! Too bad it had to come in a lost cause.

White broke the last wicket stand of 63 between Agarkar and Nehra by getting Nehra caught at third slip by Thorpe to signal the end of the match an hour or so after lunch. England had won by 170 runs. The match was a sort of personal triumph for the English captain Nasser Hussain and he was named the Man of the match as much for his brilliant batting as for his shrewd captaincy.

The Indian team was stunned by the defeat. The brilliant move of opening with Sehwag was negated by the mistake of dropping Harbhajan in favour of three quicks. Their dismal show highlighted the value of Javagal Srinath and the experience and guidance he provided. He was still very much required and no one felt it more acutely than skipper Ganguly who vowed to bring him back to the fold in the post-match press conference.

The team management's plan of using the 10-day gap before the start of the second test was hampered by rain that ruined most of the 4-day practice match against Worcestershire, though the batsmen did get some valuable batting practice, with Sachin scoring his 53rd first class hundred.

Ganguly won the toss and made the puzzling decision to bat first in conditions perfect for swing bowling at Nottingham. Luckily for him though the 5-pronged pace attack of England, except for Hoggard, failed to make use of the conditions despite starting well, and India managed to end the rain affected day1 at 210/4, thanks to a splendid 106 studded with 18 cracking boundaries by Virender Sehwag, who seemed to be relishing his new role as a test opener.

After the delayed start on the second day, Sehwag and Laxman got out early but Ganguly partnered with Agarkar to put on 67 runs for the sixth wicket, bringing India closer to 300. However, India lost 3 wickets in quick succession, including Ganguly's for 68, and slipped from 285/5 to 295/8. Harbhajan came to the rescue with a fiery 54 off 37 balls and helped India cross 350 before they were bowled out. Hoggard claimed 4 wickets and Harmison had a good debut with 3 scalps.

England's batsmen made the most of the inexperienced Indian pace attack and ended the third day on 341/5. The star of the show was Michael Vaughan who smashed 197 off 253 balls with 23 fours. It was his second consecutive and third overall hundred of the summer. His captain praised it as "one of the best innings he had ever witnessed from an English batsman". He was not exaggerating.

Next morning, the overnight pair of Stewart and Flintoff extended their partnership by another 91 runs before both fell in the same over from Zaheer Khan. Stewart played a brisk innings of 87 off 92 balls and showed his class. England's lead was only 76 runs then but India could not wrap up the tail for the second test running. Craig White frustrated India with a record-breaking stand of 103 for the ninth wicket with Hoggard. He missed his century by a whisker when Agarkar got rid of Harmison and ended England's innings at 617.

Zaheer and Harbhajan claimed 3 wickets each while Nehra and Agarkar shared 4 between them, but they all gave away too many runs and the fielding was sloppy with a few catches going down.

India were behind by 263 runs and lost both their openers in the first two overs with only 11 runs on the board but Tendulkar took charge of the situation with an assertive fifty, and along with Dravid, took India to the end of the fourth day at 99/2.

India still needed 164 runs to avoid an innings defeat but the pitch became easier to bat on and three of India's top batsmen - Dravid, Tendulkar and Ganguly - cashed in, with Dravid scoring a century while Tendulkar and Ganguly falling short by a whisker. Apart from them, it also required a very gutsy 19 not out by the 17 years old Parthiv Patel, batting for over an hour and half to rule out any possibility of a dramatic England win. Vaughan was the unanimous choice for the Man of the match.

It was rather brave of India's captain to assert in the post-match presentation that this "great escape" has opened up the series.

Before the next test, Indians played a 4-day warm-up match against Essex at Chelmsford. The match ended in a high scoring stalemate with Shivsunder Das making a strong case for a test comeback with a knock of 250, Sehwag smashing another rapid hundred and Harbhajan shining in this batsmen-dominated game with a 7-wicket haul which included the scalp of Essex's overseas star Andy Flower.

Headingley, the venue for the third test, had historically been a haven for swing bowlers. Yet the Indian thinktank decided to play both their spinners, dropping Nehra. This defiance of conventional wisdom continued at the toss as well as Ganguly chose to bat first in conditions which looked ideal for swing bowling.

The decision seemed to backfire when India lost Sehwag early for just 15 but Sanjay Bangar, who was picked in the playing eleven as an allrounder and sent in to open the innings with Sehwag, showed great temperament to put on 170 runs for the second wicket with the ever-dependable Rahul Dravid before being dismissed by Flintoff. Bangar made a very cautious 68 compiled over five hours stay at the crease. After his departure, Dravid carried on to post his second consecutive hundred of the series, and in the company of Sachin, took India to stumps at 236/2 at the end of the first day's play.

India resumed their innings on day 2 with Dravid and Tendulkar continuing their masterclass, adding another 99 runs to make it yet another 150 runs partnership between these two. Sachin Tendulkar finally managed to decode the restrictive ploy - devised against him by the wily Hussain and executed to perfection by the duo of Giles and Flintoff - and the prodigal son of Yorkshire – (In 1992, at the age of 19, Tendulkar became the first overseas player to represent Yorkshire in county cricket) - in his 99th test, finally delighted his loving fans at Leeds with a hundred of the highest calibre. It was his 30th test century and took him past Sir Don's 29. The pair looked set to bat England out of the game, but Flintoff broke their partnership by trapping Dravid lbw for a brilliant 148.

Tendulkar then joined forces with Ganguly, who was in a destructive mood from the first ball. The Indian captain unleashed his fury on the already weary English bowlers and smashed them to all corners of the ground. Tendulkar also shifted gears and reached his 150 with a six off Giles. The highlight of the day, or quite possibly the series came in the last hour of the day's play, when under sub-optimal light, the pair of Tendulkar and Ganguly went absolutely berserk hammering 96 runs in just 11 overs of the third new ball. The fireworks came to an end when Ganguly was finally dismissed, clean bowled trying to make room and hit Tudor out of the park. He creamed 10 fours and 3 sixes in his innings of 128, which came off just 167 balls. The 249 runs stand between him and Tendulkar for the fourth wicket is, to this day, an Indian record against England.

India finished the day at a massive 584/4. It was a day of utter domination by India's big three who scored a hundred each for the first time in the same innings, having come close only two weeks earlier at Trent Bridge with two nineties and a hundred; and mesmerized the crowd with their splendid batting. Their once-in-a-lifetime-show put India in a strong position to win the test and level the series at a venue it was least likely to happen.

Sachin fell in the first over the next morning just 7 runs short of his double hundred, lbw off Caddick and Ganguly declared soon after at 628/8, their highest total against England.

Faced with a mountain to climb, Rob Key and Vaughan gave them a glimmer of hope with a steady opening stand, but Zaheer struck to remove Key for 30. Vaughan looked in sublime touch and looked good for another big one, but Agarkar cut short his innings for 61. England's middle order crumbled under the pressure of the huge total, as Kumble and Harbhajan spun a web around them. Hussain, Crawley and Flintoff fell in quick succession, leaving England reeling at 164/6. Stewart was typically defiant, and found an able ally in Giles. They added 70 runs for the eighth wicket, but Kumble broke through again to dismiss Giles for 25. Caddick and Hoggard offered little resistance, as Harbhajan and Kumble wrapped up the innings for 273. Stewart was left stranded on 78*, while Kumble and Harbhajan shared six wickets between them.

England were asked to follow-on after conceding a massive lead of 355 runs to India. Key and Vaughan once again gave them a steady start, putting on 64 runs for the first wicket. However, Agarkar struck twice in quick succession to remove both the openers. Butcher and Hussain then steadied the innings with a century partnership for the third wicket. Butcher made 49 before falling to Kumble, while Hussain went on to score a fighting century. He made 110 off 196 balls, hitting 16 fours. However, he did not get much support from the other batsmen, as England lost their last seven wickets for just 89 runs and were all out for 309 in 96 overs, losing the match by an innings and 46 runs. Kumble was the pick of the bowlers for India, claiming 4 wickets for 66 runs, taking his match tally to 7, making it one of his best performances in an overseas test. However, the Man of the match honour went to Rahul Dravid, for his decisive century in adverse conditions on the first day.

The win ended a 16-year drought of no test wins in England and set up the series nicely for a decisive showdown at The Oval in the fourth and final test.

India warmed up for the decider by playing out another high scoring draw with Derbyshire in their final practice match of the tour. Ratra, under pressure from the young Parthiv, and Sehwag hit hundreds while Nehra shone with the ball.

Nasser Hussain won a crucial toss and elected to bat first on a tranquil batting wicket at the Oval. England missed Flintoff but Trescothick's comeback balanced it out somewhat. The explosive left hander smashed his way to a typically aggressive fifty with 9 fours. He was dismissed by Zaheer just before lunch, two runs shy of adding 100 with the in-form Vaughan.

The Indian bowlers had to toil for more than 50 overs to get another breakthrough as Vaughan and Butcher combined attack and defence to take their team past 200 with only 1 wicket down before tea. After the break, Vaughan reached his fourth test hundred of the summer, joining a distinguished group of great batsmen - Herbert Sutcliffe, Don Bradman, Denis Compton, Allan Lamb and Graham Gooch - with 4 test hundreds in an English summer. He needed 195 deliveries to get to the landmark and then cut loose to score his next 82 runs off just 71 balls, as he thrashed Kumble through the midwicket region repeatedly. The 174 run partnership between him and Butcher was broken when Harbhajan Singh had Butcher caught at slip by Dravid for 54. John Crawley, promoted ahead of the skipper, helped England finish the day at 336/2

Vaughan departed early on the second day caught behind off a beautiful outswinger from Zaheer. His 195 came off 297 balls and included 29 exquisite boundaries. His batting in this innings reminded one of David Gower at his peak.

Vaughan's exit so soon disrupted Hussain's plans and instead of going for the jugular, he and the other remaining batsmen inexplicably turned cautious. Perhaps it was the pressure of not only the test but also the series that made them retreat into their shells. Indian bowlers, especially the military medium pacer Bangar, exploited their hesitancy to pick up the wickets of Hussain and Crawley, reducing England to 372/5 from the overnight 336/2

A half-century partnership between Alec Stewart and Dominick Cork took England beyond 425 when Harbhajan struck and finished off the English tail with a five-wicket haul - the first in this series for either team.

India had to chase 515 and lost Sehwag in the fourth over itself. Dravid and Bangar stabilized the innings with a 69-run partnership but Bangar fell early on the next day leaving the task once again to India's big 4. Dravid and Tendulkar survived the early challenge in their own different ways - Dravid with the help of solid defence and Tendulkar displaying his wide array of shots in a four-filled 54 off just 89 balls. Their partnership added 91 runs and ended when Caddick managed to trap Sachin lbw. Ganguly took over from where Sachin left, played a nearly identical knock adding 105 runs for the fourth wicket with Dravid, who completed his third century of the series, laced with 15 fours. Their stand broke when Ganguly edged a rising delivery from Cork to the keeper's gloves. He made 51 with 8 shots to the fence. Laxman and Dravid played out the remaining 20 overs to take India to stumps on day3 at 315/4.

Still behind by 200 runs, India resumed their innings on the next day with the prolific pair of Dravid and Laxman adding another century partnership to their names. Caddick got England the breakthrough when he had Laxman caught at gully by Giles for 40. Dravid continued unperturbed to his maiden double hundred, topping off an amazing run of scores which saw him become the first to reach 1000 test runs in 2002. And it was only September!

A mix-up with Ratra, back in the side thanks to his hundred against Derbyshire, resulted in Dravid's run-out. That was the only way England could have dislodged him that day. His 217 came off 468 balls and included 28 boundaries. The ten-and-half hour that he spent at the crease during this knock took his time at the crease for the series past 30 hours, earning him the moniker of 'The Wall' in the English press.

The rest of the Indian batsmen couldn't survive much longer and India's innings ended for 508, just 7 runs short of England's first innings score. Any hopes of India's spin pair emulating the legendary Bhagwat Chandrashekhar's feat at this very ground 31 years ago were soon dashed by the very promising new English opening pair of Trescothick and Vaughan, who took their team to 114 without loss at the end of the fourth day's play.

With an outright result looking well-nigh impossible, the only point of interest left in the last day's play was whether Vaughan would be able to reach his record breaking fifth test hundred of the summer but the whole day's play was rained off, bringing a tame end to what had been an otherwise high-voltage summer for both teams.

Rahul Dravid won the Man of the match, capping off a phenomenal series for him where he amassed 602 runs in 6 innings at a Bradmanesque average of over 100. He deserved to share the Man of the series honour with Michael Vaughan, who had a margin of just 13 runs over him.

Anil Kumble and Matthew Hoggard led the bowling charts with 14 wickets apiece in the series.

Although the test series was shared, over all it was an English summer that all of India could be proud of, more so when the balance sheet also included the Natwest trophy as well.

Champions Trophy 2002

Three days later, the players from both sides found themselves in Colombo for the prestigious Champions trophy - a kind of precursor to the World cup.

India's first match of the 'Mini world cup' - as it was popularly known - was at the R. Premadasa stadium, Colombo against Zimbabwe.

Winning the toss and electing to bat first, Sehwag once again got his side off to a flyer but an inspired spell by Douglas Hondo derailed the momentum and had India reeling at 87/5 by the end of the first 15 overs. Thankfully, the team still had the always reliable Rahul Dravid and the hero of the Natwest final, Md Kaif to bail them out of this difficult situation. The two in-form batsmen did just that with a beautifully paced partnership of 117 runs, which was broken only when Dravid needlessly got run-out for a clinical 71. Batting like a seasoned finisher, Kaif managed to take the team's total from 204/6 in the 38th over to 288/6 by the end of the 50th, with able support from the experienced Kumble. He returned unbeaten, scoring 111 off 112 balls - his maiden ODI century - with the help of 8 fours and a six.

Perennial lone warrior Andy Flower kept his side in the hunt till the very end with a career-best knock of 145 as Indian bowlers were made to work hard to contain Zimbabwe. To their credit, they kept their nerve and prevailed in the end. Zaheer Khan was the star of the show, taking 4 crucial wickets and bowling a superb final over. He dismissed both the openers and then returned to break the dangerous partnership between Andy Flower and Guy Whittall. He also bowled Sean Ervine in the last over to seal the deal for India. Golden arm Tendulkar also chipped in with two wickets, including the big one of Andy Flower. India won by 14 runs and Mohammad Kaif was the player of the match for his unbeaten 111, continuing his love affair with R. Premadasa stadium, as it was here only that he had lifted the inaugural U19 world cup just 2 years back. Following his impressive performance in the Natwest final, this fantastic young talent from Uttar Pradesh continued to gain prominence within the team.

India's next match saw them resume their rivalry with England. With a place in the semi-final at stake, the match had become virtually a quarter final of sorts. Hussain won the toss and elected to bat first but the decision backfired as Nehra reduced England to 7/2, including the all-important wicket of Trescothick for a duck. The limitations of the Indian bowling line-up, however, got exposed as they let England's middle order get away from such a poor start to post a very decent 269/7 in their 50 overs. Ian Blackwell's 82 off 68 balls with 6 boundaries and 3 sixes was the highlight while Nick Knight too scored an exact 50.

No team had chased more than 244 at the Premadasa stadium and won. Indian openers, however, made a mockery of such historical stats as they tore apart the English attack with a record opening stand of 192 in just 28.4 overs. Sehwag was sensational, blazing away to his hundred in just 77 balls. He hit 21 fours and a six in his 126 off 104 balls, before he was caught and bowled by Blackwell. Ganguly was sublime, scoring an unbeaten 117 off 109 balls with 12 fours and 3 sixes, guiding India home in the company of Tendulkar, with 10 overs to spare. Sehwag was the player of the match for his breathtaking ton.

This was a display of sheer dominance, the kind that can put the fear of God in the best of the sides.

Next was the semi-final clash against the Proteas, an opponent they hadn't really faced in quite a while. Ganguly won the toss and elected to bat first. A promising start by the openers was nipped in the bud by Ntini when he had Ganguly caught in the deep trying to hook one too many. Sehwag carried on unperturbed and had taken the score past 100 in the 16th over when Donald had Laxman caught behind for 22. Kallis gave India another jolt in the very next over when he got Sehwag caught in the deep by Klusener. Sehwag made 59 off just 58 balls with 10 cracking boundaries.

This twin blow in successive overs forced Dravid and even Sachin to go into defensive mode causing the run-rate to dip slightly. Just when it seemed that he had got his eye in, Sachin was run out in brilliant fashion by that greatest-of-all-time-fielder Jonty Rhodes for 16. Yuvraj joined Dravid with the score reading India 135/4 at the halfway mark in this do-or-die semi final and the two began the repair job in the same manner as they had done a few matches earlier in the Natwest tri-series, through clever placement complemented by running hard between the wickets and hitting the odd boundary when the opportunity so presented itself. The duo took the team past 200 adding 72 runs in the next fifteen overs with minimum fuss but just as it was time to shift gears, Klusener trapped Dravid plumb in front with one that kept low, just one run short of his fifty. Yuvraj and Kaif ran hard and innovated to add 47 runs in the next 7 overs against bowlers of the calibre of Donald and Pollock before getting out in the penultimate over and India's inning ended at 261/9.

Zaheer once again provided India with the early breakthrough when he had Graeme Smith caught by an airborne Yuvraj at point. It was a catch that would have made even the great Jonty Rhodes proud. The adrenalin rush proved short-lived though as the mercurial Gibbs blew the wind out of Indian team's sails with stroke play of the highest calibre. Drives, cuts, pulls, hooks, sweep against spinners…you name the shot and Gibbs executed it, to blaze his way to the 14th hundred of his career and second in as many matches in this tournament. With Kallis once again essaying his role of a sheet-anchor to perfection, the pair had added 178 runs for the second wicket when persistent cramps in both arms forced Gibbs to retire hurt in the 37th over. He was batting at 116 off 119 balls with 16 boundaries at that point.

With just 60 more to get in 13 overs with 9 wickets in hand, it should still have been a cakewalk for a team that batted as deep as Pollock's South Africa did. But two wickets in the 39th over bowled by Harbhajan set the cat among the pigeons and the dead match came alive all of a sudden. Then, in an inspired move, Ganguly asked Sehwag - the man who could do no wrong at that point in time - to bowl the 42nd over. Sehwag responded with the wicket of Boucher - third African batter in a row falling to an attempted sweep. Here is where the tables turned. While India went on an all-out attack, Proteas inexplicably opted to play it safe taking the game deep. Asking Sehwag to bowl the 48th and 50th overs, while Zaheer sent down the 49th, was a big, big gamble but it paid off as Zaheer bowled one hell of a penultimate over, keeping a well-set Kallis and Klusener quiet, giving away just 4 runs to bring the equation down to 21 in the last over.

Kallis deposited the very first ball of the last over bowled by Sehwag over midwicket for a huge six to bring down the equation to 15 needed off 5. The next delivery he again tried to attempt the same almighty heave but ended up lobbing a skier which the keeper Dravid made no mistakes in pouching safely, sending Kallis back to pavilion 3 short of a 100. Klusener, now a pale shadow of the hero who had almost won South Africa the previous World Cup, tried his best but couldn't free his arm against the flat and quick off-spin of the street-smart Sehwag and could manage only 4 runs before lofting a catch straight to Kaif off the last ball of the innings. The heist was complete. India had managed to steal a most unbelievable win by a margin of just 10 runs and were now into the finals.

Just how the Indian team wriggled out and then reversed the stranglehold on unsuspecting Proteas is something that was going to be debated for years to come. For now though, this Indian team looked like it can walk on water.

The final was going to be contested between India and Sri Lanka, the host team that had bounced back to form in home conditions after a dismal England tour. Ganguly had a surprise in store for the hosts on the day of the final. Javagal Srinath was not part of the Indian squad that played in the group stage and the semi-final. He was flown in from Leicestershire as the last-minute replacement for Ashish Nehra who had suffered a groin injury during the semi-final and arrived at Colombo just hours before the final.

Sanath Jayasuriya won the toss and elected to bat first. The prolific opening pair of Jayasuriya and Atapattu began confidently, putting on 65 runs in 13 overs before Atapattu was caught off Harbhajan, but not before ruining Srinath's comeback, taking five boundaries off his first spell. Young Sangakkara, now the first-choice wicketkeeper for Sri Lanka, came in and played some crisp shots, but the Indian spinners Harbhajan and Sehwag tightened the screws. Still, at 155/1 in 30 overs, 300 looked very much on the cards for the hosts, especially with Jayasurya looking set for a big score. But he was caught off Agarkar for 74 in the next over, and that dried up the runs. Harbhajan bamboozled the great Aravinda de Silva and Sangakkara with his variations, while Tendulkar made up for a rare dropped catch with the wicket of Jayawardene. Pair of Russel Arnold and Vaas added some late runs to take the hosts to 244/5 in 50 overs.

Harbhajan justified his selection as the first-choice spinner over Kumble with 3/27 in his 10 overs, while Sehwag and Zaheer kept things tight. Srinath's late inclusion did not pay off however as he proved expensive and went wicketless.

India's chase started with a bang as Sehwag smashed 3 fours in the first over he faced, but then the rain came down heavily and washed out the match. The game had to be replayed from scratch on the reserve day.

Sri Lanka once again won the toss and opted to bat. Zaheer struck with the first ball of the match, dismissing Jayasuriya for a duck. Agarkar and Kumble removed Atapattu and de Silva cheaply, leaving Sri Lanka at 63/3 in 13 overs. Sangakkara and Jayawardene rebuilt the innings with a 116-run partnership, but both fell to Zaheer in quick succession. Arnold and Vaas added some late runs, but Sri Lanka could only manage 222/7 in 50 overs.

Zaheer was the best bowler for India with 3/44 in nine overs, while Harbhajan and Kumble took one wicket each. Sehwag and Tendulkar were economical.

India's chase started poorly as Dinesh Mongia was caught off Vaas for a duck. Sehwag counter-attacked with three fours and a six, while Tendulkar played cautiously. India reached 38/1 in 8.4 overs when the rain came down again and ended the match. The trophy had to be shared between the two finalists as there was no reserve day left. Ironically, had the tournament rules allowed the final to be carried over to the second day, instead of it being replayed, the contest would have been completed.

Of course, it wouldn't have been a cakewalk to chase down either of those below-par totals on *that* wicket against Muralitharan & co., yet it is fair to say that Indian team had the upper hand on both occasions and Ganguly had a valid reason to feel "robbed" of the chance to be the sole winner of this prestigious ICC tournament that boasted of the largest purse ever in cricket history.

Be that as it may, one inescapable conclusion driven home by the events in the Champions trophy was that this Indian team was now one of the top one-day sides in the world and a serious contender for the upcoming world cup which was now less than four months away.

Return duel with the Windies

The immediate next assignment, though, was the home series against the West Indies. The team hadn't forgotten the soul crushing defeat it had received at the hands of Carl Hooper and his men earlier in the year and it was time for a payback.

First up was the three match test series. The visitors, without the services of their best batsman Lara, who was getting treated for Hepatitis, stroked themselves into form in the practice match before the commencement of the test series, against an Indian board President's XI side comprised of 11 India hopefuls.

The first of the three tests, played at Wankhede stadium turned out to be a one-sided affair that saw India dominate the visitors with bat and ball.

Winning the toss and opting to bat first, Sehwag and Sanjay Bangar posted India's first 200-run opening partnership since Gavaskar's final series in 1986-87, and their best opening stand against West Indies. Bangar got out for a patient 55 while Sehwag scored a blistering 147 off 206 balls studded with 24 fours and 3 sixes. Rahul Dravid retired hurt on 100, his 4th consecutive test century, one behind Sir Everton Weekes' record. It was a typical "The Wall" innings built on the foundation of rock-solid defence combined with classical shot making. Javagal Srinath, back in whites having revoked his retirement, also contributed with a timely fifty. For Windies, Mervyn Dillon and Mahendra Nagamootoo bowled like workhorses and picked 3 wickets each.

Windies were bundled out for 157 in reply, with Zaheer Khan and Kumble claiming 4 wickets apiece. Chanderpaul was the only batsman to offer some resistance with a gritty 54. Ganguly enforced the follow-on and Windies fared slightly better in their second innings, scoring 188 runs. Chanderpaul again top-scored with 67, while Harbhajan Singh bagged 7-48 and Kumble took the remaining 3 to take his match tally to 7.

India won the match by an innings and 112 runs, their biggest victory margin against West Indies at that time. Sehwag was named the player of the match for his explosive century. India took a 1-0 lead in the three-match series.

The historic Chepauk was the venue for the second test. Hooper won the toss and elected to bat first on another re-laid pitch. In a move that reeked of a severe lack of confidence, the Windies batsmen tried to bat out time rather than looking to score. That was never going to work against Kumble and Harbhajan on a wicket that had something for the spinners from the first day itself. Kumble rang in his 32nd birthday in style by claiming 20th 5-wicket haul of his career. Bhajji chipped in with 3 wickets of his own and the Windies were bowled out for mere 167 half an hour before close, by when India had reached 31 without loss.

The still fresh opening pair of Sehwag and Bangar put on another impressive opening stand of 93 runs. Before losing his stumps to a peach of a delivery from Pedro Collins, Sehwag scored a highly entertaining 61 off just 65 balls with 8 fours and 3 sixes. The guy had felt no need of any change in approach be it ODIs or tests, and this refreshing attitude had won him a significant fan following across the cricketing world in a very short span of time. Young tearaway fast bowler from Jamaica, Jermaine Lawson did the unthinkable - breaching The Wall's defence with a 150 km/hr ball of the day, thereby ensuring Sir Everton Weeks' record of 5 consecutive test centuries stayed intact. Dillon's persistence at the other end was rewarded when he removed Bangar and Ganguly in successive deliveries. Bangar made 40 while Ganguly got another horrible decision. Tendulkar's unconvincing stay at the wicket came to an abrupt end when he dragged a wide delivery from Lawson onto his stumps. He made 43. Laxman fell early next morning but the tail wagged and took the team's total to 316.

Trailing by 149 runs in the first innings, Windies got off to a poor start losing Gayle on the fourth ball of the inning, but purposeful batting thereafter from Hinds, Sarwan and skipper Hooper took the team past 200 for the first time in the series. However, Harbhajan wreaked havoc with his spin and dismissed four batsmen in quick succession. West Indies collapsed from 208/5 to 229 all out, giving India a target of 81 runs.

Indian openers continued to impress with another half century partnership to their name before Sehwag departed after a typically entertaining 33 which included 3 fours and 2 sixes. Bangar too fell to Hooper but the pair of Tendulkar and Dravid took their side home with 8 wickets and a day to spare. Harbhajan was the Man of the match for his 7 wickets and those important runs in the first innings. India also clinched the series with this victory, their first series win against the West Indies since 1978 ie 24 years.

Another feather in the cap for this young and hungry bunch.

With the series already in the bag, the Indian team returned to where it all started for this team some fifteen months earlier- the fabled Eden Gardens at Calcutta. West Indies came into the test having played a high-scoring draw against Railways and their captain promised that they will be playing for pride in this test.

'The Prince of Kolkata' won the toss at his home ground and opted to bat first on a flat pitch. It turned out a strange sort of innings where most batsmen got starts but failed to capitalize. Bangar was the only one to cross fifty, while Srinath once again chipped in with a quickfire 46 to lift India to 358.

The visitors finally showed some fight with the bat, piling up 497 in reply. Wavell Hinds, Chanderpaul and young Marlon Samuels all scored centuries, while Gayle fell short by 12 runs. Harbhajan was the pick of the Indian bowlers, taking 5 wickets, while Kumble claimed 3.

India, trailing by 139 runs, found themselves in big trouble in their second innings, losing 4 wickets for 87; albeit a couple of them due to dubious decisions. However, Sachin and Laxman saved the day and the match with a magnificent partnership of 214. Tendulkar scored a masterful 176, combining defence and attack, while Laxman reaffirmed his love affair with Eden Gardens with a fluent 154. The match ended in a tame draw. Sachin Tendulkar was named the Man of the match and Harbhajan Singh, the Man of the series for his 20 wickets in the series.

Find of the series, however, had to be young Parthiv Patel who had been an absolute revelation, both behind as well as in front of the wicket. Team India's quest for a world class wicketkeeper seemed to have come to an end finally.

10

A 'Jolt' from the Blue

Three days later, the two sides converged in Jamshedpur for the first of the 7-match ODI series. India won the toss and elected to bat first. Openers Sehwag and Ganguly failed to get going on a belter of a wicket but Agarkar, sent in as a pinch-hitter, got the inning back on track with a 98-run stand with Laxman, who came in at number 4 in the absence of Sachin who was nursing a shoulder niggle. Laxman fell 3 short of his fifty but Agarkar shifted gears after completing his second ODI fifty to add a brisk 75 runs in the next 10 overs in the company of vice-captain Dravid, who was slowly but surely emerging as an excellent middle order batsman in the shorter format as well. Agarkar missed out on a hundred by 5 runs skying a catch to Gayle off Collins, who was the pick of the West Indian bowlers. Yuvraj too fell cheaply but Kaif and Dravid added 47 runs off the last 28 balls to take the score to 283/6 in 50 overs. Kaif contributed a breezy 31 not-out off just 18 balls.

It was a tough target but the Windies were up for the challenge, led by Wavell Hinds' tone-setting 93. He smashed 12 fours and 2 sixes, and put on 86 with Marlon Samuels, who scored a brisk 51. Ramnaresh Sarwan was the hero of the day, as he played a superb unbeaten innings of 83. He hit 6 fours and 3 sixes, and kept his cool in the final over, when six runs were needed off six balls. He hit the winning boundary off the last ball bowled by Agarkar, and sealed a memorable four-wicket victory for his team. He was rightly awarded the Man of the match for his 'coming-of-age' kind of inning. India's bowlers fought hard, but could not stop the West Indies from drawing first blood in the series.

Hooper called correctly at the toss and asked India to bat first in the rain-delayed second match at Nagpur.

India had a shaky start, losing Sehwag and pinch-hitter Agarkar cheaply. Ganguly and Laxman steadied the ship with a 98-run stand, playing some elegant strokes. Ganguly reached his fifty with a six off Nagamootoo, but fell soon after for 78. Laxman continued to anchor the inning, while Harbhajan Singh promoted up the order came and went quickly. Rahul Dravid joined Laxman and the duo added 105 runs in just 85 balls, with Dravid scoring a fluent 51. Laxman was dismissed for 99 by Gayle, just one short of his century. Losing two set batsmen in the 44th over of the innings triggered a collapse as the remaining 5 batsmen could only add 19 runs to the total to make it 279/9 in 47 overs.

West Indies were set a revised target of 280 in 47 overs by Duckworth Lewis method. Gayle and Hinds gave them a solid start, putting on 42 runs in 8 overs. Hinds was dismissed by Srinath for 27, but Gayle carried on with his aggressive intent. He found an able partner in Marlon Samuels, who matched him stroke for stroke. They added 134 runs for the second wicket, taking the game away from India. Samuels reached his fifty with a six off Sehwag, but fell soon after for 52. Gayle completed his century with a four off Nehra, but was also out in the same over for 103. Hooper and Chanderpaul came to the crease with 59 runs needed off 51 balls. They kept the scoreboard ticking with some smart running and occasional boundaries. Chanderpaul was caught by Ganguly off Nehra for 39, but Sarwan joined Hooper and finished the job. Sarwan once again hit the winning four off Srinath in the final over, and West Indies won by 7 wickets with 4 balls to spare to take a 2-0 lead in the series.

These back-to-back defeats, although close ones, were still surprising after the euphoria of the Natwest and Champions trophy. The results were also indicative of just how indispensable Sachin Tendulkar and Zaheer Khan were for this team.

But what was even more worrying was the fact that both these matches were marred by incidents of crowd trouble, something that was a rarity in India.

The nuisance continued for the third game running in the third match at Rajkot. Ridley Jacobs, standing in for the injured Hooper, won the toss and elected to bat first. Half centuries from the in-form Gayle, Sarwan and Chanderpaul propelled Windies to a handsome 300/5 in 50 overs. Srinath bowled the best among the Indian bowlers, although he had just 1 wicket to show for it.

Chasing a massive 301, Indian openers Sehwag and Ganguly showed just why they were among the most feared of their kind in the world at the moment, with a thrilling stand of 196 in a little over 25 overs. The stand was broken when Ganguly holed out to Chanderpaul at long off for 72 off 83 deliveries but Sehwag carried on unbothered. He reached his hundred off just 69 balls, his third in ODIs in less than 75 deliveries, a feat matched only by the explosive Sanath Jayasuriya. He was unbeaten on 114 off 83 balls, with 17 fours and 2 sixes, when the match was interrupted by crowd trouble. India were 200 for one in 27.1 overs at that stage, well ahead of the par score of 119.

The match was halted for over an hour before the umpires decided to award the game to India on the basis of the Duckworth-Lewis method. West Indies were unhappy with the decision and even made a written complaint to ICC against the result, but to no avail. Rumours were rife that bookies were behind the sabotage as they had bet heavily on India losing but were left flummoxed by Sehwag and Ganguly's blitzkrieg.

The ICC immediately sprang into action and sought a guarantee from the BCCI to ensure that there would be no repeat of such ruckus, while also proposing to reschedule the remainder of the series. However, BCCI President Jagmohan Dalmiya rejected the proposal and instead held meetings with the Gujarat administration to put extra safeguards in place for the next match to be played at Ahmedabad.

Ganguly won the toss and asked Windies to bat first, perhaps keeping the dew factor in mind since this was a day-night affair. The in-form Chris Gayle used the occasion to give the world an early glimpse of the kind of mayhem that would soon crown him 'The Universe Boss' with a sensational innings of 140 off 127 balls studded with 12 fours and 5 towering sixes, as he took Srinath and Nehra to the cleaners. Sarwan too continued his fantastic run with another enterprising innings but was left stranded on 99, still looking for his maiden international hundred. Carl Hooper, back after sitting out the previous match, contributed a quick 35 off 27 balls to take his team to a mammoth 324/4 in 50 overs. Ganguly tried as many as 8 bowlers but none barring Harbhajan could contain the carnage.

India's hopes were dealt a big blow when Sehwag fell in the first over itself. Ganguly tried gamely to keep abreast with the asking rate but couldn't last long, nicking one to the keeper. With 45/2 on the board after 5 overs and no Tendulkar to bail them out, India were staring down the barrel. But they had two of their most dependable batsmen at the crease: Dravid and Laxman. The duo stitched together a calm and composed partnership of 103 in 118 balls, before Laxman's perennial weakness of running between the wickets cost him his wicket yet again. He had scored a fluent 66 off 74 balls. Yuvraj struggled to find his rhythm but still managed to add 61 runs in 54 balls with his vice-captain. When Kaif fell in the 38th over, India still needed 94 runs from 75 balls and the match seemed to be slipping away from them. But Sanjay Bangar had other plans. Under the watchful eyes of Dravid, who was mastering the art of anchoring the innings in one-dayers, Bangar shed his image of a defensive test batsman and unfurled his full range of strokes on the hapless Windies bowlers, who were left stunned by this unexpected transformation. Bangar smashed 57 off just 41 balls, including 5 fours and 2 timely sixes. It was Dravid who had the last word though, as he hit the winning runs and remained unbeaten on 109 off 124 balls. His 8th ODI hundred was a masterclass in pacing an ODI chase and his ability to rotate the strike and pierce the field was evident from the fact that his inning contained only 8 hits to the fence. Jury, however, voted in favour of Chris Gayle for the Man of the match.

Ironically, it was Ahmedabad - the site of the horrible communal riots that left thousands dead - that produced the first trouble-free match of the series.

With the series levelled at 2-2, the two teams travelled to nearby Vadodara for the 5th match. India, batting first, posted a challenging total of 290/8 in 48 overs, after the match was reduced due to rain. Sehwag and Ganguly gave India a flying start, adding 88 in 10.4 overs, before both fell in quick succession after reaching their respective fifties. It was the 50th fifty of Sourav Ganguly's illustrious ODI career. Laxman and Dravid then steadied the innings with their second century partnership in as many games, but India lost momentum in the middle overs as West Indies bowlers fought back. Laxman was yet again run out for 71 and Yuvraj and Kaif failed to fire. Bangar provided some late impetus with some hefty blows, but India fell short of the 300-mark by 10 runs.

West Indies began their chase aggressively, with Gayle and Hinds tearing into the Indian bowlers. They put on 132 in 16.2 overs, with Hinds smashing 80 off 61 balls, including 10 fours and 5 sixes. Harbhajan broke the partnership by dismissing Hinds and then Samuels in quick succession. Sarwan joined Gayle and played another sensible knock, as they added 83 for the third wicket. India clawed their way back into the match by picking up three wickets in quick succession, including that of Gayle who fell for a brilliant 101 off 107 balls, his third hundred in 4 innings. West Indies still needed 52 runs from 54 balls with 5 wickets in hand. Powell and skipper Hooper then took charge and guided their team home with some calculated hitting. Powell scored an unbeaten 30 off 26 balls, while Hooper finished on a run-a-ball 21. West Indies won the match by 5 wickets and were now leading the series by 3-2.

Stand-in captain Rahul Dravid won the toss and put Windies in to bat first in the sixth match. Agarkar ended Hinds' misery at the crease - previous game's player of the match could manage just 1 off 28 balls here - and the very impressive Murali Kartik finished off the rest of the Windies top-order by dismissing Gayle, Samuels and Sarwan, to leave West Indies reeling at 74/4 by the half way mark. Chanderpaul top-scored with 58 and added 61 runs with Ricardo Powell for the fifth wicket. Hooper chipped in with 38 but the mercurial Agarkar took a couple more wickets in his second spell to restrict Windies to a modest total of 201 all out in 46.3 overs. It was a brilliant performance from bowlers. Kartik and Agarkar took 3 each while Bangar too chipped in with a couple wickets.

India had a shaky start as they lost three wickets for 48 runs in 13 overs. Dravid and Yuvraj steadied the ship with a 99-run stand. They played cautiously against the spinners and accelerated against the pacers, hitting some crisp boundaries. Yuvraj was particularly aggressive, scoring 54 off 64 balls with 7 fours. They seemed to be cruising at 147/3 in 33 overs, but then lost three wickets for the addition of just one run in a dramatic collapse. Bangar and Kaif then rebuilt the innings with a mature 39-run partnership and took India close to the target. Collins dismissed Kaif in the 43rd over, but it was too late for West Indies. Bangar displaying an ice-cool temperament took his side home in the 47th over. India won the match by 3 wickets with 22 balls to spare and levelled the series 3-3. It was third win in three matches for Rahul Dravid as the stand-in captain. Ajit Agarkar pocketed the Man of the match.

The low scoring thriller was a welcome change of pace from the usual run orgies seen in the previous matches.

With the series tied at 3-3, the seventh ODI played at Vijaywada turned into a virtual final. Sourav Ganguly had failed to recover from his thigh injury in time so Dravid was to lead again. The visitors got off to a shaky start after electing to bat first, losing Gayle and Chanderpaul cheaply to Srinath and Agarkar respectively. However, Hinds and Sarwan steadied the innings with a 116-run stand for the third wicket, playing some elegant strokes and rotating the strike.

Hinds fell for 58, caught by Kaif off Sehwag, who also dismissed Ricardo Powell and Hooper later in the innings. But the precociously talented Samuels joined Sarwan and unleashed a barrage of boundaries, taking the Indian bowlers to the cleaners. He reached his century in style, hitting Agarkar for a six over long-on.

Sarwan was trapped lbw by Agarkar in the 38th over for 83, but Samuels continued his onslaught till the end, adding 109 runs with Powell and Hooper in quick time. He finished on an unbeaten 108 which came off only 75 balls and included 11 fours and 5 humongous sixes. Samuels' stroke play that evening was a stunning blend of elegance and savagery and justified his high reputation in his homeland. He upheld the proud legacy of West Indian batsmanship and earned the admiration of the legendary Viv Richards, who cheered his century with a beaming smile from the press box. West Indies ended with their second highest total of the series setting India a target of 316.

India's chase never got going as they lost wickets at regular intervals. They were reduced to 67/4 in the 14th over, with Jermaine Lawson - called up as the cover for injured Pedro Collins - picking up 4 top-order wickets, in a devastating opening spell that evoked memories of the glory days of fearsome West Indies fast bowling. Only Yuvraj showed some guts with a fighting 68, but he ran out of partners as India were bowled out for 180 in 36.5 overs. Chris Gayle chipped in with the ball as well, with 3/22 as Windies won the match by a huge margin of 135 runs. The win helped West Indies end their tour of India on a winning note, after losing the test series badly. Samuels was adjudged the Man of the match for his unforgettable innings, while Chris Gayle pocketed the first of many Man of the series awards that were to come his way soon.

It's not very often that India loses a one-day series at home but to be fair to them, they were without Sachin Tendulkar and Zaheer Khan for the entirety of the series and lost the services of other key players like Ganguly, Kumble and Harbhajan for different reasons at various stages in the series. So, the final result need not be taken on face value. The team was still very much on track as far as the upcoming world cup was concerned. Sanjay Bangar and Murali Kartik were the two finds of the series.

Indian team's final assignment before the world cup was a lengthy tour of New Zealand where they were scheduled to play 2 tests followed by a 7 match ODI series. Barely a week after the end of the exhaustive ODI series against West Indies, the team left for Christchurch. Sachin Tendulkar and Zaheer Khan were back, having cleared the fitness test before boarding the flight.

The tour kicked off with a unique encounter - a SuperMax international - a format that was devised by the Kiwi great Martin Crowe and played mostly in his country's domestic competitions. It was a truncated version of test cricket, where each team got two innings of 10 overs each and each bowler could bowl only 4 overs in total. It was also the first format to introduce the free-hit rule for no balls. The format had a brief stint of international recognition by the ICC in the late 90s and early 2000s and India became the third team to feature in an international SuperMax game against the New Zealand Max Blacks, following England (1997) and West Indies (2000).

India put up a spirited fight but fell short in the end. They were unfamiliar with this format, unlike their opponents who had played it regularly. Sachin Tendulkar was the standout performer for India as he smashed 72 runs in just 27 balls. The master blaster showcased his versatility and class by mastering a new format in his maiden appearance and reaffirmed his status as the best batsman of his generation.

The Indians had a tough time in their only warm-up game - a three-day match against Central Districts. They struggled to save the game after their famed batting line-up failed in the first innings. It was a sign of things to come in the long and hard tour.

Test series commenced with the first test played at Basin Reserve, a happy hunting ground for the hosts. Put in to bat by New Zealand captain Stephen Fleming on a green and seaming pitch, India lost both their openers cheaply to Shane Bond and Daryl Tuffey. Dravid and Tendulkar tried to steady the innings with a 48-run stand, but Jacob Oram broke through with the wicket of Tendulkar for 8. Ganguly and Laxman followed soon after, leaving India reeling at 55 for 5. Dravid fought a lone battle and scored a gritty 76, but he ran out of partners as the lower order folded meekly. India were bowled out for 161 in 58.4 overs, with Bond and Oram taking three wickets each.

Kiwi openers Mark Richardson and Lou Vincent gave them an okay start with a 30-run partnership. Zaheer Khan struck twice in quick succession to remove Vincent and Stephen Fleming. Craig McMillan joined Richardson and added 65 runs for the third wicket, before Bangar dismissed both of them in the same over. Nathan Astle counter-attacked with a brisk 41, but Zaheer came back to claim his third and fourth wickets. New Zealand's tail wagged a bit and took them to 247 all out in 91.1 overs, giving them a lead of 86 runs. Richardson top-scored with 89, while Zaheer Khan was the pick of the bowlers with 5/53 - his first 5-wicket haul in test cricket.

India needed to bat well in their second innings to set a challenging target for the Kiwis. However, they failed miserably as they lost wickets at regular intervals. Sehwag and Dravid fell to Bond in the same over, while Bangar, Ganguly and Laxman were dismissed by Oram in quick succession. Sachin Tendulkar showed some fight and scored a fluent 51, but he was the last man out as India were skittled out for 121 in 38.1 overs. Bond was the wrecker-in-chief with four wickets including the prized ones of Dravid and Tendulkar while Oram and Tuffey took three each.

New Zealand had to chase only 36 runs to win the match. They did so without any trouble as Richardson and Vincent knocked off the runs in 8 overs. New Zealand marked their 300th test with a comprehensive 10-wicket win and took a 1-0 lead in the series. Mark Richardson was named the Man of the match.

The venue for the second test was Hamilton. Asked to bat first on a damp and seaming pitch, India got bundled out for 99 as Daryl Tuffey ran through the Indian top order in front of his home crowd. He was ably supported by Bond and Oram. Ganguly (23) and Harbhajan (20) were the only two players who managed to get into double figures.

New Zealand also struggled against the Indian pace attack, led by Zaheer Khan who bagged his second 5fer in successive matches. Captain Fleming was the only batsman to cross 20 as New Zealand were bowled out for 94, giving India a slender lead of 5 runs.

The famed Indian batting line-up fared better but only marginally so, as they were bundled out for 121 in their second innings. Rahul Dravid top scored with 39. Tuffy and Oram repeated their exploits from the first innings and took 4 and 2 wickets respectively.

Needing 160 to win, New Zealand withstood a spirited fight put up by the two Indian left arm quicks with skipper Fleming leading the way with an invaluable 32. Jacob Oram, in his second test, played a vital knock of 26 not out to seal the victory. Daryl Tuffey was awarded the Man of the match. It was the first time since 1981 that no batsman from either team could score a fifty in a test. New Zealand won the series 2-0, their first against India since 1989-90.

In the final analysis, this series would go down in history as one dictated by New Zealand's miserable early summer weather where bouncy pitches were made virtually unplayable by excessive sideways movement. Hosts New Zealand played the conditions better and were also helped by the toss going their way on both occasions.

The tour moved on to the one-day internationals, a format where India had been dominant recently. They had to shrug off the disappointment of the test series and fine-tune their world cup preparations, with the mega event just around the corner. Sachin Tendulkar, the team's ace batsman, was again sidelined by a hamstring injury for the first four games of the series, making the challenge even tougher.

First ODI got underway on Boxing day, better known as Derby day in Auckland. It turned out to be a bowler's derby as batsmen of both teams showed no signs of improvement from the recently concluded test series, failing to bat out their allotted overs even in the shorter format. India, who were put in to bat by Fleming, were bundled out for a paltry 108 in 32.5 overs, with the hard-working Jacob Oram taking a career-best 5 for 26. Only

ShivSunder Das (30) and Rahul Dravid (20) managed to cross twenty for the visitors, who struggled against the pace and bounce of the Kiwi bowlers.

New Zealand's chase was not smooth either, as they lost seven wickets for 86 runs, with the returning Javagal Srinath claiming 4 scalps. Ashish Nehra and Zaheer Khan also bowled well, but Oram (27 not out) and Kyle Mills (21) saw their team home with 74 balls to spare. Jacob Oram was named the Man of the match for his all-round performance.

To be fair, it wasn't the easiest of surfaces to bat on and both skippers complained about it after the game. However, the Indian batsmen also showed poor technique and a lack of willingness to battle it out.

Second match at Napier saw the first proper batting exhibition of the tour by both sides. New Zealand, who batted first after losing the toss, posted 254 for 9 in 50 overs, thanks to contrasting half-centuries from Astle (76) and Mathew Sinclair (78). Srinath was the pick of the Indian bowlers for the second match in a row with 3 for 34.

India's chase got off to a disastrous start as Ganguly was dismissed for a duck in the first over. Sehwag then took charge and smashed 108 off 119 balls with nine fours and two sixes. He added 57 runs with Laxman (20) and 78 runs with Dravid (18) for the second and third wickets respectively. However, once he was run out in the 40th over, India collapsed from 204 for 7 to 219 all out in 43.4 overs. Kyle Mills was the pick of the bowlers with 3 scalps while all the rest of Kiwi bowlers too chipped in with a wicket each. New Zealand won by 35 runs and were leading the series by 2-0.

2003

3rd match of the series was played on the New years' day in Christchurch. Sourav Ganguly's decision to bat first backfired as India were bundled out for their second-lowest total against New Zealand in one-dayers. 22 extras were the highest contributor in the score of 109 as none of the batsmen with the exception of Dravid could cope with the pace and swing of the New Zealand seamers. Paul Hitchcock, Jacob Oram and Daryl Tuffey shared nine wickets among them, while Andre Adams chipped in with one.

New Zealand also lost their openers cheaply, but Nathan Astle smashed Srinath for 22 runs in the 10th over of New Zealand's chase, to wrest the momentum decisively in the hosts' favour. He hit six fours and a six before falling to Harbhajan, who also removed Craig McMillan in the same over. Oram and the young wicketkeeper batsman Brendon McCullum then guided New Zealand home with 23 overs to spare. Ajit Agarkar was the only bowler who troubled the New Zealand batsmen, taking 3 wickets for 26 runs.

Daryl Tuffey was named the player of the match for his unbelievable spell of 10-2-11-2.

India, still without their batting lynchpin Sachin Tendulkar, were put into bat by the Kiwi skipper in the do-or-die fourth match of the series at Queenstown's Events centre which was hosting its first international fixture. India never got going as they lost wickets at regular intervals and were bowled out for a paltry 122 in 43.4 overs. Andre Adams was the wrecker-in-chief with 5 wickets for 22 runs, while Tuffey and Mills took two and one wicket respectively. Yuvraj Singh was the top scorer for India with 25 runs.

New Zealand had no trouble in chasing down the target as they reached 123 for three in 25.4 overs. Fleming played himself back into form with a fluent 47 off 59 balls, hitting five fours and a six. He added 73 runs for the second wicket with Sinclair, who remained unbeaten on 32. Javagal Srinath took all the three wickets to fall for India, but it was too little too late. New Zealand cruised to an unassailable 4-0 lead in the seven-match series and sealed their first ever series win over India. But the one-sided nature of the contest had left the victors feeling "a bit flat", according to the winning captain Fleming.

A day-night game at Wellington awaited India and New Zealand for the fifth ODI of the series. Having already surrendered the series 4-0, Indian team had nothing but pride to play for in the remaining three matches. Their morale was lifted by the return of their MVP Sachin Tendulkar.

Fleming won the toss and elected to bat first in the hope of giving his batsmen some much needed time in the middle ahead of the impending world cup but a fired up Zaheer Khan spoiled his plan by sending Astle, Sinclair and Harris back to the pavilion with just 3 runs on the scoreboard.

Fleming and Cairns, who was returning from an injury layoff, put on a brief fightback before Srinath bowled Cairns for 25. Nehra dismissed Fleming in the next over to reduce the hosts to 51/5 after 15 overs. Young McCullum and Andre Adams both scored 35 each in contrasting fashion to take their team past 150 but once McCullum got cleaned up by Kumble in the 39th over, the rest didn't last long and the innings folded for 168 in the 43rd over. Zak was the star for India with that sensational opening burst while Srinath, Kumble and Nehra all chipped in with 2 wickets apiece.

India's chase got off to a horrendous start as Ganguly was out for a duck, nicking the first ball of the inning to the keeper. Dinesh Mongia didn't last long either, clean bowled by Shane Bond for just 2. In his next over Bond ruined Sachin Tendulkar's return by trapping him lbw before he had even opened his account. India were reeling at 25 for 3 in 6 overs but Sehwag and Dravid revived them with a brisk 41-run stand for the fourth wicket. Sehwag hit 8 fours in his 40-ball 45 before getting out. Yuvraj batted sensibly but needed support from the other end. He found an unlikely ally in Zaheer, who helped him put on 44 vital runs in 10 overs. Yuvraj fell for a composed 54 but fittingly it was Zaheer who finished the job giving India their first win of the tour. He was awarded the Man of the match for his splendid all-round show.

Sixth match at Auckland was again a day/night affair. New Zealand were restricted to 199 for 9 in their 50 overs after opting to bat first. They had a poor start as they slumped to 50 for 4 in the 19th over. Scott Styris and Lou Vincent then revived them with an 80-run stand for the fifth wicket. Styris scored 42 off 52 balls with 7 fours and 2 sixes, while Vincent remained unbeaten on 53 off 107 balls with 3 fours and a six. Shane Bond gave the innings a late flourish with a hugely entertaining cameo of 31 off 15 balls, smashing two fours and three sixes.

As in the previous, the pitch did too much sideways, and the veteran Srinath used his knowledge superbly to end up with astonishing figures of 10 2 13 3.

The modest looking target of 200 in 49 overs - (India were docked an over for poor over rate) - proved to be a tricky chase as they kept losing wickets at regular intervals. Sehwag was once again the lone warrior for India as he played a magnificent knock of 112, keeping the scoreboard ticking with his trademark shots. He found some support from Dravid, who made 21, but the rest of the batsmen failed to cope with the pressure. Sehwag had taken India to the brink of victory but his dismissal triggered a mini-collapse as India went from 182/4 in 42 overs to 196/7 by the end of the penultimate over. Kaif and Zaheer went into the final over needing 4 runs to win. Andre Adams almost pulled off a miracle as he dismissed Kaif on the second ball and ran-out Zaheer on the very next ball to make it 198/9 in 48.3 overs. Equation now read 2 runs needed off 3 balls with number 10 and 11 at the crease. Fleming tried to unsettle the tailenders with some mind games, but Srinath and Nehra held their nerve and scampered the winning runs with a ball to spare. Virender Sehwag was awarded the Man of the match for his brilliant hundred.

It was the kind of thriller the National Bank series had been crying out for and set the stage for a similarly competitive last match in Hamilton to round off the tour on a high note.

India went into the 7th and final encounter of the series keen to take their third win on trot and head over to South Africa on a winning momentum, but it wasn't to be as, sent in to bat by New Zealand, they were soon reduced to 17/3 by Mills and Tuffey - the Kiwi Cricketer of the year. Ganguly and Yuvraj tried to rebuild the innings, but Adams and Styris ran through the middle order with 4 and 2 wickets respectively. India were bowled out for a paltry 122 in 44.5 overs, with only Yuvraj (33) and Kumble (21) managing to cross twenty.

In response, the Kiwis lost Sinclair, McCullum and Cairns cheaply, but Fleming and Styris steadied the chase with a 84-run stand for the fourth wicket. Kumble broke the partnership by dismissing Styris for 29, but Fleming remained unbeaten on 60 - his 33rd half-century in this format - and guided New Zealand to a six-wicket win with 128 balls to spare, winning him the Man of the match.

Truth be told, it had been a forgettable tour and New Zealand Cricket CEO Martin Snedden admitted that the pitches were substandard and did not produce entertaining cricket in his concluding speech at the post-match presentations.

Be that as it may, the tour was an unmitigated disaster for the Indian team, who had been on a roll before this setback. It was the worst way to prepare for the world cup and the captain and coach had their work cut out for them to try and recoup team's morale quickly. The skipper remained optimistic, hoping that the two-week break - their first after 15 months of almost non-stop cricket - would help them bounce back for the biggest event of their lives.

The only bright spot in a dismal campaign was Javagal Srinath's return to form as India's pace spearhead. Proving his detractors wrong, Srinath emerged as the leading wicket-taker of the series with 18 wickets in 7 matches, 4 more than the next bowler on the list. This was a welcome sign for India, as the world cup was to be held on the fast and bouncy tracks of South Africa.

11

World Cup Dreams

The senior selection committee, in consultation with the coach and captain, named a more or less predictable 15-men squad for the world cup, with VVS Laxman being the notable absentee. Laxman had scored more runs than Dinesh Mongia and Kaif in last ten innings, but his poor running between the wickets and substandard ground fielding may have gone against him.

India began their world cup campaign in a very unconvincing manner, as their star-studded batting line-up failed to fire against minnows Netherlands. This performance was more alarming than the failures in New Zealand, as the pitch here was a belter but the stroke-makers still struggled to get going.

Sourav Ganguly won the toss and opted to bat first. Acquiescing to Sachin Tendulkar's wishes, the team thinktank had agreed to go back to opening with the old firm of Tendulkar and Ganguly. The move failed to bear immediate fruit as Ganguly nicked one to the keeper for 8. Sehwag coming in at one down was snapped up at slip for 6 as India suffered two early blows. Sachin Tendulkar and Rahul Dravid attempted to rebuild the inning, but both perished to Tim de Leede, who bowled with exemplary accuracy and discipline. Tendulkar nicked one to the keeper for 52, while Dravid was castled for 17. Yuvraj and Dinesh Mongia then added some valuable runs for the sixth wicket, taking India beyond 150. Yuvraj played some elegant shots, while Mongia, coming in at number 7, kept the scoreboard ticking. However, both departed in the death overs, as de Leede came back to haunt India. Yuvraj was caught and bowled by Raja for 37, while Mongia was run out for 42. The tail could not wag much, as de Leede ended with four scalps. India failed to play their full quota of 50 overs getting dismissed for 204 in 48.5 overs, a disappointing show on a flat wicket.

Needing just 205 to win on a good batting wicket, Netherlands hopes of scoring a shocking upset win were dashed soon as Javagal Srinath struck in the first over, removing Feiko Kloppenburg. Henk-Jan Mol and Bas Zuiderent followed soon, as Srinath and Zaheer Khan wreaked havoc. Tim de Leede, the hero with the ball, flopped with the bat, edging Harbhajan Singh to the keeper. Anil Kumble spun a web around the middle order, as Netherlands collapsed to 54/7. Daan van Bunge showed some resistance with a valiant 62, and added 49 with Jeroen Smits for the ninth wicket. But Srinath returned to wrap up the innings for 136 in 48.1 overs. The old guard of Srinath and Kumble shared 8 wickets between them, saving the day for their side as India won by 68 runs. To their credit, the adjudicators decided to give the Man of the match award to Tim de Leede.

Three days later, India squared off against the mighty Australia in a much-awaited encounter of this world cup. Sourav Ganguly won the toss and elected to bat first but the decision backfired as Ganguly was caught behind off Brett Lee for 9, while Sehwag also perished in the same manner for just 4. Sachin Tendulkar was the only batsman who showed some resistance, scoring 36 off 59 balls. However, he was trapped lbw by Jason Gillespie, who also dismissed Dravid and Mohammad Kaif cheaply in an incredible spell as the first change, where he bowled 10 overs straight killing all hopes of a middle order revival for the Indians. Yuvraj was lbw to Glenn McGrath for a duck, while Dinesh Mongia was caught by Andrew Symonds off Lee for 13. Kumble remained unbeaten on 16, while Harbhajan scored a quickfire 28 off 32 balls. However, India were bowled out for a paltry 125 in 41.4 overs. Gillespie and Lee were the main wicket-takers for Australia, taking 3 wickets each.

Australia had no trouble chasing down the target, as Gilchrist and Matthew Hayden almost saw them home with another century partnership to their name. Gilchrist was stumped by Dravid off Kumble for 48, but Hayden and Ricky Ponting completed the chase in 22.2 overs. Hayden remained unbeaten on 45, while Ponting made 24 not out. Australia won the match by 9 wickets with more than 25 overs remaining. Gillespie walked away with the Man of the match for the stunning figures of 10 2 13 3.

If India were uneasy against Netherlands, they were positively quivering here against the mighty Australians, failing to find any fluency whatsoever in their strokeplay, except for a brief cameo from Harbhajan, who managed to hit a few lusty blows when the game was already gone. Australia, on the other hand, showed their dominance and ruthlessness, even without their star spinner Shane Warne, who had been banned due to substance abuse.

Facing the wrath of their fans back home after a string of poor performances, India needed a convincing win in their next match to keep their World Cup hopes alive.

A Remarkable Turnaround

They were up against co-hosts Zimbabwe in their own den, the Harare sports club. Zimbabwe captain Heath Streak won the toss and elected to field first. India got off to a brisk start as Sehwag and Tendulkar added 99 runs for the first wicket in 16.4 overs. Sehwag was the aggressor, hitting 6 fours in his 36 off 38 balls. He fell to Guy Whittall's medium pace, caught behind by Tatenda Taibu. Tendulkar then took charge and played some sublime strokes all around the ground. He hit 10 fours in his 91-ball knock and looked set for a century, but was bowled by Grant Flower who also claimed Dinesh Mongia's wicket in the same over. Captain Sourav Ganguly and his deputy Rahul Dravid steadied the innings after that twin blow with a 40-run stand when Ganguly and Yuvraj Singh fell in quick succession, leaving India at 184/5 in the 39th over. Dravid and Mohammad Kaif then took the team past 225 adding 45 run for the fifth wicket. Kaif scored a useful 25 off 24 balls with a four and a six before being trapped lbw by Douglas Hondo. Harbhajan (3) also departed soon after, caught by Brian Murphy off Streak but the Indian vice-captain held one end and guided India past the 250-mark with some sensible batting. He remained not out on 43 off 55 balls with 2 fours. Zaheer Khan gave him good support with a cameo of 13 off eight balls with two fours. India finished with a respectable total of 255/7 in their allotted 50 overs, helped in no small measure by a stroke of luck as Grant Flower, who had bowled superbly and picked up 2 for 14 in 6 overs, injured his finger and couldn't complete his quota of 10 overs.

Zimbabwe's reply got off to a disastrous start as they lost Mark Vermeulen for a duck in the first over, caught by Dravid off Srinath. Craig Wishart (12) also fell soon after, clean bowled by Srinath. Flower brothers then tried to rebuild the innings with a 25-run stand for the third wicket, but Harbhajan

Singh broke through with his first ball, bowling Andy Flower around his legs for 22.

Grant Flower and Dion Ebrahim added another 35 runs for the fourth wicket, but skipper Ganguly struck thrice in six balls to snuff the life out of Zimbabwe's chase, prizing out Grant Flower, Ebrahim and Andy Blignaut, to leave Zimbabwe reeling at 87/6 in the 26th over.

Taibu and Guy Whittall showed some fight with a 37-run stand for the seventh wicket, but Ganguly's lucky charm Sehwag ended their resistance by having Whittall caught by Khan for 28. Taibu remained unbeaten on 29 off 44 balls, but ran out of partners as Bhajji and Zak wrapped up the tail. Zimbabwe were all out for 172 in the 45th over, handing India a comfortable win by 83-runs, moving up to 2nd place in their group while Zimbabwe slipped to fourth. Sachin Tendulkar was declared the Man of the match for his measured knock of 81.

Indian team's next fixture was against minnows Namibia at Peitermaritzburg in South Africa. On the eve of the match, the team participated in the unveiling of a plaque at the train station where, in 1893, Mahatma Gandhi had been thrown off a train because of his skin colour. The crowd cheered loudly as they witnessed the historic moment.

As expected, it turned out to be a one-sided affair. Put in to bat first after losing the toss India got off to a fine start as Virender Sehwag and Sachin Tendulkar put on 46 runs for the first wicket in 7.5 overs. Sehwag was the first to go, caught by Danie Keulder off Rudi van Vuuren for 24. Tendulkar then joined forces with Sourav Ganguly and the duo dominated the Namibian bowling with a record partnership of 244 for the second wicket, their third partnership of over 200. Tendulkar was in sublime form, hitting 18 fours in his 152 off 151 balls. He reached his 34th ODI hundred in style with a boundary off Gerrie Snyman. Ganguly was equally impressive, playing himself back into form with a knock of 112 off 119 balls with 6 fours and 4 sixes. He completed his 20th ODI ton with a six off Bjorn Kotze. Tendulkar was dismissed by van Vuuren in the 48th over, but Ganguly remained unbeaten till the end as India amassed 311/2 in their allotted overs.

Namibia crumbled under pressure and were spun out for 130 in 42.3 overs. Yuvraj Singh was the star with the ball, taking 4 wickets for just

6 runs in 4.3 overs. India cruised to a massive 181-run win and moved back to the third slot in their group while Namibia remained at the bottom. Sachin Tendulkar walked away with his second straight Man of the match award. India's only moment of concern in the match came when Ashish Nehra had to limp off the field after spraining his ankle having bowled just one ball.

A couple of days later, Indian team squared off against Nasser Hussain's England at Kingsmead, Durban. The match started on an auspicious note for the Indian team as Sourav Ganguly won a toss that was widely expected to be influential in the eventual outcome of the game. Sehwag and Tendulkar were watchful against Anderson, who had demolished Pakistan in England's previous game. Sehwag was the first to break the shackles, hitting four boundaries before he was caught and bowled off a leading edge off Flintoff for 23. Tendulkar continued his fine form in the tournament and reached his half-century off 46 balls with 8 fours and a six before becoming Flintoff's second victim for a run-a-ball 50. Ganguly followed soon after, caught by Trescothick off Craig White for 19, leaving India in a spot of bother at 107/3 in 22 overs.

Dinesh Mongia and Dravid then stabilized the innings with a patient 48-run stand. Mongia scored a laborious 32 before being lbw to Collingwood, while Dravid forged a bustling partnership of 62 runs for the fifth wicket with Yuvraj, who smashed 42 off 38 balls. India's ever reliable vice-captain reached his half-century with a clipped six off Anderson and looked set for a big score. However, both he and Yuvraj fell in the final overs as India lost their last five wickets for just 33 runs. Dravid was caught by Collingwood off Andy Caddick for 62, while Yuvraj was caught by Hussain off Anderson. India were restricted to 250/9 in their allotted overs. Caddick picked 3/69 but it was Flintoff who bowled the best ending up with 2-14.

England faced a stiff target of 251 on a seaming track under lights and lost their way early as Kaif's direct hit sent back Knight for just 1 in the second over. Trescothick struggled to get going and edged Zaheer to Tendulkar at slip for eight, leaving England at 18/2 after 7 overs. Hussain tried to hit his way out of trouble but the introduction of Ashish Nehra as the first change in the 13th over turned out to be the killer blow. The lanky left-arm quick from Delhi, who was in doubt of even playing this match due to the ankle sprain he sustained in the previous game, produced a sensational straight spell of 10 overs of nagging seam bowling to rip through England's batting line-up. He struck twice in two balls to remove Hussain and Stewart and then added Vaughan's scalp in his next over. Flintoff fought a lone battle with a gutsy 64 off 77 balls, hitting 5 fours and 3 sixes, but it was not enough, as Nehra dismissed Collingwood, White and Irani to finish with a dream haul of 6/23 in 10 overs, which, to this day, remains the best bowling figures by an Indian in a World Cup. Srinath dismissed Flintoff and Zaheer wrapped up the innings as India cruised to an 82-run win and almost sealed their place in the Super Six stage. Nehra was the undisputed Man of the Match for his career-defining spell. He rightfully gave credit to team physio Andrew Leipus and trainer Adrian Le Roux for getting him fit in time for this match.

12

Epic 'Encounters'

The stage was set for the most keenly awaited marquee encounter of the tournament - India vs Pakistan at Centurion. The two arch-rivals had not faced each other on the cricket field for more than two years, as political tensions had put a freeze on their bilateral ties. The atmosphere was electric, the stakes were high, and the pressure was immense. In such a scenario, having players like Yuvraj and Sehwag in the Indian dressing room proved to be a blessing, as they kept the mood light with their witty remarks and jokes. India's coach John Wright had a clear strategy to counter Pakistan's fiery passion with calm and calculated cricket. He wanted his team to play smart, disciplined and fearless cricket, and not get carried away by the emotions of the occasion.

The Pakistan team were being led in this world cup by the great Waqar Younis. The Burewala Express had taken over the reins of the team in 2001, but his captaincy record was mixed at best. He needed a strong showing in the world cup to silence his doubters and began this all-important match on a positive note by winning a vital toss and electing to bat first on a surface that promised a fair contest between bat and ball.

After the toss, the match referee Mike Procter, on the special request of ICC chairman Dr. Ali Bacher, had arranged a symbolic gesture of goodwill between the two teams - a handshake and a souvenir exchange on the ground, just before the openers walked in. One of India's senior players however was not too keen on this idea. He felt that it would undermine the intensity of the contest and questioned why the ICC was acting like the UN. There was a delay as the players debated whether to go ahead with the plan or not. The photographers waited impatiently at the foot of the stairs, ready to capture the historic moment.

Finally, with time running out, the Indian team decided to put aside their reservations and oblige the match referee. They did not want to risk being seen as snubbing their opponents. So Waqar and Sourav swapped ties, the players shook hands, and Centurion erupted in cheers. It was a brief but powerful display of sportsmanship.

Waqar's decision to bat first was rewarded by a splendid opening partnership between Saeed Anwar and Taufeeq Umar, who added 58 runs in the first ten overs with some fluent strokes and smart running. Anwar was especially impressive, playing with grace and authority, enroute his 20th ODI hundred. Zaheer gave India the first break-through with a delivery that angled into Umar and beat his defence. Ashish Nehra followed up with the wicket of Abdul Razzaq sent in as a pinch-hitter thanks to a superb diving catch by the makeshift wicketkeeper Rahul Dravid. In the very next over, Inzamam-ul-Haq was run out by a direct hit from Virender Sehwag after attempting a risky single. Pakistan had lost 3 wickets for 40 runs and were in danger of squandering their advantage. Yousuf Youhana and Younis Khan steadied the innings with a sensible partnership of 73 runs in 14 overs. They played cautiously at first, then gradually increased the tempo as the overs ran out. Yousuf was elegant and composed, while Younis was busy and inventive. They looked set to launch a final assault when Srinath removed Yousuf with a slower ball that he could only chip to deep midwicket. Shahid Afridi came in with his usual intent, but could not last long as he holed out to Kumble off Mongia's gentle off spin. Younis carried on till the penultimate over, when he fell to Zaheer's slower ball as well, caught by Mongia at deep square leg. Rashid Latif and Wasim Akram added some useful runs in the final overs, taking Pakistan to 273 for 7 in their 50 overs. It was a respectable total made even more daunting by the fact that the Pakistani bowling attack boasted of the two Ws, Shoaib Akhtar, Abdul Razzaq and Shahid Afridi. This might have prompted the venerable Raj Singh Dungarpur, a stalwart of Indian cricket who was in audience, to ruefully quip, "too big to chase" with a furrowed brow. He was certainly not alone to feel that way at the innings break.

The match had haunted Sachin Tendulkar for a year before it happened. He could not escape the reminders of the date, the 1st of March, when he would face Pakistan. He confessed later that he had trouble sleeping for twelve nights in a row.

None of that showed, however, as the little maestro launched the Indian chase with an almighty bang, as he and Sehwag tore into the Pakistani bowlers with some audacious strokes. They added 53 runs in just 5.4 overs, with Tendulkar upper cutting Akhtar for a breathtaking six over third man and three glorious fours in one over, forcing Waqar to take him off the attack after just 1 over. Sehwag was equally aggressive, hitting Waqar for a six over midwicket and 2 fours in another over. But then Waqar Younis struck twice in two balls, first having Sehwag caught at point by Afridi, then trapping Ganguly lbw with a swinging yorker. India were 53 for 2, and Pakistan sensed an opening.

But Tendulkar was unfazed by the double blow. He continued to bat with sublime skill and supreme confidence, finding gaps and boundaries with ease. He found an able ally in Mohammad Kaif, who played sensibly and rotated the strike. They added 102 runs for the third wicket in 15 overs, keeping up with the required run rate. Tendulkar reached his fifty off just 37 balls, and looked set for another hundred. He was particularly severe on Akhtar, whom he hit for four more boundaries in his second spell. He also played some exquisite shots against Akram and Afridi, showing his mastery over all kinds of bowling. Pakistan needed a breakthrough to stem the flow of runs, and they got it from an unlikely source. Afridi, who had been expensive and erratic in his first spell, came back to bowl a quicker delivery that skidded through and hit Kaif's off stump. Kaif was out for 35 off 60 balls, and India were 155 for 3 in 21.4 overs.

Tendulkar was still going strong at 93 off 68 balls, but was now visibly struggling with severe leg cramps. Perhaps those sleepless nights had finally taken a toll on the old warhorse's body. Dravid joined him at the crease, and they had added another 22 runs for the fourth wicket in 6 overs when a rising ball from Akhtar put an end to one of the great ODI knocks of all time, just 2 runs short of what would have been his third century of the tournament. The master blaster had scored 98 off 75 balls, with 12 fours and an immortal six, and had taken India to 177 for 4 in 27.4 overs. He walked back to a standing ovation from the crowd and his teammates, knowing that he had played one of the defining innings of his long and illustrious career. But the maestro was in no mood to celebrate, knowing better than anyone else that the job was far from done. With the target still nearly a hundred runs away, Pakistan still had a chance to win the match, if they could pick some quick wickets and put pressure on the Indian lower order. But they were denied by a calm and composed partnership between vice-captain Rahul Dravid and Yuvraj Singh, who batted with maturity and skill ensuring Tendulkar's outstanding work at the top wasn't wasted. Following the template they had rehearsed and perfected on more than a couple of occasions in the past 18 months, the seemingly odd pair of Dravid and Yuvraj added another unbeaten 99 runs for the fifth wicket in 18 overs, playing each ball on its merit and picking up singles and twos with ease, while also punishing the odd loose balls. Dravid was solid and steady at one end, scoring a composed 44 not out off 76 balls with 2 fours. Yuvraj was fluent and stylish at the other end, scoring 50 not out off 53 balls with 6 boundaries. The duo completed the chase with 6 wickets and 26 balls to spare, sealing India's fourth consecutive win over Pakistan in World Cups.

But it was not just another win over the arch-rivals. It was much more than that. It was a statement of intent, a display of skill and a celebration of spirit. It was a win that marked another huge turning point in the history of Indian cricket and specially in their rivalry against their arch-nemesis Pakistan. It was a win that repaid the faith of their fans, roused their nation and inspired a whole new generation.

Under the heaviest burdens of pressure and expectations, the Men in Blue rose to the occasion and delivered a performance that will be remembered for generations. It was not just a win, it was a legend.

Such a seminal event was bound to have huge repercussions. Pakistan's World Cup campaign ended in the first round itself after that crushing and demoralizing loss to their arch-rivals. India, meanwhile, progressed to the Super Six stage on a high note and with a lot of momentum.

In their first Super Six encounter at Capetown, Ganguly's men were up against Kenya who were replicating their exploits from the 1996 edition of the World cup. They had made the Super Six with a stunning victory over Sri Lanka and thus could not be taken lightly.

Batting first after winning the toss, Kenyan batsmen batted with patience and put on a decent 225/6 in their allotted 50 overs. Opener Kennedy Otieno was the key architect behind that score which was built on two vital partnerships of 75 runs each with Ravi Shah (34) and Thomas

Odoyo (32) for the first and fourth wickets respectively. Kenya could have scored more but for some tight bowling by Javagal Srinath and Harbhajan Singh in the death overs. The resurgent Srinath claimed 2 wickets for 43 runs while Harbhajan justified his inclusion over Kumble by claiming 2 for 41. Dinesh Mongia also picked up a wicket with his part-time spin. India's fielding was sloppy though as they dropped three catches, including two of Otieno.

India's chase got off to a shaky start as they lost 3 quick wickets for just 24 runs within the first 10 overs. Martin Suji and Thomas Odoyo bowled with accuracy and swing to trouble the Indian batsmen. Sachin Tendulkar, who had been in sublime form throughout the tournament, fell for a rare failure as he edged Martin Suji to a diving Tony Suji at slip for just 5 runs.

However, India's captain Sourav Ganguly stepped up and took the onus of taking his side home upon himself. He first steadied the innings with a solid 84-run stand with his deputy, the ever-reliable Rahul Dravid (32) for the fourth wicket and then accelerated the scoring with a flamboyant 118-run partnership with Yuvraj Singh for the fifth wicket. Ganguly reached his century in style by smashing Collins Obuya over long-on for a six in the 45th over.

India reached their target of 226 runs with 6 wickets and 13 balls remaining. Yuvraj remained unbeaten on a breezy 58 off just 64 balls with 7 fours while Sourav Ganguly was named the Man of the match for his brilliant unbeaten 107 off 124 balls with 11 fours and 2 huge sixes. With this hundred, his 21st, Ganguly moved past Saeed Anwar to become the second-highest century-maker in this format, behind only Sachin Tendulkar who was miles ahead with 34 hundreds.

In their second Super Six encounter, Ganguly & co. took on a familiar foe in the form of Sri Lanka. The pitch at New Wanderers was damp after heavy showers that lashed Johannesberg over the weekend, and Jayasuriya had no hesitation in putting India in to bat. But his gamble backfired spectacularly as Tendulkar and Sehwag unleashed a batting masterclass, tearing apart the Lankan attack with a 153-run opening stand. They were watchful against Vaas and Murali, but ruthless against the rest. Sehwag reached his maiden World Cup fifty and celebrated by launching Jayasuriya for two massive sixes. He tried to repeat the dose against Murali, but holed out for a sparkling 66. Sri Lanka breathed a sigh of relief, but it was short-lived as Ganguly joined Tendulkar in the middle. The pair added another 61 runs with ease, taking India past 200. Tendulkar looked set for his third World Cup hundred, but fell agonisingly short when he edged de Silva to the keeper for 97. It was a rare lapse of concentration from the master batsman, who had missed out on a ton against Pakistan as well. He had the minor consolation of breaking his own record for most runs in a world cup when he crossed the 526 runs mark that he scored in the 1996 edition. India were still in a commanding position at 214/2 in the 39th over, but Sri Lanka fought back with some clever bowling from Vaas and Murali. They removed Ganguly for 48 and then dismissed Kaif and Yuvraj cheaply to stem the run flow. India ended up with 292 thanks to some quick runs towards the end by the multifaceted Rahul Dravid.

In response, the Lankan chase never got off the ground, as they were blown away by a fiery spell of fast bowling from Srinath and Zaheer. Srinath struck in the second over, removing the in-form Atapattu for a duck with a sharp catch by Kaif at point. Two balls later in the same over he induced an edge from the hapless Jehan Mubarak for a duck. Zaheer joined the party by trapping a woefully out of form Jayawardene lbw for a duck, leaving Sri Lanka reeling at 3/3 the third over. It soon became 15/4 as Srinath trapped the veteran de Silva, playing his last world cup, plumb in front for a duck in the very next over. An injured Jayasuriya tried to counter-attack with a few boundaries, but he too fell to Srinath, caught by Kaif again at point for 12. Sangakkara and Arnold tried to rebuild the innings with a 50-run stand, but Nehra broke through by having Sangakkara caught by Yuvraj for 30. Nehra then got rid of Vaas for 9, leaving Sri Lanka at 95/7. The tailenders offered some resistance, but it was too little too late. Kaif took his fourth catch of the match, a world cup fielding record as Sri Lanka were eventually bowled out for 109 giving India a massive victory by 183 runs. It was India's biggest victory margin in World Cups till then. Srinath earned the Man of the match award for his match winning spell of 4/35, his best in World Cups. He proved that Ganguly was right to persuade him to come out of retirement for this tournament.

This win left India level with Australia on 16 points, guaranteeing them a place in the semi-finals regardless of the result in their final Super Six match against New Zealand. It also reinforced the growing belief among experts and fans alike, that this Indian team was the only side in the competition which looked capable of challenging the all-conquering Aussies.

India faced New Zealand in their final Super Six match at Centurion, but the tables had turned since their last face-off. A month earlier, India had to endure soul crushing ignominy in New Zealand, but now they were on a roll, winning six matches in a row. New Zealand, on the other hand, were on the verge of elimination, having lost two of their three Super Six games.

Zaheer Khan gave India a dream start after Sourav Ganguly opted to field first. The left-arm pacer struck on the second and third ball of the match, removing Craig McMillan and Nathan Astle for ducks and reducing New Zealand to 0-2 in 0.3 overs. The Kiwis never really recovered from that twin blow and were bundled out for a paltry 146 in 45.1 overs. Only skipper Fleming showed some resistance with a gritty 30, but he found no real support from the other end. Sourav Ganguly's bowling changes worked like a charm and the Indian bowlers were relentless and accurate, with Harbhajan Singh and Ashish Nehra too chipping in with a couple of wickets each.

Shane Bond and Tuffey tried to bowl their side back into the game by reducing India to 21/3 inside the first 5 overs with Sehwag, Ganguly and Tendulkar all back in the pavilion. But team India's tried and tested crisis manager Rahul Dravid once again came to the rescue, stitching together a vital partnership of 129 runs in 35 overs with Mohammad Kaif who played himself back among runs with a solid unbeaten 68 with 8 fours. Dravid remained unconquered on 53 with 7 boundaries, his 44th half century in this format, underscoring his importance to this Indian side. India's seventh consecutive win was achieved with 7 wickets and 56 balls to spare. Zaheer Khan pocketed the Man of the match but the most heartening sight from the team's point of view was the timely return to form of Mohammad Kaif, the only player from the eleven who had been misfiring in his primary role.

Six days later, India met Kenya in the second semi-final of the world cup at Durban. Australia had already made it to the final beating Sri Lanka by 48 runs in the first semi-final.

India chose to bat first after Sourav Ganguly called correctly at the toss. Sehwag and Tendulkar started cautiously, putting on 74 for the first wicket before Sehwag fell for 33, caught by Odumbe off Ongondo in the 19th over. Tendulkar then teamed up with his former opening partner Ganguly and they added another 103 runs in the next 20 overs. Tendulkar was looking good for a hundred, but perished for 83, caught by Obuya in the deep. Ganguly, however, shifted gears and took on the spinners with disdain. He smashed four sixes off them and reached his hundred - his 22nd in ODIs and third in this tournament, taking him level with Mark Waugh's record of three hundreds in a single edition of a world cup (1996) - with a huge six off Martin Suji. He remained unbeaten on 111 off 114 balls with five fours and five sixes. It was a splendid knock from the skipper that took his team to 270 for 4 in 50 overs.

Kenya's chase never got going as they lost wickets at regular intervals. It was Zaheer Khan once again who gave India a perfect start by trapping Ravindu Shah lbw for 1 in the third over. He then returned to dismiss Hitesh Modi and Obuya to finish with 3 for 14 in 9.2 overs. Ashish Nehra also bowled with pace and accuracy, removing Peter Ongondo and Thomas Odoyo in quick succession. He ended with 2 for 33 in 10 overs. Srinath and Harbhajan were economical and picked up a wicket each. The only bright spot for Kenya was the knock of captain Steve Tikolo who fought valiantly with a 83-ball 56. He hit 5 fours and 2 sixes and shared a 57-run stand with Collins Obuya for the eighth wicket. However, it was too little too late as Kenya were bowled out for 179 in 46.2 overs, handing India a comprehensive 91-run victory, setting up a dream final with defending champions Australia. Sourav Ganguly was declared the Man of the match for his captain's knock of 111.

Now it was time for the Grand Finale.

The One That Got Away

The stage was set for the ultimate showdown in cricket as the two most dominant teams in the tournament were ready to lock horns in the final of the ODI world cup at Johannesberg on 23rd of March 2003. India came into the final on a seven-match winning spree, their sole defeat in the tournament coming against Australia only in the first round. Australia stormed into the final on the back of a 16-match winning streak that spanned before and during the world cup. It was an Indian team led by Sourav Ganguly that had halted a similar Aussie Juggernaut of 16 consecutive test wins a couple of years back in 2001. This gave hope to the billions of cricket fans back home in India that their team could repeat the feat at the grandest stage of them all, the World Cup final.

The final promised to be a thrilling contest between two evenly matched sides, having some of the best players in the world. Indian team boasted of a formidable batting line-up, led by the master blaster Sachin Tendulkar, who was the leading run-scorer in the tournament with 669 runs at an average of 66.90. He was supported by the likes of Sourav Ganguly, Rahul Dravid, Virender Sehwag and Yuvraj Singh, all of whom had been amongst runs in the tournament. India also had a balanced bowling attack, with Javagal Srinath, Zaheer Khan, Ashish Nehra and Harbhajan Singh sharing the wickets.

Australia, on the other hand, had McGrath, Brett Lee, Jason Gillespie and Andy Bichel forming a fearsome quartet of fast bowlers. McGrath was the leading wicket-taker in the tournament with 21 scalps at an astonishing average of 14.76, followed by Bichel, who had taken 16 wickets at an even more mind-boggling average of 9.31. Australia also had a strong batting line-up, with Ricky Ponting, Adam Gilchrist, Matthew Hayden and Damien Martyn all scoring heavily; Ponting being the second-highest run-scorer in the tournament with 415 runs at an average of 83.

The final promised to be a test of nerves and skills for both teams, who had a growing rivalry that had the potential to surpass Australia-England and India-Pakistan as the biggest in cricket in the coming years. India was hoping to lift their second World Cup trophy after 1983 ie 20 years while Australia was aiming to retain their title and become the first team to win three World Cups.

So, it was on Sunday, March 23rd in front of a capacity crowd of almost 33000 at New Wanderers stadium, Johannesberg, Indian captain Sourav Ganguly won the toss and chose to bowl first, hoping to exploit the slightly damp conditions after some early morning showers. However, his decision sparked a lot of controversy and debate among the fans and experts as the game unfolded.

Australia got off to a flying start as Adam Gilchrist and Matthew Hayden attacked the Indian bowlers with a gusto. They added 105 runs for the first wicket in just 14 overs, with Gilly smashing 57 off 48 balls with 8 fours and a six. He was dismissed by Harbhajan, who caught and bowled him after he tried to slog-sweep him over the leg side.

Hayden followed soon after, scoring 37 off 54 balls with five fours. He was also caught behind by Rahul Dravid off Harbhajan, who got the ball to turn sharply across him. Australia were 125/2 in the 20th over and India seemed to have pulled things back.

However, that was when the Australian captain Ricky Thomas Ponting took charge of the innings. He was joined by Damien Martyn, who was playing despite a broken finger. The duo put on a batting masterclass, as they tore apart the Indian bowling with clinical precision. They mixed aggression with caution, finding gaps with ease and clearing the boundaries at will.

Ponting was particularly brutal, as he thumped 11 fours and 8 sixes in his unbeaten knock of 140 off 121 balls. He reached his century off just 74 balls, the fastest in a world cup final. He spared no bowler, but was especially brutal on the in-form Srinath and Zaheer Khan, who leaked runs at over 9 runs per over.

Martyn too was at his elegant best, as he scored an unbeaten 88 off 84 balls with 7 fours and a six. He played some delectable strokes on both sides of the wicket and supported Ponting well. The pair added an unbroken 234 runs for the third wicket, a record for any wicket in a world cup final.

Australia finished their innings at a mammoth 359/2 in 50 overs, setting India a daunting target of 360 to win. It was the highest total ever scored in a world cup final and the second-highest in any world cup match. Ponting walked off to a standing ovation from the crowd and their teammates, having played perhaps, the finest innings in world cup history. One couldn't help but feel sorry for the Indian bowlers, especially the old warhorse Srinath who had been absolutely phenomenal throughout the tournament only to falter at the final hurdle in what was, in all probability, his last match.

India had a mountain to climb as they hoped to hunt down that target of 359 to win the final. However, their hopes were dashed in the very first over of their innings, as Glenn McGrath got the better of his old rival Sachin Tendulkar, the leading run-scorer and Player of the tournament, for just 4. Tendulkar tried to pull a short ball from McGrath, but only managed to sky it to mid-wicket, where McGrath took a simple catch. It was a crushing blow for India and their fans, who had expected Tendulkar to lead the chase.

Virender Sehwag and Sourav Ganguly, the Indian captain, tried to rebuild the innings with some aggressive strokes. They added 54 runs for the second wicket in just 9 overs, with Sehwag hitting some crisp boundaries and a six. However, Ganguly fell for 24 off 25 balls, as he holed out to Darren Lehmann at mid-off off Brett Lee.

Mohammad Kaif followed soon after, edging McGrath to Gilchrist for a duck. India were reduced to 59/3 in the 11th over and in deep trouble. Rahul Dravid who, like Martyn, was playing with an injured finger and Sehwag then put on a brave fightback, as they added 88 runs for the fourth wicket in 13 overs. Sehwag was particularly aggressive, as he reached his half-century off just 38 balls. He hit 10 fours and 3 sixes in his defiant knock of 82 off 81 balls.

However, his innings came to an end in the 24th over, as he was run out by Lehmann after a mix-up with Dravid. It was a crucial breakthrough for Australia, as Sehwag was the only batsman who looked capable of taking on their bowling attack. His dismissal triggered a collapse, as India lost their last seven wickets for just 77 runs.

Dravid tried to soldier on, as he scored a gritty 47 off 57 balls with 2 fours. However, he did not get much support from the other batsmen, as Yuvraj Singh (24), Dinesh Mongia (12), Harbhajan Singh (7), Zaheer Khan (4) and Javagal Srinath (1) all fell cheaply. Dravid was eventually dismissed by Andy Bichel, as he tried to clear long-on.

India were bowled out for 234 in 39.2 overs, losing the final by a massive margin of 125 runs. Ricky Ponting was named the Man of the final for his epic hundred.

It was an anti-climactic end to a brilliant world cup campaign for Sourav Ganguly's men. They had come so close to achieving their dream of winning the world cup for the second time in their history, only to be outclassed by a superior Australian team. They had to settle for the runners-up trophy, while Australia celebrated their third world cup title and their second consecutive one.

The only solace was Sachin Tendulkar winning the Player of the Tournament award, but he said he would happily trade it for another crack at the Aussies.

The loss in the final was a crushing blow and a collective heartbreak for the billion plus Indians. Some fans cursed Sourav Ganguly's decision to bowl first for the disaster, but it was a small minority. Most fans were appreciative of the '*jazbaa*' shown by the team in making it to the final after a poor start and had high hopes for the team's future.

13

Moving On

The team took a brief two-weeks break before flying to Dhaka for the final assignment of their season, the TVS cup, a one-day tri-series featuring hosts Bangladesh, India and South Africa. Some of the senior players like Tendulkar, Dravid, Kumble and Srinath decided to skip the tournament and rest their weary bodies. This opened up the doors for some fresh faces in the squad, the most notable among them being Gautam Gambhir, a young and explosive left-handed opener from Delhi who had been scoring heavily in the domestic circuit for quite a while.

India took out the frustrations of losing the world cup final upon Bangladesh thrashing the hosts by a whopping margin of 200 runs in the opening match of the TVS Cup 2003 at Dhaka.

Batting first after winning the toss, India's innings was built around two blistering knocks - a typically stroke-filled 63 off 51 balls with 11 fours and a six at the top of the order by the stand-in vice-captain Virender Sehwag followed by a brilliant unbeaten century by Yuvraj Singh, who scored 102 off just 85 balls with 9 fours and 4 towering sixes. He came to the crease when India were in a spot of bother at 144 for 4 and added 120 runs with Agarkar for the seventh wicket, 92 of those coming in the last 10 overs. For Bangladesh, Tapash Baisya took 3 wickets while Alok Kapali and Sanwar Hossain took two each.

Bangladesh's chase never got going as they lost wickets at regular intervals. They were reduced to 3 for 11 inside the first 5 overs and never recovered, getting bundled out for a paltry 76, their lowest ever total. Only Mohammad Rafique showed some resistance with an unbeaten 18 off 21 balls. For India, Zaheer Khan was the pick of the bowlers with 4 wickets while young fast bowler Avishkar Salvi had an impressive debut claiming 2 as did a returning Agarkar. Harbhajan Singh also chipped in with a wicket.

It was India's biggest win in terms of margin of runs. The dashing Yuvraj earned the Man of the match for his maiden hundred.

The team continued in the same dominant vein two days later in the day-night game against a new look South African side. Batting first after winning the toss, India posted a handsome 307/4 in their 50 overs on the back of a couple of big partnerships - a 86 run stand for the third wicket between captain Ganguly (75) and Kaif, followed by a whirlwind unbroken stand of 103 for the fifth wicket between Kaif and Dinesh Mongia (55 not out) in the final ten overs. Kaif top scored with an enterprising 95 not out off just 103 balls with 7 fours and 3 sixes but was unlucky to miss out on a well-deserved hundred. Rookie Alan Dawson with 2 wickets was the pick of the South African bowlers. 21 years old Graeme Smith, standing in his first game as captain, came in for some deserved criticism for his puzzling decision to relegate his predecessor, the formidable Shaun Pollock to the role of a third change bowler instead of giving him the new ball.

The inexperience in South Africa's batting stood exposed in the absence of mainstays Kallis, Klusener and the just-retired Jonty Rhodes and Gary Kirsten, and they never looked comfortable in their chase after being reduced to 13/2 inside the first 6 overs by a fired-up Agarkar. Only Jacques Rudolph (49) and Mark Boucher (36) showed some fight, but they could not avoid a crushing defeat. South Africa were all out for 154 in the 35th over, giving India their second straight win by a margin of over 150 runs. Part-timers Sehwag and Ganguly shared 5 wickets between them while Agarkar and Harbhajan took a couple each. Amit Mishra, the debutant leggie, also claimed his maiden wicket.

More seniors including the captain sat out the next game against Bangladesh giving Sehwag his first chance to lead the side. Batting first after winning the toss, the hosts could only manage a mere 207 with only Habibul Bashar showing some fight with a gritty 50. Agarkar continued his red-hot form with the new ball with another 3-wicket haul while Sarandeep Singh picked 2. In reply, India cruised home in the 43rd over with the new opener Gautam Gambhir picking up his first Man of the match award in his third outing in Indian colours, for his well-paced knock of 71 with the help of 9 fours.

Sourav Ganguly returned but coach John Wright's ploy to use the last league match against the Proteas as one more opportunity of testing the bench strength turned the otherwise inconsequential game into a keen contest. Choosing to bat first, India lost their first wicket, that of Gambhir at the score of 7. Then, at 32, Sehwag got hit on the forearm by a snorter from Ntini and had to retire hurt. Captain Ganguly tried to rebuild the inning in the company of Mohammad Kaif but his departure at the score of 124 triggered a collapse, as India lost its last 7 wickets for a mere 91 runs to get bundled out for 215 in 49.1 overs. It was an inspired performance by the Proteas bowlers led by the fiery Ntini who picked 3 and the in-form Alan Dawson who claimed 4 with his prodigious swing.

In reply, Avishkar Salvi removed Graeme Smith and Harbhajan struck twice in two balls to reduce South Africa to 42/3 but a steadying stand of 63 runs for the fourth wicket between Rudolph and the in-form Neil Mckenzie followed by another vital partnership of 107 runs for the fifth wicket between McKenzie and the tenacious Boucher (44 not out) proved to be decisive as the Proteas reached home with 8 balls to spare. Harbhajan's 3-fer went in vain as Neil Mckenzie was named the Man of the match for his composed knock of 80.

It was a morale boosting win ahead of the final for the young South African side trying to come to grips with the simultaneous retirement of their stalwarts Alan Donald, Jonty Rhodes and Gary Kirsten following the world cup semi-final heartbreak.

The final got washed out without a single ball bowled. It was the second time in three tournament finals that the Indian team watched from the pavilion as the rain pummelled down and washed out the entire game. The rain decided to play spoilsport again on the reserve day and the match had to be abandoned altogether after only 17.1 overs of play at Dhaka. India had won the toss and elected to bat first, but they were reduced to 46/3 when the rain interrupted the match. Though the rain stopped towards the evening, the outfield was still wet, prompting the match referee Sir Clive Lloyd to decree that the safety of the players would be compromised if play was resumed. India and South Africa were declared joint winners of the TVS Cup. Alan Dawson of South Africa was named the player of the series for taking 11 wickets in 4 matches.

In a way it was a fitting end to a tournament that was a dull affair after the highs of the world cup.

This marked the end of a roller coaster of a season for Indian cricket. The next season would not begin until October, giving the Indian cricketers a much-deserved break. They had been on the road pretty much non-stop in the past three years so such a lengthy lay off of almost 4 months came as a welcome relief.

Sachin Tendulkar and Ashish Nehra utilized the time-off to have surgeries and rehab while workhorses Dravid, Ganguly, Srinath and Kumble rested and healed. Yuvraj flew to England to play county cricket for Yorkshire while other big names like VVS Laxman stayed in form by playing in domestic tournaments like the Irani trophy and India A matches, along with other aspirants like Gautam Gambhir etc.

In August, coach John Wright conducted two preparatory camps that lasted for a month. The first camp opened with 36 probables who were narrowed down to 25 for the second camp. The squad for the upcoming 2 test series at home against New Zealand was selected by the Syed Kirmani led senior national selection committee based on the two camps and the domestic season performances. Yuvraj and Aakash Chopra were somewhat of a surprise inclusions in the test squad. Yuvraj had an indifferent season at Yorkshire and Chopra faced stiff competition from the likes of Sadagopan Ramesh and Deepdas Gupta. Agarkar missed out perhaps a bit unfairly. But the real shocker was the omission of Sanjay Bangar who had done little wrong in the few chances that came his way.

The first test at Ahmedabad turned out to be a high-scoring draw. India batted first and piled up 500/5 declared, on the back of Rahul Dravid's masterful 222 which contained 28 boundaries and 2 sixes, well supported by a solid 64 from VVS and an unbeaten even 100 by the Indian captain Sourav Ganguly.

New Zealand were staring at follow on after being reduced to 41/3 at the close on day2 thanks to a lively spell from Zaheer Khan, but fought back gallantly the next day with Nathan Astle's defiant 103 aided by a gritty 54 from Craig Mcmillan and a handy 60 from a bespectacled Daniel Vettori coming in at number 9, still conceding a 160-run lead.

Paul Wiseman claimed 4 wickets as India declared again at 209/6 setting New Zealand a daunting target of 370. Laxman scored a breezy 44 off just 35 balls that even contained a rare six and Dravid scored another 73 becoming the second Indian after the legendary Sunil Gavaskar to score a double hundred and a fifty in the same test.

The Kiwis faced an uphill battle having to deal with two of the world's best spinners on a fifth day track in India but showed great character and resilience to save the match, reaching 272/6 on the final day. Lou Vincent scored a patient 67 and Craig Mcmillan and an ailing Astle remained unbeaten on 83 and 51 respectively. Anil Kumble added 4 more to the 2 he took in the first inning taking his match tally to 6 wickets. Rahul Dravid was named the player of the match for his splendid batting display.

Of the two debutants, Aakash Chopra did well while the Tamilnadu seamer Lakshmipathy Balaji failed to impress.

India faced a major setback before the second and final test of the series as their captain Sourav Ganguly was ruled out due to a serious infection in his right thigh. Ganguly had developed an abscess that needed two surgeries to heal, leaving him unfit to play. In his absence, Rahul Dravid took charge of the team for the first time in his career in tests. Ganguly's misfortune also opened the door for a precocious young talent to make his mark in test cricket. Yuvraj Singh, who had already impressed in the shorter format, got his maiden test cap and a chance to prove himself in the longer version of the game.

Team India paid a heavy price for going in with only two seamers on the traditionally seamer-friendly Mohali pitch, as the Kiwis piled up a mammoth 630/6 virtually batting India out of the match. Four of their batsmen - the in-form Lou Vincent, his opening partner Mark Richardson, Scott Styris who was promoted to one down and the enigmatic Craig Mcmillan coming in at number 6, all scored superb centuries and Daniel Vettori added to Indian bowlers' misery with another handy knock of 48 not out before his captain declared. The two Indian seamers, Zaheer Khan and Balaji, were ineffective and failed to take a single wicket. Only Anil Kumble showed some determination and claimed 3 of the 6 wickets to fall with his tireless bowling.

Faced with the daunting task of chasing 630, Sehwag and Aakash Chopra, in their second test together as openers, gave India the perfect opening with a 164 run opening stand with Chopra contributing a solid 60 while Sehwag went on to score a fabulous 130 with 14 fours and 2 sixes. After his departure at 218, senior pros Tendulkar and Laxman added 112 for the fourth wicket before Vettori snared Tendulkar for 55. Laxman carried on gamely, batting with great skill and patience to score his fifth test century. He remained unbeaten on 104, but did not get much support from the lower order as India were bowled out for 424. Daryl Tuffey was the star bowler for New Zealand, taking four wickets for 80 runs.

Following on, another excellent spell by Daryl Tuffey had India in a big trouble at 18/3 before lunch on the final day but Aakash Chopra and VVS Laxman put their heads down and batted sensibly for almost four hours to save the day for India. Chopra scored his second fifty of the match, a gritty 52 off 160 balls while Laxman returned unconquered on 67 which consumed 183 balls.

Daryl Tuffey won the player of the match for his match haul of 7 wickets while 'Very Very Special' Laxman earned the player of the series for scoring 279 runs in 2 tests at an astonishing average of 139.5.

The series may have ended in a draw but it was an undeniable moral victory for the Kiwis, made all the more special by the fact that it was achieved without the services of two of their most charismatic cricketers, Chris Cairns who chose to skip the test series to be present for the birth of his child, and Shane Bond who failed to recover from an ankle injury.

After the test series, India hosted a one-day tri-series with world champions Australia as the third side beside New Zealand. Laxman was rewarded for his superb performance in the test series with a spot in the one-day side replacing the under-performing Dinesh Mongia. Hemang Badani also made a comeback, along with one-day specialists Kaif and Agarkar. Murali Kartik and Avishkar Salvi were the new faces in the 15-man squad, with Salvi filling in for Ashish Nehra who was still some way away from being match fit.

The second TVS Cup tri-series of the year began on a disappointing note as rain played spoilsport in the opening match between India and New

Zealand at Chennai. India were 141 for 3 in 26.5 overs when the match had to be abandoned due to the late monsoon. Tendulkar was batting on 48, just 2 short of another half century. One positive takeaway for the Kiwis from this game was the comeback of Cairns, who removed an ominous looking Sehwag for 31 before he could really cut loose. Cairns' heroic comeback proved to be short-lived, however, as he appeared to have injured his hamstring after sending down only three overs.

The tri-series really got going with the second match at Gwalior, which was a day-night encounter between India and Australia. It was the first time the two fierce rivals met since that fateful final of the world cup six months ago, where India suffered a crushing defeat that still haunted them and their fans. India were eager to settle the score and redeem themselves for that painful loss.

India chose to bat first on a good batting strip at Captain Roop Singh stadium, but suffered an early setback as Sehwag was dismissed for a duck in the first over. However, Tendulkar and Laxman repaired the inning with a very, very special 190-run stand for the second wicket. They batted with flair and finesse, setting it up nicely for the rest of the batters to go hell for leather in the final ten. Sachin registered his 35th ODI hundred and his 7th against Australia in 36 matches. He scored an even hundred off 119 balls with 9 fours and a six. Laxman also celebrated his ODI comeback with his second hundred in this format, against his favourite opposition, the kangaroos. He scored 103 off 134 balls with 9 fours. After his stellar show in the tests, this was a triumphant return for a cricketer who had almost quit the game, feeling heartbroken by his world cup snub.

89 came off in the last ten overs, thanks to some explosive hitting from Yuvraj and Agarkar. Yuvraj smashed 44 off 33 balls, while Agarkar blasted 22 off 10 balls justifying stand-in captain Dravid's move of promoting them ahead of himself and Kaif. India ended up with a formidable total of 283 for 5 in 50 overs.

It looked like the replay of the world cup final all over again as Gilly and Haydos started off in their by-now customary fashion. If anything, they were even more ruthless this time, smashing 132 runs in the first 25 overs. But then, Zaheer Khan struck a vital blow by clean bowling Gilchrist for 83 off 79 balls. Kumble followed up with 2 quick wickets and suddenly

Australia were in trouble at 140 for 3 in the 28th over. Zaheer made it 141/4 in the very next over by trapping Symonds lbw with a late inswinger for just 1. Martyn and Bevan tried to steady the ship with a budding partnership of 35 runs, but Sehwag turned the game on its head by dismissing them both in the same over, giving further proof of his golden arm while also making up for his failure with the bat earlier. Australia had lost half their side for 176 and there was no coming back from there. The lower order tried hard but could not chase down the target of 296 falling short by 37 runs in the end.

India had avenged their humiliating loss in the final, though to be fair to the world champions, they had to field a second-string bowling attack in the absence of their three best bowlers, Lee, Mcgrath and Warne. Sachin Tendulkar walked away with the player of the match for his magnificent hundred and a wicket.

Australia bounced back from their sobering defeat by bowling out New Zealand for 97 and then getting there with 8 wickets and 200 balls to spare in their next match. They were now primed to take India on again in the day-night game at Wankhede Stadium next.

Ricky Ponting won the toss and chose to bat first. India got an early breakthrough when Zaheer Khan bowled Haydos for a duck. But Gilly didn't let that stop him from getting his team off to a flyer, smashing 8 fours in his 30 balls 41, before being dismissed by Harbhajan in the 6th over. Agarkar came on as the fifth change in the 14th over and immediately got rid of the Aussie skipper for 31, trapping him lbw with a full delivery. Damien Martyn and Andrew Symonds then steadied the innings with a 78-run stand for the fourth wicket. Symonds was caught by Bhajji off Yuvraj for 48, just two runs short of his half-century. Martyn then took over and put on a masterclass on pacing the innings, enroute a sublime even hundred. He creamed 9 fours and a six and justified his tag of 'the most aesthetically pleasing batsman in the world at the moment'. He got good support from the brilliant Michael Bevan, who scored 42 runs without much fuss. Australia finished with 286 for 8 in their 50 overs. Agarkar was the best bowler for India with 4 wickets for 37 runs in 9 overs.

In reply, Nathan Bracken removed Sehwag for a duck in the first over for the second game in a row. Laxman too failed to convert a start into something substantial so it once again fell down to the old firm of Tendulkar and Dravid to get the chase back on track. The two did manage to do that with a 99-run stand for the third wicket but Punter had a surprise weapon in store for Indians. Part-time offie Michael Clarke turned out to be the surprise package as he broke India's back with key wickets of the well-set Tendulkar (68), Dravid (59) and Yuvraj (9). Bracken returned to polish off the tail and India were skittled out for 209, losing to Australia by 77 runs. Damien Martyn walked away with the player of the match for his splendid hundred.

India next faced New Zealand in game 6 of the TVS Cup which was once again a day-night affair at Cuttack. Ganguly was still recovering from his surgeries, so Dravid continued to lead the side. He won the toss and decided to bat first. VVS Laxman had to return to opening duties with Sachin, as Sehwag was also out injured.

India suffered an early setback when Tendulkar was dismissed for 14 by Kyle Mills in the sixth over. Kaif was promoted to number three but it was slow going as he and Laxman could manage only 50 runs in the next 12 overs. Laxman was caught and bowled by Styris for 31.

Dravid joined Kaif and the two stitched together another 50 runs, but then disaster struck. Dravid and Yuvraj Singh were both out in the same over, bowled by Vettori. India were reduced to 136 for 4 in the 32nd over.

Hemang Badani, who was making a comeback to the team, played a useful knock of 41 off 45 balls. But the real impetus was provided by a delightful cameo by Zaheer Khan, who smote 3 fours and 2 sixes in his 13 ball 33, 20 of which came off the 50th over bowled by Jacob Oram as India finished on 246/9.

In reply, India had New Zealand on the mat at 68/4 by the 15th over but a decisive 127 run stand for the 5th wicket between the in-form Craig Mcmillan and Scott Styris took the game away from India. Styris made a fine 68 while Mcmillan finished the job with an unbeaten 82 as the Kiwis opened their account in the triangular with their first win. Scott Styris won the player of the match for his splendid all-round show.

These back-to-back defeats had made a huge dent in India's chances to qualify for the finals but their hopes were boosted by the return of their regular captain Sourav Ganguly for their third and final round-robin encounter against Australia at Bangalore.

Australia batted first on a flat pitch at the Chinnaswami stadium and repeated their world cup final heroics. Gilchrist and Hayden tore into the Indian bowling with a blistering opening stand of 119 in 16 overs, with Gilly smashing 111 off 114 balls. Ponting and Martyn then took over and added an unbeaten 149 in the last 16 overs to take Australia to a mammoth 347/2. Ponting was in a murderous mood, hitting 7 sixes in his unbeaten 108 off 103 balls, while Martyn played a classy knock of 61 not out off 49 balls. The Indian bowlers were helpless, except for Kartik who bowled well until Ponting ruined his figures in his final over.

Faced with the daunting task of chasing 347, Indian openers Sehwag and Tendulkar came out firing, with Sachin playing the aggressor for a change. They put on 103 for the first wicket before Sehwag was bowled by Harvey's clever military medium pace. Clarke then showed that his spell at Wankhede was no fluke with the important wicket of Laxman. But the biggest blow for India was Tendulkar's dismissal for 89 in the 29th over, which dashed their hopes of pulling off a miracle. Ganguly, Dravid and the rest fought bravely but fell short by 61 runs in the end.

In a high-scoring game, the unsung Michael Kasprovicz stood out with a spell of 10 overs for 37 runs and Dravid's wicket. Player of the match however was rightly awarded to Adam Gilchrist.

India and New Zealand played for a spot in the final at Hyderabad in the last match of the round-robin stage. Ganguly won the toss and chose to bat first. Sehwag and Tendulkar gave India a flying start with a 182-run stand in 30 overs, their second hundred plus partnership in a row, before Tendulkar departed after posting his 36th ODI hundred, a superb 103 off 91 balls with 12 fours and a six. Sehwag continued his onslaught and signalled his return to form with a splendid 130 off 134 balls with 15 fours and 2 sixes. But the real fireworks came from Dravid, who seemed a bit pissed off for some reason, perhaps because he was again saddled with the added responsibility of keeping wickets in the name of team balance. Or, it might have something to do with his batting position. Whatever be the case, he took out his wrath on the Kiwi bowlers and smashed a 22-ball 50 - which, to this day, remains the joint-second fastest fifty by an Indian and the fastest by an Indian keeper. Dravid's carnage, which included 5 fours and 3 massive sixes, lifted India to a massive 353/5 in 50 overs.

The Indian captain's fitness issues continued as he had to opt for a runner during his knock of 33 after pulling a groin muscle while taking a run. He also did not come out to field so Dravid had to take over on his behalf.

In the absence of their two best batsmen, Fleming and Astle, who were both out injured, New Zealand had no chance of chasing down such a huge target and they folded for 208 in the 47th over, losing by a massive 145 runs. Zaheer was the star of the Indian bowling with 3 wickets, while Agarkar, Kumble and the increasingly impressive Murali Kartik, all took a couple of wickets each. Sehwag won the player of the match for his match-winning hundred - the 6th of his ODI career as India marched into the final in style.

Thus, it was India vs Australia again in a final, this time for the TVS cup, at the iconic Eden Gardens at Kolkata; the same venue where it all started for this Indian team against this very opposition two and a half years back. But the Prince of Kolkata had failed to recover in time so his deputy Rahul Dravid had to stand-in for him once again. Australia chose to bat first, hoping to set a huge target on the board like they did in the world cup final. But India had other plans this time. They managed to get rid of their tormentors Hayden and Gilchrist for just 32 runs inside the first 8 overs for a change. Ponting and Martyn tried to rebuild the innings with an 80-run stand, but Kartik outsmarted the Aussie captain and got him caught in the slips. Harbhajan soon joined the party and removed Symonds cheaply. Australia were in trouble at 129/4 in the 28th over. Martyn and Bevan had to play cautiously as the Indian spinners bowled with accuracy and guile on a turning track. They could only score 41 runs in the next 13 overs. The golden arm of Sehwag came into play again as he broke the partnership by dismissing Martyn for 61. Young Michael Clarke, aptly nicknamed 'Pup', came to the crease and injected some much-needed life into the Australian innings. He danced down the track to hit the spinners and ran hard with the never-say-die Bevan. They added an unbroken 65 runs in the remaining 9 overs to take their side to a respectable 235/5 by the end. Dravid read the wicket well and used his bowlers brilliantly. He tried seven bowlers and all except Salvi and part-timer Badani chipped in with a wicket each. The four

Indian spinners, including the two part-timers Sehwag and Badani were all economical, conceding only 122 runs in their 33 overs.

India had a golden chance to upset the world champions and clinch the TVS cup. All they had to do was chase down a very gettable target of 235. But they stumbled at the first hurdle. Sehwag's problems against the bowler of the tournament Nathan Bracken continued and he was caught and bowled by the lanky left-arm seamer for a paltry 5. Laxman showed some flair, but he was undone by Brad Williams for 22. Tendulkar and Dravid joined forces and launched a counterattack. Tendulkar was unusually slow to start, but then he opened up with some glorious shots. He looked set for a big score, but Andy Bichel had other ideas. He produced a peach of a delivery that cut back and shattered Tendulkar's stumps. He walked back for 45, leaving India in a spot of bother. Yuvraj soon followed him, and India were reeling at 110/4 in 25 overs. Dravid and Badani tried to revive the innings with a sensible partnership. They added 49 runs and kept India in the hunt. But then the golden boy Clarke struck a double blow. He removed both Dravid and Badani in quick succession, leaving India gasping for breath. Ian Harvey then delivered the knockout punch. He ripped through the lower order with 4 wickets in 2 overs. Agarkar fought valiantly, but he ran out of partners. India were bundled out for 198 in 41.5 overs. Australia won by 37 runs and showed why they were the world champions, snatching victory from the jaws of defeat, even with a second-string bowling attack. With this emphatic win, Aussie captain Ricky Ponting proved once and for all that he was more than just a lucky inheritor of a team loaded with matchwinners from top to bottom.

Michael Clarke was named the player of the match for his all-round brilliance. This was neither the first nor the last time that the lively 'Pup' had clinched a memorable win against India in India with his bowling. He had an even bigger surprises in store for an already startled India in about a year's time from now.

The tournament that just ended also marked the end of a glorious career in Indian cricket. The great Javagal Srinath had been hinting at retirement for a while and he finally confirmed it on the eve of the India-Australia match in Bangalore during the tournament. The hardships and rigours of bowling on lifeless Indian pitches for more than 12 years finally caught up with the self-effacing speedster from Karnataka and he had to bow out with a heavy heart and a battered body, but with immense pride and respect. With over 551 international wickets to his name - 236 in 67 tests and 315 in 229 ODIs - 'The Mysore Express' was a rare breed of Indian fast bowlers who could bowl consistently above 140 kmph and swing the ball both ways. He was also a handy lower-order batsman who scored four fifties in Tests and one in ODIs. But above all, he was one of the unsung heroes of Indian cricket, a tireless performer who gave it his all on the field and was an excellent role model-cum-mentor for the young fast bowlers emerging in India, off it.

14

Onwards & Upwards

Five days later, a 16-member Indian squad flew to Australia for an 82 days long tour down under.

Yuvraj Singh and Hemang Badani missed out while S Ramesh and Deepdas Gupta were back as reserve opener and keeper respectively. The biggest debate was about who should be the second spinner with Harbhajan. Anil Kumble had not been at his best since his return from injury and the selectors seemed to have made up their minds to put him out to pasture and pick a left-arm spinner, the very promising Murali Kartik instead. Their rationale was that Aussies are historically known to struggle against left-arm spin. While the Indian captain himself saw great promise in Kartik, for this important tour he insisted on having the experienced Kumble by his side. He refused to sign the final team sheet until Kumble's name was there. The selectors had to back down and let 'Dada' have his way, but they warned him that he would be held responsible if the move failed. Ganguly accepted the terms.

The most exciting selection, however, was that of a young left-arm fast bowler hailing from Baroda, Irfan Pathan. It was a sweet and just reward for the promising 19 years old, who had been performing consistently at the junior level and played a stellar role in India's title triumph in the under-19 Asia Cup in Pakistan a couple of weeks ago. The left-arm quick's sterling performance in Pakistan capped by a record 9-wicket haul against Bangladesh and crucial 3 wickets in the final had made him a hot contender for the fifth bowler's spot besides Zak, Agarkar, Nehra and Lakshmipathy Balaji. Kirmani led selection panel decided to strike while the iron was hot and picked him in hope of capitalizing on the red-hot form of the youngster.

First item on the tour itinerary was the 4-test Border Gavaskar trophy, aptly named after the top two run-scorers in test cricket. Indian team warmed up for the first of the 4 tests by playing out two hard-fought draws against Victoria and Queensland Academy of sports XI.

The series got underway with the first test at the Gabba in Brisbane, where Australia had a formidable record of dominance. Sourav Ganguly made a bold decision to bowl first on a green top under cloudy skies, but his pacers failed to exploit the conditions and Australia dominated the first day, scoring 262/2 at a brisk rate. Justin Langer led the way with a gritty hundred. The next morning, however, Zaheer Khan turned things around with a superb spell of swing bowling, taking five wickets and Agarkar also chipped in with three to dismiss Australia for 323.

Rain interrupted play for most of the second and third days, but India fought back with the bat in the most unexpected fashion. They were in trouble at 62/3 after losing their openers cheaply on the fourth morning, but the captain Sourav Ganguly came to the rescue with a glorious century that silenced his critics. He played with aggression and flair, hitting 18 boundaries in his 144 off 196 balls. It was an inning which can easily qualify as his finest hour under the sun. He was well supported by Laxman and Parthiv and India took a lead of 86 runs after scoring 409. Australia came back strongly in their second innings, with Hayden smashing 99 off 98 balls. Steve Waugh tried his best to keep it interesting by declaring at 284/3, setting India a tantalizing target of 199 in 23 overs. It was a gamble that almost paid off, as Bracken removed both openers early giving further evidence that he indeed had Sehwag's number. But Dravid and Laxman held firm with an unbeaten partnership of 67 runs and ensured a draw for India. Ganguly was named the player of the match for his inspirational knock and captaincy.

The match may have ended in a draw but it was a remarkable start for India, who were notoriously slow starters on overseas tours. The credit for that solely belonged to the captain who had led from the front in the most awe inspiring of manners setting the tone for the rest of the series.

The caravan moved to Adelaide - the home of the mythical Sir Donald Bradman. India made two changes, bringing in Anil Kumble and Irfan Pathan for Harbhajan Singh, who had a poor first test, and Zaheer Khan, who was injured. The changes paid off, as Kumble removed the previous match's centurion Langer, and Pathan claimed Hayden as his maiden test wicket. Nehra then dismissed Martyn and Waugh in quick succession, and

Australia were reduced to 242/4. But then India's hopes of bowling them out cheaply were dashed, as Ponting played a masterful innings of 242. He was well supported by Simon Katich and Gillespie, who made 75 and 48 respectively, and Australia amassed 556 in their first innings.

In reply India found themselves in familiar situation with their backs against the walls, losing 4 top order wickets for just 85 runs. But then Dravid and Laxman did an encore of their once in a lifetime heroics from Kolkata '01 adding a massive 303 runs for the 5th wicket. This time though the roles were reversed with Dravid scoring a magnificent double hundred - his fourth in test cricket - and Laxman made a classy 148. India managed to limit the deficit to 33 runs. A brilliant bowling performance in the third innings could give them a chance to win the match, and Ajit Agarkar delivered just that with a sensational spell of swing bowling. He took 6 wickets for 41 runs, including two early strikes and four tail-enders. Australia were bowled out for 196, leaving India a target of 230.

India chased down the target with confidence, thanks again to Dravid's solid half-century. The Wall stood tall and ensured that India overcame their usual middle-order collapses. He hit the winning runs and sealed a historic victory for India. The win gave India the edge in the series - they had shown their intent and determination to win.

Australia were desperate to bounce back in the series with a win in the Boxing day test at Melbourne but India started strong with a century stand for the first wicket and a scintillating 195 from Virender Sehwag. However, the rest of the batsmen failed to capitalise and India were bowled out for 366. Most worrying was Sachin's lack of runs so far in the series. He went for a duck, once again falling to an attempted cover drive, this time off Lee.

Australia responded with a massive 558, thanks to a hundred from Matthew Hayden and another double century from Ricky Ponting who was in the midst of a purple patch. Anil Kumble put in another lion-hearted effort with the ball, taking 6 wickets with his leg-spin.

India's second innings was another flop show, as they managed only 286 despite half-centuries from the captain and the vice-captain. Australia's bowlers were relentless, with Brett Lee, Nathan Bracken, Brad Williams and Stuart MacGill sharing the wickets. They left Australia with a meagre target of 95, which they chased down easily. Ricky Ponting was named the player of the match for his Bradmanesque batting.

The series was tied at 1-1, setting up a thrilling finale at Sydney.

2004

The fourth and final test at Sydney was more than just a series decider - it was Steve Waugh's farewell. The 'Ice Man' was revered not just in his own country but all over the cricketing world for his mental toughness, shrewd captaincy and gritty batting.

The venue for the final showdown, the SCG had always been a favourable venue for the Indian teams over the years and it proved so this time as well. Sourav Ganguly won the toss and India piled up a gigantic 705, with Sachin Tendulkar roaring back to form with a sublime 241 not out with 33 fours in over 600 minutes of batting without playing a single cover drive! It was a masterclass in self-restraint by one of the greatest to ever grace the game; something that today's pretenders to the throne can learn from. VVS Laxman too maintained his dominance over Australia with another daddy hundred, scoring 178 with 30 hits to the fence.

India thought they had batted Australia out of the match, but Australia managed to score 474 on the back of fighting centuries from Justin Langer and Simon Katich, despite the indefatigable Anil Kumble putting in another herculean performance, claiming 8 wickets in 48 tireless overs. India batted again and raced away to 211/2 declared, setting Australia a target of 443 in the fourth innings.

Australia started aggressively but lost wickets regularly as Kumble continued his magic with another 4 wickets. But he could not dislodge the great Steven Waugh, who played a typically defiant innings to save the match for Australia. It was a fitting "last dance" for the legendary Tasmanian, who received a standing ovation from the crowd for the yeoman services he had rendered to Australian cricket over the years.

The series ended in a 1-1 draw and India retained the Border Gavaskar trophy. The last time an Indian team had succeeded in drawing a series in Australia was way back in 1980-81. The spirit and the fight shown by Sourav

Ganguly's India were praised all over. While Sourav lamented some missed chances to clinch a first ever series win down under, even his opposite number Steve Waugh had to admit that no other visiting team had shown as much grit and chutzpah as this Indian team in a long time.

It was a collective performance from the team with everyone contributing at some stage or the other in the series. Having said that, the two individuals who ended the test series with their reputations and stature enhanced were Rahul Dravid and Anil Kumble. Kumble, whose selection was questioned by many, proved his captain right by finishing the series as the leading wicket-taker with 24 wickets in just 3 tests, 10 more than his Australian counterpart, Stuart McGill. While Ricky Ponting topped the run charts with 706 runs, Rahul Dravid wasn't too far behind with 619 runs, finishing as the team's leading run scorer in yet another test series. The Wall was now challenging the great Sachin Tendulkar for the mantle of the team's best batsman, at least in tests.

The proud tradition of Karnataka cricket had found its finest ambassadors in this duo.

The action shifted to the white-ball leg of the tour with the VB series - a triangular tournament involving Australia, India and Zimbabwe. The first match was between the hosts and India at the MCG. Ricky Ponting, now the all-format Australian captain following the retirement of Steve Waugh, won the toss and opted to bat first. Australia were in trouble at 89/4 in the 16th over with Agarkar taking 3 of those wickets. But a 143 runs stand for the fifth wicket between Andrew Symonds and Michael Clarke lifted Australia to a formidable 288. Agarkar registered his second 6 wicket haul of the tour with 6 for 42 while Irfan Pathan had an underwhelming debut.

India started their chase strongly with another century stand between the openers Sehwag (35) and Tendulkar (63), followed by Sourav Ganguly who top-scored with 82 off 83 balls. But the middle order squandered the opportunity and could not build upon the solid foundation laid by the top three. Ganguly's run-out in the 46th over was the final blow as India fell short by 18 runs. Ian Harvey was the most effective of the Aussie bowlers with 3 wickets, while Symonds also took two wickets to go with his 88 runs. He was named the player of the match for his all-round performance.

India faced Zimbabwe in their second match of the tournament at Hobart. Heath Streak, the Zimbabwean captain, chose to bat first, but his top order let him down and Zimbabwe were struggling at 115/6 after 38 overs. A brilliant cameo from Sean Irvine, who was well supported by Streak himself, helped Zimbabwe recover and reach 208/6.

India chased down the target with ease, thanks to another century partnership between Sehwag and Tendulkar. Sehwag was the player of the match, scoring 90 runs after taking two wickets earlier. Ganguly and Laxman completed the chase with 12 overs to spare, giving India a comfortable seven-wicket win.

In their third match of the tournament, India faced the hosts Australia once again. Sehwag had to sit out due to a back injury, so Ganguly opened the innings with his old partner Sachin. But he couldn't make much of an impact and got out for 18. Sachin and Laxman then took charge and added 110 runs for the second wicket. Sachin played a brilliant knock of 86 despite being limited by a sprained ankle, before he was caught and bowled by Symonds. Laxman was then joined at the crease by his favourite batting partner Rahul Dravid and the duo put on 133 runs for the third wicket, helping India cross the 300 mark for the first time on Australian soil. Dravid scored a fluent 74 off 64 balls while Laxman stayed unbeaten on 103, his third ODI hundred, all coming against Australia. Brett Lee registered his second worst figures in ODIs, giving away 83 runs in his 10 overs.

Chasing a challenging target of 303, Australia got off to a galloping start and despite losing Gilly in the 6th over, they were looking in control at 86 for 1 in the 11th over, until Balaji struck a double blow, removing Ponting and Martyn in quick succession. India tightened their grip on the match with some disciplined bowling and lively fielding. Australia started to fall behind the required rate and felt the pressure. Hayden played a superb innings of 109 off 110 balls, but his wicket in the 34th over was the turning point of the match. India wrapped up the lower order and restricted Australia to 284, winning by 19 runs. It was their first ODI victory on Australian soil in 12 years. VVS Laxman walked away with the player of the match for his delightful unbeaten hundred.

The most encouraging aspect of the win was the performance of two young seamers, Balaji and Irfan Pathan. They bowled with skill and confidence and shared 7 wickets between them. Rohan Gavaskar, son of the legendary Sunil Gavaskar, too made a decent impression on debut with 9 overs of left-arm spin and a brilliant diving return catch to dismiss the dangerous Symonds in his first over.

Buoyed by this huge morale booster, India hoped to brush aside Zimbabwe easily in their next match but Zimbabwe put up a spirited fight in both the innings and made India sweat before going down by 24 runs.

India were missing Tendulkar, who joined Sehwag on the injury list. They lost three early wickets and were in trouble at 74 for 3 in the 17th over. But then the designated troubleshooter of this team, vice-captain Rahul Dravid and Yuvraj Singh came together and steadied the ship with a 114-run partnership for the fourth wicket. Yuvraj scored a stylish 69 while Dravid anchored the innings brilliantly with a sensible knock of 84. They helped India reach a decent total of 255.

Zimbabwe did not give up in their chase, even though one of their openers, Vermeulen, had to retire hurt after being hit by a Pathan bouncer. They had some useful contributions from Grant Flower and Carlisle, who both scored in the 30s. It was an unexpected double assault from Sean Irvine and Dion Ebrahim aided by a few lusty blows from Ray Price, coming in at number 8, 9 and 10 respectively by that threatened to snatch the game away from India's grasp out of nowhere. But to their credit the relatively inexperienced Indian bowlers held their nerve and wrapped up the match in the 48th over. Pathan and Balaji were excellent again, as was the captain Sourav Ganguly who bowled 10 overs and picked 3 wickets. Yuvraj Singh was named the player of the match for his valuable knock.

Barely 36 hours later, the Indian team found itself on the field again to play their fifth match of the tournament and third inside five days, against the hosts at Sydney. It was a classic case of poor scheduling and to make matters worse they were missing Tendulkar and Sehwag due to injuries.

India were in trouble again when they lost three top-order wickets, including those of captain Ganguly and vice-captain Dravid, inside the first 15 overs. They were reeling at 80 for 3 and looked doomed. But then Laxman and Yuvraj rose to the occasion and staged a remarkable comeback. They put on a mammoth 213-run partnership for the fourth wicket and took the attack to the Australian bowlers. They both scored sparkling centuries and lifted India to a fighting total of 296. Yuvraj was in a destructive mood and smashed 139 off 122 balls with 16 fours and 2 sixes. He fell in the last over, trying to hit another boundary. Laxman remained calm and composed and carried his bat through the innings, scoring 106 not out. It was his fourth ODI century, all against Australia, his favourite opponents.

Gilchrist seemed to be in a hurry to finish the game before the expected storm hit. He took just 31 balls for his fifty and was close to a stunning hundred when the storm interrupted the chase. When the play resumed, Australia's target was revised to 225 from 34 overs. Gilly was beaten in flight to be caught and bowled by Kartik, missing out on a sure shot hundred by just 5 runs. Ponting scored a quick 42, but India kept finding ways to pick wickets and made it close. Australia needed 11 runs off the last over, bowled by Balaji. Brett Lee redeemed his poor performances earlier in the series by hitting a six off the fourth ball to tie the scores, and then hitting the winning run off the next ball to take his team home by 2 wickets with just 1 ball remaining, in the closest finish seen in the tournament so far. Player of the match still went to Yuvraj Singh for his brilliant hundred, his second in this format.

India faced another tough challenge when they had to play their fourth match in a week against Zimbabwe at the Adelaid Oval with barely any rest. To add to their woes, they lost Yuvraj Singh to injury, joining Sachin and Sehwag on the sidelines. On top of it all, they got off to their worst start in the tournament, at 3 down for just 4 runs in the fourth over. But to their immense credit, they overcame all this and still managed to post a respectable 280/7, thanks to yet another pristine century by VVS Laxman, aided by two industrious half-centuries by crisis man Dravid and the newbie Gavaskar Jr. For Zimbabwe Streak led from the front with 3 wickets.

Zimbabwe too began poorly and lost 3 wickets with just 46 runs on the scoreboard. But they did not give up and staged a remarkable recovery with two superb centuries from Craig Ervine and Stuart Carlisle. They added 202 runs for the fourth wicket, a record partnership for Zimbabwe in ODIs. It was also the first time that two Zimbabwean batsmen scored hundreds in the same innings.

But the turning point came when Ervine was run out by a brilliant throw from skipper Ganguly in the 46th over followed by the other centurion Carlisle in the 48th. A couple of streaky boundaries in the penultimate over bowled by Pathan took the game right down to the wire. With 7 needed off 4 balls, Blignaut lofted a ball towards midwicket. Laxman, who was at deep midwicket, had to cover a lot of ground to reach it. But the man could do no wrong that day, pulling off a stunning catch diving forward, to add to another superb diving catch he took at slip to dismiss Travis Friend earlier. It proved decisive as India managed to sneak through by a mere 3 runs in a nail-biting finish. Agarkar with 3 wickets for 39 runs was the best Indian bowler on show. Bangar too bowled well and kept his nerve in the final over. Laxman was named the player of the match for his splendid 131 - his third hundred in the ongoing tournament and fifth overall.

The result ensured that Australia and India would play in the finals.

India had a week-long break before their last league match against Australia, but it did not help them at all. They faced a rampant Brett Lee, who bowled with searing pace and swing on a lively WACA pitch. He ripped through the Indian batting line-up and dismissed them for 203 in 49 overs. Australia too had some early hiccups in their chase, but Gilchrist and Symonds smashed the Indian bowlers all over the park. They added 122 runs in just 16 overs and finished the game with 18 overs to spare. Gilchrist got the player of the match award, but Lee deserved it more.

The last league match before the finals was a dull affair between India and Zimbabwe, with little at stake. Zimbabwe skipper was once again let down by his batsmen after electing to bat first at the toss. Pathan was the star of the show, taking 4 wickets with his pace and bounce, restricting them to a paltry 135. Even that proved challenging to India as they stuttered to 105 for 5 in 23 overs before Badani took them home with a mature unbeaten 34. Irfan Pathan won his first player of the match award, confirming that he indeed was the find of the tour for India.

Zimbabwe ended the tournament with another heavy defeat - and without a single win in seven completed games. India's unconvincing performance too did not bode well for the finals, which was to be contested in a best-of-three format.

India hoped to change their luck by batting first on a good wicket at the new look MCG, but it was not to be as the Aussie seam attack led by the brilliant Jason Gillespie bowled intelligently on a largely unresponsive track by varying their line, length and pace to to reduce India to 75/6 in no time. Hemang Badani and Agarkar showed some resolve and added 102 runs for the seventh wicket to take India past 200. Agarkar hit 2 sixes and 4 fours in his entertaining 53 off 62 balls while Badani remained not out on a sensible 60 as India were bundled out for 222 in the 49 overs. For Australia, Gillespie, Brett Lee and Ian Harvey took two wickets apiece while Symonds and Brad Williams too chipped in with a wicket each.

A target of 223 proved to be too meagre for the Australian batsmen, who came out all-guns blazing. They hit 12 boundaries in the first 12 overs, with Gilchrist leading the charge as usual. Hayden played a solid innings of 50, while Ponting, who won the player of the match award, played a brilliant knock of 88 off 80 balls. With the sole exception of Balaji who took all the 3 wickets that fell, the rest of the Indian bowlers had no answer to the onslaught as Australia cruised home with almost 10 overs to spare, to go one up in the best of three finals. In that kind of mood, the Australian batsmen could have easily scored 350.

That's precisely what happened in the second final at Sydney as electing to bat first, Australia piled up a massive 359/5 in their 50 overs - the same total that they posted in the world cup final. What was most impressive was that they managed to post that total despite losing Gilchrist and Ponting inside the first ten overs. Matthew Hayden led the charge with a magnificent 126 off 122 balls with 11 boundaries and 3 sixes, aided by a stylish fifty by Damien Martyn. Andrew Symonds unleashed his fury with a blistering 66 off just 39 balls, and Michael Clarke added some quick runs with a 20-ball 33. The final onslaught saw 70 runs scored in the last 5 overs, with Symonds smashing 3 sixes. Ashish Nehra picked 2 wickets and was the least expensive of the Indian bowlers.

In reply, Indian batsmen could not offer even token resistance in the face of some inspired bowling, succumbing to 59/6 by the 17th over. Sachin and Sehwag fell in identical fashion to Gillespie while Laxman popped a simple catch back to Lee. Ganguly threw his wicket away with a reckless shot off Harvey, who also had Yuvraj caught behind in his next over. Dravid's run of 120 consecutive innings without a duck came to an end with a terrible mix-up with Badani resulting in a run out. None of the Indian batsmen crossed 30 and the whole team folded for just 151 in the 34th over, losing by 208 run-margin. It was a total rout as evidenced from the fact that this was India's second worst defeat in terms of runs in ODIs - and Australia clinched the VB Series in the most emphatic fashion.

The most troubling thing about the two losses was not the losses themselves but the fact that they were so expected. While this Indian team was regularly going toe-to-toe with Australia in tests, when it came to the ODIs, there still remained a huge gulf between the two sides.

Despite losing the VB tri-series final, the tour was a success overall. India achieved their first test win in Australia in 22 years, drew the test series in Australia for the first time in 22 years thereby stopping the Border Gavaskar trophy from changing hands and reached the finals of the VB series by winning 5 out of 8 league matches, including their first ODI win over Australia on Australian soil in 12 years. VVS Laxman made a triumphant return to the ODI side topping the batting charts in the VB series with close to 450 runs with 3 hundreds. Irfan Pathan and Balaji, while still a bit raw, showed enough promise to be termed the discoveries of the tour.

15

The Peak

Next up on the Indian cricket calendar for the season 2003-04 was the much-awaited tour to Pakistan.

It was announced in early January 2004 that India would tour Pakistan in March-April that year to play 5 ODIs and 3 tests. The Indian team and its management had some doubts about the security situation in Pakistan, so the BCCI sent a three-member team in February to assess the situation and reported that they were "satisfied with the security measures being planned by Pakistan". Based on their report, the Indian government gave a go-ahead to the tour after a few days.

The team selection for the tour was moved up by three days in Kolkata so that the players could have a three-day training camp before leaving. The selectors did not spring any surprises. Harbhajan was still recovering from his hand injury, so Murali Kartik replaced him in both the test and ODI squads. Kaif returned for the ODIs, while Agarkar was given a break from the ODIs to heal his minor injury in time for the tests. The Indian team management had asked for the test series to be played after the ODIs. The only newcomers in the ODI squad were Mumbai spinner Ramesh Powar and Delhi pacer Amit Bhandari, while Powar was the sole new face in the test squad.

Before embarking on the tour, The Prime Minister of India, Shri Atal Bihari Vajpayee, hosted a high tea for the entire team at his official residence. He spent an hour with them, treating them to a stirring rendition of *Hum Honge Qamyaab* by the naval band and sending them off with a message to win not only matches but also hearts.

Both the Pakistan government and their cricket board pulled out all stops, rolling out the red carpet for the Indian team as they landed in

Lahore. The tour was not just a cricketing event, but also a diplomatic one for both countries and everyone wanted it to be a huge success.

The tour started on a sobering note for the Indian team as they narrowly lost the only 50-over tour game against Pakistan A.

The first ODI at Karachi was going to be the first time the two teams met since their thrilling world cup clash at Centurion almost a year ago. Pakistan cricket had undergone a major overhaul since that high-profile defeat. The great Saeed Anwar and the two Ws - Wasim and Waqar - were gone; Anwar and Akram retired while Waqar was sidelined. Rashid Latif, who took over as captain after the world cup disaster, was also out. Inzamam was the new captain while the great Miandad managed to retain his position as the coach, which he took up following the exit of Dav Whatmore after the world cup debacle. This home series against the arch rivals was going to be an acid test for the new captain-coach *jodi*.

Inzamam made a surprising decision to bowl first on a good batting pitch after winning the toss. He regretted it as India scored a massive 349/7 against a weak Pakistan bowling attack. Sehwag and Sachin continued their form from Centurion, putting on 69 in 9 overs before Shoaib dismissed Tendulkar for 28. Sehwag went on a rampage and hit 73 runs in the next 5 overs with Ganguly, before he chopped a poor ball from Rana Naved onto his stumps. Sehwag scored a fiery 79 off just 57 balls with 14 fours and a six. Ganguly was joined by his vice-captain and they slowed down a bit but still managed to add 72 in 12 overs for the third wicket when Ganguly was caught and bowled by Rana for 45. He hit 3 fours and 2 sixes in his knock. Rana struck again in the next over as he had Yuvraj caught at point for just 3. Dravid and Kaif came together and batted smartly while still keeping the run rate high, adding 118 in 19 overs for the fifth wicket when Dravid sacrificed his wicket for the team's cause in the 48th over. He was bowled by an Akhtar slower ball for 99 as he tried to hit a six. His 99 had only 8 boundaries but came off just 104 balls, showing his transformation as a limited-overs batsman. Kaif also missed his fifty by 4 runs, lbw to a Sami yorker but India had set Pakistan a daunting target of 350 in 50 overs. Rana Naved took 3 wickets but was expensive as was Sami who took 2. Akhtar redeemed himself from his world cup thrashing by taking the prized scalps of Sachin and Dravid while giving away only 55 runs in his 10 overs.

Pakistan had a shaky start in their chase of 350 as they lost both their openers by the 8th over for just 34 runs. But their reliable middle-order of Yousuf Youhana, Inzamam and Younis Khan, cheered on by a 33000 strong passionate crowd, rescued them with two consecutive century partnerships - 135 for the third wicket between Inzamam and Yousuf, who played a stunning hand of 73 off 68 with 4 of his trademark inside-out lofted sixes before falling to Sehwag's golden arm; followed by 109 for the fourth wicket between Inzi and Younis Khan who took the score to 278 in the 42nd over. Inzamam was in sublime form and scored a majestic 122 before he was caught by Dravid off a sharp turner from Kartik. Kartik struck again in his next over and bowled Younis who had just hit a six to take the score past 300. Younis made 46. This twin blow by the wily Kartik proved to be the game changer in the final analysis. Abdul Razzaq and Moin Khan tried hard to keep up with the required rate and brought it down to 9 off the last over bowled by Nehra. Nehra bowled superbly and made it 5 off the last ball. There was no encore of Miandad heroics this time and Moin was caught on the last ball to give India a thrilling win by 5 runs. The Indian pacers led by Zaheer took 5 wickets while Kartik took the vital wickets of Inzimam and Younis. Sehwag also contributed with the wicket of an ominous looking Yousuf. Inzamam deservedly won the player of the match award.

Inzamam learned from his mistake and decided to bat first in the second match at Rawalpindi. Yasir Hameed and Shahid Afridi gave them a flying start with 138 for the first wicket in 18 overs before Yuvraj bowled Afridi for a smashing 80 off 58 balls with 10 fours and 4 sixes. Only a maverick like Shahid Afridi could have played such a knock on his comeback after being sidelined for more than a year. Hameed also fell in the 80s after a mix-up with Inzi. The middle-order trio got starts but could not capitalize and it was Shoaib Malik and Abdul Razzaq's late assault that lifted the score to 329/6, smashing 45 runs in the last 4 overs. Nehra, who braved a swollen ankle to play in this match, was the best bowler for India with 3 for 46 but then split his webbing and had to be sent back home. Yuvraj also bowled well picking up a couple but the other bowlers, especially Zaheer, were thrashed mercilessly.

India had a good start to their chase with Sachin and Sehwag adding 56 in 8 overs when hometown hero Shoaib cleaned up Sehwag with a jaffa. Laxman, back in the side after sitting out the first game, was lbw soon after and India were 71/2 in 12 overs. Sachin who was in sublime touch at the other end, rebuilt the chase with Ganguly and Dravid, scoring a dazzling 141 with 17 fours and a six, also becoming the first man to go past 13000 ODI runs along the way. He added 69 with Ganguly and 105 with Dravid before he was out to a mistimed slog sweep off Malik. The game changed when a well-set Dravid was bowled by a fast and furious Sami in the 42nd over. Afridi completed a fairytale comeback by ending Yuvraj's promising cameo, his second wicket to go with the 80 odd he made with the bat. Shoaib Akhtar, who was playing his 100th ODI in front of his home crowd, then came back for his final spell and removed Kaif and Zaheer in two balls, leaving India 46 runs short with just 4 overs left. Debutant Ramesh Powar and Balaji tried valiantly, hitting 30 runs in 15 balls but could not finish the job falling short by 12 runs. Pakistan won and levelled the series 1-1. Player of the match went to a player from the losing side for the second game in a row as it was awarded to Sachin for his fabulous hundred. It was his 37th ODI ton and the first scored by an Indian on Pakistani soil.

Next day, the Indian team was treated to a tea with the Pakistani President General Parvez Musharraf. He praised Balaji and Powar for not going down without a fight in the final overs.

It had been bat versus bat in the three matches that India played so far on the tour, including the practice game against Pak A, with both the teams easily going past 300 in all the three games.

That was to change in the third match at Peshawar. Pakistan captain elected to bowl first for the second time in three matches and this time his seamers, especially Shabbir Ahmad, did a great job of destroying India's top order. He took three early wickets, including the centurion from previous game, Sachin for a duck, and left India reeling at 37 for 3 after 8 overs. The captain and his deputy then steadied the innings with a 68-run partnership for the fourth wicket, followed by a fighting 65 from Yuvraj. Some brave hitting from the tailenders, especially Balaji, took India to a respectable 244/9 in 50 overs. Shabbir Ahmad was the pick of the bowlers with 3 for 33, while Razzaq and Malik also took two wickets each.

In reply, Pakistan lost two early wickets to Irfan Pathan, who bowled with pace and swing. Yasir Hameed was the only batsman who looked comfortable against the Indian bowlers. He anchored the innings with a superb 98 off 129 balls, hitting 11 fours and a six. He got some support from Yousuf Youhana, who made 39 off 51 balls, and Inzamam, who scored 25 off 35 balls. However, India kept taking wickets at regular intervals and reduced Pakistan to 173/6 in the 35th over, when Pathan dismissed the well-set Hameed just 2 short of a well-deserved hundred in front his home crowd. Pakistan still needed 72 runs from 15 overs with just 4 wickets in hand. It looked like India had the upper hand, but the experienced pair of Abdul Razzaq and Moin Khan had other ideas. They played sensibly and aggressively, rotating the strike and finding the boundaries when needed. They added an unbeaten 74-run partnership in a little over 12 overs and took Pakistan home with 16 balls to spare. Razzaq remained not out on 53 off 52 balls, hitting 7 fours, while Moin Khan was unbeaten on 22 off 29 balls. Yasir Hameed was named the player of the match for his sensible knock. Pakistan took a 2-1 lead in the five match series with this win.

The fourth match of the series at Lahore had become a must-win game for the Indian team if they wished to stay alive in the series. The hosts had the advantage of batting first after winning the toss yet again. However, Irfan Pathan struck early with his lovely swing, dismissing Afridi and Youhana for low scores. Pakistan could manage only 59/2 in 15 overs on a good batting track, as Indian seamers kept the pressure on. Inzamam-ul-Haq, the Pakistan skipper, took charge of the innings and found an ally in Yasir Hameed, who was also in good nick. They added 74 runs before Murali Kartik outfoxed Hameed with a clever delivery and had him stumped for 45. Inzamam then joined forces with Younis Khan and they accelerated the scoring rate. They put on 105 runs for the fourth wicket before Kartik struck again, trapping Younis lbw for 50. Inzi was unstoppable though, and he unleashed his power-hitting in the final overs. He smashed Balaji for two sixes in an over, but the bowler got his revenge by bowling him for a glorious 123 off 121 balls with 9 fours and 4 sixes. It was the 10th ODI hundred of his career and fourth against India. Abdul Razzaq also chipped in with a quickfire 32 off 24 balls as Pakistan reached a formidable total of 293/9 in 50 overs.

Each of India's four main bowlers - Pathan, Balaji, Zak and Murali Kartik - claimed two wickets, though Balaji was expensive. Kartik stood out as the most impressive of the lot with his variations of flight and trajectory.

India started their chase well and kept up with the required rate. But they paid a heavy price for their aggression and lost their top order quickly. After 13 overs, India were 94 for 4, with their big guns Sachin, Sehwag and Ganguly all back in the pavilion. They still had a mountain to climb with 200 runs to get in 37 overs.

However, Rahul Dravid again showcased his evolution as a limited overs batsman, as he forged two crucial partnerships with Yuvraj Singh and Mohammad Kaif. He added 68 runs with Yuvraj for the fifth wicket, and then an unbeaten 132 runs with Kaif for the sixth wicket. Dravid scored a brilliantly paced 76 not out from 92 balls, hitting 9 fours, while Kaif played a gem of an innings, scoring 71 not out from 77 balls, with 8 hits to the fence. The duo took India home with 5 overs to spare, stunning the hosts and their fans while enhancing their reputations as the finishers for India in tough situations. This win was also a testament to the great chemistry that Rahul Dravid had managed to develop with Yuvraj and Kaif in the past couple of years.

The series was levelled at 2-2 after this match. Pakistan captain Inzamam was named the player of the match for his magnificent hundred.

The series decider was played at the Gaddafi stadium Lahore in front of the largest contingent of Indian fans owing to Lahore's proximity to the Indian border. Inzamam won the toss for the fifth time and put India in for the third time in the series. Sehwag started with a flurry of boundaries but fell for 20, caught behind off Shabbir Ahmad. Sachin and Laxman added 45 runs in 8 overs before Sachin too perished, edging Sami to the keeper for 37. He had hit 7 fours in his 48-ball innings. Laxman and Ganguly then steadied the innings with some elegant and sensible batting. They put on 91 runs for the third wicket before Ganguly was out for 45, caught behind off Shoaib Akhtar. Laxman was in sublime touch and kept the scoreboard ticking even though Yuvraj and Kaif did not last long. He scored a brilliant 107 off 104 balls with 11 graceful boundaries. This was his sixth ODI hundred overall and 4th in last 11 innings. He was out in the 46th over, but the endearing duo of Pathan and Balaji again provided the innings a final boost by smashing 30 runs in the last 3 overs. Balaji even hit a six, that too off Akhtar no less, to take India's total to 293 for 7. For Pakistan, Sami took three wickets and Shabbir two, but they were all expensive, barring Akhtar.

Pathan and Balaji then wreaked havoc with the ball to leave the Pakistani chase tottering at 96 for 6 by the end of the 24th over with all their stalwarts back in the hut. Old warhorse Moin Khan and Shoaib Malik tried to revive the innings with a gutsy 99-run stand for the seventh wicket and gave some hope of a miraculous win. But Sehwag furthered his growing reputation as a partnership-breaker by getting Malik caught by Kaif for 65. Pakistan were 195 for 7 in the 41st over and the game was almost over. Moin Khan fought till the end but ran out of partners. He was the last man out for a brave 72 in the 48th over. Pakistan were all out for 253 and India won by 40 runs to clinch the five match series 3-2. Pathan and Balaji both took 3 wickets each, though Balaji was a tad expensive. Murali Kartik again bowled a nagging spell in the middle overs and took one wicket, as did Zaheer and Sehwag.

VVS Laxman was awarded the player of the match for his superb century while Inzamam was the player of the series for scoring 340 runs, which was almost a hundred more than the next best, Rahul Dravid, with 248.

This historic first ODI series win on Pakistani soil was another feather in the cap of Sourav Ganguly-John Wright partnership. Irfan Pathan and Balaji solidified their positions as the finds of the season, Murali Kartik more than made up for the absence of Kumble and Harbhajan, VVS Laxman, with 4 hundreds in 11 innings, looked ready to fill a Mohammad Azharuddin-sized hole in the middle order now in the ODIs too; Yuvraj and Kaif kept going from strength to strength as ODI batsmen and Rahul Dravid was now a proper force to reckon with in the shorter format as well. All in all, things were looking up for the Indian ODI unit with only one missing piece: a specialist wicketkeeper batsman to free Rahul from the dual burden.

The next challenge for India was the three-test series against Pakistan. The last time India played a test series in Pakistan was in 1989, when they drew 0-0 in four tests, thanks to some superlative batting by Sanjay Manjrekar and Mohammad Azharuddin. That series also saw the debut of a teen prodigy, a 16-year-old boy wonder named Sachin Ramesh Tendulkar. After that series, there was a gap of ten years before the two teams would meet again in a test series, when Pakistan visited India in 1999. Pakistan dominated that tour, winning two out of three tests and also the ODI tri-series. India had taken revenge for the ODI loss by winning the ODI series in Pakistan. Now they had a chance to do something that no other Indian team had done before - win a test series in Pakistan.

There were only two notable changes from the squad that toured Australia. Yuvraj Singh replaced Sadgoppan Ramesh and Ramesh Powar was picked as an extra spinner instead of a backup wicketkeeper. The selectors did the best they could as Harbhajan and Nehra were still injured.

The first test at Multan turned out to be a one-sided affair, with India dominating from the start. Rahul Dravid, standing-in for the injured Sourav Ganguly, won the toss and elected to bat first on a flat pitch. They piled up a massive 675 for 5 declared, thanks to a sensational triple century by Virender Sehwag. He became the first Indian batsman to score 300 in a test match and the seventh overall. He smashed 39 fours and 6 sixes in his 375-ball innings and shared a record 336-run stand with Sachin Tendulkar for the third wicket. Tendulkar also scored a handsome unbeaten 194, missing out on his fourth double century by just 6 runs due to a controversial declaration call made by the acting-captain Dravid. Tendulkar carved 21 boundaries in his 348-ball knock, and went past Steve Waugh on the list of most Test hundreds with his 33rd ton. Yuvraj Singh also chipped in with a quick-fire 59 off 66 balls.

Pakistan's bowling was ineffective and expensive, with only Mohammad Sami and Saqlain Mushtaq taking a wicket each. Shoaib Akhtar went wicketless and conceded 119 runs in 32 overs.

Pakistan faced a daunting task of avoiding the follow-on and they failed miserably. They were bowled out for 407 in their first innings, despite half-centuries from Yasir Hameed and hometown hero Inzamam. Hameed scored 91 off 151 balls with 14 fours, Inzamam scored 77 off 118 balls with 13 fours and was the victim of a poor umpiring call by the otherwise astute Simon Taufel of Australia. Razzaq also played a hand of 47 off 109 balls with 6 fours. They were the only batsmen to offer some resistance to India's bowling attack led by an inspired Irfan Pathan who took 4. Kumble and Sachin also picked a couple of wickets each, with Sachin's googly to clean up Moin Khan being the highlight of the day. Zaheer also chipped in with the important wicket of Yousuf but suffered a hamstring injury leaving India a bowler short for the rest of the match.

India enforced the follow-on and Pakistan collapsed to 216 all out in their second innings. They lost wickets at regular intervals and never looked like saving the match. Only Yousuf Youhana fought bravely with 112 off 165 balls, but he could only manage to delay the inevitable.

Kumble was the star of the show, taking 6 wickets for 72 runs in 30 overs. He also completed 450 test wickets in his career. A staggering 34 of those 450 had come in the last 4 away tests only, capping off a remarkable turnaround for the veteran of 15 years. This gentle giant of Indian cricket had reclaimed his rightful place as its greatest match-winner in Tests.

Kumble was well supported by Irfan Pathan who claimed 2 wickets for 26 runs in 21 overs (12 of which were maiden) to finish with a match haul of 6 wickets. This was a remarkable feat on a dead track where all the other seamers struggled.

India won the match by an innings and 52 runs with more than a day to spare and registered their first ever test win in Pakistan in 49 years. It was also their second biggest win by an innings margin and they took a 1-0 lead in the three-match series. Sehwag was not only named the player of the match but also crowned 'The Sultan of Multan' for his record-breaking knock of 309, which was also the highest individual score by an Indian batsman in tests, overtaking the 281 by VVS Laxman.

A huge controversy towards the end of the second day had almost threatened to rob India of this historic feat. Sachin Tendulkar was in great form and had reached 165 by tea. India were 588/4 and planning to declare soon. Sachin was told he had 15 overs to get 200. But after tea, things changed quickly. Sachin couldn't quite accelerate despite a message from the dressing room. Dravid, the stand-in captain, declared with India at 675/5 when Yuvraj got out on the fifth ball of 75th over of the day, leaving Sachin stranded on 194. Sachin was left stunned and fuming. He felt betrayed by his captain and teammate. He walked back to the dressing room with a look of disbelief and anger on his face and did not take the field for the remaining overs citing ankle pain. He expressed his displeasure at the press conference and said he felt let down by the abrupt declaration implying that he was not properly informed.

The declaration sparked off a huge uproar among fans and media. Many questioned Dravid for being selfish and insensitive. Some wondered if there was a rift between Dravid and Sachin. Some even blamed Ganguly for the mess, as he was seen involved in an animated discussion with Dravid right before the decision was made. Dravid, on his part, stood by his decision saying it was nothing personal, strictly business and he did it to give ample time to his bowlers to get Pakistan out twice on a flat, unresponsive pitch. Sachin later confided in coach John Wright - who had backed Dravid's decision - that he felt he deserved more respect after 16 years of selfless service to Indian cricket.

But Dravid and Tendulkar, being the consummate professionals, cleared the air after an honest heart-to-heart the next morning before the third day's play. Tendulkar went on to take 2 important wickets in Pakistan's first innings, including Moin Khan, with a brilliant googly. He celebrated with unbridled joy and hugged Dravid, who was fielding at slip putting an end to speculations of any lingering rift.

Any two lesser men than Sachin Tendulkar and Rahul Dravid and the issue would have snowballed and derailed the momentum the team had for many years to come. But thankfully, saner heads prevailed and the potentially volatile situation was averted.

Facing a lot of flak specially from ex-players, Pakistan made 4 changes to their playing eleven going in to the second test at Lahore. They replaced injured Razzaq and Moin with left-hander Asim Kamal and young Kamran Akmal. They also brought in leg-spinner Danish Kaneria for the out-of-depth Saqlain and a matchstick-thin fast bowler from a remote village on the Afghan border, Umar Gul for the struggling Shabbir. India brought in Agarkar for the injured Zaheer.

Ganguly was still unfit so Dravid continued as the stand-in captain. He won the toss and chose to bat first on a wicket that had some moisture. It turned out to be a mistake as India's batting crumbled on the first day. The wrecker-in-chief was the lanky Umar Gul who, just 9 days short of his twentieth birthday, bowled a dream spell of 12 overs on either side of lunch, taking the wickets of Sehwag, Sachin, Dravid, Laxman and Parthiv Patel. Tendulkar's dismissal was his first in four test innings in 2004, in which he had amassed a record 497.

It was Yuvraj Singh who saved India the blushes with his maiden test hundred - a stunning 112 off 129 balls with 15 fours and 2 sixes. Coming in at 94/4 which soon became 147/7, the 22 years old dashing southpaw from adjoining Punjab launched a counter-attack, adding 117 runs for the 8th wicket with young sensation Irfan Pathan, who played a fine knock of 49 in front of his parents who had flown in from India. India were all out for 287 in 64.1 overs.

Pakistan replied strongly with Imran Farhat and Inzamam-ul-Haq scoring centuries. Youhana and Asim Kamal also chipped in with solid fifties. Pakistan amassed 489 in their first innings, taking a huge lead of 202 runs. Pathan and Balaji took 3 wickets each and Kumble took 2.

India's batting didn't fare much better in their second innings either. Only Virender Sehwag from the top six scored a quickfire 90. Parthiv Patel's fighting unbeaten 62 and his 75-run stand with Agarkar saved India from innings defeat. However, once Agarkar got out for 36, India's second inning folded up for 241, setting Pakistan a target of mere 40 runs, which they chased down in just 8 overs with 9 wickets to spare. Pakistan won by 9 wickets and levelled the series 1-1. Umar Gul was the player of the match for his sensational 5-wicket haul in the first innings but he injured his back during the second innings and was ruled out for the third and final test.

Pakistan bouncing back so strongly made the third and final test a thrilling contest. The two fierce rivals faced each other at Rawalpindi for the series finale. Sourav Ganguly was still not a hundred percent, but determined to lead his team in such a defining moment of his career. He won a good toss and decided to bowl first on a pitch that offered some assistance to the seamers. His seamers Balaji, Pathan and Ashish Nehra rewarded his decision by removing both the Pakistani openers Imran Farhat and Taufeeq Umar for 34 runs. Yasir Hameed and Inzamam-ul-Haq tried to rebuild the innings with a 43-run stand, but both fell for 26 and 15 respectively. Yousuf Youhana, Asim Kamal and Kamran Akmal also failed to make an impact as Pakistan slumped to 137 for 8. Mohammad Sami showed some defiance with a gritty 49 and added 70 runs for the ninth wicket with Fazl-E-Akbar. But Kumble broke the partnership and Pakistan were eventually dismissed for 224 in their first innings. Lakshmipathy Balaji was the most successful with 4 wickets for 63 runs in 19 overs. He was well complimented at the other end by Irfan Pathan and Ashish Nehra who took a couple wickets each.

India's reply was dominated by Rahul Sharad Dravid, who scored a colossal 270 and batted for over 12 hours to help India post a mammoth 600 in their first innings. He came to the crease after Sehwag was sensationally dismissed for a duck by Shoaib Akhtar on the first ball of India's inning. He shared a 129-run stand with Parthiv Patel, who responded with a career-best 69 upon being sent in to open. The Rawalpindi Express dealt another huge blow to India by having Sachin Tendulkar caught behind for just 1. Dravid then forged a partnership of 131 runs with VVS Laxman, who scored a delightful 71, and another 152 runs with Sourav Ganguly, who contributed a handsome 77 on his return from injury. Dravid reached his fifth double century, overtaking the legendary Sunil Gavaskar on the list of Indian batsmen with most test double centuries, and went on to score his highest test score of 270 before he was bowled by Imran Farhat. He faced 495 balls and hit 34 fours and a six. Yuvraj Singh continued his impressive initiation into test cricket with another handy knock of 47 as India piled up a monumental 600 in their first innings.

Faced with a huge deficit of 376 runs, Pakistan failed to cope with the pressure and collapsed in their second innings as well. Led by the crafty Balaji, the Indian seamers ripped through their top order reducing them to 94 for 5 in less than 25 overs. Youhana and Asim Kamal tried to resist with a 81-run partnership for the sixth wicket, but Kumble broke their stand by catching Yousuf for 48 off his own bowling. The veteran leg-spinner then cleaned up the tail as Asim Kamal ran out of partners after scoring a brave 60. Pakistan were bowled out for 245, giving India a massive victory by an innings and 131 runs. Kumble was once again the most successful Indian bowler with 4 wickets, but Balaji was the one who inflicted the maximum damage with 3 top order scalps, including the captain Inzi, taking his match tally to 7 wickets.

Rahul 'The Wall' Dravid was named the player of the match for his marathon knock of 270. 'Nawab of Najafgarh' Virender Sehwag won the player of the series for scoring 438 runs at an average of 109.50, including a triple century in the first test at Multan. Anil Kumble ended second successive away tour as the leading wicket taker with 15 wickets. He got excellent support from Pathan and Balaji, who took 12 wickets each and outperformed the best Pakistani bowler by 5 wickets. So much for the pre-series hype of it being India's batting versus Pakistan's fast bowling. India clinched the series 2-1 and made history by achieving their first-ever test series win on Pakistani soil. It was also their first major away series win since 1993.

Basking in the glory of the historic feat, captain Sourav Ganguly dedicated the achievement to the whole squad including coach John Wright and the support staff. Irfan Pathan was the star of the tour, but Lakshmipathy Balaji turned out to be the surprise package. The smiling assassin won hearts with his cheerful visage and courageous cricket, emerging as an unlikely cult figure even among Pakistani fans and people.

For most Indian cricket fans, it was a painful experience to watch their team ending up on the losing side more often than not against their arch rivals in the 70s, 80s and 90s. Things started to change after Ajay Jadeja's stunning assault on Waqar Younis in the quarter-final of the 1996 world cup at Bangalore. That was like breaking a psychological spell that was cast by Javed Miandad's last-ball six, which haunted India for almost a decade. After that Jadeja blitz, India began to win more frequently against Pakistan, especially in the shorter format, with Sourav Ganguly himself leading the way with two Sahara cups and memorable wins in 1999 and 2003 world cup. But the 1998 home series defeat was a huge setback, which erased the progress made. Therefore, defeating Pakistan in their own backyard was the holy grail for the average Indian fan and now that it was finally achieved, whole of India erupted in uninhibited joy.

The dressing room was a scene of jubilation and champagne as the young guns like Yuvraj, Sehwag and Pathan shared their happiness with the senior stalwarts like Ganguly, Dravid, Sachin, Kumble and Laxman, who also let loose and enjoyed the moment. The celebration went on in the bus ride to Islamabad, where team manager Ratnakar Shetty had hosted a lavish dinner for the whole team. The party then shifted to discotheques, where the elated Indian team danced their hearts out till the dawn, just before flying back home to Delhi, where they were given a rapturous reception upon landing at the Indira Gandhi airport by thousands of adoring fans.

Following days were no less heady, as the team received praise from the highest echelons of power, including the President of India, the eminent Dr. Abdul Kalam, Prime Minister Atal Bihari Vajpayee and the leader of opposition Mrs. Sonia Gandhi, who all congratulated them on their historic achievement.

By any standard, it was a tour for the ages, filled with political significance, thrilling cricket, and a range of emotions. The Sourav Ganguly-John Wright partnership was never stronger than it was in this moment.

Few would have guessed that the *jodi* had reached the peak of their glory and it was all downhill from here.

Section 2

THE DESCENT

16

The Unravelling

Pakistan tour concluded one of the most remarkable seasons for the Indian team. The cricketers got a three-month break to heal their injuries and relax after a tough season. They also got a lot of endorsement deals as they had once again become the cynosure of all eyes after beating Pakistan.

The next season commenced with the Asia cup in Sri Lanka. This edition was a six-team tournament with teams from Bangladesh, Hong Kong and UAE also participating alongside the big three - India, Pakistan and host Sri Lanka.

India faced UAE in their opening match, a team that had not played an ODI in eight years. Ganguly won the toss and chose to bat first. But the Indian batsmen looked rusty and struggled against the UAE bowlers who bowled with discipline and accuracy. India lost three quick wickets, including Sehwag and Tendulkar, and were in trouble at 65 for 3 in 8 overs. Dravid was the only batsman who looked in touch and he rescued India with a brilliant century. He first shared a 88-run partnership with Ganguly, who scored a scratchy fifty, and then added another 100 runs with Yuvraj and Kaif, who also found it hard to score freely. Dravid scored 104 off 93 balls with only 8 fours again showing you don't have to be a Sehwag or a Jayasuriya to score at a good clip in one-dayers. It was his 9th ODI hundred and he now had an average of over 40 in a format that he was once considered unsuitable for. He was the last man out as India made 260.

Chasing 261, UAE had no answer to the Indian pace attack of Pathan, Balaji and Zaheer Khan, who was coming back after a long injury lay-off. The three pacers shook off their rust and ran through the UAE batting line-up. Only Mohammad Tauqir at number 8 put up some fight but Tendulkar wrapped up the innings quickly by taking three wickets. UAE were bowled out for 144 in 35 overs and India won by 116 runs. Rahul Dravid was the player of the match for his brilliant century.

India next took on hosts Sri Lanka at Dambulla in a day/night match. It was the first high-profile clash in the first round of the tournament, but a dead rubber, as both teams had already qualified for the next round. Marvan Atapattu, who had been leading Sri Lanka since their early exit from the 2003 world cup, won the toss and elected to bat first on a sluggish pitch. His batters proved him right with number 3, 4 and 5 all scoring a fifty while opener Gunawardhene missed out on his by just 1 run. It was, however, the frenetic 116 run stand for the fourth wicket between Jayawardene and Sangakkara in less than 15 overs that really propelled the hosts to a very impressive 282/4 in their 50 overs. This partnership showed that Sri Lanka had finally found two superb middle order batsmen who could take over from the legendary Ranathunga and de Silva and serve Sri Lankan cricket for many years to come. Jayawardene, in particular, played some really cheeky shots in his unbeaten 49 ball 58. Indian bowlers still showed signs of rust as evident from the 27 extras. Pathan and Balaji took a wicket each, but Balaji was expensive.

India's chase was derailed by an inspired Nuwan Zoysa, who took a couple of early wickets including that of Tendulkar and ran out Sehwag with a direct hit. At 71 for 4 and missing Laxman who was out nursing a swollen left-knee, India were in trouble. Crisis men Dravid and Yuvraj revived the innings with a mature 133-run stand, but Muralitharan bowled Dravid via an inside-edge for 82 just when he was beginning to up the ante. The tail wagged, but Sri Lanka's bowlers led by the experienced Chaminda Vaas held their nerves and sealed a 12-run win. Zoysa walked away with the player of the match for his lethal spell of 3 for 49 plus the crucial direct hit.

India bounced back from their loss to Sri Lanka with a comfortable 8 wicket win over Bangladesh in their most convincing performance in the tournament so far. Opting to bowl first, Irfan Pathan sliced through the top order putting Bangladesh on the back foot from the outset with his prodigious swing. He struck twice in his third over and came back later to finish off the innings with Tendulkar, who used his mixed bag of tricks to outfox the Bangladeshi lower order. Ashish Nehra and Harbhajan also marked their comeback to cricket with nice, probing spells picking up a wicket each while Pathan and Tendulkar bagged 3 apiece.

In reply, India lost Sehwag on the fifth ball of a dramatic first over which yielded 23 runs but then Tendulkar and Ganguly knuckled down and played themselves back into form, guiding India to a comfortable 8 wickets win with more than 11 overs to spare. Ganguly made 60 off 100 balls with 3 fours and 3 trademark sixes while Sachin stayed unbeaten on 82 off 126 balls with 10 fours and a six. He was named the player of the match for his all-round brilliance.

India's next match was against their arch-rivals Pakistan at Colombo, rightly billed as the clash of the tournament. Laxman failed to pass the fitness test on the morning of the game so Parthiv Patel had to be included in the playing eleven. It was a high-voltage encounter, but Pakistan dominated from the start. Shoaib Malik, promoted to one-down, rode his luck to play a stunning knock of 143 off 127 balls, the highest individual score in the tournament, and took Pakistan to 300 for with some help from Inzi and Yousuf. India's bowlers had no answer to Malik's onslaught though Pathan and Sachin did manage to take 3 wickets each.

India lost Sehwag early, but Tendulkar and Ganguly braved a really hostile spell from Shoaib Akhtar to keep the chase alive. But Kaif's run-out at 151 for 5 exposed the tail, forcing India to give up on the win and aim for the bonus point instead by reaching the 240 runs mark. They managed that thanks to the bye the ninth-wicket pair stole off the last ball. Losing by 59 runs rather than 60 ensured India gained - and Pakistan lost - a bonus point. And results in the remaining second-phase games meant India finished 2 points ahead of Pakistan - though behind on net run-rate; meaning Pakistan's fate was no longer in their own hands: they would progress only if Sri Lanka, already guaranteed a place in the final, beat India.

The bonus point system in this tournament was confounding to say the least and Pakistan's coach Bob Woolmer, who had just taken charge, had a valid point when he termed it 'flawed'.

Be that as it may, it was still a remarkable turnaround by the Pakistani team that had lost so squarely at home just three months ago. Shoaib Malik was named the player of the match for his superb century and 2 wickets, including Tendulkar's, who scored a ponderous 78. This was the beginning of a string of matches where the young Pakistani all-rounder would perform exceedingly well against India.

With a place in the final at stake, India took on host Sri Lanka at the same venue, still without Laxman. Ganguly called correctly at the toss and chose to bat first. India managed to post a healthy 271 on the scoreboard despite losing Sachin early, thanks to Sehwag coming good for the first time in the tournament with a measured knock of 81. He and Ganguly (79 off 120 balls) added 134 runs and India looked on course for a score above 300 but lost momentum towards the end despite a quick 50 by Yuvi.

Jayasuriya then played a vintage knock of 130 from 132 balls and took Sri Lanka close to a stunning win. But Ganguly used his part-time spinners well, especially Sehwag and his off-spin. Extracting sharp turn from a crumbling pitch, Sehwag broke a 103-run stand between Jayasuriya and Dilshan by clean bowling Dilshan for 39, leaving Sri Lanka 35 to get from 37 balls. Then, with 18 needed from 18, Sehwag caught and bowled an exhausted Jayasuriya. Pathan delivered a brilliant penultimate over giving away just 4 runs. It came down to 11 from the last over, and the experienced Zaheer Khan kept his cool and sealed the win and with it, a place in the final. Sehwag was named the player of the match for his 82 runs and 3 wickets.

VVS Laxman's left knee had a history of injury and it got worse when he was hit on it twice in the nets. He sat out three group matches and hardly got a chance to spend time in the middle in the other two. He almost flew home the previous Sunday after failing a fitness test for the Pakistan match. The team management had already asked for a replacement, likely Gautam Gambhir from India A that was on tour in Zimbabwe. But Ganguly changed his mind and kept him, hoping he would recover by the final. He did and Team India was back to full-strength with a fit-again VVS.

The hitherto slumbering Premadasa stadium in Colombo came alive for the final which was to be a day/night affair between the hosts and India. Marvan Atapattu won a good toss and elected to bat first on a typical slow, low and turning Premadasa track. They got off to a shaky start as Irfan Pathan and Ashish Nehra bowled with pace and swing, reducing them to 31/2 in the eighth over. Atapattu and Sangakkara then steadied the innings with a 116-run partnership for the third wicket, both scoring half-centuries. Atapattu was run out for 65 and Sanga was bowled by Sehwag for 53, triggering a middle-order collapse. Sachin Tendulkar showed his magic with the ball again, taking 2 crucial wickets in the middle order taking his tournament haul to 12, as Sri Lanka were restricted to 228/9 in 50 overs. Pathan took 2/33 in 7 overs and ended up as the leading wicket-taker in the tournament with 14 wickets to his name.

India's chase began poorly as they lost Sehwag and Ganguly inside the first 13 overs. Tendulkar held one end up and played some fluent strokes, but wickets kept falling at regular intervals. The Sri Lankan spin quartet of Muralitharan, Jayasuriya, Upul Chandana and Tillakaratne Dilshan - bowled with accuracy and guile, choking the Indian batsmen. Chandana was the most successful among them, taking 3/33 in 10 overs. Tendulkar was the only batsman who looked capable of negotiating the Lankan spinners, but he fell for 74 in the 40th over, leaving India at 140/7. Zaheer Khan and Harbhajan tried to revive the hopes with some big hits, but it wasn't meant to be. Sri Lanka won by 25 runs and lifted their third Asia Cup title. Atapattu was named the Man of the match for his captain's knock as well as for his astute marshalling of his resources. His predecessor Sanath Jayasuriya was chosen as the Man of the series for his 293 runs and 4 wickets over Tendulkar who had 274 runs and 12 wickets.

India had a dismal record in finals dating back to 1999 with only one solitary win in 18 previous attempts. Under Sourav Ganguly's leadership, they had won only 1 out of 13 finals. This loss was a rude wake-up call for the team that had done so well in the previous seasons. Ganguly was frank and furious, and he said it was "unacceptable" to come up short in so many finals. But it was not just the final that was disappointing. India had looked below par throughout the tournament.

The only bright spots were Irfan Pathan's brilliant form and the decent comeback of Harbhajan Singh and Ashish Nehra from injuries. Issues were aplenty: VVS Laxman's dodgy knee, persistent rustiness in most batsmen, Balaji leaking a lot of runs. Dravid too had been making more errors than usual as a keeper, some that cost the team dearly. The experiment seemed to have run its course and it was time to look for a specialist keeper-batsman and relieve Dravid of the extra burden. Tamilnadu's Dinesh Karthik had been performing well for a while and was the clear frontrunner, but he faced a strong challenge from MS Dhoni, a young and flamboyant keeper-batsman from Ranchi in Jharkhand, who had dazzled everyone with a brilliant 119 for India A against Pakistan just a few days back. Luckily, the chairman of the senior selection committee was Syed Kirmani, a great wicket-keeper himself. There was no better person to make that call while picking the Indian team for a 40-day European tour, where they would be taking part in three ODI tournaments including the ICC Champions Trophy.

The squad for the tour had no major surprises. Zaheer was injured again during the Asia cup, so he was rested. Agarkar replaced him. Rohan Gavaskar also returned to the team, while Dinesh Karthik got his much-deserved call-up as the second wicketkeeper, though Ganguly made it clear that there were no guarantees that he'd get a look-in. Another good news was that coach John Wright had agreed to a contract extension for another year, till September 2005.

The first challenge on the 40-day European tour was the hastily conjured Videocon cup, a three-way contest between India, Australia and Pakistan. The tournament was organized jointly by the BCCI, the PCB and Cricket Australia on a very short notice, and it was held in Netherlands, as part of the ICC's efforts to popularize cricket in Europe.

The tournament began with the marquee clash of India versus Pakistan, watched by a packed crowd of 10,000 passionate fans of both teams. India suffered a huge setback before the match, as Sachin Tendulkar was ruled out due to injury. Sachin had been playing with a debilitating pain in his right arm for a long time, dating back to his magnificent 241 in Sydney earlier that year. But here the pain became intolerable and he had to undergo tests. He was diagnosed with 'Tennis elbow', a serious injury that affects some athletes. Team think-tank had to make a call between Rohan Gavaskar and Dinesh Karthik and they went with Rohan to fill-in for Sachin for this big match.

Overnight rain had reduced the match to 33 overs a side contest. Ganguly won the toss and chose to bowl first, hoping to take advantage of the overcast conditions. His seamers, especially Balaji who came on as first change, did well by reducing Pakistan to 58/3 in 14 overs. But Shoaib Malik played a sensible innings of 68 off 67 balls and got good support from Yousuf, Razzaq and Moin. They took Pakistan to a respectable 192/6 in their 33 overs. India were happy to see Balaji back at his swinging best taking 3/27 in his 7 overs, though Irfan had a rare off day at the office.

India started their chase strongly taking 30 off the first 3 overs, but soon suffered a double blow. Ganguly threw away his start like Sehwag and Dravid was caught in a horrible mix-up with Laxman that resulted in his run out by Inzamam, who displayed remarkable agility in the field. This derailed India's chase and allowed the Pak spinners Afridi and Malik to apply the choke on the rest of the Indian batsmen. They bowled India out for 127 in 27 overs, winning the match by 66 runs as per the Duckworth Lewis method. This was the second match in a row where Shoaib Malik had almost single-handedly sank India, earning him the player of the match award.

This was Pakistan's 21st win in 30 ODIs under Inzamam, which showed that this was not just a young team, but a resurgent one. Bob Woolmer had joined as coach only recently, but his impact was already visible, especially in the fielding. Ganguly & co. would have to raise their collective game significantly if they hoped to overcome this Pakistan team that was on a roll in their upcoming clash in the Champions Trophy.

India's chances of still making it to the Videocon Cup final were dealt a severe blow by rain, which forced the abandonment of their match against Australia after they had put up a spirited performance in the field to keep them to 175 for 7 in 32 overs. Balaji was the pick of the bowlers, taking 3 wickets with his clever variations, and Sehwag pulled off a spectacular catch in the deep to dismiss Clarke, who had smashed 42 off 28 balls to lift Australia from a precarious position. India now needed a huge favour from Pakistan, who had to beat Australia by a big margin and earn a bonus point, to qualify for the final ahead of them.

The match was washed out by heavy rain without a single ball being bowled, which ended India's hopes and sent Australia to the final without fielding even once. The organisers proposed to reschedule the two abandoned games, and maybe push the final for a day, but Australia rightly refused, citing 3 matches in 4 days would be too hard for their players and went on to sneak a 17 runs win over Pakistan in a low-scoring final to prove they were world champions for a good reason.

India's woes worsened as Sachin and Dravid also succumbed to viral fever, joining Harbhajan and Nehra on the sick list, as the team was getting ready to embark on the English leg of their euro trip.

They all recovered from the viral fever by the time the team landed in England, but Sachin's elbow pain was still bothering him. He failed the fitness test before the first match of the NatWest Challenge trophy, which had three ODIs and came before the Champions Trophy. The team decided to stick with Rohan Gavaskar and have Dravid keep wickets, even though Dinesh Karthik was available.

There was one major change in the England side that last played against India. Nasser Hussain had bowed out and Michael Vaughan had taken over as the captain. He won the toss and chose to bowl first in the first ODI at Nottingham. India started well with Sourav and VVS adding 52 runs for the second wicket after Sehwag fell for 4. But then Alex Wharf ripped through the middle order, taking 3 wickets in 3 overs. Ganguly, Laxman and Dravid were all dismissed with only 80 runs on the board. Yuvraj was run out soon after, leaving India reeling at 89 for 5. Kaif fought hard and made 50, but he had no support from the other end. Steve Harmison cleaned up the tail and India were all out for 170 in the 44th over.

England had no trouble chasing down the low target in 32.2 overs despite a terrific effort from Balaji. Vikram Solanki, who was making a comeback to the team, scored a fluent fifty and Trescothick, Strauss and Flintoff chipped in with useful runs. Wharf was the player of the match for his superb spell of 3 for 30 in 8 overs.

The second match was at the Oval. Ganguly chose to bowl first after winning the toss. England had lost 11 matches in a row when batting first and they looked in trouble again when they slipped from 71 for no loss to 105 for 4 in 20 overs thanks to Bhajji and Sehwag making up for the poor showing of the seam trio. But Flintoff and Collingwood turned things around with a brilliant 174-run partnership in the next 27 overs. Flintoff fell for 99 hitting 9 fours and 4 sixes, while Collingwood stayed unbeaten on 79 off 85 balls. Jones added some quick runs and England finished on 307 for 5. Harbhajan was the most economical bowler, giving away only 14 runs in 10 overs and taking 2 wickets. Sehwag also took 2 wickets, while the seamers had a bad day.

India's chase started badly as they lost both their openers for 10 runs. Laxman and Kaif steadied the innings with a 89-run stand, but Laxman yet again threw his wicket away in the thirties. Dravid's low run of scores continued as he was out for 1. Kaif fought on with a gritty 50, but the rest of the batsmen failed to build on their starts. Yuvraj and Rohan Gavaskar got out cheaply and the tailenders tried to hit some big shots, but it was not enough. India were bowled out for 237 in the 47th over with Darren Gough, fuelled by the prospect of becoming the first English bowler to 200 ODI wickets, taking a 4-fer. England broke their 11-match run of defeats after batting first with an emphatic 70 run victory over India to clinch the NatWest challenge 2-0 with one game still to go. Freddie Flintoff was the player of the match, resuming his rivalry with Sourav Ganguly's India.

With nothing but pride to fight for in the third and final match at Lords, India batted first after winning the toss, but were again haunted by the absence of Sachin Tendulkar in the top order as they collapsed to 48 for 3 in 14 overs. The captain and his deputy then stepped up and revived innings with a 93-run stand. Ganguly led from the front with a fabulous innings of 90, smashing 5 fours and 3 sixes, before he fell to Steve Harmison, who was the outstanding English bowler. Yuvraj fell cheaply and Dinesh Karthik too had a forgettable debut with the bat becoming the fourth victim of a fiery Harmison for just 1 run. Dravid was out for a sluggish 52 in the 46th over and India were bundled out for 204 in 49.3 overs. Harmison was the pick of the English bowlers with 4 scalps while veteran Darren Gough, in the sunset of his career, etched his name in history as the first English bowler to reach 200 ODI wickets.

It was a modest target, but India bowled and fielded out of their collective skins to bowl out England for 181 and win the match by 23 runs and salvage some pride. The two left-arm seamers, Pathan and Nehra finally delivered in the series, sharing 5 wickets between them. Bhajji also bowled a splendid spell of 3 for 28 in the middle overs to wreck England. Debutant Dinesh Karthik redeemed himself with the gloves, taking a sharp catch and a brilliant stumping to dismiss Vaughan, who crawled to 74. Sourav Ganguly was the player of the match for his captain's knock, while Steve Harmison was the player of the series.

In theory, India should have been well-prepared for the Champions trophy having played two tournaments in English conditions, but they were far from it. They were still rusty after a long break and out of form. Most worrying was Sehwag who had gone from being the toast of the country to woefully out of form in a matter of months. To make matters worse, players were hit by injury and health concerns. India received the biggest blow when Sachin Tendulkar was ruled out of the Champions trophy because his tennis elbow injury turned out to be more serious than previously thought. Balaji was also ruled out due to an abdominal injury, forcing the team management to seek replacements for both. The selectors wanted Dinesh Mongia, who was in good form in county cricket, to fill in for Sachin, but they were overruled by the office of the BCCI President who insisted that Rohan Gavaskar, who was already with the team, be persisted with. Amit Bhandari, who last played for India in the VB trophy last year, was flown in as Balaji's replacement.

All in all, the Indian cricket team was in disarray before the start of the big tournament. They had to face several challenges and setbacks before they even stepped onto the field.

In the midst of such gloom, Rahul Dravid and Irfan Pathan brought some cheer to the struggling Indian team by winning big at the inaugural ICC Awards. The awards ceremony, dubbed as the 'Cricket Oscars', was held at Alexandra Palace in London and was a glittering affair. Dravid won the coveted Sir Garfield Sobers 'Player of the Year' trophy and was named as the best Test player, pipping the likes of Hayden, Harmison and Muralitharan. Meanwhile, Pathan was named the 'Emerging Player of the Year', edging out Yasir Hameed and Michael Clarke. Dravid's impressive performance included scoring 1241 runs in 9 Tests at an average of 95.46; while Pathan took 16 wickets in 5 tests and 36 wickets in 18 ODIs. They were the only Indians to win individual awards, as Sachin Tendulkar narrowly lost out to Freddie Flintoff in the 'ODI player of the year' category. However, Tendulkar and Sehwag both made it to the one-day team of the year.

Champions Trophy 2004

Team India's opening match in the 'Mini World cup' was against Kenya at the picturesque Rose Bowl in Southampton. Kenya captain Steve Tikolo won the toss and decided to bowl first, pleasing the mostly Indian crowd who wanted to see their heroes bat for 50 overs. Sehwag failed to get a big score, but Ganguly and Laxman knuckled down on a tricky pitch. To their immense credit, the Kenyan bowlers bowled well, and boundaries were hard to come by in the first 20 odd overs. But Ganguly upped the ante before he fell for 90, trying to steer Martin Suji to third man. He missed out on his fourth hundred in a row against Kenya, and so did Laxman, who was stumped for 79 after charging at Tikolo. But they had laid the platform and the Indian innings ended with a bang. Kaif showed his power-hitting skills and the newly crowned Test player of the year Dravid proved his versatility in one-dayers as well.

Dravid (30 off 16 balls) and Kaif (49 off 29) smashed the Kenyan attack in a 77-run stand that came in just 41 balls, and took India to 290. The match was over as a contest, as Kenya had no hope of chasing such a huge total. They lost 3 wickets for 21 runs in 9 overs. Pathan and Harbhajan shared 5 wickets between them. Only Maurice Ouma, a young debutant, batted with some sense, but he could not do much, as Kenya finished on 192 for 7 in 50 overs, losing by 98 runs. Sourav Ganguly was the player of the match for his superb 90, two catches and astute captaincy. It was his second player of the match award in a row.

Although it was only Kenya, India's impressive performance with both bat and ball gave them a much-needed confidence boost ahead of their match against Pakistan. The stage was set for another thrilling encounter between two of the biggest rivals in cricket.

The tournament, which had been a snooze fest so far, finally came to life as India and Pakistan clashed at Birmingham in front of a sea of 20,000 passionate fans from both sides. The game lived up to its billing as the biggest spectacle in world cricket: it had the kind of drama and twists that low-scoring matches are known to provide sometimes. India, who were put in to bat, saw their batsmen crumble at 28 for 3, which worsened to 106 for 6 by the 34th over. But a defiant 67 from vice-captain Rahul Dravid, which started in stoic resistance and ended in aggression - he glared back at Shoaib Akhtar even giving him a piece of his mind - offered a glimmer of hope, as did some fearless hitting by the unpredictable Agarkar who scored 47 in 50 balls with 3 fours and a six. Rana Naved and Shoaib Akhtar, who came on as fourth-change claimed 4 wickets apiece.

Even a target of 201 was tricky under these conditions, and Irfan Pathan kept India in the hunt, swinging the ball with great skill to reduce Pakistan to 27 for 3 by the 11th over. Mainstays Inzamam and Yousuf Youhana steadied the ship with a stand of 75. When he went past 23, Inzamam became only the second batsman in the history of ODI cricket to go past 10,000 runs, after Sachin. India, however, kept chipping away and at 152 for 6 at the end of the 40th over, the match was on a knife's edge. Then came Shahid Afridi, who was held back until No. 8, to thump two massive sixes, that too off Pathan no less, providing the needed impetus for the final push. Player of the match, the ice-cool Youhana played flawlessly despite cramps throughout his unbeaten 81 guiding Pakistan to a win with 4 balls to spare. India, on the other hand, had to cope with the humiliation of being dumped out of the tournament by their arch-rivals, who had beaten them in Sri Lanka, Holland and now England in the space of 3 months.

In a pleasant surprise, Brian Lara-led West Indies defied the odds and won the Champions trophy, proving right the adage that cricket is indeed a game of glorious uncertainties.

A heartbroken Team India returned home to get ready for a tough test cricket season, starting with the much-awaited Border-Gavaskar trophy against Australia. Seeing how the Aussies always seemed to bring out the best in this team, coach John Wright and the captain Sourav Ganguly hoped that this series would help the Indian team bounce back from their recent slump.

Meanwhile Jagmohan Dalmiya's term as the BCCI President had come to an end, but he still pulled the strings in Indian cricket. He made sure his loyalist Ranbir Singh Mahendra beat the influential Sharad Pawar in the election to become the 27th president of BCCI. Pawar claimed the election was rigged, but did not go to court. He chose to bide his time, which was not far away.

The Indian team prepared for the big showdown by playing a four-day match against India A, where they were made to work hard for a win. S. Sriram, D. Jadhav and Mohammad Kaif scored centuries for India A, while Yuvraj and Sehwag scored match-winning centuries in the fourth innings for India seniors. Contenders Gautam Gambhir and MS Dhoni failed to impress the selectors with their batting, though Dhoni did well behind the stumps.

The selectors announced the squad for the first two tests, with Kaif and Murali Kartik earning their test recalls and Ajit Agarkar getting the nod over Nehra due to his better record against Australia and a slight injury to Nehra. Sachin Tendulkar, who was still recovering from tennis elbow, was also included in the 15-man squad, hoping that he would be fit for the second if not the first test.

Australians too had a good practice game against Mumbai, with Langer scoring a century and Hayden, Martyn and Gilchrist spending some valuable time in the middle. McGrath also took 4 wickets. There was no notable performance from Mumbai.

The first test match was played on a dry and cracked pitch in Bangalore that promised plenty of turn and reverse swing throughout the match, making it a challenging contest for both teams.

Adam Gilchrist, who took over as captain from Ponting after the latter suffered a thumb injury during the Champions Trophy semi-final, won the toss and chose to bat first, hoping to make use of the conditions. However, they soon ran into trouble at 149 for 4, as India's spinners wreaked havoc. That's when Michael Clarke made a sensational debut, scoring 151 with 18 fours and 4 sixes. He played with audacity and confidence, especially against the spinners of the calibre of Kumble and Harbhajan. He was well supported by Simon Katich, who made 81, and Gilchrist, who smashed 104 off 109 balls, his 11th test hundred. Australia piled up 474, despite Harbhajan Singh's 5-wicket haul.

India's response was marred by a couple of poor umpiring decisions and superb bowling by McGrath and Kasprowicz, who exploited the reverse swing and cut on offer. Warnie too chipped in with the most prized wicket for Australia, that of VVS Laxman whom he bowled for the first and only time in his career with an absolute beauty. Only Parthiv Patel, increasingly under pressure for his poor showing behind the wicket, showed some fight with a determined 46, but India were bowled out for 246, falling short of the follow-on target. With memories of Kolkata 2001 still fresh in their collective psyche, Australia decided not to enforce it, and extended their lead to 456 with a second-innings total of 228, despite another excellent effort from Bhajji who took 6 for 78 in 30 overs - his sixth successive five-wicket haul against Australia in home tests.

India's chase was doomed from the start, when Sehwag was wrongly given out lbw by Billy Bowden. Only Irfan Pathan, who scored his maiden test fifty, and Harbhajan delayed the inevitable. Australia eventually dismissed India for 239, giving them a comprehensive victory and a 1-0 lead in the series.

The match was not without controversy, with several umpiring decisions going against India, with Billy Bowden himself admitting to being wrong about the Sehwag dismissal in the second inning. However, it was a roller-coaster ride of emotions, with Australia coming out on top by 217 runs, thanks to some memorable performances by Clarke, Gilchrist and McGrath. The match shall also be remembered for Anil Kumble becoming only the ninth bowler overall and the third spinner to 400 test wickets.

The action shifted from Bangalore to Chennai for the second test of the series, with the best batsmen from both sides - Sachin Tendulkar and Ricky Ponting - still missing from action. Indian captain had been dropping hints for some time now, and he finally made the bold move of dropping the struggling Aakash Chopra to fit-in Yuvraj Singh as a test opener. Perhaps inspired by the success of Sehwag's transformation from a middle-order batsman to a dashing opener, Ganguly was hoping that Yuvraj would provide the same kind of fireworks at the top of the order.

The match was played on a dry and dusty Chepauk pitch that favoured the spinners. Australia, who won the toss and opted to bat first, looked in control at 189/2, with Langer and Hayden both scoring half-centuries. But then Anil Kumble, India's ace spinner, turned the game on its head with a sensational spell of 7/48 in just 17 overs. He ripped through the Australian batting line-up, bowling with accuracy and guile. He was well supported by Harbhajan, who took 2 wickets. Australia lost their last 8 wickets for just 46 runs, and were bowled out for 235.

India's response was spearheaded by Virender Sehwag, who roared back to form with a spectacular knock of 155, laced with 21 boundaries. He tore apart the Australian bowlers, especially Shane Warne, whom he hit for three consecutive fours in one over. Dravid and VVS fell cheaply, but Kaif and Parthiv Patel showed a lot of determination and added 102 runs for the seventh wicket, both scoring solid fifties. India scored 376, taking a lead of

141 runs. Warne, despite being thrashed by Sehwag, still managed to take 6 wickets, his best bowling figures on Indian soil.

Australia fought back in their second innings, with Australian cricket's new man for a crisis - Damien Martyn scoring a sublime century against a rampaging Kumble who bagged another 6-fer to take his match tally to 13 wickets. Martyn batted with patience and poise, and stitched together useful partnerships with Clarke, Lehmann and Gillespie. He scored 104, his eighth hundred in tests and helped Australia reach 369, setting India a target of 229 to win.

It wouldn't have been easy against a resurgent Warne on a fifth day Chennai wicket, but India were up for the challenge as they had Sehwag, Dravid and VVS - all masterful players of spin - in their ranks. However, they did not get a chance to bat, as rain played spoilsport and washed out the entire fifth day's play. The match that was shaping up as another Chepauk classic ended in a damp squib, leaving the Indian fans and players heartbroken. India had bounced back from a defeat in the first match with a strong showing in the second, and were on the verge of levelling the series. However, they had to settle for a draw. Anil Kumble was the player of the match for his 13-wicket haul.

In a major setback, Irfan Pathan was ruled out from the third test due to a side strain.

Biggest headache for the Indian team, however, was Parthiv Patel's poor wicketkeeping, which had been a cause of worry for some time. The young lad had impressed with his batting, but his glove work had gone from bad to worse in recent times. He dropped a crucial catch of Martyn when he hadn't yet opened his account, and Martyn made India pay by scoring 104 runs. Despite the growing clamour for his replacement, Sourav Ganguly backed him to bounce back in the next test at Nagpur.

After a mid-series mini break, both teams assembled at the VCA stadium in Nagpur for the third test.

The build-up to the match saw a lot of controversy and speculation, as the pitch turned out to be a green top, much to the surprise of many. The curator had reportedly been instructed by someone in the BCCI to prepare such a track, which would suit the Australian pace attack more than the Indian spinners. Many felt that this was a suicidal move by the hosts, who were already trailing 1-0 in the series and were going into this match without their spearhead Irfan Pathan who could have exploited the wicket.

Indian team management asked the curator to remove the grass from the wicket on the eve of the match but the curator stuck to his guns and refused. To add to the drama, captain Sourav Ganguly and Harbhajan Singh pulled out of the match on the morning of the match, citing a thigh injury and gastroenteritis respectively. This raised many eyebrows, as some in the media suspected that it was more a case of "greentrackitis" and those two were not keen to play on such a pitch. This seemed a bit far-fetched as both Ganguly and Harbhajan were not ones to back down from a challenge.

Agarkar filled-in for Irfan Pathan, left arm spinner Murali Kartik came in for Harbhajan, Yuvraj Singh replaced Ganguly in the playing XI and Rahul Dravid took over the captaincy. In the midst of this bleak situation, Team India received a welcome boost from the long-awaited comeback of their Talisman, Sachin Tendulkar, whose availability was the other hot topic of discussion ahead of this match.

For a third game in a row, Australia elected to bat first with Martyn continuing his rich vein of form by scoring his second consecutive century (114) and Michael Clarke contributing 91. India's bowlers struggled on the green track and could only manage to dismiss the visitors for 398 runs. The batsmen fared even worse, as they were bowled out for a paltry 185 runs with only Mohammad Kaif showing some steel. Jason Gillespie was the pick of the bowlers with 5 wickets, while Glenn McGrath chipped in with 3.

The second half of the game would be just as one-sided. Australia declared on 329/5 in their second innings, setting India an imposing target of 543 runs. Simon Katich missed out on a much deserved hundred by just 1 run, Damien Martyn fell short of what would have been his third hundred in three innings by 3 runs and Michael Clarke belted out a highly entertaining unbeaten 73 as the Aussies took the attack to the Indian bowlers. India's bowlers struggled to make any inroads with Agarkar being a serious disappointment on a green track. Australia sensed history in the making and unleashed their bowling attack on India's batsmen. Jason Gillespie, Glenn McGrath and Shane Warne shared 9 wickets among them in India's second innings, including that of Tendulkar who had a disappointing comeback.

Sehwag waged a lone battle with a valiant 58 but it was not enough to stop Australia from achieving their first series win in India since 1969-70; thereby conquering the 'Final Frontier' with a clinical 342-run win. Adam Gilchrist, the stand-in captain, had accomplished what Kim Hughes, Alan Border, Mark Taylor and Steven Waugh - four times - had failed to do, by guiding Australia to the promised land. Damien Martyn was named the player of the match for his superlative batting. It was a historic moment for Australian cricket and a bitter pill to swallow for Indian fans.

India, desperate to restore some pride by winning the last test, made a couple of long-awaited changes to their playing eleven for the fourth test to be played at the historic Wankhede stadium. Left-handed opening batsman from Delhi Gautam Gambhir from Delhi and the Tamil Nadu wicket-keeper Dinesh Karthik came in for their test debuts in place of Aakash Chopra and Parthiv Patel, who had both lost form and all confidence. Harbhajan returned for Agarkar. Sourav Ganguly had failed to recover in time so Rahul Dravid carried on as the stand-in skipper. Meanwhile, Australia had to do without Warne, who broke his right thumb batting in the nets on the eve of the match. Ricky Ponting returned to lead the side after missing the first three games through injury.

India won their first toss of the series, electing to bat first. The first day was washed out after only 34 balls were bowled, with India losing 2 wickets for 22 runs. The second day saw India collapse to 104 all out, with only Rahul Dravid (31*) showing some fight. Jason Gillespie was the main destroyer with 4 for 29, while Nathan Hauritz, the rookie off-spinner who replaced the injured Shane Warne, took 3 for 16.

Australia then took a commanding lead of 99 runs, thanks to Damien Martyn's 55 and some useful contributions from the lower order. Martyn played the spinners with confidence and skill, while the others chipped in with vital runs. India's spinners, led by the great Anil Kumble - who took another 5-for to finish yet another series as the top wicket-taker - and Murali Kartik, shared 8 wickets, but they could not prevent Australia from gaining a substantial advantage.

India fought back in their second innings, with Sachin Tendulkar (55) and VVS Laxman (69) putting on an invaluable 91 for the fourth wicket. Tendulkar and Laxman, promoted to one down, found their form for the first time in the series and played some trademark shots on a difficult wicket where even a part-timer like Clarke was making the ball talk.

India managed 205 in their second innings and set Australia a modest target of 107, but it proved to be too much for the visitors. Kartik and Harbhajan ripped through the Australian batting line-up, taking 7 wickets between them. Kartik bowled with accuracy and variation, while Harbhajan extracted turn and bounce to claim yet another 5-fer against the Aussies. Michael Clarke, who had taken 6 wickets for just 9 runs with his part-time spin in India's second innings, was bamboozled by Kartik's arm ball and bowled for a duck. Adam Gilchrist swept to deep square leg and was caught by Zaheer Khan for 4. Glenn McGrath edged to slip where Sehwag took a sharp catch to seal India's victory by just 13 runs. The adjudicators made a great choice to award the player of the match to Murali Kartik, who outshone even the great Anil Kumble and Harbhajan in this match.

The match was a fitting farewell for David Shepherd, the veteran English umpire who retired after this game. He was given a guard of honour by both teams and received a standing ovation from the crowd. The match was marred by rain, bad light and poor floodlighting, but it produced a dramatic finish that left the fans on the edge of their seats. Damien Martyn was named the Man of the series for his 444 runs at an average of 55.50. He scored two centuries and two fifties in four matches and was the most consistent batsman on either side.

The wicket for this match came in for a lot of criticism from both captains as well as experts, with even then-Mumbai Cricket Association president and former India great Dilip Vengsarkar describing it as unsuitable for test cricket. As many as 40 wickets fell in a little over two days' time with even a part-timer like Clarke looking as unplayable as Muralitharan in his pomp.

That said, this historic series win by Australia was the culmination of three years of painstaking preparation and meticulous planning by the team think-tank and the coaching staff led by John Buchanan. As Rahul Dravid generously accepted in the post-match press conference, Australians were the worthy winners. With the final frontier conquered, the set was complete for Australia's golden generation - Hayden, Langer, Ponting, Martyn, Gilly, Mcgrath, Warne, Gillespie and the indefatigable Kasprovicz. They had earned their place among the all-time great teams such as Sir Don Bradman's Australia of the 1930s and Clive Lloyd's West Indies of the late 70s-80s.

India, on the other hand, had a lot of soul searching to do before their next big assignment, a two-test home series against the Proteas.

But before that, the Men in Blue had to square off against Pakistan in a one-off one day international, organised by the BCCI as part of its platinum jubilee celebrations. The match was the brainchild of Jagmohan Dalmiya and was to be played at his home turf, the iconic Eden Gardens.

Selectors made one change to the Indian team, dropping Rohan Gavaskar and giving Sridharan Sriram his first call-up in 4 years. Sourav Ganguly and Irfan Pathan, who had both missed the last two tests against Australia due to injuries, passed the fitness test and were ready to take part in the one-off affair. Selectors also announced Board president XI side to play the visiting South Africans in their only tour game before the first test. Suresh Raina was the one name to watch out for, along with strong contenders Gambhir and Dhoni, in a team otherwise full of India discards.

India batted first and posted 292 for 6, bookended by two brilliant half-centuries - one at the start of the innings by Sehwag, who smashed 53 off 65 balls with 6 fours and 2 sixes, and the other towards the end by Yuvraj, who blazed 78 off just 62 balls with 10 fours and 2 sixes. Laxman and Ganguly also contributed valuable forties although Ganguly's was a bit slow perhaps owing to his lack of match fitness. Afridi bowled a tight spell in the middle and took a couple wickets, while Shoaib, Rana Naved and Razzaq all chipped in with a wicket each.

Pakistan's chase got off to a shaky start as they lost Younis Khan, who was promoted to open, for a duck in the fourth over. However, Salman Butt and Shoaib Malik revived Pakistan with a 113-run stand for the second wicket at a brisk pace. Malik continued his terrific run against India with another fluent knock of 61 off just 55 balls with 5 fours and 2 sixes, before he fell to Sehwag trying to clear the boundary. India sensed an opening, but the great Inzamam slammed it shut with another nonchalant innings of 75, while Salman Butt reached his maiden ODI century and carried his bat to see his team home with 6 wickets and 6 balls to spare. He was declared the man of the match. Ashish Nehra took a couple of wickets, but was expensive.

This was India's fourth consecutive loss against their arch rivals, and the wins at Centurion and in Pakistan series seemed like a distant memory for the fans now.

To add insult to injury, India's captain was banned for two test matches by the match referee Sir Clive Lloyd for slow over-rates. This meant that Ganguly, who had already missed the last two Tests against Australia due to injury, would also miss both the tests against South Africa. BCCI decided to appeal to the ICC against this decision, and said they would only name a replacement if the appeal failed. However, the ICC's appeals commissioner Tim Castle realised that the appeal could not be heard before the first Test, which was too late. So he cleared Ganguly to play the first test.

The upcoming two-test series presented a fantastic opportunity for both the hosts and the visitors to reverse a slump in form and start afresh.

Proteas started off the tour with a hard-earned draw against the Indian board President XI side led by Sairaj Bahutule who shone with the ball along with Dinesh Mongia who slammed a handsome 148. MS Dhoni did his chances no harm with another decent outing with both bat and gloves.

D. Jadhav and SS Das made way for the return of Sourav Ganguly and Irfan Pathan for the first test played at the Green Park stadium in Kanpur.

The match turned out to be a dull draw because of the absolutely lifeless pitch. Two contrasting innings stood out however. Batting first after winning the toss, Andrew Hall - asked to open for the first time at any level by coach Ray Jennings - ground out a dour 163. Hall batted for almost 10 hours, the fourth-longest by a South African, his marathon effort virtually ruling out a defeat for his side. He got some support from de Bruyn, who made a solid 83 on debut. Kumble tried hard to break through with a 6-wicket haul, but the pitch was too dead for him to skittle out the opposition.

When South Africa finally declared their first innings at 510/9 on the third morning, Sehwag tore into their bowling with a vengeance. He got a life on 29, and made them pay, stroking a dazzling 164 studded with 24 boundaries and a couple of sixes. Gambhir, his Delhi teammate, playing only his second test, matched him stroke for stroke with a stylish 96, as they added 218 for the first wicket. It was India's best opening stand in 49 years. Sehwag carried on after Gambhir fell, smoking 46 in 3 overs after lunch on the fourth day. But once Sehwag was out, India collapsed. Ntini bowled with fire and took 3 wickets as did Hall, giving South Africa a slender lead of 44 runs.

The fifth day was a formality, as South Africa batted out time. Murali Kartik and Harbhajan bowled well, but there was no excitement. The only drama came when a man with a gun was caught near the boundary. He turned out to be the son of the Kanpur Cricket Association president, and claimed it was normal to carry a gun there. The police disagreed, and took him away. It was a bizarre end to a highly mediocre game.

Sourav Ganguly got a reprieve from the ICC, who lifted his two-match ban and allowed him to play the second Test against South Africa in Kolkata. He had a lot to prove in the series decider at his home ground, as India's home record, which was already dented by the loss to Australia earlier in the season, was now under threat from Graeme Smith-Ray Jennings' underdogs, who would be content with a draw. It was a tense situation for the whole Indian team, but especially for Ganguly, who faced immense pressure to justify his position both as a captain as well as a player, as it had been a year - Brisbane in December 2003 - since his batting had a major effect on a test match. India needed nothing less than a win.

Graeme Smith won the toss and decided to bat first, but he was soon regretting his decision. Pathan, who replaced Kartik as the third seamer, struck with his second ball, getting Smith caught behind for a duck. Zaheer then removed Hall, the centurion from the previous match, and South Africa were in trouble at 21 for 2. They recovered thanks to a century stand between the two Jacques - Kallis, who made a superb 121, and Rudolph, who chipped in with 61. Hashim Amla, on debut, showed some promise with 24, but South Africa were bowled out for 305, well below par on a flat pitch. The Baroda firm of Pathan and Zaheer Khan shared 6 wickets, while Ganguly got the big one of Kallis, who shouldered arms to a straight one on the second morning.

As expected, India took the first innings lead which was built upon the brilliance of Sehwag, who smashed 88 off 95 balls with 11 fours and 2 sixes, and the resilience of Dravid, who made 80 off 247 balls. Sehwag was in a league of his own, hitting Ontong for 19 in an over and playing some breathtaking shots. Ntini finally got him with a bouncer, but by then he had set up India's advantage. The Wall was less fluent, but more determined, as he battled against Ntini and co., who bowled with fire and skill. Ganguly and Dinesh Karthik too contributed valuable forties.

South Africa fought hard in the second innings, with Smith leading from the front with a classy 71 before falling to a superb delivery from Harbhajan. But once Kallis was caught and bowled by Harbhajan on the final day, the end was near. Kumble joined Kapil Dev as India's highest Test wicket-taker, with 434 scalps, as he finished off the tail but the real hero was Harbhajan Singh, who continued his love-affair with the Eden Gardens, bagging 7 for 87 to bowl out South Africa for 222. India chased down the paltry target of 117 with ease, despite losing Sehwag early. Bhajji was named the player of the match while Sehwag walked away with the player of the series.

It was a satisfying win for Ganguly & co. who were under immense pressure before the match but managed to end a difficult home season on a winning note by clinching the series 1-0.

India's last assignment of the season was a short tour to Bangladesh, where they would play two tests and three ODIs. Syed Kirmani's term as the chairman of selection panel had come to an end and he was replaced by another one of India's finest glove men, Kiran More. More, like Kirmani, valued the role of a specialist keeper. He decided to use the low-key Bangladesh tour as a chance to try out another exciting wicketkeeping prospect - MS Dhoni, the long-haired Jharkhand player who had been very impressive of late. Dhoni was picked for the ODIs, while Dinesh Karthik kept his place for the tests.

The first test at Dhaka turned out to be a one-sided affair. The tone was set on the first day, when India won the toss and elected to field. Pathan, the left-arm seamer, produced a sensational spell of swing bowling, as he reduced Bangladesh to 50 for 5 in no time. He finished with 6 for 51, his best figures in tests, as Bangladesh were bowled out for 184. Only Mohammad Ashraful showed some resistance, scoring an unbeaten 60. Another highlight of the first day was Anil Kumble overtaking the great Kapil Dev as India's highest wicket-taker in tests with his 435th scalp, Mohammad Rafique whom he trapped leg before wicket. What made Kumble's feat even more remarkable was the fact that he achieved this record in 40 fewer tests than Kapil!

India replied strongly, reaching 348 for 7 at stumps on the second day. Tendulkar was the star of the show, scoring his 34th Test hundred and drawing level with his hero Sunil Gavaskar as test cricket's most prolific centurion. He was dropped thrice before reaching 50, but made the most of his chances and batted with authority and grace. He was well supported by Sourav Ganguly who contributed 71 and added 164 for the fourth wicket, rebuilding the innings from 68 for 3.

The third day belonged to Tendulkar and Zaheer Khan, who added a record 133 runs for the tenth wicket. Tendulkar went on to score his fourth double hundred in tests, ending with an unbeaten 248, his highest score in tests. He faced 379 balls and hit 35 fours in his marathon innings, which lasted for more than 9 hours. But more than the numbers, it was the fact that he was able to bat so long that came as a major relief to himself as well as all true connoisseurs of the game. Tennis elbow was still there but the finest batsman of his age had found a way around it and was going nowhere anytime soon. Zaheer played a remarkable cameo, smashing 75 off 115 balls with 8 fours and 4 sixes. It was the highest score by a No. 11 batsman in tests, and also Zaheer's maiden test fifty. India declared their innings at 526, a lead of 342 runs.

Bangladesh fared no better in their second innings, as they collapsed to 202 all out. Pathan was again the chief tormentor, taking 5 for 45 and completing his first 10-wicket haul in tests. He was ably assisted by Kumble who chipped in with a couple of wickets. Nafis Iqbal (54) and Manjural Islam Rana (69) offered some fight for Bangladesh, but it was too little too late.

The match ended on the fourth day, when Pathan had Mashrafe Mortaza caught behind to seal India's emphatic victory by an innings and 140 runs and walk away with the player of the match award for his 11 wickets in the match.

Second test at Chittagong followed a similar script, only difference being India batted first after winning the toss. They lost Sehwag early, but Gautam Gambhir and Rahul Dravid steadied the ship with a massive partnership of 259 for the second wicket. Gambhir scored his maiden test hundred, a fluent 139, while Dravid returned to form with a solid 160, becoming the first batsman to score a century in all ten test-playing countries. Tendulkar was again looking good but fell on 36 to Mashrafe Mortaza, who was the only Bangladeshi bowler to trouble the Indians. Sourav Ganguly chipped in with a valuable 88, as India finished their innings at 540.

Bangladesh were in trouble at 54 for 3, before Ashraful lit up the stadium with a scintillating knock of 158 not out. He took on the Indian attack with flair and aggression, hitting 24 fours and 3 sixes in his 194-ball innings. He became the highest scorer for Bangladesh in tests, surpassing Aminul Islam's 145 in their inaugural test against India. But he received no support from the other end, as Bangladesh fell short of the follow-on target by 8 runs. Kumble was the pick of the Indian bowlers, taking 4 for 75 while Irfan and Zaheer picked a couple each.

India enforced the follow-on and Pathan ran through the Bangladeshi batting again, taking 5 for 32 in the second innings. Harbhajan Singh too chipped in with a couple of wickets but got reported for 'suspect action' by match referee Chris broad. Bangladesh were bundled out for 124, losing by an innings and 83 runs as Indian completed a 2-0 clean sweep over the hosts. Ashraful was named the player of the match while Irfan Pathan won the player of the series for his staggering 18 wickets in just 2 matches.

It was a series that witnessed some memorable individual performances by the likes of Pathan, Kumble, Tendulkar, Gambhir, Dravid and Ashraful but also one that highlighted the huge gulf between the two sides when it came to Tests. The three-match ODI series that followed was expected to be more evenly contested, as Bangladesh were more of a challenge in the shorter format.

The series was a chance for India to experiment with their reserves, as the team think-tank decided to give opportunities to the youngsters. VVS Laxman was unhappy to be 'rested' for the series, while other key players like Sehwag, Tendulkar, Kumble and more were also rotated out of the playing eleven during the three games. India fielded some fresh faces like Joginder Sharma, MS Dhoni and others.

Series got underway with the first match at Chattogram. After being put in to bat, India recovered from a shaky start, thanks to a 128-run stand for the fourth wicket between Rahul Dravid and Mohammad Kaif, who both scored patient fifties. India posted a competitive total of 245, as Bangladesh missed their strike bowler Mashrafe Mortaza.

Bangladesh never looked like chasing down the target, as they batted with a defensive mindset. Habibul Bashar, the captain, played an inconsequential knock of 65, consuming 96 balls and ignoring the required run-rate. He was dismissed in the 41st over, with Bangladesh still needing 90 runs from 54 balls. Khaled Mashud provided some late urgency with a frenetic 50, but it was too little too late. Bangladesh finished on 234 for eight, falling short by 11 runs. Sridharan Sriram picked 3 wickets with his part-time off spin as India cruised to a comfortable 11-run win despite resting some of their key players like Sehwag, Kumble and Zaheer Khan. Mohammad Kaif who top-scored with 80 was adjudged the player of the match.

The match also marked the debut of MS Dhoni, who had a forgettable outing. He was run out for a duck on the very first ball he faced. Not even the most astute cricket pundits could have foreseen the tectonic shift this seemingly ordinary talent would bring about in world cricket in the not-so-distant future.

The two teams met in Dhaka for the second match. Bangladesh were in trouble at 88 for five, after being put in to bat by India, who were missing their stars like Tendulkar, Dravid, Harbhajan and Pathan. But Aftab Ahmed played a gem of an innings, scoring 67 off 62 balls with 5 fours and a six. Mortaza played an invaluable late cameo of 31 as Bangladesh reached 229 for 9 in their 50 overs, giving themselves something to defend.

India's chase started poorly, as they lost their top three batsmen for 39 runs. Sridharan Sriram tried to steady the innings with a slow 57, but he consumed 91 balls for it and put pressure on the other batsmen. Dhoni eased some of it with a couple of good blows but then threw away his wicket with a reckless shot. Mohammad Kaif hustled for 49, but his run out in the 42nd over triggered a collapse. India lost their last six wickets for 34 runs, and were bowled out for 214 in the final over. Bangladesh's bowlers and fielders showed tremendous spirit and skill, as they kept India on a tight leash throughout. Mashrafe Mortaza, Tapas Baishya, Khaled Mahmud and Mohammad Rafique all took two wickets each. Mortaza was named the player of the match for his inspired all-round performance.

It was a historic day for Bangladesh cricket, as it was their first ever win at home, first against India and only their third against a test-playing nation, the other two being Pak and Zimbabwe. The jubilant crowd of 40,000 at Bangbandhu stadium witnessed a remarkable come-from-behind victory but the moment was overshadowed by the tragic events of the Asian tsunami, which devastated many parts of the continent. The result was barely noticed by the rest of the world, but it was still a much awaited and deserved moment of pride and glory for the Bangla tigers and their loyal fans.

Peeved by the humiliating defeat and faced with a real prospect of an ignominious series loss against low-ranked Bangladesh, India decided to take no chances and fielded a near full-strength eleven for the series decider at Dhaka. Batting first after winning the toss, Sehwag and Tendulkar unleashed their fury on the Bangladeshi bowlers, smashing 70 and 47 respectively in quick time. They added 106 for the first wicket in 14 overs, setting the tone for a big score. The captain and vice-captain then built upon that foundation, playing sensibly and punishing the bad balls. Both Ganguly and Dravid scored fifties and put on 98 for the third wicket in 19 overs, before falling in quick succession. But the real carnage came from Yuvraj Singh, who blasted a breathtaking 69 off just 32 balls, with 8 fours and 3 sixes. He tore apart the Bangladeshi attack before falling with 3 balls to go. Dhoni faced 2 of those and muscled a six to take India to a formidable 348 for 5.

Bangladesh had no option but to go for broke, but they were up against a clinical Indian bowling unit. Rajin Saleh played a gutsy knock of 82, but he got no support from the other end as Agarkar and Zak shared 3 top order wickets between them. Bangladesh kept losing wickets at regular intervals, 4 of those to the mystery spin of Tendulkar and never really threatened to chase down the target. They were eventually bowled out for 257 in the 47th over, giving India a comfortable win by 91 runs. Dhoni delivered his most assured performance behind the wicket in the three games he had kept so far, with 5 dismissals in the match. Sehwag was chosen as the player of the match over Sachin while Mohammad Kaif was the unanimous choice for the player of the series for his consistent batting.

It was a convincing performance by India, who showed their class and character after a shocking upset. They won the series 2-1 to end a mixed bag kind of year on a winning note.

2005

Rematch with the arch-rival

The team enjoyed a much-needed extended break from new year to mid-February, before gearing up for the Challenger trophy - a prestigious domestic one-day tournament that served as a warm-up for the much-awaited home series against Pakistan.

Rahul Dravid led India A to victory in the Challenger trophy, defeating India seniors led by Ganguly in the final. Dravid's captaincy credentials were enhanced by his performance. Another performer who strengthened his case was Dhoni, who belted out a blistering hundred under Ganguly's watch in an earlier game.

Pakistan arrived in India without their spearhead Shoaib Akhtar, who had pulled out of the test series citing injury as the official reason. Real reason, however, was his long simmering feud with the Inzamam-ul-Haq-Bob Woolmer management. A relatively inexperienced Pakistan began their tour with a three-day practice match against an Indian Board President's XI side led by Kaif, who had been inexplicably dropped from the first two tests of the series. The match was a close contest, but rain played spoilsport on the third day and it ended in a tame draw.

The series was a sequel to India's historic tour to Pakistan less than a year ago, which had enhanced the cricketing and diplomatic relations between the two countries. The series had a lot to live up to, as both teams wanted to repeat their feats and thrill their fans. A lot had changed in India since then, and not just in cricket. A new government had come to power, as the Congress-led UPA alliance dethroned the BJP-led NDA coalition, crowning Dr Manmohan Singh the new Prime Minister replacing Atal Bihari Vajpayee.

The series began on an unpleasant note for Sourav Ganguly, whose position as the captain and player was already under scrutiny like never before. Coach John Wright, the co-architect of many of Sourav's successes, announced that he was quitting after the Pakistan series. He said he wanted to spend more time with his family, but he might have also felt burnt out by the extremely demanding job.

The first Test at Mohali was a roller-coaster ride that ended in a thrilling draw.

India had the upper hand right from the coin toss, as Balaji swung his way to a 5-wicket haul in the first innings, his first in tests. The smiling assassin, who was coming back from a serious injury, also dismissed Asim Kamal for 91, who had anchored Pakistan's innings of 312.

First half of the second day was washed out. India then took control with the bat, as Sehwag smashed 173, making the most of two reprieves in slips. He added a century stand with each of the top three batsmen, a first for an Indian. Dravid made an even 50 and Tendulkar missed out on his record-breaking 35th Test hundred, falling for 94, but Laxman pushed India to 516 and a lead of 204, with a neat 58. All four Pakistani bowlers conceded over a hundred but leg spinner Danish Kaneria had the small consolation of 6 wickets to show.

Pakistan were in deep trouble on the fourth morning, losing their top 3 for 10 runs. But Inzamam and the newly-converted Mohammad Yousuf revived them with a century stand, and took the game into the final day. India still fancied their chances of victory, but they were denied by a remarkable rescue act by 23 years old wicketkeeper batsman Kamran Akmal and veteran Abdul Razzaq. The duo added 184 for the seventh wicket, a record for Pakistan against India, and batted out the day. Kamran scored his maiden test hundred, a sparkling 109, while Razzaq played an uncharacteristically dour knock of 71 not out off 260 balls. Pakistan declared at 496 for 9 and secured a draw. Akmal was named the player of the match for his match-saving hundred.

It was a frustrating result for India, who had let the game slip away from their grasp. Balaji was the star performer with 9 wickets in the match, but he lacked support from the other bowlers, except Kumble who took 4 in the second innings but couldn't force a victory for once.

The venue for the second Test was Eden Gardens, where India swapped Harbhajan Singh for Zaheer Khan, trusting his outstanding record at the ground. India opted to bat first and started strongly, with Sehwag blasting a typically belligerent 82. After both openers were back in the hut and the score was 156, Rahul Dravid took centre stage and scored 110 in just over five hours, hitting 15 fours and a six. He added 122 with Tendulkar, who became the fifth batsman after Border, Gavaskar, Steve Waugh and Lara to 10,000 Test runs, enroute his 52. Dravid was out in the last over of the day, but India had already reached 344. The tail took them to 407 in the first innings.

Pakistan needed a big reply, and they got it from newly-appointed vice captain Younis Khan and Mohammad Yousuf, who put on 211 for the third wicket. Both scored fluent centuries, with Yousuf more flamboyant and Younis more patient. But none of their team-mates could support them, and Pakistan fell short by 14 runs.

India were in trouble in their second innings, as Sami bowled a hostile spell claiming both openers and Tendulkar (52) was given out controversially by Umpire Steve Bucknor, standing in his world record 100th test. Laxman and Ganguly also fell cheaply - Ganguly to a chorus of boos at his home ground! - and India were only 170 ahead. But The Wall came to the rescue again, scoring his second hundred of the match and his 20th overall. He batted with authority and elegance, and received a standing ovation from the same crowd that had once booed him for his ultra-defensive approach. He found an unlikely partner in Dinesh Karthik, who played a sterling knock of 93 - the best he had batted since debut. They added 166 for the seventh wicket, and helped India declare at 407 for 9.

Pakistan had a daunting target of 422 to chase, but they crumbled under Kumble's pressure on the final day when he had Younis stumped on the very first ball of the day, and never let Pakistan recover. India's greatest matchwinner lived up to his billing, bagging 7 wickets for 63 runs in the second innings with his remarkable accuracy and guile - his 29th 5-wicket haul in Tests. Only Asim Kamal showed some resistance with a fighting 50, but he too couldn't delay the inevitable for too long. Pakistan were bowled out for 226, giving India a huge win by 195 runs. Rahul Dravid was adjudged the player of the match for his twin hundreds.

It was a near-perfect display by Team India, marred only by Harbhajan Singh getting reported again by match referee Chris Broad, despite the remedial work he had undergone in Australia to fix the same.

Caravan moved down south to Bengaluru for the third and final test of the series. Pakistan had won the toss and batted first on a flat pitch. They lost an early wicket, but then Younis and Inzamam joined forces and put on a mammoth 324-run partnership, the third-highest against India. Younis played a marathon innings of 267, his highest Test score and the highest by any visiting batsman in India. He batted for nearly 12 hours, hitting 32 fours and a six. Inzamam celebrated his 100th Test with a majestic 184, hitting 20 fours and 2 sixes. He became the fifth batsman to score a hundred in his 100th Test. Pakistan piled up 570, their highest total in India.

India replied with Sehwag's counter-attacking double hundred, his second of the series. He scored 201 off 262 balls, with 28 fours and 2 sixes. He reached 3,000 Test runs in his 55th innings, an Indian record. But he did not get much support from the other batsmen, except for Laxman who made 79. Kaneria took another fifer, and Pakistan had a lead of 121 runs.

Pakistan extended their lead with Afridi's blistering fifty, which came off just 26 balls, only two short of the test record. He smashed 58 off 34 balls, with 7 fours and 4 sixes. Younis also scored a fluent 84, showing his versatility and rapid strides as a batsman in the last six months or so. Inzamam declared at 261 for 2, setting India a target of 383.

India started well, with Sehwag scoring a quick 47. But he was run out by a direct-hit from Afridi. Sachin Tendulkar overtook his childhood idol Sunil Gavaskar as India's leading run-scorer in Tests, in two fewer tests. The 31-year-old modern master was dismissed in the final session however for 16, caught by Asim Kamal at forward short-leg off leg-spinner Shahid Afridi and that triggered a collapse. India adopted a strange ultra-defensive approach, which backfired badly. They crawled to 100 for 3 at lunch on the final day, and never recovered. Pakistan's bowlers kept chipping away at the wickets, and India were bowled out for 214 with just 6 overs to spare. For the second time in two tests, Ganguly was booed by an irate crowd, as he failed twice in the match. Naved-ul-Hasan took 4 wickets in the second innings, while Kaneria took 3 to take his series haul to 18, outperforming both Kumble and Harbhajan!

It was a thrilling win for Pakistan, who had shown great character and skill to level the series. Younis Khan was the player of the match for scoring close to 350 runs in the match while Sehwag was named the player of the series for his aggregate of 555 runs in 3 tests at an average of 90.

India were left stunned and disappointed, as they had let the series slip away from their grasp, after dominating it for most part.

Energized by their series levelling act at Bangalore, Pakistan carried the momentum to launch the ODI leg of their tour with an easy win over India A in Hyderabad, thanks to a brilliant partnership of 137 runs between Salman Butt and Shoaib Malik, the two match winning heroes of the last India-Pak encounter - the BCCI platinum jubilee match back in November. The lone bright spot for India A was the dazzling half-century by Suresh Raina, a 19-year-old southpaw hailing from Uttar Pradesh. The budding star, who had been part of India's under 19 world cup squad in 2002 and 2004, looked ready for the big league even at that young an age.

He would have to wait for his time, though, as the selectors didn't ring in too many changes while picking the team for the first two one-dayers. Murali Kartik was in for the injured Anil Kumble. But the most surprising and perhaps unjust omission was that of VVS Laxman whose one-day career now seemed to be in real jeopardy after he was dropped to give another run to Dinesh Mongia. M.S. Dhoni's hundred in the challenger trophy helped him hold on to his place as the preferred wicketkeeper for the ODIs, despite that brilliant 93 by Dinesh Karthik in the second test.

No one - not even those who made this choice: the selectors and the team management - could have envisaged how this 'one' selection call would turn out to be the game changer for Indian cricket in the coming years.

The one-day series kicked off with the first match in the sweltering heat and humidity of Kochi. Sourav Ganguly chose to bat first, but soon regretted it as Rana Naved removed him and Tendulkar in the same over, leaving India reeling at 4 for 2. India's recovery was led by two contrasting yet equally valuable centuries from Virender Sehwag and Rahul Dravid. Sehwag, who had a lean 2004 in one-dayers, cashed in on the two early reprieves to smash an explosive 108 off 95 balls, his 7th ODI hundred with 9 fours and 3 sixes, while Dravid anchored the innings with 104 off 139 balls with just 6 fours. It was the 10th ODI hundred for a guy regarded as misfit for this format early on in his career. They braved the extreme heat and humidity, but India lost momentum in the slog overs with Yuvraj, Kaif and Dhoni all failing to provide the final impetus, as 32 years old off-spinner Arshad Khan bowled a nagging line to claim 4 wickets.

Pakistan started well, with Salman Butt hitting some boundaries, but India's seamers struck back with 4 quick wickets. Some experts questioned the wisdom of going in with a three-pronged pace attack in these conditions but Nehra, Balaji and Zaheer Khan bowled with fire and skill in adverse conditions to dismiss the top order.

Inzamam and Mohammad Hafeez steadied the innings with a 48-run stand, but they fell behind the required rate. Sachin Tendulkar, who had a rare failure with the bat, made up for it with his golden arm. He spun a web around Pakistan's middle order, taking his second 5-for in one-dayers with his legbreaks, googlies and faster ones. Incidentally, Tendulkar had grabbed his first 5-wicket haul also at the same venue, a match-winning 5 for 32 against the Australians in 1998.

Pakistan folded for 194 in 45.2 overs, handing India an emphatic win by 87 runs and a 1-0 head start in the 6-match series. The victory was India's first at home against the arch rivals since that famous Ajay Jadeja-inspired 1996 world cup quarter-final win at Bangalore. It also helped India narrow their win-loss record against Pakistan at home to 5-11 and buck the sequence of 4 consecutive ODI defeats. Sehwag was named the player of the match, but Dravid and Tendulkar were equally instrumental in India's victory.

From Kochi, the two teams travelled to Vizag for the second match. Ganguly was going through a lean patch with the bat, but he had no such problems with the toss. He won it for the second time in a row and elected to bat first on a belter of a pitch. Sehwag had got India off to a flyer as usual, but ran out Tendulkar for just 2 runs in the fourth over.

It was then that Ganguly decided to gamble by sending Dhoni, who was being wasted lower down the order in his 4 previous innings, as a pinch-hitter at one down. It turned out to be an epochal masterstroke as Dhoni seized the opportunity with both hands. He signalled his arrival with a cracking straight drive off his first ball, and then unleashed a barrage of shots that left Pakistan shell-shocked, mixing conventional strokes with cheeky ones, such as the ramp shot over the keeper's head off Razzaq. He even outshone the mighty Sehwag, who sizzled to 74 off 40 balls, in their 96-run stand that came off just 64 deliveries, and then dominated a 149-run partnership off 134 balls with the great Rahul Dravid, who posted his 57th fifty. Dhoni's fiery ambition and desire to perform was evident even in the way he sprinted between the wickets like a man possessed, a trait that was to serve him well throughout his career. By the time he finally holed out to midwicket, he had clobbered 4 sixes and 15 fours in his 123-ball 148, the highest individual score by an Indian against Pakistan in this format. The 23 years old walked off to a deafening applause, his burgundy locks sparkling in the sun.

With his flowing locks, confident and purposeful strut, brutal stroke play and that iconic gun-toting celebration, the rebel from Ranchi had captured the imagination of the masses and emerged as an instant hero.

Only Rana Naved escaped unscathed from the carnage with 3 for 54 in his 10 overs. Even the usually economical Afridi was hammered for 82 runs in his 9 overs.

Pakistan tried to chase down the daunting target, but fell behind the required rate early on. Razzaq played a valiant innings of 88, but he was involved in a crucial run-out of Inzamam in the 20th over which proved to be very costly, perhaps even decisive in the final analysis, as Yousuf and Akmal tried their best but fell short in the end by 59 runs. Nehra was the pick of the bowlers with 4 wickets followed by Yuvraj who claimed 3, though both were expensive. India took a 2-0 lead in the series and celebrated their new hero, the player of the match Mahendra Singh Dhoni, who had burst onto the big stage with an almighty bang.

The next match was at his home ground in the steel city of Jamshedpur, where he received a rousing welcome from the packed crowd. They had come to see their local hero, who had dazzled them with his explosive innings in the previous match. Pakistan captain won a crucial toss and decided to bat first on a good pitch. Salman Butt justified his captain's decision with a sublime century, his second against India. He stroked the ball with with left-hander's grace and timing, scoring 101 off 111 balls with

10 fours. He was well supported by Shoaib Malik, who contributed a brisk 75. Yousuf added some late fireworks with a 31-ball 43, and Pakistan posted a daunting 319 for 9. Nehra was the pick of the Indian bowlers, taking 3 for 57 in his 10 overs while Irfan looked completely off-colour.

India's chase never got going, as they lost wickets at regular intervals. Rana Naved was the wrecker-in-chief, taking a career-best 6 for 27 with his clever variations of length and movement. He was aided by Mohammad Sami, who bowled with pace and accuracy, and claimed Tendulkar as his 100th one-day scalp. Younis Khan also shone in the field, taking four catches for the second time in one-dayers, a unique feat. India were reduced to 82 for 6, and the game was virtually over. Pathan played a valiant innings of 64, his maiden fifty in ODIs, but it was in vain. Pakistan bounced back in style to win by a big margin of 106 runs and keep their hopes alive in the series. The low key and balding Rana Naved - who lacked the flair and flamboyance of the typical Pakistani strike bowlers - earned the player of the match award.

Afterwards, Ganguly was fined 70% of his match fee for slow over-rate.

Fourth match was at Ahmedabad. Batting first after winning the toss, Sachin Tendulkar roared back to form after three single digit scores with a masterful century - his 38th in one-day internationals and first since March 2004 against the same opposition. He batted with vintage flair, grit and authority, hitting 12 fours and 2 sixes in his 130 ball 123. He was ably supported by Dhoni in the middle stages and Yuvraj towards the end, who chipped in with 47 and 35 respectively. India posted a challenging 317 for 6, with Malik taking 3 wickets with his seemingly harmless off spin.

Pakistan went about the daunting chase in uncharacteristically clinical fashion. Afridi gave them a flying start with a blistering 40 off 23 balls, and then the middle order kept the scoreboard ticking with singles and doubles. They hit only 4 boundaries in 20 overs, yet never let the required rate get out of hand, their coach Bob Woolmer's stamp of smart and composed cricket plainly obvious. Malik and Inzamam played mature innings of 65 and 60 respectively, and took Pakistan to the brink of victory. In the final over, bowled by Tendulkar, Pakistan needed 3 runs. The miracle worker almost pulled off another memorable heist but Inzamam kept his nerve and sliced the last ball through point for four, sparking wild celebrations.

It was Pakistan's highest successful chase in one-dayers, and they staged a remarkable comeback to level the series from a 2-0 deficit. Inzi won the player of the match for his ice cool finishing while Ganguly - who seemed to get nothing right at the moment - was banned for 6 matches, later reduced to 4, for his perennial issue, slow over-rate.

Pakistan had regained their confidence and swagger and India felt the heat in the fifth match of the series. With Ganguly suspended, Rahul Dravid took charge and chose to bat first on a sluggish Green Park wicket at Kanpur. But India soon found themselves in trouble at 59 for 4 in the 17th over, losing their top order to Rana Naved's crafty spell of 3 wickets. Dravid then joined forces with Mohammad Kaif, who played a crucial knock of 78 off 88 balls after a long lean patch, and added 135 runs for the fifth wicket to steady the ship. Dinesh Mongia provided the much-needed late flourish with a quick-fire 33 as Dravid fell for a valiant 86 on the second last ball, taking India to a respectable total of 249/6 in their fifty overs.

It was by all means a defensible target on this wicket but Shahid Afridi demolished their chances with a blistering attack that only he could pull off in world cricket. He unleashed his fury in the third over, hammering Balaji for 23 runs, and did the same to a returning Anil Kumble in the fifth and Mongia in the 11th. The unpredictable Pashtun made light work of the difficult pitch, the two world-class spinners and the daunting target with a sensational 102 off 46 balls; his fourth one-day international ton and the joint-second quickest ever, just behind his own record, hitting 10 fours and 9 sixes in a savage display of brute power. He got to his hundred with a fierce pull over the top, and was bowled next ball - playing a rare defensive shot. Pakistan were cruising at 131 for 1 in the 15th over by then. The other batsmen found it hard to bat on the pitch, showing how remarkable Afridi's knock really was, as Pakistan chased down the seemingly difficult total with 8 overs to spare and took a 3-2 lead in the series with only one game remaining. Boom Boom Afridi was the undisputed player of the match.

India faced a must-win situation in the final match of the series, after squandering a 2-0 lead and facing the prospect of a series defeat. In front of their president, Pervez Musharraf, and Indian prime minister Manmohan Singh, Pakistan won the toss, elected to bat first and put up their most ruthless performance of the series with both bat and ball. Shahid Afridi gave them a blazing start with 44 off 23 balls, threatening to repeat his Kanpur carnage. Shoaib Malik then anchored the innings with another calm innings of 72, while Yousuf and Inzamam added some flair with stylish fifties, both falling to dubious calls. Younis Khan came good with the bat for the first time in the series, scoring a quick 40 as Pakistan posted a daunting 303/8.

India's chase never got going as Rana Naved struck early to remove Sehwag - fourth time in the series. Pakistan's bowlers kept up the pressure and picked up wickets at regular intervals, with the unheralded Arshad Khan claiming 3 precious scalps. The pitch also deteriorated and made batting difficult. The crowd showed their frustration by throwing bottles on the field when Kaif was dismissed at 94. The match resumed after a brief delay, but India's hopes were dashed as they were bowled out for 144 in the 37th over, giving Pakistan their biggest one-day win by runs over India, a margin of 159 runs.

Shoaib Malik, who had emerged as Team India's biggest headache in the past year or so, won the player of the match award, while Rana Naved, who had exceeded all expectations with 15 wickets in the series, bagged the player of the series honour.

Coach Bob Woolmer and captain Inzamam's young team had played like "cornered tigers" to complete an astonishing turnaround in the series, winning 4-2 after being 2-0 down. India and their outgoing coach John Wright, on the other hand, were left lamenting the chances they squandered in both test and the one-day series, which they failed to clinch after being ahead at one point.

The team could not give Wright the winning farewell that he deserved, but they did give him a warm and intimate farewell dinner, led by the seniors who expressed their gratitude for his mentorship and grooming that made them more professional as a team and as individuals. John Wright's four-and-a-half-year tenure may have ended on a sour note, but it was one hell of a ride with many more highs than lows, that much was indisputable. He instilled more fire and fitness in his gifted but erratic players. His contribution wasn't just limited to overseeing the training drills and delivering pep talks, but also on the strategic front, with quite a few tactical masterstrokes like promoting VVS to one down in that famous Kolkata test and turning Sehwag into an opener. For a low-key and gentlemanly coach, he could also be a strict disciplinarian when needed, as shown by the infamous Sehwag incident[3]. What made him different from some other hard taskmasters, though, was his skill to reconcile with the player after such a heated incident. These qualities ensured he left as a much loved, respected and admired coach of Team India.

Thus, ended a long and agonizing season of disappointment for the Indian team.

---

[3] **Footnote** - Sehwag has been on record narrating an incident which happened during the Natwest trophy in England, 2002; where an infuriated Wright, frustrated by Sehwag's repeated failures to rash shots after good starts, grabbed him by the collar in the dressing room. An incensed Sehwag threatened to leave, but manager Rajiv Shukla and senior BCCI official Amrit Mathur stepped in to mediate and facilitate a patch-up between the two.

17

Freefall

The players had a welcome break of 100 days at the end of the season before the next one began in July. After such a disappointing season, most of them used it to relax and unwind, while four - Ganguly, Harbhajan, Irfan and Dinesh Mongia chose to sharpen their skills by playing in county cricket. Dinesh Karthik flew to Australia to get wicketkeeping training under Australian Cricket Academy, while Sachin Tendulkar decided to use this window to undergo surgery in London for his tennis elbow, hoping to cure the persistent problem for good.

First order of business for the BCCI was to appoint a new head coach. There were several more experienced names in the fray, like Dav Whatmore, Tom Moody, Mohinder Amarnath and Desmond Haynes, but the BCCI-appointed panel chose the legendary Greg Chappell to take over from John Wright as the head coach of India for a two-year term till the 2007 ODI World Cup. Ganguly himself was keen on having Greg as the next coach of India, as he had developed a great rapport with him after the legendary Australian had helped him fix some technical flaws in his batting before the 2003 Australia tour with wonderful results.

India had been decent in tests, despite losing the latest series against Pakistan, but their decline as a one-day side since reaching the World Cup final had been alarming and sharp, as shown by 28 losses in 55 games since the last World Cup. Last season was particularly dismal with just 9 wins in 22 matches. And even that was a flattering statistic, because 5 of those 9 wins came against weaker opponents like Kenya, the UAE and Bangladesh, who even managed to defeat them once. So, the new head coach Greg Chappell's first priority was to arrest this downfall in one-dayers.

He wasted no time in assembling his team of support staff - Assistant coach-cum-biomechanics expert Ian Frazer, trainer Gregory King and physio John Gloster, and got down to business with three short camps at the NCA in Bengaluru - first one exclusively for fast bowlers focusing on how they could avoid frequent injuries - something that had been a recurring issue in last couple of seasons, second one focusing on physical conditioning and third one cricket specific - with 30 probables prior to flying out for his first assignment. In the third and most important camp, Greg shared his 'vision' for Indian cricket for his two-year tenure.

VVS Laxman made a strong case for his recall by scoring a quick hundred in a practice match that also served as a benefit match for former India bowler David Johnson, before the squad selection for the Indian Oil Cup - a tri-series in Sri Lanka with West Indies as the third team - which was the season opener for India. He earned his place in the side announced by the selectors, which had three new faces - two exciting young batsmen, Suresh Raina and Venugopal Rao, and Jai Prakash Yadav as an all-rounder. The rest were the regulars, with Sachin being the only notable absentee, but it was to give rest to his still healing tennis elbow. Rahul Dravid was named the captain for the tri-series, as Sourav Ganguly was still serving a reduced four-match ban, but he was selected provisionally as the 16th member and was to join the team midway in the tournament if his appeal against the ban before ICC got settled in his favour.

India played two warm-up games to prepare, with Dhoni shining in both games with two scores of 80s.

India, under new coach and captain, wasted no time in granting debuts to Suresh Raina and Venugopal Rao on a sluggish Sri Lankan pitch, but they soon found themselves in trouble at 64 for 5, as debutant Dilhara Lokuhettige bounced back from Sehwag's onslaught to remove Dhoni and Yuvraj sent in as opener and one-down respectively. Skipper Dravid held the innings together with a gritty 54, and got some support from Venugopal and the tailenders, as India managed to reach 205 for 9. Muralitharan was the chief tormentor with 3 wickets while Lokuhettige made up for Vaas' absence with 2 for 31 on debut.

In their pursuit, Sri Lanka struggled against some tight and disciplined bowling from India's four specialist bowlers - Pathan, Zaheer Khan, Nehra and Harbhajan- and was on the verge of collapse at 112 for 5, needing 93 more runs to win. But then the Matara mauler emerged from the pavilion like a wounded gladiator resolved to rescue his side. He had suffered a dislocated shoulder while fielding and was in immense pain. But the 38 years old was not ready to let that stop him from guiding his team to victory. He wielded his bat like a sword, slashing and cutting his way to a heroic 43 not out. He was ably supported by Lokuhettige - who completed a handsome debut and exacted revenge for the first over pasting by hitting Sehwag over long-on for a six on the third ball he faced in international cricket - and Maharoof, who batted with the skill and confidence of a specialist batter, as Sri Lanka won comfortably by 6 wickets with 10 balls to spare. The evergreen Jayasuriya showed once more why he was a true ODI legend by still being able to win matches off his bat even when half-fit, and deservedly won the player of the match award.

In a bad case of poor scheduling, India had to play their next match the very next day against West Indies who were not to be underestimated as they had won Champions trophy last season. However, they were missing quite a few of their key players including their inspirational captain who led them to that glorious victory, the charismatic Brian Lara because of a stand-off with their board owing to contractual issues. Stand-in captain Chanderpaul chose to bat first and regretted it as his inexperienced team could only score 178, that too, only thanks to some late hitting by Dwayne Smith and a couple of responsible 20s from wicketkeeper Denesh Ramdin and tailender Tino Best, as Indian bowlers including part timers bowled well in tandem with Harbhajan, Nehra and Sehwag taking two wickets each and Pathan, Zaheer and even Raina chipping in with a wicket apiece.

India's chase was not without drama, as they lost Sehwag in the second over and were let off by some shoddy fielding from Windies. Raina, who had a nightmarish debut the previous day, got two reprieves and made the most of them by scoring a fluent 35. He was well supported by Dravid, who also survived a run out chance and went on to anchor the innings with a calm 52. Yuvraj and Dhoni added some quick runs to finish the game with 14 overs to spare and earn a bonus point. Dhoni sealed the win with a six off Lawson. It was a comprehensive victory for India, led by their captain's fifty and their bowlers' collective effort. Rahul Dravid was adjudged the player of the match as much for his innings as for his refreshing captaincy.

India's prospects for their next match looked bright as Sourav Ganguly returned to the side, albeit only as a player. He had been playing county cricket for Glamorgan with middling results and flew over to join the team mid-tournament after his ban was reduced by two games. VVS Laxman also made a comeback, while Sri Lanka were missing their key bowlers Vaas, Murali and Jayasuriya - all injured - for this match.

Rahul Dravid chose to bat first, but India's famed batting line-up was put to the sword by Sri Lanka's makeshift spin attack and their innings never got going, as they lost wickets at regular intervals and failed to accelerate. Ganguly top-scored on his return with a painfully slow 51 off 110 balls, and in the process crossed 10,000 ODI runs, joining the elite club of Sachin and Inzamam. But it was not an inning he could be very proud of. He got no support from the other batters, as Sehwag, Laxman and Dravid all departed early, Dravid for a rare duck to a questionable lbw decision. Dhoni and Raina also fell to Dilshan's crafty off spin, leaving India in trouble. Only Kaif and Pathan showed some fire, with Pathan hitting 17 runs off Fernando's final over to take India to 220 for 8. It was a below-par total and Sri Lanka's rag-tag bunch of spinners deserved all the praise for their tight bowling. Dilshan was the star of the show, with 4 wickets for 29 runs in his 10 overs.

Chasing 221, India's pace trio of Nehra, Pathan and Balaji had Sri Lanka on the mat at 95 for 6. But Jayawardene and Chandana refused to give up, and played with calmness, intelligence and spirit to turn the game around.

The pair saw off the threat of Nehra, who bowled his full quota of 10 overs straight, and then launched a counterattack against India's part-time bowlers. Ganguly, Sehwag and even Harbhajan were all taken to the cleaners, as Jayawardene and Chandana scored at a brisk pace and kept the required rate under control. By the time Dravid brought back his remaining quicks Pathan and Balaji, it was too late. Jayawardene had a career-rebirth with a splendid 94 not out, his first fifty in 19 innings and highest score in 4 years, and Chandana made an invaluable 44 not out. They added an unbroken 126 runs for the seventh wicket, the highest partnership for that wicket in ODIs. They took Sri Lanka to victory with two balls to spare, leaving India stunned and shell-shocked.

In the last qualifying match of the triangular that would determine which team would meet Sri Lanka in the final, India chose to bat first against a further weakened but spirited Windies. Their young and inexperienced bowlers, buoyed by their sensational win over Sri Lanka the previous night, bowled with fire and skill, tearing through India's formidable top four, leaving them reeling at 51 for 3, with Ganguly rushed to hospital after suffering a body blow from a Powell bouncer.

But the reliable duo of Yuvraj and Kaif engineered a stunning comeback, putting on 165 runs for the fifth wicket in a replay of their heroic stand in that Natwest trophy final at Lords three years ago that had etched itself in Indian cricket lore. 23 years old Yuvi scored a brilliant hundred, his third in ODIs, while 24 years old Kaif played a solid supporting role with an unbeaten 83. Dhoni provided the finishing touches with a cameo of 28 off 13 balls with a couple of sixes, as India posted 262 for 4, their highest total in the tournament so far.

West Indies, further weakened by the injury to their captain Chanderpaul, faced a daunting chase. They lost wickets at regular intervals and were reduced to 112 for 6, with only opener Morton showing some intent. But he found an unlikely ally in Ramdin, the talented young wicketkeeper, who joined him in a spirited partnership of 83 runs for the seventh wicket. Morton scored 83, his highest ODI score, while Ramdin made 51 not out, his maiden ODI fifty. They kept Windies in the hunt till the end, but fell short by 8 runs. Nehra bowled a superb final over, conceding only 4 runs when 12 were needed. Anil Kumble justified his return to playing eleven with 3 middle order wickets for 38 in his 10 overs. It was a thrilling finish to a see-saw match, which India won by a narrow margin to book their spot in the final. Yuvraj was named the player of the match for his scintillating hundred.

This impressive team performance was a nice birthday present to their new coach Greg Chappell who celebrated his 57th birthday that day.

For the final to be played at the storied Premadasa stadium in Colombo, hosts Sri Lanka were bolstered by the return of their three big guns - Jayasuriya, Vaas and Muralitharan. Skipper Atapattu won the toss and opted to bat first, but India's best bowler in recent times, Ashish Nehra once again bowled a nippy and intelligent spell, rocking them to 67 for 3 in 14 overs. Jayasuriya and Jayawardene, however, rebuilt the innings with a 52-run partnership, before Jayawardene and Arnold took charge with a

125-run stand for the fifth wicket. Jayasuriya scored 67, joining the elite club of 10,000 ODI runs, the fourth batter to do so after Sachin, Inzamam and Ganguly. But the hero of the day was Jayawardene, who played a dazzling knock of 83 off 97 balls, with Arnold supporting him with a breezy 64. Nehra took his second 6 wicket haul in ODIs, but Sri Lanka still amassed a formidable 282 for 7, thanks to some atrocious fielding by India with Sehwag spilling a couple of chances in slips and Dhoni being sloppy behind the wicket. The Jharkhand lad had played a couple of useful knocks with the bat but his keeping had been below par throughout the tournament and needed a lot of improvement if he wished to make that position his own.

India had to chase the highest total of the tournament, and they began aggressively, with Sehwag hammering Lokuhettige for 26 runs in an over. He perished soon after though, trying to do the same to the wily Vaas but Ganguly and Dravid took India past 100 when Ganguly too departed after a ponderous 26. Yuvraj joined Dravid and they put India in a strong position at 186 for 2 in 36 overs. But then Yuvraj's dismissal sparked a dramatic collapse, as Sri Lanka's spinners, led by the great Muralitharan spun a web around the Indian batters. Dravid was run out for 69, and the rest of the batting folded under pressure. The crowd went wild as Sri Lanka dismissed India for 264, winning by 18 runs. Jayawardene was awarded the Man of the Match and the Man of the Series, though Nehra also had a strong case with 12 wickets at 16.50 and an economy rate of 4.12.

It was a match that showcased the contrast between confidence and nerves. Sri Lanka had the home advantage and showed why they were the second-ranked side in ODIs at that time. They continued their impressive record of winning finals - they had won 12 out of 14 finals before this one - while India continued their tradition of choking in tournament finals, even under a new coach and captain.

Tom Moody, who had settled for Sri Lanka's offer to coach after missing out on India's coach job, basked in the adulation of his team and fans. Greg Chappell, on the other hand, faced a tough challenge to transform the no.7 ranked ODI team into a competitive force in two years' time.

The decision-makers in Indian cricket responded by making some bold changes to their one-day squad for the upcoming tri-series in Zimbabwe, dropping four senior players - Kumble, Laxman, Zaheer Khan and Balaji.

However, all four were retained in the test squad along with test opener Gautam Gambhir, test wicketkeeper Dinesh Karthik and Sachin Tendulkar, who would play if fit.

Zaheer and Laxman had failed to impress in Sri Lanka, but Kumble and Balaji's omission came as a surprise, as Kumble had bowled well in one of the two matches he played, while Balaji had featured in only one game. The selectors brought back Ajit Agarkar and Murali Kartik, to replace Balaji and Kumble, and gave a maiden call-up to Rudra Pratap Singh, the left-arm swing bowler from Uttar Pradesh, who had a stellar domestic season with 41 wickets in eight games. Suresh Raina, Venugopal Rao and Jai Prakash Yadav managed to retain their places. Sourav Ganguly was back as captain for both formats.

India took on New Zealand - the third side making up the Videocon tri-series at Bulawayo after a scheduling oversight had them arriving at Bulawayo less than 24 hours before the match, their first in the tri-series. Stephen Fleming won the toss and elected to bat first but Nehra and Pathan exploited the swing and seam to rip through the Kiwi top order, leaving them reeling at 36 for 5. But McMillan and McCullum showed grit and resilience to rebuild the innings and take them to a respectable 215.

Then it was Bond's turn to unleash his fury. He bowled with pace and venom, making the ball bounce and zip past the Indian batsmen. He put Ganguly out of his first-over misery with a vicious bouncer in his second, and then ran through the middle order with ease. India were reduced to a hopeless 44 for 8, staring at a humiliating defeat. However, Jai Prakash Yadav and Pathan refused to give up. They counterattacked with flair and courage, smashing boundaries and frustrating the Kiwis. They stitched together a record-breaking ninth-wicket partnership of 118, bringing India within sight of a miraculous win. But Bond had other plans. He came back for his final spell and broke the stand, dismissing Pathan with a yorker. He finished with 6 for 19, the best figures by a New Zealander, and made history by becoming the first cricketer to earn the player of the match award as a *supersub*, a new innovation by the ICC to spice up the ODIs.

India had faced many a fiery spell from fast bowlers in the past, but never had they been so clueless and helpless against them as they were here. It was a complete shambles and, like Miandad's legendary last-ball six, had the potential of leaving a deep and lasting scar on a batting line-up already woefully short of confidence.

That lack of confidence was on full view in the way India batted in their next game against the hosts at Harare. Against a Zimbabwean bowling attack that had been thrashed to the tune of 397 runs in 44 overs by New Zealand in the opening match of the tourney, India's top four managed to crawl to 123 in 40 overs, with Kaif scoring a painstaking fifty, before Dhoni and Yuvraj unleashed a late onslaught to propel them to a somewhat decent 226. Dhoni blasted 4 sixes in his 46-ball 56, while Yuvraj, who had struggled earlier, found his touch and finished with an unbeaten 53. They put on 103 in 87 balls, the first of many such rescue acts this dashing duo would perform in the future. Heath Streak was the only bowler who bowled well, especially in his opening spell when he dismissed Venugopal Rao for a duck in the first over. Rao was India's makeshift opener as Sehwag was rested.

Zimbabwe's reply was a disaster from the start. Pathan and Agarkar swung and seamed the ball at will, and the batsmen had no clue how to cope. Pathan took his maiden 5-wicket haul in a devastating spell, while Agarkar chipped in with 4. Only Streak and Utseya reached double figures, as Zimbabwe were bundled out for 65, their lowest total ever. Pathan was named the player of the match for his excellent spell. It was another crushing defeat for the hosts Zimbabwe, and a win by a whopping margin of 161 for India, though question mark over their batting still remained.

India met New Zealand again but this time at Harare, where Fleming chose to bat first on a belter of a pitch - the first such in the tournament thus far. Kiwi batsmen made the most of it and piled up 278 runs in a collective team effort. Skipper Fleming laid the foundation, Lou Vincent set the tempo, and Styris anchored the innings in his 100th match. The trio of McMillan, McCullum and Oram provided the fireworks, as Nehra, Pathan and Agarkar all took a couple of wickets each but India clawed their way back with Jai Prakash Yadav's miserly military medium pace - reminiscent of Kiwi's own Gavin Larsen - Bhajji's guile, and two brilliant run-outs by Agarkar and Yuvraj.

India's chase was off to a blazing start, as Sehwag feasted on a weakened Kiwi attack badly missing Bond. Ganguly showed glimpses of his old form too, before falling to a poor shot to make it 66 for 1 in 7 overs. Oram got rid of the dangerous Sehwag soon after but New Zealand sorely missed their other star bowler, Vettori, in the middle overs, as Kaif took control of the situation with rare grace and fluency, along with his usual virtues of intelligent placement coupled with frenetic running between the wickets. Rahul Dravid, back to his role of vice-captain, played a fine support act in a 101-run stand which was the foundation of the run-chase. After Dravid departed, India still needed 103 runs at a challenging rate, but Kaif held his nerve and steered India to victory with the help of Yuvraj and Dhoni. Dhoni sealed the deal with 2 massive sixes off Patel. Kaif remained unbeaten on a superbly paced 102 off just 121 balls with 11 boundaries - his second hundred in ODIs, winning him the player of the match award.

Guru Greg must have felt a sense of relief as it was the first time that his wards had put up such a near-flawless and complete team performance since he had taken charge.

The otherwise inconsequential final league game was spiced up by a spirited show from the hosts Zimbabwe, who were without their captain Heath Streak. First, they batted well with stand-in captain Tatenda Taibu leading from the front with a splendid knock of 71 and Charles Coventry smashing 3 sixes in his 74 - his maiden ODI fifty. Andy Blignaut then blasted 41 in just 26 balls, to take Zimbabwe to a healthy 250. Agarkar was the most successful Indian bowler with 3 for 34 in 10 overs. RP Singh, the tall left-arm quick from Uttar Pradesh, too made a favourable impression on debut with a couple wickets to his credit.

Zimbabwe continued their good work with the ball, as they reduced India to 36 for 4 and then 91 for 5, thanks to a combination of some accurate bowling, rash shots, a stunning catch by Sibanda and a smart run-out of Venugopal Rao. But Yuvraj Singh rose to the occasion, with a magnificent 120 with 12 sweetly timed boundaries and a glorious six. He batted sensibly at first, and then unleashed his full array of shots, as he and Dhoni added a brisk 158 runs - just 3 runs short of the sixth-wicket record in one-day internationals. Player of the match Yuvraj was out trying to finish the match, but Dhoni did it with his third six to return unbeaten on 67 off 63 balls, as India won by 4 wickets with 11 balls to spare.

India faced a full-strength New Zealand in the final, and Ganguly decided to bat first on a good pitch. Sehwag was in a destructive mood, taking on Bond and the other bowlers with a flurry of boundaries. He and Ganguly gave India a brisk start, adding 72 in 13 overs before Ganguly threw away another decent start going after Oram. Kaif joined Sehwag and played second fiddle, as India were cruising at 155 for 1 in the 25th over. But then Vettori changed the game, with two wickets in three balls and a tight spell of spin bowling. He choked the runs and created pressure, as the other batsmen fell around Kaif, who was left stranded on 93. Oram picked up 4 wickets, but Vettori was the real game changer with 2 for 35. India finished with 276, which looked slightly below par.

New Zealand's openers outdid India's. After Pathan started with a maiden, Fleming and Astle went berserk on all three seamers, smashing 62 in 6 overs, and then 121 in 18 overs, before Fleming was dismissed for 60. Though the spinners put the brakes on, Astle continued to attack from his end and steered New Zealand to a comfortable win by 6 wickets with 11 balls to spare with a glorious unbeaten 115 - his 15th hundred in ODIs, a feat achieved by only 9 other batsmen in the world. He deservedly won the player of the match award, while Shane Bond was aptly named the player of the series for his tally of 11 wickets in just 4 matches at an astounding average of 8.63.

India's chokejob in the finals continued, as they suffered their 11th defeat in 15 finals since 2000 (with just 1 win and 3 no-results). Their record was even worse if we go back further, losing 16 out of 21 finals since 1998. This time it was the turn of their bowlers to let them down after Sehwag and Kaif had set them up with the bat.

Gregory Stephen Chappell was a bona fide legend of the game and his appointment as India's coach had created a lot of buzz in the cricket world. Greg had tried to take the early setbacks in his stride, but such repeated poor performances were unacceptable for someone of his stature and had started to test his patience. Something had to change and change quickly.

A Clash of Personalities

The test leg of the tour was about to begin, with the first test starting a week after the final. India had only one three-day practice match at Mutare to get ready. It was in this warm-up game against Zimbabwe board XI that the seeds of a discord that would engulf Indian cricket in the days ahead were first sown.

The game itself ended in a draw, with India getting what they wanted out of the match: good batting practice for their batsmen and decent outings for their bowlers. Gambhir, Sehwag and Dravid scored hundreds, while Kumble took a 5-fer. But the coach felt that the captain, who scraped a 46, was trying to dodge the prospect of facing the opposition's quick bowlers, perhaps in a bid to avoid another low score going into the first test.

After the game, Chappell, who had helped Ganguly overcome a previous slump before his triumphant tour of Australia in 2003-04, had a candid chat with a vulnerable Ganguly. He insisted Chappell for his honest opinion on his batting, and Chappell, being the straight-shooting Aussie, did not mince words - saying on current form, he does not feel Ganguly deserves a place in the playing eleven ahead of the in-form Kaif and Yuvraj. Ganguly was stunned and asked Chappell if he was serious. Chappell said he was, as Ganguly had insisted on the truth.

Then next day, upon being asked about Ganguly's slump by a media personnel, Chappell acknowledged that his poor form was bound to affect "the other areas of his game", but expressed confidence that the left-hander should regain his touch soon, adding he had no doubts about his ability to score runs again.

Things really came to a boil when the matter of team selection came up again on the eve of the first test. Ganguly sought Chappell's opinion on who to pick between Kaif and Yuvraj. Chappell said India should pick the best XI and when Ganguly pushed him for a frank opinion, Chappell told him that left to him, he would pick both Yuvraj and Kaif in the team ahead of Ganguly. A taken aback Ganguly again asked Chappell if he really means it. Chappell told him he does, and urged Ganguly to think about his legacy and Indian cricket's future, not his own. He said Ganguly should choose when to bow out gracefully.

Ganguly was enraged and stormed off to the dressing-room. He told Dravid and Chowdhary, the manager, that he was done and leaving since the coach doesn't want him in the team. Chowdhary called Chappell and they all came to an agreement that Ganguly leaving in this manner in the middle of the tour would be a catastrophe.

Next morning the test series finally got underway with the first test being played at Bulawayo. The hosts batted first and reached 279, thanks to a gritty 71 not out from their captain Taibu and a solid debut from opener Duffin. India's bowlers struggled to find their rhythm, with Zaheer Khan bowling 9 no-balls and the spinners failing to make an impact until late in the day.

India's reply was swift and ruthless, as their openers Sehwag and Gambhir raced to 88 before lunch. Dravid and Laxman then took over, with Dravid helping himself to a 77 and Laxman scoring a sublime century that lasted until the third morning when Ganguly refused his call for a quick single.

Ganguly, under pressure for his poor form and captaincy, also laboured to a hundred which took 261 balls, his first in 14 tests since that epic one at Brisbane in December 2003, 22 months to be precise. En route, he also completed 5000 test runs and broke the Indian record for most tests as captain (47) - jointly held by Sunil Gavaskar and Azharuddin - this being his 48th, but was out soon after reaching three figures. Pathan backed up his fifer with a fine fifty and Harbhajan added some quick runs by smashing 3 sixes in 18 balls. Mahwire was the pick of the Zimbabwean bowlers, taking 4 wickets as Heath Streak, Zimbabwe's most experienced bowler had a rare poor outing.

Zimbabwe's second innings was a disaster, as they collapsed to 67 for 6 by the end of the third day. At the press briefing that evening, Ganguly dropped a bombshell by revealing that he was asked to step down before the match. He said that this served as "extra motivation" for him to score a century and prove his worth. Truth be told, Zimbabwe's bowling attack in this test was so pedestrian that a candid Sunil Gavaskar had slammed it on air as '*Popatwadi*', meaning akin to a club-level side. But Ganguly's statement sparked a shitstorm in the gossip-hungry Indian media, as rumours and stories flew around thick and fast, overshadowing the ongoing match.

Tatenda Taibu was once again the lone fighter for his team the next morning, scoring another fifty and putting on some resistance with the tail but Zimbabwe were eventually bowled out for 185 in little under 2 hours on the fourth day, giving India an innings victory and a 1-0 lead in the series. Pathan was the destroyer-in-chief, taking 4 wickets in a brilliant spell of swing bowling and won the player of the match for his all-round brilliance. Harbhajan also claimed 4 wickets, becoming the fastest Indian to 200 Test wickets in the process.

This was Zimbabwe's seventh successive innings defeat against the senior test nations since their player rebellion of April 2004 had left them further depleted.

After unleashing a media frenzy by going public on third evening, Ganguly refused to comment on the conflict while the BCCI and the coach Chappell tried to downplay the controversy. The board vice-president Rajiv Shukla blamed the media for blowing things out of proportion and urged all parties to focus on the task at hand which was to win the series. Chappell, on the other hand, took a diplomatic stance and avoided any direct criticism of Ganguly or his performance.

Afterwards, the coach and captain quite literally went separate ways before the second test at Harare which was due in 3 days' time. While Chappell headed for the venue of the match with four other players, Ganguly took off to catch a glimpse of the famous Victoria Falls.

After reaching Harare, Chappell rubbished reports that he threatened to resign, saying neither did he threaten to resign nor does he intend to. Weighing in on the controversy in the aftermath of the media storm, the usually reticent Sachin Tendulkar said that dressing-room conversations should be kept private. He said it would not be right for him to comment as to what really transpired but the board should talk to the players when they come back and find out the real story. Looking as the issue was spiralling out of hand, BCCI finally sprang into action constituting a six-member panel to investigate the matter after the team returned home. But for now, the priority was to win the second test and the series.

The next morning, Ganguly and Chappell met for a talk initiated by Amitabh Chowdhary, the team manager, at the board's request. They tried to patch things up and were seen discussing the pitch and conditions at the Harare sports club. They also played a game of pool and posed for the cameras.

On the eve of the second test, Chappell read out a written statement professing his respect for Ganguly and desire to work with him, remarking that the private discussion was meant to motivate Ganguly for the Bulawayo test.

India kept the same team for the second and final test of the series. Ganguly decided to bowl first on a green pitch at the HSC. Zimbabwe were blown away for 161 by Pathan's brilliant swing bowling. He took 7/59 in the first innings, as he made the ball move both ways and troubled the Zimbabwean batsmen. None of them could score a fifty, while Charles Coventry, who made his debut in the previous test, top-scored with 37.

India's openers Sehwag and Gambhir gave them the customary flying start. Gambhir fell just 3 runs short of a hundred and Dravid missed his by a mere 2 runs, as Zimbabwe fought back with some quality bowling and fielding. Former captain Heath Streak, their only world-class bowler, redeemed himself from the first test with a 6-wicket haul. He was supported by Mahwire and some sharp catches, as Zimbabwe managed to restrict India to 366 in their first innings.

Zimbabwe's second innings was a disaster, as Pathan and Zaheer Khan ran through their top order. They were 39 for four at the end of the second day, with Pathan taking three wickets and Zaheer dismissing Taibu, their best batsman. Zaheer added three more wickets on the third day, but Blignaut and Masakadza showed some fight with some big hits. Pathan came back to wrap up the innings. He took his 12th wicket of the match, a record for an Indian seamer overseas, and denied Blignaut a hundred as Zimbabwe were all out for 223. Taibu's men did however succeed in breaking their run of innings defeats by making India bat again. India needed only 19 runs to win, which they did without losing a wicket, winning the match by 10 wickets - their first test win at Harare in four attempts - and with it, the series 2-0. Irfan Pathan walked away with both player of the match as well as series honour for his incredible 21 wickets in just 2 tests.

This was India's first test series win outside the subcontinent in 19 years and came as a welcome boost for a team struggling with too many problems on and off the field. It did not matter that Zimbabwe was missing some of their key players; India had finally broken the jinx that had haunted them since Kapil's Devils triumphed over England in the summer of 1986. The next challenge for this Indian team was to become a consistent force in foreign conditions.

But to attain that, it was of paramount importance to resolve the conflict between the captain and the coach urgently, once and for all.

Section 3

THE TRANSITION

18

All Hell Breaks Loose

With both Chappell and Ganguly being equally stubborn and proud characters, the chances of that happening were pretty remote. In a climactic twist towards the end of the second test, coach Chappell sent a private e-mail to the BCCI President and secretary, criticizing Ganguly's captaincy skills and making other pretty scathing comments. But in classic BCCI fashion, it got leaked to the media by an unknown source, and an influential Kolkata newspaper published a report of Chappell's allegations. The BCCI President, Mahendra, confirmed receiving the e-mail, but did not reveal its contents, saying it was confidential. An infuriated Ganguly refused to comment on the allegations. He said he would only talk to the board, but questioned Chappell's character for writing such an e-mail after they had agreed to a truce.

He reiterated the same position upon returning home the next day, adding that it is between him and the coach and the whole team should not be dragged into it.

The board had constituted a six-member review committee to discuss the row at a meeting in Mumbai three days later. The committee included former BCCI president Jagmohan Dalmiya, current president Ranbir Singh Mahendra and S K Nair, the board secretary, apart from the three former captains: Sunil Gavaskar, Ravi Shastri and Srinivas Venkataraghavan.

Two days before the crucial meeting, a couple of media outlets dropped a bomb by revealing the full text of Greg Chappell's e-mail to the BCCI, which contained more damning allegations against Ganguly, accusing him of being a cunning schemer who manipulated the team and the board to extend his captaincy and career. The e-mail created a huge uproar in the cricketing world, with Harbhajan Singh openly coming out in Ganguly's defence slamming Chappell's methods. Some other team members also sided with Ganguly, but off the record, prompting BCCI to issue a gag order asking them not to speak out of turn.

The controversy had split the cricket world into two camps. Chappell had his fair share of backers too, both in the team as well as outside of it, including his brother the great Ian Chappell and erstwhile BCCI President, the venerable Raj Singh Dungarpur, who openly blamed the Dalmiya camp for the e-mail leak to save Ganguly from being sacked.

The clock was ticking with less than a day to go for the all-important meeting. Ganguly's fanatical fan base, especially in his home state of West Bengal, took to the streets, burning effigies of Greg Chappell, as the "devil incarnate" who was out to destroy Indian cricket. They demanded that the BCCI should stand by their idol and fire Chappell.

The review committee met for four hours in Mumbai, surrounded by a media frenzy at the Taj Mahal Hotel. They heard the views of Chappell and Ganguly independently before calling them both in for a joint discussion. In the end, the committee decided to retain both Ganguly and Chappell, and asked them to work out a way to coexist professionally. The BCCI president, Ranbir Singh Mahendra, told the media that they had demarcated and clarified the roles of the captain and the coach, and that each of them had to do their own job.

Ganguly expressed his relief and satisfaction after the review meeting. He thanked the BCCI and his fans for their love and support and indicated that he was ready to move on from the controversy and focus on cricket.

As the dust settled on one of the most unsavoury incidents in Indian cricket, everyone left for a desperately needed two-weeks break. Indian team had a month before their next international assignment, which was a seven-match ODI series against Sri Lanka. But before that, they had to assemble for the Challenger Trophy, country's most important domestic 50-overs tournament that would help the selectors pick the squad for the series.

A bold new direction

The review committee decision notwithstanding, Ganguly's fate as captain was still hanging in the balance, as the national selection committee, headed by Kiran More, were set to meet on October 13, the last day of the Challenger series, to first decide who would lead India in the upcoming home series against Sri Lanka, and then pick the rest of the squad the next day, as told to the PTI by a "highly-placed source close to the board"

For all these reasons, the 2005 edition of the Challenger trophy had assumed more significance than any previous one. However, some of the biggest stars of Indian cricket were missing from the event. Dravid and Sehwag were off to take part in the first ever Super series - a historic one-off test between an ICC World XI and Australia - while Ganguly was sidelined due to his niggling elbow injury. The only silver lining was the highly anticipated return of Sachin Tendulkar, who had been out of action for six months after undergoing surgery - the longest he had ever been away from the game.

In Ganguly, Dravid and Sehwag's absence, the three teams in the tournament - India seniors, India A and India B - were led by Mohammad Kaif, VVS Laxman and Dinesh Mongia respectively. They all had an equal record of one win and one loss each, but India seniors emerged as the champions by defeating India B by 3 wickets in the final. The tournament saw some brilliant batting performances from Venugopal Rao, who scored the most runs, VVS, Yuvraj Singh and Robin Uthappa, who all smashed dazzling centuries. The bowling honours were shared by Murali Kartik and Sreesanth, who took 7 wickets each. Sreesanth also earned the player of the tournament award for his impressive bowling, including the fiery spell where he managed to dismiss the great Tendulkar, who had an underwhelming comeback in terms of runs but gained some valuable match practice before the upcoming series.

Sourav Ganguly made the selectors' job easy by making himself unavailable for the first two games of the seven-match series due to his ongoing elbow issue. They appointed Dravid as the skipper and Sehwag as his deputy for the upcoming two limited-over series and rewarded Sreesanth for his impressive showing in the Challenger trophy. Laxman was once again ignored despite scores of 48 and 108, as the selectors persisted with Venugopal Rao and Raina. Zaheer Khan was also left out of the squad, even though he had shown glimpses of his fiery form in some matches of the series. The selectors preferred the young left-arm pacer from Uttar Pradesh, RP Singh. Kaif missed out due to the injury he sustained during the final, while JP Yadav got another chance to prove his worth.

The series against Sri Lanka kicked off with a sensational display by the great Sachin Tendulkar, who made a heroic return from a long injury layoff with a vintage innings in the first match at Nagpur. Wearing a bandage on his left arm, Tendulkar played like his old, carefree self, stroking 93 runs off 96 balls with the help of 9 sublimely timed fours and a glorious six, silencing any doubts about his form and fitness and reminding everyone why he was still the very best in the business. He was well supported by Irfan Pathan, who smashed 83 runs off 70 balls as a pinch hitter, hitting 4 sixes and 8 fours. Skipper Rahul Dravid also joined the party, racing away to 85 runs off 63 balls with his trademark shots. MS Dhoni added some late fireworks, blasting 38 runs off 28 balls with 3 fours and 2 sixes as India piled up a mammoth total of 350 for 6 in their 50 overs.

India's spin trio of Harbhajan, Murali Kartik and Sehwag proved too much for Sri Lanka, who crumbled in pursuit of a huge target. They had a promising start despite losing their captain early, thanks to Jayasuriya and Sangakkara, who smashed the debutant Sreesanth all over the park. But once they fell to an early introduction of spin, the rest of the batsmen crumbled under the pressure and threw away their wickets, Murali Kartik spun a web around the Sri Lankan middle order, claiming 3 wickets and reducing Sri Lanka to 126 for 8. A late flourish from Vaas and Lokuhettige added some respectability to the score, but it was never going to be enough. Sri Lanka were bowled out for 198 in 35.4 overs, losing by a massive margin of 152 runs. Dravid was adjudged the player of the match, not only for his batting, but also for his refreshing captaincy. He caught the Sri Lankans off guard by bringing Harbhajan early, and the move paid off handsomely as the Turbanator dismissed the dangerous looking Jayasuriya, Chandana and Arnold inside the first fifteen overs. Dravid also gave Sreesanth a chance to redeem himself at the end, and the youngster picked up the last 2 wickets to end his debut on a decent note. Sending Irfan Pathan at one down was another bold move, though Dravid gave the credit for that to Tendulkar and Greg Chappell.

As far as statement of intent go, it was as emphatic as they come, as the seventh-ranked team in the world humiliated the current second-best.

The number 2 side in the world slipped to a new low in the second match at Mohali. Dravid won the toss and chose to make first use of the most seamer-friendly wicket in the country. Pathan, who had been a revelation with the bat in the first game, followed it up with a sensational spell of swing bowling that ripped through the Sri Lankan top order. He took 4 wickets for 37 runs in 8 overs, including the prized scalps of Jayasuriya and Dilshan for ducks. He made the ball talk, as he swung it late and at pace, leaving the batsmen clueless. Sri Lanka never recovered from his onslaught, and were bundled out for a paltry 122 in 31.4 overs on a good batting pitch, with Harbhajan and JP Yadav also chipping in with a couple of wickets each.

India had no trouble chasing down the target, as Tendulkar continued his fine form with another classy half-century. He scored an unbeaten 67 off 69 balls, hitting 11 exquisitely timed boundaries. He looked in supreme control, winning another duel against the great Muralitharan. He reached his fifty with a six over long-on off the spinner, and finished the game with a boundary through point. India reached 123 for one in the 21st over, winning with more than 29 overs to spare. It was another comprehensive performance by India, who took a 2-0 lead in the series. Pathan was rightly adjudged the man of the match, for his match winning spell with the new ball. The Baroda youngster who had just turned 22 the previous day was again being hailed as the "new Kapil Dev" by the media. The level-headed Rahul Dravid, on his part as the captain, downplayed such comparisons terming him a "bowler who could bat well" and urged everyone not to put such extra pressure on the young talent.

With 5 matches still to go, it was still early days in the series but the signs had been so encouraging that the national selectors kept the faith in the same combination and announced an unchanged squad of 15 for the next three games, overlooking Sourav Ganguly despite him proving both his form and fitness with a Duleep Trophy century for East Zone against North Zone.

Batting first after winning the toss, Sri Lanka put up their best batting performance in the series in the third match at Jaipur, on the back of a magnificent innings of 138 not out off 147 balls by Kumar Sangakkara who carried his bat, and was well supported by Jayawardene, who made a stroke filled 71 off 70 balls. The two brightest batting talents of Sri Lanka added 151 runs for the third wicket, and set the stage for a late flourish from Maharoof, who smashed 33 off 16 balls, as all Indian bowlers barring Harbhajan proved expensive. Sri Lanka reached a formidable total of 298 for 4 in 50 overs, and looked confident of defending it.

But they had not reckoned with one Mahendra Singh Dhoni, who unleashed a stunningly brutal assault on the Sri Lankan bowlers. He was promoted to one down, and took the game away from Sri Lanka with his fearless and uninhibited stroke play. He scored 183 not out off 145 balls, the highest score by a wicketkeeper in ODIs, eclipsing the 172 by the great Adam Gilchrist - with 15 fours and 10 sixes, a record for the most runs in boundaries in an innings (120). Dhoni was simply unstoppable, as he cleared the ropes with ease and played some truly audacious shots, finishing the match with a six over long-on, giving India a thumping 9-wicket win - and a 3-0 lead in the seven-match series - with 23 balls to spare. It was one of the greatest ODI innings ever played, and Dhoni was rightly named the man of the match, proving that his hurricane 145 against Pakistan earlier in the year was no fluke and he was much more than just another biffer of the cricket ball.

Emboldened by the 3-0 lead, Dravid decided to test his team's chasing skills by opting to field first in the fourth match at Pune. He was rewarded by Agarkar and Sreesanth, who utilized the early swing on offer to reduce Sri Lanka to 51 for 3. However, Sri Lanka recovered thanks to their captain Atapattu, who signalled a timely return to form with a composed 87. He got support from Dilshan and Arnold, who chipped in with 52 and 32 respectively. Sri Lanka looked set for a big total, but Agarkar came back strongly in his second spell and cleaned up the tail. He was the star for India taking 5 wickets for 44 runs in his 10 overs, besides taking a catch and effecting a brilliant run out through a direct hit. Sri Lanka managed to reach 261 for nine in 50 overs, a competitive but not daunting score.

India lost Tendulkar and Yuvraj early in their chase - Tendulkar falling for the ninth time to Chaminda Vaas in ODIs and Yuvraj failing to cash in on a promotion to one down - but Dravid and Sehwag steadied the ship with a 78-run stand before Sehwag fell 2 short of his fifty. Venugopal Rao joined Dravid and added 64 runs for the fourth wicket, playing with positive intent. India were cruising at 176 for 3, needing 86 from 19 overs. But then the great Muralitharan, who had had a quite series so far, struck a double blow, and Fernando dismissed Dravid for a brilliant 63, leaving India in a spot of bother at 180 for 6.

That's when MS Dhoni and Suresh Raina joined forces. Dhoni, who had hammered 183 not out in the previous match, showed his versatility by playing a clinical innings of 45 off 43 balls, shepherding the 18-years old Raina, who showcased great temperament and skill to carve 39 not out in just 30 balls, in what was only his fifth innings at this level. Dhoni and Raina shared a magnificent 82-run unbeaten stand for the seventh wicket - the first of many more such match-winning partnerships these two were going to script in the years to come. Dhoni finished the match in stirring fashion hitting two sixes in a row off Arnold, as India won by 4 wickets with 26 balls to spare, thereby sealing the series with an unassailable 4-0 lead. Agarkar was declared the player of the match for his fifer.

Four wins on trot against the second-ranked team in the world was a remarkable turnaround for a team that had started the series as underdogs. The work Chappell and his support staff had put in, in the last four months had started to pay dividends.

The circus moved to Ahmedabad for the fifth match of the series. An upbeat India rested three of their key players - Sachin Tendulkar, Irfan Pathan and Harbhajan Singh - with an eye to keep them fresh for the challenges that lie ahead. Marvan Atapattu won an important toss, ensuring India's bowlers would have to contend with heavy dew in the evening, a factor that could potentially end up being decisive. India scored 285 for 8 in 50 overs, with Gambhir and Dravid scoring scintillating centuries. Gambhir, who was playing his first ODI in two and a half years, made his maiden hundred at this level, scoring 103 off 97 balls. He added 128 runs for the fourth wicket with Dravid, who also scored 103 off 104 balls - his eleventh hundred in this format. Dhoni, who had been in sensational form, was out for a golden duck, but Gambhir and Dravid kept the scoreboard ticking. Sri Lanka fought back with Maharoof, who took 4 wickets as a supersub, and restricted India to a par score.

Sri Lanka had a shaky start to their chase, as they lost 5 wickets for 155 runs. India bowled well and picked up regular wickets, but they were hampered by the dew factor, which made the ball difficult to grip. Dilshan and Arnold took advantage of the conditions and launched a calculated counter-attack. They added 121 runs for the sixth wicket in just 15 overs, and took Sri Lanka closer to the target. Dilshan was the aggressor, scoring 81 off 67 balls with 9 fours and 2 sixes. Arnold played the supporting role, scoring 50 not out off 57 balls. They took Sri Lanka home with 5 wickets and 14 balls to spare. It was Sri Lanka's first victory on tour and it gave them hope to finish the series at an honourable 3-2. The mercurial Tillekaratne Dilshan turned a corner as a limited-overs player with this inning and deservedly walked away with the player of the match honour.

India made two changes to their squad for the remaining two matches of the series, as they continued to experiment with their bench strength. Mohammad Kaif and VRV Singh, regarded by many as the fastest bowler in the country, replaced Venugopal Rao and JP Yadav while Sourav Ganguly continued to be ignored by the selectors.

The win at Ahmedabad turned out to be a momentary respite as the Sri Lankans were back at the receiving end in the sixth match at Rajkot. Virender Sehwag, who was leading the team in the absence of the rested Dravid, won the toss and opted to field first on a sluggish pitch. He was rewarded by his pace trio, particularly Rudra Pratap Singh, the 19-year-old left-arm pacer, who bowled a brilliant spell of swing and bounce, claiming 4 wickets for just 35 runs in 9 overs, including the key wicket of Atapattu. He was well supported by Murali Kartik who took 2 for 31 runs in 10 overs. Sri Lanka were all out for 196 in the 43rd over, with only the in-form Dilshan showing some resistance with a fighting 59 off 65 balls.

India had no trouble chasing down the target despite some early hiccups, as the old firm of Kaif and Yuvraj took them home with another handsome unbeaten hundred runs partnership. Yuvraj Singh returned to form with a stylish unbeaten 79 off 67 balls. He hit 3 sixes and 9 fours, and played some elegant strokes all around the ground while Kaif completed a fine comeback with a good supporting hand of 38 not-out to go with the catch and run-out while fielding. India reached 197 for 3 in 35.4 overs, winning by 7 wickets and extending their lead to 5-1 in the series. RP Singh, in just his fourth appearance, won the player of the match.

The series reached its climax at Baroda, where India and Sri Lanka assembled for the seventh and last match. Sri Lanka were without their two biggest match winners - Jayasuriya sitting out due to a lack of runs and Muralitharan nursing an injury - and they struggled on a tricky pitch after opting to bat first. India's new ball bowlers drew first blood, dismissing both the openers inside the first 6 overs. Then Rudra Pratap Singh, who bowled with fire and venom for the second match in a row, ripped through the middle order, taking the wickets of Sanga, Mahela and Dilshan in successive overs. Sri Lanka were in deep trouble at 85 for 5 at the halfway stage, but skipper Atapattu and Arnold saved them from a collapse with an amazing partnership of 133 runs in 20 overs. They batted with flair and aggression, with Atapattu making 59 and Arnold 64. Both fell to Pathan in the same over, but they had taken Sri Lanka to a respectable total of 244 for 8 in 50 overs.

But it turned out to be a walk in the park for an Indian team that was on rampage mode. Tendulkar and Sehwag gave them a flying start, scoring 50 runs in 8 overs. Sehwag made 35, while Tendulkar scored 39. Then Pathan, the prodigal son of Baroda, entertained his home crowd with a cameo of 35 off 23 balls, hitting 4 fours and 2 sixes. He was followed by Dhoni, who continued his incredible form with another explosive innings of 80 off 73 balls with 9 fours and 3 massive sixes, and took India close to the target. He fell trying to finish the match with a six, but fittingly it was Dravid - who had a very satisfying series both as a captain as well as a batsman, scoring 312 runs at an astonishing average of 156 - who completed the job with a classy off-drive off Vaas. India won by 5 wickets with more than 10 overs to spare, and took the series 6-1. Pathan was the player of the match for his all-round performance, while Dhoni won his first player of the series honour for his series aggregate of 356 runs at an incredible average of 115.

It was an utterly dominant and ruthless performance by India, who outplayed Sri Lanka in every department of the game. Sachin was back with a bang, Dravid was batting like a dream, and Dhoni had emerged as the new poster-boy of Indian cricket. With his wicketkeeping also showing marked improvement, the maverick from Jharkhand was now vying for a place in the test team as well. Sehwag, Gambhir, Yuvraj, Kaif, and Raina had also shone with the bat at different points in the series, and Irfan had dazzled with his all-round skills, raising hopes of evolving into the genuine all-rounder that Indian cricket had been desperately looking for, for over a decade. The fast-bowling reserves were also abundant, with RP Singh, Sreesanth, Agarkar, Nehra, Zaheer, Balaji and VRV Singh in the fray. Munaf Patel was another Baroda speedster who had begun making waves in the domestic circuit impressing everyone with his pace and accuracy. Harbhajan was doing a decent job as the first-choice spinner, but Kartik had not been very effective, except for the one game where he took three wickets. The talented left-arm spinner needed and deserved more opportunities to prove himself. With the likes of Kaif, Yuvraj, and Raina replacing some slow movers, India's fielding had never looked sharper than it did in this series. All in all, India had rebounded well from the disappointments of the past year and a half, and looked primed to take on the formidable South Africa. The Proteas, under Graeme Smith and coach Mickey Arthur, had been unstoppable lately and had just climbed to the second spot in the world rankings, leaving behind the struggling Sri Lanka.

In an interview with a Kolkata newspaper, Sourav Ganguly lauded Rahul Dravid's excellent leadership and expressed his desire to make a comeback clarifying that he had no problems playing under Dravid. But the former captain had to face another disappointment when the selectors retained the same squad for the first three matches of the upcoming series, leading to another round of protests by a section of fans alleging a conspiracy against their beloved Dada.

The five-match ODI series against the Proteas had been hastily conjured and sandwiched between the ODI and test legs of Sri Lanka's tour of India. The first of these was in Hyderabad, where the visitors had already warmed up with an easy 8-wicket victory over a local team in their only practice match. It was the first international match at the new Rajiv Gandhi Stadium in Uppal, a suburb of Hyderabad, where big games were previously staged at the Lal Bahadur Shastri Stadium. But the home crowd had little to cheer as India's top order collapsed under the fiery pace of Pollock and Ntini. Sehwag was caught brilliantly by Prince off the first ball of the match, and Gambhir gave Mark Boucher his 300th catch in one-dayers, a feat only matched by the great Adam Gilchrist. India were reeling at 35 for 5, and only Yuvraj's heroic century saved them from humiliation. He fought back with aggression and patience, scoring 103 out of India's 249 with the lower order also chipping in with some useful cameos. But it was not enough to stop the South African juggernaut. Graeme Smith led the way blasting Pathan for 7 fours in a quickfire 48, and the great Jacques Kallis anchored the chase with a clinical unbeaten 68 with Prince and Kemp also contributing vital 40s. Despite nagging spells from RP and Harbhajan in the middle overs, South Africa won by 5 wickets with 7 balls to spare, extending their amazing unbeaten streak to 20 matches. Yuvraj Singh was named the player of the match for his hundred in a losing cause - his third this season and fifth overall.

Smarting from their loss in the series opener, India elected to field first in the second match at Bangalore and came up with a much improved bowling performance. The Chinnaswamy pitch was slow and low, and favoured the spinners, but Pathan was the one who struck early, moving the ball both ways and taking the first 3 wickets, including the valuable wicket of Kallis, who was outfoxed by a late outswinger. The spinners then spun a web around the batsmen and took wickets at regular intervals, with Kartik being the most frugal, conceding only 16 in his 10 overs. Kemp and Pollock dug in with uncharacteristic patience, but could only muster 169 for 9 in their 50 overs.

India's chase was sluggish at first, and Tendulkar departed early, but Sehwag, batting at number 4, soon ignited the fireworks with his explosive shots, smashing 11 fours in his 77. He found more than handy support in Pathan, who displayed his batting finesse once again with a very fine 37, highlight being the straight six off Andre Nel. They stitched together 88 for the fourth wicket and steered India to a comfortable win with plenty of overs to spare. Pathan was the player of the match, with his 3 wickets and vital runs, as South Africa's unbeaten streak of 20 matches came to an end.

On the eve of the third ODI, the selectors announced that Rahul Dravid would lead India in the three tests against Sri Lanka in December, bringing an end to Sourav Ganguly's eventful five-year tenure as not only India's most successful captain yet, but also its most impactful.

The third ODI between India and South Africa in Chennai had to be called off without a ball being bowled due to rain, leaving the series level at 1-1. This was the third time in a row that Chennai's weather had played spoilsport in an international game. In 2003, only 27 overs were played in an ODI against New Zealand; then, in 2004, a test against Australia was drawn when rain washed out the final day, with India chasing 210 with all wickets intact.

The series now hinged on the last two matches in Kolkata and Mumbai respectively.

Next day the selectors met for five hours behind closed doors and decided to keep the same squad for the last two ODIs against South Africa. But they did pick Sourav Ganguly in the capacity of a "batting allrounder" for the first two tests against Sri Lanka starting in a week, owing to Ganguly's impressive bowling returns in recent domestic matches. Anil Kumble and VVS Laxman also returned for the tests. As expected, MS Dhoni replaced Dinesh Karthik as the first-choice keeper in tests as well, but Zaheer Khan missed out on both formats despite his excellent showing in the Duleep Trophy, where he took a bagful of wickets. RP Singh was preferred over him for the tests.

Ganguly's fans were not satisfied with his test selection and continued to protest against his ODI exclusion. The same fans who booed Ganguly the last time India played at Eden, now burned effigies of Greg Chappell and Kiran More, accusing them of conspiring against the cultural icon of West Bengal. The protests became so intense that security had to be increased around the Eden Gardens stadium for the fourth ODI between India and South Africa, to prevent any disruption by the angry fans.

It was a shocking sight, as the Eden Gardens crowd turned against their own team, booing them and cheering for the South Africans, in a blatant display of their fury at the way their prodigal son, who had hit a timely 159 for Bengal in the Ranji trophy earlier in the day, was being snubbed. Local anger may have been further fuelled because of a video clip that was widely circulated on news channels, showing Greg Chappell giving a middle finger salute to Ganguly fans who were shouting slogans outside the team hotel the previous evening.

To make matters worse, Smith won a crucial toss and put India in to bat first, leaving them to contend with the treacherous dew later while bowling.

India wilted under the pressure of the hostile crowd and the metronomic Shaun Pollock, who ripped through their batting with 3 for 25 in 10 overs, 4 of them maidens. Pollock also claimed Tendulkar's wicket for the third time in succession. Only Yuvraj and Kaif showed some gumption, putting on 81 for the sixth wicket. Yuvraj hit 53 and Kaif fell short of his fifty by 4 runs. Hall also grabbed 3 wickets as India were skittled out for 188 in 47 overs.

To rub salt into India's wounds, South African openers Graeme Smith and Andrew Hall raced to the paltry target of 189 with 14 overs to spare. Smith played a captain's knock of 134 in 124 balls, smashing 20 fours and a six - his fifth and best ODI hundred - to the delight of the 80000 strong Eden crowd who cheered him on. He walked off with the player of the match award as his side beat India by 10 wickets to go 2-1 up in the series. The crowd did not stop their hostility even during the post-match ceremony. They booed Rahul Dravid, Chappell and didn't even spare Sachin Tendulkar, who had another poor outing in his record-breaking 357th appearance.

Thankfully, the fans at Wankhede stadium were fully behind the Indian team in the decisive fifth and final match of the series, largely due to the presence of Tendulkar. Rahul Dravid won the toss and took the brave decision of bowling first. He was rewarded by a superb opening spell from Pathan who dismissed both openers for 32 in 9 overs. Kallis held the innings together with a patient 91 off 146 balls, but India kept the pressure on with some brilliant fielding and smart bowling changes and fields by Dravid. They restricted South Africa to a below par 221 for 6 in 50 overs on a decent batting pitch at Wankhede. Pathan was the pick of the bowlers with 3 for 20 in 8 overs and Harbhajan also bowled well, taking 2 for 32 in 10.

Tendulkar set the tone with a blazing start, delighting his home crowd with his flair and finesse. Sehwag matched him with some daring shots, and the fans went berserk with every stroke. It was a welcome change from the boos they faced in Kolkata. But the chase hit the roadblocks after their departure, as Charles Langeveldt and Andre Nel bowled superbly in the middle, testing the Indian batsmen. Dravid, who had led brilliantly in the field, rose to the occasion with a calm and classy 78 not out. He found a perfect partner in Yuvraj, who was in splendid form, averaging a Bevanesque 50 in his last 16 ODIs. Here too, he missed his fifty by just one run, hitting

7 fours in his 64-ball knock. But fittingly, it was Dravid who hit the winning runs with 15 balls left, taking India to a 5 wicket win to level the series 2-2.

Dravid was named the player of the match for his captain's knock while his counterpart Graeme Smith and Yuvraj shared the player of the series honour, for their series aggregate of 209 runs apiece.

It was a tremendous comeback by the Indian team to level the series 2-2 against an ascendant South African team after being behind 2-1.

After playing 12 one-dayers in a row, the players and the fans were ready for a change of pace with the three-test series against a familiar opponent beginning in a week's time. Sri Lanka had been doing well in the shorter format and had risen to second in the ICC rankings, before India thrashed them 6-1. But they were not as strong in tests, so India started as favourites.

During the break week, a major event that would change the course of Indian cricket took place. BCCI's long-delayed and bitter 2005 annual election were finally held, with Sharad Pawar faction sweeping all the major seats, including the president's post, in BCCI'S annual general meeting held in Dalmiya's own den, Kolkata. Pawar himself beat Ranbir Singh Mahendra by 20 votes to 11, ending Jagmohan Dalmiya's almost two-decade grip on BCCI power. It had taken a Union cabinet minister, the support of the ruling national party, a Supreme Court decision, a former election commissioner overseeing the whole electoral process, 10 lawyers and 16 court cases to bring about this change in India's richest but most secretive sporting bodies. Pawar was the only man who could have toppled Dalmiya, and he did it. It was the end of an era for Indian cricket and the beginning of a new one, with "transparency" and "transformation" being the buzz words of the new regime. This was to be done through a "generational change" and one of the faces driving this generational change was a certain Lalit Modi - the young scion of the 8000 crore K.K. Modi group - who fought with the old guard like Dungarpur, ousted the Rungtas from the Rajasthan Cricket Association, used his legal and political savvy to get into the working committee and was now in a position to realize his long-cherished vision of an Indian cricket league and a more professional BCCI complete with a CEO and all.

First heads to roll after the new regime took over were of three selectors widely seen as pro-Sourav Ganguly - Yashpal Sharma, Pranob Roy and

Gopal Sharma - who were sacked and replaced by Bhupinder Singh, Ranjib Biswal and Sanjay Jagdale, none of whom had played test cricket. Chairman Kiran More and V.B. Chandrasekhar retained their positions. One of the deposed, Yashpal Sharma blamed Greg Chappell for his ouster and also accused him of carrying a hit-list with more names on it.

The first test in Chennai turned out a damp squib, however, as Cyclone Baaz washed out most of the play. The match had been keenly anticipated, especially in India, as ex-captain Sourav Ganguly was making his comeback after being dropped from the one-day team. It was also Sri Lanka's first test in India in 8 years, and the phenomenal Muttiah Muralitharan - Chennai's son-in-law - showed his class in the brief action that was possible.

Sri Lanka had the upper hand in the truncated game. India batted timidly after winning the toss, scoring at a snail's pace on a slow and low pitch. They were bowled out for 167, with Vaas bowling 11 consecutive maidens and taking 4 wickets. The pitch eased on the last day, and Sri Lanka raced to a small lead, with Jayawardene batting superbly. The game ended in a draw, with Vaas being the player of the match, once again proving that he was much more than just a supporting act to the great Muralitharan.

The series truly got going with the captivating second test at Delhi, where three modern greats of the game put on a dazzling exhibition of their skills.

India, led by their new full-time captain Rahul Dravid, chose to bat first on a typical dry and dusty Kotla wicket that favoured the spinners. However, they lost both their openers, Gambhir and Dravid, cheaply to Vaas and Muralitharan respectively. VVS Laxman then steadied the innings with a stylish 69, and was well supported by Sachin Tendulkar, who made history by scoring his 35th test century surpassing his idol Sunil Gavaskar's record of most test hundreds. Tendulkar also shared a vital century stand with former captain Sourav Ganguly, who scored a gritty 40. India looked set for a big total at 245 for 3 at stumps on day one.

But the next day, the Sri Lankan wizard Muttiah Muralitharan spun a web around the Indian batsmen and dismissed them for 290, taking 7 wickets in the process. His 48th five-wicket haul in tests included the prized scalps of Tendulkar, Ganguly and Dhoni, and showed why he was the most successful spinner in the world. India's own spin legend, Anil Kumble, who was back at the same ground where he had taken all 10 wickets in an innings in 1998, responded with a four-wicket haul of his own and reduced Sri Lanka to 198 for 6 by the end of day two. He took a couple more wickets on the third morning to take his innings tally to 6 for 72 and wrapped up Sri Lanka's innings for 230, giving India a 60-run lead. Only skipper Marvan Atapattu and Mahela Jayawardene offered some resistance for Sri Lanka with half-centuries each.

India's second innings started with a surprise move by Dravid, who promoted Irfan Pathan to open the batting to build quickly on the 60-run advantage. Pathan justified his captain's faith with a brilliant 93, hitting 10 fours and 2 sixes. He lost his opening partner Gambhir early, whose wretched run of single digit scores continued, falling lbw to Vaas for just 3 runs. Vaas also dismissed Laxman cheaply, and India were in trouble when Tendulkar fell lbw to Bandara for 16. But Pathan found a solid ally in Dravid, who scored a fluent 53 and added 92 runs for the fourth wicket. After Pathan's dismissal, Ganguly played another decent anchoring knock of 39 runs and supported Yuvraj, who smashed a quick 77 not out to make amends for his first innings duck. Dhoni also chipped in with an unbeaten run-a-ball 51 with the help of 2 sixes - his maiden half century coming in his third test innings. Dravid declared the innings at 375 for 6, setting Sri Lanka a daunting target of 436 runs to win.

The visitors crumbled under the relentless spin attack of India. Anil Kumble, who was playing his 99th Test, added 4 more wickets to his 6 in the first innings and completed his eighth 10-wicket haul in tests. He was the deserving winner of the player of the match award for his match-winning performance. Harbhajan Singh also chipped in with 3 wickets and kept the pressure on the Sri Lankan batsmen. Once again it was only Atapattu and Jayawardene who showed some fight with 67 runs each, but they could not prevent Sri Lanka from being bowled out for 247. India won by 188 runs and took a 1-0 lead in the series.

The team celebrated a well-deserved win, but their joy proved short-lived as later the same evening, the selectors made a debatable selection call that cast a shadow over the triumph. They axed Sourav Ganguly, the former skipper despite scores of 40 and 39 in the two innings, and brought in Wasim

Jaffer as an extra opener for the third test. The move sparked another round of protests and outrage in Kolkata and other parts of Bengal, where Ganguly enjoyed a cult following. Many former cricketers and eminent politicians like Bengal CM Buddhadeb Bhattacharya and Defence Minister Pranab Mukherjee also came out in support of Ganguly, calling his exclusion unjust and an insult to him and his fans. The issue also reached the Parliament, where the Speaker Somnath Chatterjee allowed a discussion on Ganguly issue next week.

The public outrage was so huge that the BCCI top brass, including President Sharad Pawar, had to clarify that they had nothing to do with Sourav's exclusion. They also said they were surprised by the selectors' decision and promised to review it.

Sourav Ganguly, for a change, showed restraint and said he accepted the selectors' choice. He also urged his fans and supporters to calm down and not to resort to violence.

Suffice to say, the saga of the dethroned Maharaja continued to haunt Indian cricket and split the nation with rumours and speculations.

The third and final test of the series in Ahmedabad was overshadowed by the off-field drama involving Ganguly's exclusion. Dravid, who had played 93 consecutive tests since his debut, was hospitalized with gastroenteritis and missed the match. Sehwag, who had just recovered from a throat infection, took over as captain for the first time in tests. He won the toss and chose to bat, but India soon lost three wickets, including Tendulkar, to Malinga and Muralitharan. Laxman then steadied the innings with a patient century, and got valuable support from Dhoni and Pathan, who both scored attacking fifties. India reached 398, a competitive total on a turning pitch. Laxman's ninth test hundred was a contrast to his usual style: he batted for more than 6 hours and curbed his natural flair. Dhoni counter-attacked after Muralitharan struck twice in 3 balls, while Pathan showed once again showed his range as a batsman. He added 125 with Laxman and fell just short of a hundred once again, but not before putting India in a commanding position.

Sri Lanka never recovered from their first-innings collapse on the second day, when they were bowled out for 206, trailing by 192 runs. Only the in-form Dilshan resisted with a fluent 65, as Harbhajan found his rhythm and took 7 wickets. India then lost wickets against Murali & co. in their second innings, but Yuvraj Singh justified his selection ahead of Ganguly with a powerful half-century. The tail also chipped in with some runs, and Sehwag declared on the fourth morning with a lead of 508.

Sri Lanka showed some fight in their second innings, with half-centuries from Jayawardene and Dilshan. But the target was too daunting and the Indian spin twins too relentless. The great Anil Kumble, playing his 100th Test, took another five-wicket haul, taking his series tally to 20 wickets. Harbhajan was named the player of the match for his 10-wicket haul and some useful runs down order. Kumble was awarded the player of the series for his outstanding performance with the ball. India won the match by 259 runs and the series 2-0.

This emphatic series win lifted Team India to number 2 in ICC Test rankings for the first time since the ranking system was put in place in 2001. It was a remarkable end to a year of great turmoil in Indian cricket.

Amidst backroom efforts to rehabilitate him, Sourav Ganguly flew over to New Delhi to meet BCCI President Sharad Pawar and state his case. The two had an amiable meeting. Two days later, he was named in the 16-man squad for the Pakistan tour starting on 13th January. Zaheer Khan also returned to the team after a three-month absence, while Mohammad Kaif and Murali Kartik had to be left out. Parthiv Patel was the 16th player in the squad, as a backup keeper for MS Dhoni. He was chosen over Dinesh Karthik based on their recent performances in domestic cricket.

With the announcement of the squad, the players and the coaching staff embarked on a well-earned two and a half week break to cherish the festive season with their respective families and get ready for the highly anticipated round three of the most epic showdown in cricket - India vs Pakistan.

2006

This was going to be the third series between the two neighbours in less than 24 months. Both teams were on a high at the moment. Pakistan, led by Inzamam and coached by Woolmer, had just beaten England in both tests and ODIs at home. India, under the new regime of Dravid and Chappell, had won a test series against Sri Lanka and 8 out of their last 11 ODIs. The clash of the arch-rivals was expected to be a sensational spectacle, to say the least.

It kicked off with the only tour game - a three-day match against a decent Pakistan A side that ended in a high-scoring draw.

Incessant rain ruined the first test at Gaddafi Stadium, Lahore, as it wiped out most of the play. Only 220 overs were bowled in the five days, with no chance of a result. The match ended in a dull draw, but the batsmen had a field day on a lifeless pitch. Batting first after winning the toss, Pakistan piled up a mammoth 679 for 7 declared, with four centuries, including a record-breaking 199 by vice-captain Younis Khan. He ran himself out, one short of his second double hundred against India. Mohammad Yousuf too helped himself to 173 in just 199 balls. Shahid Afridi and Kamran Akmal smashed 80-ball hundreds, adding to the misery of the Indian bowlers.

India responded with 410 for 1, thanks to a mammoth opening stand between the captain and his deputy. It was one hell of a counter attack considering the monumental total India were up against. Rahul Dravid was his usual solid and steady self, even as a makeshift opener for this match and scored his first test hundred as captain. Sehwag was sensational and savage, scoring his second double hundred in a row against Pakistan. He hit 48 boundaries, mostly on the off-side, in a breathtaking display of stroke play. He fell just three runs short of breaking the world record for the highest opening partnership in tests. The match ended with no result, but plenty of runs and records with Virender Sehwag walking away with the player of the match award for his scintillating 254.

The second Test at Faisalabad in 2006 was another run orgy, as the pitch offered no help whatsoever to the bowlers. Pakistan chose to bat first and scored a massive 588, thanks to some excellent batting from their middle order giants. The two Ys added 142 runs for the third wicket, and were looking good for their second successive hundreds each, but fell in quick succession to uncharacteristic loose shots. Inzi and Afridi then took charge and smashed the Indian bowlers all over the park. Afridi hammered his fastest and highest test ton, off just 78 balls, while Inzamam caressed his 25th. Shoaib Akhtar also chipped in with a cameo of 47. RP Singh, making his test debut, was the most successful bowler for India, taking 4 wickets on a completely dead pitch.

In reply, India lost Sehwag early, but Dravid and VVS Laxman steadied the innings with a record partnership of 190 for the second wicket against Pakistan. Dravid scored his second successive hundred, while Laxman scored a fluent 90. They batted for more than 5 hours and took India past 200. However, they both fell in the same session, triggering a mini-collapse. The match came alive for a brief but electrifying period of play as Shoaib Akhtar, the fastest bowler in the world, came charging in and unleashed a barrage of bouncers at the Indian batsmen. He was furious and fearless, and he made the ball fly past the batsmen's noses and helmets. He even got the mighty Sachin Tendulkar out with a vicious snorter that grazed his glove.

But there was one man who stood up to Akhtar's challenge. MS Dhoni, the new sensation of Indian cricket, decided to fight fire with fire. He hooked and pulled Akhtar's bouncers with disdain, sending one over the boundary for a six. He was fearless and flamboyant, played some of the most audacious shots seen in the series and announced himself as a test batsman, scoring his first test hundred in style, off just 93 balls. Irfan Pathan supported him well, and showed his class as a batsman but missed out on a hundred yet again. They added 210 runs for the sixth wicket, and took India past Pakistan's huge total of 588 to finish on 603. It was a spectacular riposte, and it made the match worth watching.

The fourth day was another dreary affair, as Younis Khan and Mohammad Yousuf piled on the runs for Pakistan. They both scored centuries, and shared a stand of 242 runs for the third wicket. Zaheer Khan had a late burst of wickets and took four in a row. Inzamam decided to declare at 490 for 8. Dravid and Laxman batted out the last 8 overs without any trouble. The match ended in a dull draw, with no joy for the players or the spectators.

The match saw a total of 1,702 runs scored for the loss of 28 wickets, with six centuries and four half-centuries. It was a forgettable affair for the fans who wanted to see some contest between bat and ball. The adjudicators did well to award the player of the match to RP Singh, who had an impressive debut, taking 5 wickets on that nightmare of a pitch.

The series had been a massive letdown so far. The previous three series between these teams - going back to the 1998 - were full of excitement and drama, and made us forget the boring draws of the past. But now, they seem to have gone back to the old ways, where playing safe was more important than playing to win. This was not a good advertisement for the India-Pakistan rivalry and was hurting the health of the game. Ashes 2005 had revived test cricket, but the pitches at Lahore and Faisalabad threatened to kill it again. The game and its lovers deserved better.

The third and final test at Karachi in 2006 was a dramatic turnaround from the previous two matches. The pitch was green and lively, and the conditions were overcast. Rahul Dravid won the toss and decided to bowl first, hoping to exploit the swing and seam. He was proved right, as Irfan Pathan stunned Pakistan with a hat-trick in the first over of the match. He dismissed Salman Butt, Younis Khan and Mohammad Yousuf with three absolute gems of deliveries that moved in the air and off the pitch. Butt edged to slip, Younis was trapped leg-before, and Yousuf was bowled by a ball that almost spun back from outside off. It was the earliest hat-trick in the history of test cricket, and it left Pakistan in tatters at 0 for 3. Pathan had been struggling with a mysterious loss of pace for a while, but he made up for it with prodigious banana swing here, reminding many of the Sultan of swing himself, Wasim Akram.

Zaheer Khan joined the party with a couple of strikes of his own and when RP removed Imran Farhat, Pakistan had collapsed to 39 for 6 by the 11th over of the match. Even reaching 50 seemed like a distant dream.

Enter Kamran Akmal. The diminutive keeper-batsman played one of the great back-to-the-wall classics in the annals of test cricket, smashing 18 fours and adding valuable stands with Abdul Razzaq and Shoaib Akhtar. He scored his seventh international hundred in the past year, and took Pakistan to a respectable 245.

India could not capitalize on their early advantage, as they were bowled out for 238 by Pakistan's versatile pace trio of Mohammad Asif, Abdul Razzaq and Shoaib Akhtar. Asif and Razzaq shared 7 wickets, while Akhtar hit Sachin Tendulkar on the helmet with a bouncer. Yuvraj Singh and Irfan Pathan fought hard with 40s, while Sourav Ganguly made a gutsy 34 on his return to the team after being dropped for the Faisalabad test in favour of an extra seamer. Pakistan were a bowler short but Younis Khan, captaining the side in absence of injured Inzamam, impressed with his bowling changes and attacking field placements.

Pakistan then batted superbly in their second innings, piling up 599 for 7 declared. All of their top seven batsmen scored more than fifty, with Faisal Iqbal scoring his maiden test century. Mohammad Yousuf and Abdul Razzaq fell short of their hundreds by just 3 and 10 runs respectively.

India faced an impossible target of 607 runs to win, and never showed any intent to chase it down. They lost wickets at regular intervals, and were eventually dismissed for 265. Asif and Razzaq again did the damage, taking 7 wickets between them. Shoaib Akhtar also picked up two wickets, including Rahul Dravid's in the second over. Only the in-form Yuvraj Singh showed some spine, scoring a brave century in the second innings - his second in tests - but it only delayed the inevitable.

Pakistan won the match by 341 runs, and the series by 1-0. It was their first test series win over India since 1986-87. Kamran Akmal was named the player of the match for his heroic century in the first innings. Younis Khan was named the player of the series for his phenomenal batting performance, scoring 553 runs at an average of 184.33.

The 2005 return series in India may have ended in a stalemate but a determined Pakistan had finally managed to avenge the 2004 home series loss. The victory also meant they had now vanquished not one but two second-ranked test sides at home back-to-back. Coach Bob Woolmer's wards were clearly on a roll, and ready to face India in the upcoming five-match one-day series.

India, on the other hand, had some major worries to contend with. Their batting lynchpin Sachin Tendulkar and their lead spinner Harbhajan Singh were struggling with indifferent form. That sensational first over hat-trick notwithstanding, Irfan Pathan, too, had lost his pace and edge as a strike bowler. The stats too were in Pakistan's favour, as they had won 10 of their last 12 ODIs, while India had won 8. Pakistan had also dominated India in their recent clashes, winning 8 of the last 10 ODIs between the two teams. In short, India were the underdogs and needed to find their collective mojo quickly.

Sourav Ganguly was once again left out from the ODI squad after failing to impress in the test series. The only change in the team that drew 2-2 with South Africa was the inclusion of Zaheer Khan. The selectors termed it a "collective decision to retain a winning combination". The team got a fresh dose of youth as Kaif, Raina, Murali Kartik and Sreesanth joined the squad, while Ganguly, Kumble and VVS returned to India.

Kaif (as captain) and Raina had just guided the unfancied Uttar Pradesh to their first ever Ranji Trophy title, and were expected to bring some much-needed spark and zest to India's fielding and batting. Left-arm spinner Kartik was selected as a back-up for the struggling Harbhajan. Sreesanth was expected to add some bite and fire to India's attack.

The ODI series kicked off at Peshawar, just five days after the end of the test series. Inzamam won the toss and opted to bowl first, hoping to exploit the overcast conditions at the Arbab Niaz Stadium. India suffered an early blow, as Sehwag was dismissed in the first over. Sachin Tendulkar, who was facing growing criticism for his poor form, silenced his critics with a masterful even hundred. He became the first batsman to score 14,000 runs in ODIs, enroute his 39th ODI century. He was well supported by Irfan Pathan, who came in at No. 3 and smashed 65 off 65 balls. Mahendra Singh Dhoni also played a blistering knock of 68 off 53 balls, hitting 11 fours and a six. Yuvraj Singh chipped in with a quick-fire 39 off 28 balls. India looked set for a total in excess of 350, but Tendulkar's wicket triggered a collapse. India lost their last 6 wickets for just 23 runs in 28 balls, and were bowled out for 328. Rana Naved took 4 of those but Mohammad Asif with 3 for 30 was the best bowler on show for Pakistan.

Pakistan's run-chase was set up by a brilliant 101 by opener Salman Butt and the flowing 151-run second wicket stand in 142 balls he shared with another established tormentor of Indian team, Shoaib Malik, who slammed 90 off just 67 balls with 9 fours and 3 sixes. India did not give up easily, and took some crucial wickets under rapidly fading light. But Pakistan, to their credit, made sure they were ahead of the required score under the Duckworth/Lewis method at all times. They were 311 for 7 in 47 overs when the umpires offered them the option of bad light which they readily took, winning the match by 7 runs as per the D/L method. Salman Butt was named the man of the match for his strokefilled hundred - his third against India.

The match had its fair share of drama, as Inzamam-ul-Haq became only the third batsman in history to be given out for obstructing the field. He tried to stop a throw from Raina with his bat, while standing outside his crease. He argued with the umpires, but had to walk back to the pavilion. Inzi felt that the appeal was against the spirit of the game, but Dravid disagreed. He said that it was a legitimate dismissal, and that the umpires had made the right decision. It was a controversial moment that sparked a heated debate among the fans and experts alike and may have had a bearing in Pakistan readily accepting the umpire's offer of bad light.

Pakistan's decision to bat first after winning the toss backfired in the second ODI at Rawalpindi, as India's new ball bowlers exploited the seam-friendly conditions to rattle their top order. Pakistan were reduced to 68 for four, with Irfan Pathan taking 3 wickets and Zaheer Khan one. Sreesanth too bowled a very impressive first spell. Pakistan's hopes rested on Shoaib Malik and Younis Khan, who staged a remarkable recovery with a timely century partnership. Malik played a fluent knock of 95, while Younis was more adventurous with his 81. They took Pakistan to a respectable total of 265, but it proved to be inadequate against India's batting firepower.

India's chase was spearheaded by Virender Sehwag, who always found his mojo against Pakistan. He and Sachin Tendulkar launched a blistering assault on the Pakistani bowlers, adding 105 runs in just 15 overs. Sehwag was in sublime form, hitting 10 fours and a six in his 60-ball 67. He had to retire hurt after injuring his shoulder while trying to hit Naved-ul-Hasan for another six. Tendulkar also creamed 8 boundaries in his 43-ball 42. Yuvraj Singh then took charge of the chase and played a superb innings of unbeaten 82 off just 89 balls with 8 fours and 2 sixes in the company of his captain Rahul Dravid who contributed a typically unfussy 56. Yuvi finished the game in style as India won by 7 wickets with almost 7 overs to spare, to make it 1-1. Irfan Pathan was declared the player of the match for his match winning opening spell.

This was India's tenth consecutive victory while chasing. This was a remarkable turnaround in their fortunes, as they had lost 9 out of 10 matches while batting second before this streak. The much-maligned captain & coach pair of Dravid and Chappell deserved some credit for the way they engineered this overnight turnaround, with their flexible approach to batting order and the novel concept of a 'floater', which the captain often took upon himself.

Injured duo of Sehwag and Harbhajan were sent back home to recover in time for the upcoming home series against England beginning next month. Rahul Dravid won his first toss of the series and opted to bowl first on a greenish track. India's pacers made early inroads, with Pathan dismissing both openers and RP Singh getting rid of Akmal and Yousuf. Pakistan were in trouble at 82 for 4 in the 18th over, and things got worse when Tendulkar, not for the first or the last time, got the better of Inzamam with a clever googly. Younis also fell cheaply to RP Singh, leaving Pakistan at 158 for 6 in the 33rd over. However, Malik and Razzaq staged a remarkable recovery, adding 86 runs at better than a run a ball. Malik scored his fifth ODI hundred and third against India, hitting 11 fours and a six, while Razzaq smashed 64 off 56 balls with 7 fours and 2 sixes. They lifted Pakistan to a respectable total of 288 for 8. Pathan and RP Singh were the pick of the bowlers for India, taking three wickets each.

The pitch was still tricky and the Pakistani bowlers, especially Mohammad Asif, exploited the conditions well. He dismissed Gambhir and Pathan in the same over, reducing India to 12 for 2. He also troubled Dravid and Tendulkar, who struggled to cope with his swing and seam. Dravid fell for 11, but Tendulkar showed his class and skill to overcome the initial difficulties and play a stellar knock of 95. He hit 16 fours and a six, and kept India in the hunt but missed out on a most deserved hundred by just 5 runs, falling to his old nemesis Abdul Razzaq for the sixth time in ODIs. When Umar Gul removed Kaif in the next over, India were 190 for 5 in the 35th over, and the match seemed to be slipping away from them.

But then, Dhoni and Yuvraj came together and changed the whole complexion of the game with their fearless and flamboyant batting. Dhoni was ruthless, smashing 72 off 46 balls that contained 13 hits to the fence. He attacked the Pakistani bowlers with disdain, and made the target look easy. Yuvraj was elegant, scoring an unbeaten 79 off 87 balls with 10 fours. He complemented Dhoni well, and played some gorgeous shots of his own. The duo added an unbroken stand of 102 runs in just 12 overs, and took India to a comfortable five-wicket win with 14 balls to spare. It was their second match-winning partnership of over a hundred runs, after their 154-run stand against Zimbabwe a few months ago. They showed a great chemistry that hinted at future accomplishments.

Rahul Dravid opted to chase again after winning the toss in the fourth ODI at Multan. Pakistan's batting crumbled against a spirited and skilful Indian seam attack, who exploited the pitch and the poor judgment of the batsmen to reduce Pakistan to 29 for 4 by the 13th over. Hometown hero Inzamam tried to salvage the innings with a fighting 49, but he was yet again outsmarted by Tendulkar's genius.

India's chase was not without drama, as Mohammad Sami bowled a hostile first spell to remove both openers cheaply. However, Dravid and Yuvraj steadied the ship with a solid 85-run partnership. Skipper Dravid scored another unruffled fifty, while Yuvi contributed 37. Suresh Raina finished the game with a breezy unbeaten 35, as India reached the target in 32.3 overs, to clinch the match and with it, the series with one game still to go. R. P. Singh was named the player of the match for his impressive 4-wicket haul.

With the series already in the bag, India rested Sachin for the fifth and final match of the series, played at Karachi where they had succumbed to one of their biggest test defeats just 18 days ago. Pakistan were put in to bat by Rahul Dravid, who won his third toss of the series. They got off to a steady start, with Kamran Akmal and Imran Farhat adding 62 for the first wicket. However, Sreesanth, brought in as first-change turned the game on its head with a terrific spell of fast bowling. He removed both openers and Shoaib Malik in quick succession, reducing Pakistan to 77 for 3. Ramesh Powar, playing his first match of the series, added to Pakistan's woes by trapping Inzamam lbw with a straighter one. Pakistan were in trouble at 115 for 4, and needed a rescue act from their middle order.

Mohammad Yousuf and Younis Khan did just that with a 95-run partnership for the fifth wicket. Yousuf was the aggressor, scoring 67 off 59 balls with 9 fours and a six. Younis provided the late impetus, scoring an unbeaten 74 off 79 balls with 6 fours to take Pakistan to a decent 288. Sreesanth with 4 wickets for 50 runs was the pick of Indian bowlers.

Dravid, opening the innings in absence of the rested Sachin, and Gambhir gave them a steady start, but Pakistan's seamers kept them in check. Dravid scored another tranquil fifty, but his wicket gave Pakistan a glimmer of hope.

That hope was soon dashed by the dynamic duo of Yuvraj and Dhoni, who took charge of the chase. They ran hard, hit hard, and put Pakistan under pressure. Yuvi played some glorious cover-drives, while Dhoni waited for his chance to strike. Pakistan's fielding and bowling fell apart, as Yuvraj and Dhoni plundered the runs. Yuvraj survived a drop on 64, and went on to score his first ton against Pakistan and sixth overall. He was in pain from a hamstring injury, but he battered the bowling with powerful punches. Dhoni was his usual unbridled, explosive self, scoring 77 not out off 56 balls with 8 fours and 3 sixes. He unleashed his trademark shots - swivel pulls, lofted drives and the 'helicopter' flick - and made a mockery of Pakistan's bowling attack. He finished the match with a six over long-on off Asif.

India ended their tour of Pakistan with a resounding 8-wicket win, sealing the series 4-1. The brilliant Yuvraj Singh was rightly adjudged the player of the match as well as series.

It was a dominant performance from the visitors, who once again proved their superiority in all departments of the game - batting, bowling and most of all fielding. They also showed their excellence in chasing, as they won their 13th match in a row batting second, now just one short of the legendary Windies team of the mid-80s.

Loss in the third test notwithstanding, the tour, on the whole, had been a success for the Indian team, thanks to the 4-1 drubbing in the one-dayers. Fab four of Sachin, Dravid, VVS and Sehwag all scored valuable runs at different stages of the tour. Yuvraj Singh and MS Dhoni announced themselves as test batsmen in memorable fashion and followed it with a couple of match-winning partnerships in the ODIs to boot. This emphatic performance by Dhoni sealed his position as the team's first-choice keeper in all formats, putting a conclusive end to India's five-year search for a world-class wicketkeeper-batsman since Nayan Mongia's departure. Irfan Pathan also had his moments with both bat and ball, highlight being that unforgettable first-over hattrick. Sreesanth's gradual evolution was another heartening development. But the real find of the tour had to be RP Singh, who shone with the ball in both formats, claiming 3 player of the match awards in his first 10 international matches.

The test team still had some lingering issues, but the limited overs squad was doing fantastically well. The results spoke for themselves - the unflappable Rahul Dravid, in his own understated manner, had silenced the critics and the controversies that had plagued this team for some time, and ushered in a new chapter of excellence and dominance, guiding India to 12 wins out of 16 against some of the world's best teams since taking over as the captain five months earlier. The previous two seasons of dullness and mediocrity were forgotten, as the team looked forward to build on the momentum.

19

Forward March

England had just achieved a historic Ashes win after 19 years of waiting, about six months back. They had lost their next series to Pakistan, but they were still expected to come hard at India, a team they had a growing rivalry with since 2001. They had enough time to get used to the conditions and started the tour well by beating a weak CCI XI with Collingwood and Blackwell doing well. But the visitors faced a setback when they lost to India board president XI, who had Gambhir starring with the bat with a timely hundred and Baroda pacer Munaf Patel with the ball with 5-wicket hauls in both innings. England's preparations for the first test received a further, major double jolt as they lost their Ashes winning captain Vaughan and the experienced Marcus Trescothick to knee injury and depression respectively, leaving them with a depleted squad. They also had some other players struggling with fitness issues and doubts before the first test on March 1.

Unlike the visitors, the hosts had a problem of plenty, as they picked their team for the first test. Former captain Sourav Ganguly, who had already lost his place in the one-day side, failed to make the cut in the test squad as well, ending the speculation about his future, at least for now. India picked two youngsters, VRV Singh, a tall fast bowler from Punjab, and Piyush Chawla, a promising leg spinner from Uttar Pradesh. Wasim Jaffer, who impressed with 48 runs for the Indian Board President's XI, also kept his spot in the team.

The first test at Nagpur turned out to be a tale of two debutants and two contrasting captaincy approaches. England, who had lost 3 key players before the match, were led by Andrew Flintoff who won the toss and chose to bat first. India's new ball bowlers had them in trouble at 136 for 4, but Paul Collingwood played a gutsy knock of 134 not out to lift them to 393. He was well supported by the young Alastair Cook, who arrived in India just two days before the match and scored a composed 60 on debut. He wasn't the only one who did well on test debut, however, as Sreesanth too bowled with sustained intensity to claim 4 wickets, including that of the dangerous Kevin Pietersen. Pathan too chipped in with 3 wickets.

Despite a solid 81 by opener Wasim Jaffer, India's reply was rocked by Matthew Hoggard, who swung the ball both ways and claimed 6 wickets on the third morning, including that of Jaffer. Hoggard reduced India to 190 for 7, before Mohammad Kaif and Anil Kumble staged a remarkable recovery. Kaif, playing only because Yuvraj was out injured, missed out on his maiden test century by a mere 9 runs. Kumble's hard work on his batting in the nets finally paid off, as he reached his first test half-century in nine years. He and Kaif added 128 runs for the eighth wicket, frustrating the English bowlers and reviving India's hopes. India were eventually dismissed for 323, conceding a lead of 70.

England batted aggressively to set up a declaration. Cook continued his impressive debut with an unbeaten 104, becoming the 16th player to score a century in his first test, the youngest Englishman to do so in 67 years; and possibly the first cricketer to receive a marriage proposal on debut, from a fan in the crowd who held up a sign with her offer. He was joined by England's best batsman, Kevin Pietersen, who played with his usual flair and aggression, blasting 87 off 110 balls. England declared at 297 for 3, leaving India a daunting target of 368 in about 3 sessions on the final day.

Any hopes of an unlikely Indian win faded away as soon as Sehwag was dismissed for a duck by his bête noire Hoggard, as Dravid opted for a defensive approach, putting on 82 runs with Jaffer for the second wicket. It was a slow and steady partnership, but it lacked the urgency and intent required to chase down a big target. Jaffer reached his second test century and Dravid scored 71, but both perished in a sudden burst of aggression in the last session. But the crowd was treated to a dazzling cameo from Tendulkar, who, perhaps irked at being pushed down the order, played some outrageous shots to express his displeasure. His brilliance was short-lived though, as the clock ran out for him to pull off a miracle win. India ended at 260 for 6, escaping with a draw from a tricky situation they had created for themselves. Matthew Hoggard was the man of the match for his 6-wicket haul that turned the game on its head on the third day.

This was the first occasion that Rahul Dravid's captaincy came under fire for being too defensive.

Munaf Patel's ten-wicket haul in the tour game earned him a place in the test squad for the remaining two matches. He got his maiden test cap when Sreesanth was ruled out with a viral infection. India made a daring decision to go with 5 specialist bowlers for the first time in ages in the second test at Mohali. It was a bold move that showed their intent to win the series.

The move was rewarded as England, who again opted to bat first, were bowled out for 300, with only Pietersen offering some fight with 64. Captain Flintoff and keeper Geraint Jones added some respectability to the score with a century partnership, their fifth in the last two years, but Kumble wrapped up the innings with a 3-wicket burst, enroute his 32nd fifer in tests, also going past the Himalayan milestone of 500 test wickets in his 105th test, in the process. Only the phenomenal Muralitharan had taken fewer tests to reach there than India's gentle giant. India replied with 338, taking a slender lead of 38 runs. Dravid missed out on a century by mere 5 runs - his ninth score in the nineties - while Irfan Pathan scored another fluent test fifty. Flintoff led from the front for England with 4 wickets.

England's second innings was a disaster, as they collapsed against the spin of Kumble and swing of Munaf Patel. Kumble took 3 crucial wickets of Andrew Strauss, Ian Bell and Pietersen as England's batsmen showed no application or intent, and crawled at a snail's pace, losing half their side for 112 runs at stumps on day 4, still trailing by 74 runs. The only bright spot for them was Flintoff, who remained unbeaten on 51. The final day saw no respite for England, as they lost their last 5 wickets for just 15 runs. Debutant Patel produced a lethal spell of reverse swing bowling that evoked memories of the great Waqar Younis, claiming the wickets of Geraint Jones, Shaun Udal and Hoggard in a span of just 9 balls, leaving Flintoff stranded on 51 not out. England were all out for 181, setting India a target of 144 runs to win.

India had no trouble in chasing down the target, as Sehwag unleashed his trademark aggression. He smashed 76 runs off just 89 balls, hitting 9 fours and 2 sixes, signalling a welcome return to form. His opening partner Jaffer departed early but Sehwag and Dravid completed the formalities without any fuss. India won by 9 wickets with more than a session to spare, and took an unassailable lead of 1-0 in the three-match series.

It was a memorable win for India, as they celebrated Kumble's landmark achievement and Munaf Patel's impactful debut. Kumble was named the man of the match for his match haul of 9 wickets for 144 runs.

Munaf's match figures of 7 for 97 were the best ever for an Indian fast bowler on debut. The 22 years old's remarkable cricketing journey - from Ikhar, a small and non-descript Gujarat village of 10,000 people, to a ceramic factory where he worked hard for a paltry salary of 1200 rupees, to this stunning performance on test debut made for a fascinating underdog story.

The third and final test of the series, played at the storied Wankhede stadium began with a surprising decision by Dravid, who won the toss and chose to bowl first on a seemingly good batting surface. England made the most of the opportunity and reached 400, thanks to a solid 128 by Strauss, an aggressive 88 by debutant Shah and an even 50 by captain Flintoff. India's fielding was sloppy, as they dropped several catches. Sreesanth and Harbhajan were the only bowlers who troubled the batsmen, taking 4 and 3 wickets respectively.

England took control of the match with a superb bowling display on the third day. Hoggard struck early with a couple of bouncers that dismissed the Indian openers, while Jimmy Anderson made a brilliant comeback with 4 wickets, including the prized scalps of Dravid for 52 and Tendulkar for just 1. MS Dhoni top-scored with 64 as India were bowled out for 279, giving England a lead of 121 runs.

England then batted cautiously in their second innings, scoring at a slow rate of 2.06 runs per over. They lost wickets at regular intervals, as India's spin twins exploited the turning pitch with Kumble picking up 4 wickets. Flintoff was the only batsman to show some aggression, scoring his second half-century of the match. He was dropped thrice by the Indian fielders, who had another poor day in the field. England were eventually dismissed for 191, setting India a target of 313 in 98 overs to win the match.

The last day of the test saw a sensational display of bowling by England, who skittled out India for a paltry 100 runs and won by 212 runs. It was a dramatic turnaround, as India had looked comfortable at 75 for 3 at lunch, chasing 313 to win. But after the break, England, fired up by listening to Johnny Cash's 'Rings of Fire', unleashed their fury, led by the inspirational Flintoff, who bowled with pace and venom to take 3 wickets for just 14 runs in 11 overs, including the key wicket of Tendulkar. Shaun Udal, the 37 years old off-spinner, matched his captain's feat with 4 wickets for 14 runs, as India collapsed in a heap, losing their last 7 wickets for just 25 runs in 15 overs, showing poor shot selection and judgement. Dhoni's reckless dismissal off Udal, caught at mid-off by Panesar, epitomised India's lack of application.

This memorable, series-levelling win was England's first win in India in 21 years and also their biggest by runs on Indian soil. Flintoff was named the player of the match as well as the series for his outstanding all-round performance and inspired leadership in the face of great odds. It was a stunning achievement for England, who overcame the loss of several key players from their Ashes glory, such as Vaughan, Trescothick, Giles, Simon Jones and, for the final match, Steve Harmison. They showed remarkable resilience and determination to beat India in their own backyard, despite being written off by many.

The Wankhede was a scene of contrasting emotions. While the 3000 strong Barmy Army celebrated their team's series-levelling act, the Indian fans were furious and frustrated. They demanded the return of Sourav Ganguly while booing Rahul Dravid at the post-match presentation. Some of them even had the gall to boo Mumbai's very own Sachin Tendulkar for his continued dismal run. The atmosphere was so hostile that some English players had to face vulgar abuse from the crowd, prompting an apology from the great Farokh Engineer, who had settled in England.

Dravid admitted that he made a wrong call by opting to field first in the press conference later.

After the test series, both teams shifted their focus towards the one-day format which was a whole different ballgame. England played and lost their only warm-up game against a decent Rajasthan Cricket Association XI, led by the brilliant Ajay Jadeja - regarded by many as 'the best captain India never had' - who was back playing domestic cricket after clearing his name from the match-fixing scandal.

Sachin Tendulkar faced another setback in this ongoing injury-plagued phase of his career, as he was ruled out of entire seven-match one-day series due to a shoulder injury that required urgent surgery. He was expected to be out of action for at least a couple of months. The Indian selectors made a couple of changes to their squad for the series, bringing in the young fast bowler Munaf Patel, who had impressed in the test series. They also recalled the middle-order batsman Venugopal Rao and retained Sehwag, who had missed the last few ODIs against Pakistan because of a back injury. Gautam Gambhir, who had scored a century in the tour match, was also retained as the other opener. However, the selectors again left out the experienced duo of Zaheer Khan and Anil Kumble, who was India's leading wicket-takers in tests, citing their intent to "not disturb a winning combination too much" as the reasons for their continued exclusion.

The series was expected to be a close fight between two well-matched sides. England and India had an equal record of 5 wins each in their last 10 matches with a result. England had also won more than half of their 22 matches in India. The overall score was 25-24 in England's favour. However, India had a clear edge in recent form, winning 15 of their last 20 games, while England had only 7 wins, 3 of which were against low-ranked Bangladesh.

English captain Flintoff decided to bowl first on a pitch that favoured the bowlers in the first ODI at Delhi. His bowlers did not disappoint him, as they ripped through the Indian top order and reduced them to 80 for 5 in 20 overs. However, the Indian lower order showed some fight and added 123 runs for the last 5 wickets. Harbhajan, who came at number 9, was the highest scorer with a gutsy 37. Little known Kabir Ali was the star of the England bowling, taking 4 wickets, while Anderson and Liam Plunkett took a couple each. India were all out for 203 in 47 overs.

England's chase got off to a terrible start as Irfan Pathan struck twice in the first over, leaving them at 4 for 2. However, the other two seamers - Sreesanth and RP's inexperience showed as they leaked too many runs at the other end. Harbhajan struck in the 11th over to dismiss Matt Prior, but England were still in a good position at 117 for 3 in 20 overs. Then Yuvraj changed the game by removing Pietersen, who was looking dangerous on 46. Harbhajan then took over and ran through the England batting line-up, taking 4 more wickets, including the key one of the well-set Flintoff for 41.

England collapsed from 117 for 3 to 164 all out in 40 overs, giving India a thrilling 39-run victory. Harbhajan won the player of the match with his all-round performance, scoring 37 runs and taking 5 wickets - his second fifer in ODIs. More importantly, he regained his form and confidence after a lean patch.

England, who won the toss and chose to bat, struggled to cope with the spin-friendly pitch and the variety of Indian spinners. Only Kevin Pietersen showed some flair and aggression, scoring 71 and equalling the great Sir Viv Richards' record of reaching 1000 ODI runs in just 21 innings. He was well supported by Strauss, who made 61, but the rest of the batting line-up failed to fire. Ramesh Powar, the Mumbai off-spinner playing only his fifth match, was the pick of the Indian bowlers with figures of 3 for 34 in his 10 overs. Sreesanth, though still a little wayward, also picked up 3 wickets nevertheless.

India, chasing a modest target of 227, looked in trouble when they lost their top 5 with just 92 runs on the board. Plunkett and Ian Blackwell bowled with discipline and accuracy, putting pressure on the Indian batsmen. But then came the turning point of the match, as Raina and Dhoni joined forces and put on a splendid partnership of 118 runs. Raina, barely 19 years old leftie hailing from Meerut in Uttar Pradesh, played a gem of an innings belying his age, scoring an unbeaten 81 in 89 balls with 8 fours and a six. He displayed a full range of shots, from powerful drives to delicate paddles, and kept the scoreboard ticking. Dhoni gave him solid support with a sensible knock of 38. They took India to the brink of victory, before Dhoni fell in the penultimate over. But Raina finished the match with a boundary off Anderson, giving India a 4-wicket win with 6 balls remaining. The plucky southpaw was rightly named the player of the match for his scintillating knock.

This was the second time Dhoni and Raina had scored a hundred runs together to chase down a target. Hardly two years into his international career, Dhoni had shown a knack of building strong bonds with his fellow batsmen, especially the left-handed ones. He had a similar chemistry with Yuvraj, another stylish and aggressive left-hander. Together these three were to serve as the backbone of the Indian middle order in the shorter format for the next decade.

It was a day of contrasts at the Nehru Stadium in Margaon, Goa where India and England played the third ODI of the series. In a stadium more used to football than cricket, the pitch was uneven and unpredictable, but one man rose above the conditions and produced an absolute masterclass of batting. Yuvraj Singh smashed a brilliant century, his seventh in ODIs, and powered India to a comfortable 49-run win over England. He hit 10 fours and 3 sixes in his 76-ball 103, and shared a match-winning partnership of 142 with Suresh Raina, who made a fluent 61. England had no answer to Yuvraj's onslaught, as their bowlers lost their line and length and conceded too many extras. Sajid Mahmood was the most expensive, leaking 66 runs in 8 overs on his return to ODIs.

Without KP, who was sitting this one out with a stomach bug, England's chase was doomed from the start, as Irfan Pathan struck 3 early blows with his clever variations of pace, leaving England reeling at 47 for 3. When their skipper Flintoff fell to Ramesh Powar, it became 5 for 83. Collingwood was the only batsman who showed some steel, scoring a fighting 93 in 84 balls. He added 105 runs with wicketkeeper Geraint Jones, who made 39, but it was not enough. England were bowled out for 245 in 48.5 overs, giving India the win by 59 runs and a 3-0 lead in the series with 4 matches still to go.

Yuvi was named the player of the match for his splendid hundred. He had been on a roll in ODIs, averaging a staggering 85 in his last 13 innings with 3 hundreds and 3 fifties, also winning the player of the series against South Africa.

Another man who was in red hot form for India was Irfan Pathan, who had been on a wicket-taking spree in his last 6 ODIs, claiming 17 wickets. He had a knack of getting early breakthroughs, and he did it again here as well. He could not do much with the SG ball in tests, but he was a different bowler with the white Kookaburra that he could swing at his will.

However, despite the winning streak, not everything was rosy for India, as they had some concerns with their batting. Sehwag and Kaif were going through a prolonged slump, failing to score runs consistently. Kaif, in particular was in the midst of a horror run with 4 ducks and a score of 4 in his last 5 innings since coming back from an injury. Coach Greg Chappell backed them both to come good soon. Munaf Patel, who made his ODI debut, also had a quiet day, as he went wicketless in his 8 overs. He had made an instant impact on his test debut, but he could not replicate his performance in the shorter format.

Fourth match at Kochi was again a one-sided affair, as India thrashed England by 7 wickets to seal the series with 3 games to spare. England, who won the toss and batted first, wasted a good start by losing their key batsmen in quick succession. Pietersen, who returned to the side after missing the last game due to illness, was the top scorer with 77, but he fell to Yuvraj, who also dismissed Flintoff in his next over. Jones tried to revive England's innings with a patient 49, but he injured his thigh and had to bat with a runner. He also gave up his keeping duties to Prior, who made his ODI debut. England could only manage 237 on a good batting pitch, which was never going to challenge India.

India's chase was smooth and swift, as Dravid and Pathan added 76 runs for the second wicket after Sehwag's early dismissal. Dravid played an aggressive knock of 65, hitting 9 fours and a six. Pathan also scored 46, before falling to Blackwell. Yuvraj then took over scoring a breezy 48 and finished the game with a six off Collingwood, as India reached their target in 42.5 overs. Yuvi was named the player of the match for his all round show. Dravid's men also broke the record of the mighty West Indies team of the mid 80s for the most consecutive successful run-chases in ODIs, achieving their 15th win in a row while chasing. India's dominant performance in the series earned them high praise from Matthew Hoggard, who called them the best one-day team in the world at the moment. Hoggard was certainly not the only one who felt that way.

The selectors decided to stick with the same squad for the rest of the series, as India had already clinched the series with three wins in a row. Rahul Dravid was given a break for the next couple of games and Virender Sehwag was handed the opportunity to lead the team in his absence.

The fifth ODI was a disappointing affair, as heavy rain prevented any play from taking place. The match was called off without a ball being bowled, leaving the fans frustrated and angry. Some of them vented their fury by throwing bottles and stones at the ground, injuring two policemen who were trying to control the situation. The crowd trouble cast a shadow over Guwahati's status as an international venue, as the ICC asked for a report on the incident.

England registered their first win of the series in the scorching heat of Jamshedpur thanks to their new stand-in captain Andrew Strauss. Strauss, leading the side for the first time in absence of the rested Flintoff, won the toss and chose to field first, and his decision paid off as his seamers, led by Jimmy Anderson, restricted India to a modest 223 in 48 overs. India's batsmen struggled on a true but slow wicket, and only Dhoni, who opened the innings in front of his home crowd, scoring an excellent 96, and Powar, who scored his maiden fifty, showed some resolve. Anderson was the pick of the England bowlers, taking 3 wickets for just 28 runs. Sajid Mahmood too made up for his poor performance at Goa with figures of 3 for 37.

England's chase was smooth and swift, as Strauss and Ian Bell put on a century stand for the first wicket. Strauss played a captain's knock, scoring 74 in 85 balls, before he had to retire exhausted and dehydrated. He was taken to the dressing room and given a saline drip. Bell also made a solid 46, before he was caught off a no-ball by VRV Singh who was making his limited overs debut. Pietersen then came in and finished the job with a quick-fire 33, as England reached their target with 5 wickets and 44 balls to spare, laying waste to a fine spell of 3 for 30 by Harbhajan. Strauss was named the player of the match for his superb innings and leadership.

With an eye on testing their bench strength, India made 4 changes to their team for the next game, resting Sehwag, Kaif, Harbhajan and Dhoni, and giving a debut to an exciting young talent from Karnataka, Robin Uthappa. Dravid, who returned as captain, won the toss and opted to field first. The move seemed to have backfired as England started well, with Pietersen, Collingwood and Jones scoring fifties. KP was especially aggressive, hitting 50 in 39 balls, including 23 runs off one over from the unimpressive VRV Singh. However, he injured his knee while batting and lost his momentum. England also lost their way in the end, as Sreesanth ran through their batting line-up with 6 wickets in the death overs. England were bowled out for 288 in 49.1 overs.

India's chase was smooth and swift, as Uthappa and Dravid put on a record opening stand of 166 runs. Uthappa, who was playing his first match, impressed with his strokeplay and temperament. He hit 12 fours and a six in his 96-ball 86, and became the highest scorer for India on ODI debut. He missed out on a century, as he was run-out by Anderson's direct hit. Dravid also played an excellent knock of 69 in 79 balls with 9 boundaries, before getting out lbw. Yuvraj and Raina then took over and added 115 runs for the third wicket - their second century partnership of the series. Yuvraj scored a quick-fire 63 in 57 balls, while Raina made an unbeaten 53 in 66 balls. They took India close to the target, before Yuvi fell to Collingwood in the last over. Raina then finished the game with a nerveless boundary off the first ball of the final over, as India won the match by 7 wickets and the series by 5-1.

Sreesanth was named the player of the match for his 6-wicket haul, while Yuvraj Singh was named the player of the series for his all-round performance - 237 runs and 6 wickets. This was his second player of the series honour in last three bilateral series.

Another player who had been equally prolific off late was Mahendra Singh Dhoni, whose consistent brilliance was rewarded when he pipped Ponting to be crowned the number 1 ODI batsman in the latest ICC rankings. Remarkably, this long-haired maverick achieved this feat just 38 innings into his ODI career, making him the fastest batter to reach the top spot.

Even though it came against a depleted England, the 5-1 margin was still a remarkable feat for India who were also without their finest - Sachin Tendulkar. Sourav Ganguly's fans and supporters were still fuming over his unceremonious ouster. But the facts couldn't be denied any longer. India had become a powerhouse in one-day cricket under the new regime of Rahul Dravid and Greg Chappell. They had a stunning record of 20 wins out of 27 matches since October, with only 5 losses and 2 no-results. The World Cup was less than a year away, and India looked like the team to beat. The only glitch was the worrying slump in form of Sehwag and Kaif, who needed to rediscover their mojo soon.

India and Pakistan were set to face each other again in a short two-match one-day series in the UAE. The matches were arranged at the last minute to raise funds for the victims of the devastating 2005 Kashmir earthquake. The same fifteen who had played the last few games against England flew to Dubai to play on back-to-back days.

India chose to bat first for a change, but their innings never got going on a Sheikh Zayed wicket that was not very conducive to batting, in the first match. They lost 4 wickets to run-outs, and 3 more to Shoaib Malik's clever off-spin. The only bright spot for India was the partnership between Raina and Rao, who showed some courage and skill in the middle overs. But they too could not accelerate in the end, as Raina holed out to Iftikhar in the deep, and Rao was left stranded on 61. India were all out for a paltry 197.

Pakistan chased down the target with ease, thanks to Younis Khan and Inzamam. Younis played with flair and finesse, using his supple wrists and sublime timing to score runs all over the ground. He was especially strong on the leg side, where he flicked and pulled with ease. He was well supported by Inzi, who was calm and composed at the other end. He played the anchor role, rotating the strike and hitting the occasional boundary. Together, they took Pakistan close to the target, before the Pakistan captain was dismissed by Ramesh Powar for 40. Him, Agarkar and Sreesanth bowled their hearts out but it was too late for India as Pakistan won by six wickets with just 9 balls to spare. Pakistan's president Pervez Musharraf watched the match and congratulated his team. Younis was named the player of the match for his superb 71 not out. India looked drained after a long, tough and rewarding season, but nothing can be taken away from Pakistan's fiery performance. It was their first win against the arch rivals after 4 straight losses earlier in the year.

Dravid's men showed their class and character, as they turned the tables on Pakistan in the next match. They batted with skill and patience on a difficult pitch, where the ball did not come on to the bat. Dravid and Sehwag stitched together a fantastic opening partnership, as they played with caution and confidence. Sehwag, who was rested for the last two games and was back into the side for this one in place of Robin Uthappa, was finally dismissed for 73, when Afridi's quick delivery beat his defence and hit the off stump. It was only his third fifty-plus score in last 22 innings and couldn't have come at a better time. The newly crowned *numero uno* MS Dhoni came in at one-down and kept the momentum going, with a series of inventive strokes. He dabbed, pushed, whipped and swept the ball to all parts of the ground, scoring a breezy 59, before he was deceived by a slower ball from Naved. Dravid also fell short of a century, when Asif's yorker crashed into his stumps. His 116-ball 92 was his 71st half century in this format and was a masterclass in anchoring the innings. Yuvraj then came in and smashed some thumping blows, scoring 24 off just 10 balls. He hit 3 consecutive fours and a six, and gave India the final push they needed. India finished with 269 for 5, a formidable total on that pitch.

Pakistan's chase was doomed from the start, as they lost wickets at regular intervals. Pathan and Powar were the wreckers-in-chief, as they bowled with accuracy and guile sharing 6 wickets amongst them. Pathan got rid of Farhat and Afridi with his inswingers, while Powar trapped Malik and Yousuf with his flight and turn. Yuvraj also chipped in with a stunning catch at short fine leg, as he plucked the ball out of thin air. Inzamam was the only batsman who offered some resistance, as he batted calmly and sensibly. He scored 79, before he was run out in a bizarre fashion off a direct-hit from Dravid. It was the final nail in Pakistan's coffin, as they were bowled out for 218.

India ended a long and successful season on a high note, as they beat Pakistan by 51 runs and squared the series 1-1. It was their 18th win in 24 completed matches, a stunning turnaround for a team that had suffered too many defeats in the previous two seasons. The captain who led this transformation, Rahul Dravid, was rewarded with the Man of the match award for his superb 92. His opposite number, the equally inspirational Inzamam received the Man of the Series award for scoring 119 runs in 2 innings.

20

A Season of Ups & Downs

The players enjoyed a 25-day break before they embarked on a long tour to the Caribbean, where the next world cup would be held. This Indian team had a lot of newcomers and it was crucial to give them a taste of the conditions, although the world cup was still a long way away. The tour began with a 5-match ODI series. Sachin Tendulkar opted out of the ODI leg, so the selectors retained the same 15-member squad that had played against England and Pakistan.

Brian Lara had taken over the captaincy of the Windies for the third time in his career, after Chanderpaul stepped down due to poor results, and began well by leading his team to a crushing victory against lowly Zimbabwe, winning all 5 matches in the series. The Prince of Trinidad now awaited a real test of his leadership against India.

West Indies still had a better overall record in ODIs, with 46 wins and 30 losses against India. But recent form pointed to India. They had beaten West Indies in 9 of their last 15 encounters, including a historic first ODI series win when they last visited these shores back in 2002 under the captaincy of Sourav Ganguly. And the gap was even wider when comparing the last 25 matches for each team - India had 18 wins and 7 losses, while West Indies had only 8 wins and 16 defeats.

Rain had threatened to wash out the series-opener at Kingston, but the Sabina Park staff worked wonders to get the ground ready for play. The match was reduced to 45 overs per side, and India chose to bowl first again in the hopes of exploiting the conditions. But their plans were laid to waste as Jamaica's very own Chris Gayle unleashed a storm of his own, putting on 74 in the first 10 overs with Runako Morton. India fought back with two quick wickets but Gayle carried on unperturbed, adding 80 with Lara for the fourth wicket, and reached his century off 116 balls. He was finally dismissed for 123 off 130 balls with 18 fours and 2 sixes - by Agarkar, who was India's best bowler with 2 for 38. West Indies lost their way after Gayle's departure, but still managed a decent 251 for 6 in 45 overs.

India chased down the target with some gritty batting and some luck, as Windies let them off the hook with poor fielding. Sehwag and Dravid gave India a steady start, adding 56 for the first wicket, before Sehwag was run out for 22. Bradshaw then struck twice in quick succession, removing Irfan and Yuvraj, to reduce India to 86 for 3 after 18 overs. But Dravid and Kaif got the chase back on track with a 123-run stand for the fourth wicket. Dravid played a masterful knock, scoring his 12th ODI hundred and keeping India in the hunt. He fell soon after reaching his century, leaving India 42 runs to get from 37 balls. Taylor bowled a superb over, giving away just one run, and putting the pressure back on India. Dhoni tried to break free, but only succeeded in holing out to long-on. Kaif was struggling to find the boundaries, but he got some lucky breaks: an edge flew past the keeper for a four, a wild swing landed safely in the outfield, and a run-out chance missed by a whisker. He remained unbeaten on 66, and took India home with 4 balls to spare. It was a patchy innings, but a crucial one for India and for Kaif's own form.

The win started India's new season on a winning note and extended India's winning streak in chases to 17. Rahul Dravid was named the player of the match for his splendid match winning hundred. He was now averaging a whopping 58.01 with 2 centuries and 9 fifties in 23 games since taking over as captain full-time. The Wall had finally proved, beyond a shadow of any doubt, that he was not only a master of test cricket, but also one of, if not the best one-day batsmen in the world at the moment.

Ironically, this is where things suddenly started going haywire for him and his team in the shorter format, somewhat inexplicably.

A Sudden Ambush

The 17-match winning streak when batting second finally came to an end with an agonising 1-run defeat in the second match played at the same venue a couple of days later. Dravid chose to field first on a slow and low pitch, and his bowlers did a fine job of restricting West Indies to 198. Pathan was the pick of the bowlers, taking 3 for 45 with his clever variations. Agarkar and Powar also took two wickets each. The only batsman who defied India was Ramnaresh Sarwan, who played an extraordinary innings of 98 not-out. He started slowly, but accelerated towards the end to give West Indies a fighting chance despite yet again missing out on a most-deserved hundred.

India's chase was a mirror image of West Indies', as they also lost early wickets to the left-arm swing of Bradshaw, raw pace of Jerome Taylor and part-time off spin of Marlon Samuels. In-form Yuvraj was the lone warrior for India, as he played a fabulous knock of 93. He almost pulled off a sensational win, as he hit 2 fours in the last over with 10 runs needed. But Dwayne Bravo bowled him with a perfect slower yorker, and West Indies celebrated a thrilling victory as India's 17-match chasing juggernaut finally came to a halt. Sarwan was deservedly named the player of the match for a knock which his captain, the great Brian Lara himself termed as "extra-ordinary".

The first-ever international game at Warner Park, St Kitts turned out to be an affair to remember. Batting first for a change, India lost Dravid for a duck in the first over, but Sehwag and Raina kept the score ticking with some fluent strokes. Sehwag was especially aggressive, as he cut and drove the pacers with ease. He hit 2 huge sixes, one over point off Bradshaw and one over mid-on off Bravo. Raina threw away a promising start but another batsman who was struggling for runs, Mohammad Kaif took over the supporting role, as he ran hard between the wickets. India looked on course for a total in excess of 300 but once Bravo bowled Sehwag for 97, the innings went downhill, as the spinners applied the choke. India sorely missed the commanding presence of Yuvraj who had to sit this one out due to back spasms, as Dhoni was run out by Gayle, and the rest of the batsmen failed to accelerate. Kaif was stuck on a patchy 63 not out, as West Indies bowled and fielded superbly. Samuels and Gayle were especially economical for part-timers, giving away only 64 runs in 18 overs.

West Indies had a shaky start in their chase, as they lost 3 wickets for 65. Sreesanth and Agarkar bowled well, and got some help from the umpires, who gave two dubious lbw decisions. But Sarwan and Chanderpaul steadied the ship with a brilliant partnership of 106. Sarwan played a gem of an innings, scoring an unbeaten 115 in his 100th ODI. He hit 11 fours and 2 sixes, and kept West Indies in the hunt at all times. Fellow Guyanese Chanderpaul was equally classy, scoring 58 despite a hamstring injury. He retired hurt after his fifty, but came back to bat in the final over.

The match went down to the wire, as West Indies needed 6 runs off the last over, bowled by Sreesanth. Bravo was run out off the first ball, but Dravid made a costly error in the field, giving Sarwan 2 runs instead of 1. Sarwan then finished the game with a glorious cover drive for four, sealing a 4-wicket win as West Indies took a 2-1 lead in the series. Sarwan was rightly named the Man of the Match for his match-winning knock. He was now averaging a mind boggling 84 in 16 games against his favourite opponents, India.

India had expected a smooth victory in the series, but they were in for a surprise. All 3 matches so far had been nail-biters, with the outcome decided in the last over. India were trailing by 2-1, and needed a miracle to turn things around. The only bright spot was Sehwag's return to form, scoring runs with his trademark aggression. Kaif, on the other hand, struggled to find his rhythm, despite hitting two half-centuries.

Indian batsmen found the going tough, after being put in to bat by Lara on a tricky wicket, in the fourth match of the series, played at Port of Spain. Windies bowlers bowled with pace, swing, and spin, and kept the visitors on a tight leash. Only Yuvraj and Kaif showed some spark in the middle overs with fluent fifties, while Dhoni managed to hit some late blows. However, their efforts were not enough to lift India to a competitive total, as they finished with a modest 218. Fidel Edwards bowled the best, bowling with speed and accuracy, troubling even a batsman of the calibre of Rahul Dravid, though it was Dwayne Bravo who was the most successful taking 3 wickets for just 32 towards the end.

Windies chase began with a bang as Chris Gayle unleashed his power and flair. He smashed the Indian bowlers all over the park, hitting a one-handed six and a defensive four that defied physics. He slowed down after his initial onslaught, but by then Brian Charles Lara had taken over. Playing in front of his home crowd for the second-last time, the Prince of Trinidad dazzled with his sublime stroke play and superb timing. He outwitted the Indian spinners with his nimble footwork and audacious shots, hitting them for fours and sixes with ease. He stitched a match-winning partnership with Bravo, who played a mature knock of 61 not out off just 62 balls and supported Lara well.

Lara's innings was a masterclass of batting, as he paced it perfectly. He started cautiously, nudging singles and getting his eye in. Then he exploded, dancing down the track and lofting the ball over the infield. He took a special liking to Harbhajan, whom he hit for 3 boundaries in an over, including a majestic six over long-on. He fell for 69, but by then he had done enough to seal the game and the series for West Indies. Bravo finished the job with a six off Powar, as West Indies romped home to a 6-wicket win to seal the series with an unbeatable 3-1 lead with one match still to go. Dwayne Bravo was named the player of the match for his all-round impact.

In the fifth and final match of the series, India won the toss and chose to field first, hoping to restrict West Indies to a low total. West Indies, who had rested four of their key players for this match, lost their new opener Chattergoon early but Gayle gave West Indies a flying start with 51, while Sarwan anchored the innings with 52 - his seventh fifty against India. The star of the show, though, was Dwayne Bravo, who smashed a brilliant 62 off 44 balls. He lifted West Indies to a formidable 255 for 6. Agarkar was once again the pick of Indian bowlers with 2 wickets taking his series tally to 9. Sehwag also chipped in with the wicket of Gayle while giving away just 29 runs in his 10 overs.

India's chase never got going, as they lost Uthappa for a duck and then kept losing wickets at regular intervals. Only Sehwag showed some fire, scoring a defiant 95 off 103 balls. However, he lacked support from his teammates, as none of them crossed 26. West Indies' bowlers were on top of their game, especially Jerome Taylor and new spinner Dave Mohammed, who shared 6 wickets between them. Brian Lara, in what was likely his last ODI appearance at his home ground, had a quiet day with the bat earlier, scoring only 36, but he had the satisfaction of leading his team to a convincing victory by 19 runs to take the series 4-1. Dwayne Bravo won the player of the match while Ramnaresh Sarwan walked away with the player of the series honour for his series aggregate of 273 runs.

It was a bitter pill to swallow for India, who had been on a winning streak for the last eight months. The only silver lining was the resurgence of some of their key players, such as Sehwag, Agarkar and, to an extent,

Kaif. Captain Rahul Dravid looked dejected after the loss, and admitted that their fielding let them down. However, he urged the fans and critics not to be too harsh on his young team, and hoped that this experience would stand the team in good stead when they return here for the World Cup in nine months' time. Brian Lara, the West Indies captain, was gracious in victory and praised his team for their superb performance. He also said that India missed the presence of one man - Sachin Tendulkar, suggesting that Tendulkar's absence was a major factor in India's defeat. This was not good news for India, who would be without Tendulkar for the upcoming test series as well. They faced a tough challenge ahead, as West Indies were high on confidence and morale.

Before the test series began, India had a chance to warm up with a two-day match against Antigua and Barbuda XI. India's bowlers did well, dismissing the hosts for 300 runs. India's batsmen also got some valuable practice, as four of them scored fifties. Jaffer, Laxman, Kaif and Dhoni all looked in good touch, and prepared themselves for the tougher challenge ahead. It was a useful outing for India, as they drew the game and gained some confidence for the test series.

The venue for the first test was Antigua Recreation Ground in St. Kitts, which was a batsman's paradise. This test was supposed to be its last international, and it lived up to its reputation, producing a high-scoring draw with a thrilling finish.

The first day was an exception, when the pitch had some grass and bounce, and the West Indies bowlers exploited it to the fullest. They reduced India to 235 for 9, with Collymore and Bravo sharing 7 wickets. Dravid fought hard for 49, but was unlucky to be dismissed off a no-ball. Then the pitch flattened out, and the batsmen took over. West Indies took a 130-run lead, thanks to fifties from Gayle, Sarwan and Bravo. For India, Munaf Patel and Kumble took 3 wickets apiece while Sehwag and debutant VRV Singh chipped in with a couple each.

India bounced back in the second innings, with opener Wasim Jaffer scoring a magnificent double-century. He started nervously, but grew in confidence and fluency as he batted for more than 8 hours, to become only the fourth Indian after the legendary Sunny G, Dilip Sardesai and Navjot

Singh Siddhu to score a double century in the Caribbean. He hit 24 fours and a six in his marathon knock off 399 balls.

India set West Indies a daunting target of 392, after some explosive batting by Dhoni, who smashed 69 off 52 balls with 4 fours and 6 sixes. His innings ended in controversy though, when he was caught at the boundary, but the fielder's foot may have touched the rope. The TV replays were inconclusive, and Lara angrily asked Dhoni to walk off. Dravid declared soon after, and India had a whole day to bowl out West Indies.

India started well, taking 3 quick wickets, including Lara for a duck. However, Gayle and Chanderpaul dug in, and batted for more than a session. They frustrated the Indian bowlers, who could not find a way to break their partnership. After tea, India struck again, and reduced West Indies to 9 down, with Kumble bagging 4 wickets. However, the last pair of Edwards and Collymore held on for 19 balls, with Ganga running for the injured Edwards. It was a nerve-wracking finish, as the crowd watched in rapt attention. Sreesanth bowled the final ball, and Collymore defended it. West Indies had saved the match by the skin of their teeth. It was a fitting farewell for the Antigua Recreation Ground, which had witnessed many a memorable match. Wasim Jaffer, who scored 212 in the second innings, was named the player of the match.

India dominated the first day of the second test, played at Gros Islet, St. Lucia, thanks to a sensational innings by Sehwag, who tore apart the West Indies bowling with his fearless stroke play. He smashed 180 off 190 balls, including 25 fours and 2 sixes, and almost reached a hundred before lunch. He was unstoppable, hitting the ball with power and precision, and making a mockery of the five-man pace attack. He was well supported by his captain Rahul Dravid, who scored a composed 146 - his 23rd test hundred and Mohammad Kaif, who scored his maiden test century with 148. Only Pedro Collins managed to leave some impression taking 4 wickets as India piled up 566 for 8 declared, and put West Indies under immense pressure.

West Indies had no answer to India's bowling, as they collapsed twice in two days. Munaf Patel and Kumble struck early, removing the openers, one-down Sarwan and Lara, who was trapped lbw by a straighter one from Kumble. Chanderpaul and Bravo tried to resist, but Pathan broke their partnership with a superb delivery that nipped back and hit the stumps.

Sehwag then wrapped up the lower order with his guile and accuracy, taking 3 wickets with his off-spin. Windies were bowled out for 193, and India enforced the follow-on.

Windies were staring at defeat, with two days left and a huge deficit to overcome. They needed a miracle, and they got one. The rain came to their rescue, washing out the fourth day and most of the fifth. India were frustrated, as they had to wait for a chance to bowl out West Indies. Greg Chappell, the Indian coach, joked that "God is a West Indian".

When play finally resumed, West Indies had one man to thank for saving the match - Brian Lara. The Prince of Trinidad played one of his finest rearguard innings, showing grit and determination that he had often lacked in the second innings. He batted for more than 6 hours, scoring 120 runs in 262 balls. He adjusted his technique, standing well outside his crease and playing forward to negate any movement. He survived some close calls, as India dropped 4 catches and missed a couple of lbw appeals. Indian bowlers, especially Kumble bowled his heart out, but Lara stood firm and showed just why he was the leading run-scorer in tests. He reached his slowest test hundred, but it was also one of his most valuable ones. With some help from Chanderpaul and Bravo, he denied India a victory, and earned himself the renewed respect of his opponents. Sehwag, who had scored a blistering 180 in the first innings and also claimed 4 wickets was rightly named the player of the match.

After the 4-1 drubbing in one-dayers, many had written India off for the test series, expecting them to be outplayed by the hosts. However, India surprised everyone with their fighting spirit and resilience. They dominated the first two tests, coming close to winning both matches, but were denied by rain and West Indies' stubborn batting. West Indies were fortunate to escape with two draws, as India showed that red-ball and white-ball are two different ballgames.

The third test of the series - and the first staged at Warner Park - turned out to be a run-fest, as the hosts turned the tables on the visitors. The match was also marred by a contracts dispute between the West Indies players and their board, which threatened to derail the series. However, the issue was resolved just in time, and the match went ahead as scheduled.

Lara won his first toss of the series and chose to bat first, and his batsmen feasted on the Indian bowling. Darren Ganga scored a patient century, his third in tests, while Gayle and Sarwan played attacking knocks. Sarwan was especially impressive, hitting 6 fours in an over off Munaf Patel, who had a forgettable outing. Chanderpaul missed out on a hundred by just 3 runs, running out of partners, as Harbhajan cleaned up the tail with his cunning spin, taking a fifer on his return to the playing XI. It was a rare feat for West Indies, who had not scored more than 560 in the first innings of a test outside Antigua for over a decade.

India started their reply confidently, but were rocked by a burst of pace and swing from Jerome Taylor, who ripped through their top order with 3 wickets in 6 balls. But this time it was Windies' turn to be thwarted by rain that ate up close to two full sessions. Upon resumption, Laxman held the innings together with a resilient hundred, and the lower order chipped in with some valuable runs.

India were still 219 behind, but Lara decided not to enforce the follow-on, fearing for his bowlers' fitness on a scorching day. Windies batted again, and extended their lead to 391, with Ganga scoring his second fifty of the match. They gave themselves 88 overs to bowl out India, but the pitch had no demons in it. India went for the chase, with Sehwag blasting a 75-ball 65 before lunch. Dravid and Laxman added a century stand, and Dhoni joined the party with a six off his first ball. India needed 149 from 25 overs with 7 wickets in hand, and a sensational win was on the cards. Only once in history had a team lost after making more than 580 in the first innings - England at Sydney in 1894-95. But the West Indies captain switched to survival mode, and packed the field with close-in fielders. They managed to stop the run-flow and save the match. It was a thrilling finish to a high-scoring draw. Darren Ganga was named the player of the match for his batting in both innings.

The fourth and final test at Sabina Park was a thrilling climax to a series that had been marred by three back-to-back high-scoring draws. The wicket here, for a change, was a challenge for the batsmen, as it offered bounce and unpredictability. It required technique and application to survive and score runs. And there was one man among the 22 who had both in abundance

- the Indian captain Rahul Dravid. He put on a masterclass of batting, showing his class and skill in tough conditions.

Calling it right at the toss, Dravid elected to bat, but his decision soon looked questionable as Jerome Taylor ripped through the Indian line-up with his pace and swing. He took his maiden five-for in tests and reduced India to 200 all out. Dravid was the only one who resisted, scoring a masterful 81 and holding the innings together with a 93-run stand with his fellow Karnataka stalwart, Anil Kumble. West Indies had a chance to take a big lead, but they squandered it as Harbhajan spun a web around them with his off-spin. He took five wickets in just 27 balls, his second five-for in as many matches, as West Indies collapsed for 103, giving India a vital lead of 97.

India's second innings was also a struggle, as Collymore and Taylor bowled with accuracy and hostility. They shared 9 wickets, as India managed only 171. Three batsmen, including Dravid, were undone by low shooters that skidded off the pitch. But by then The Wall had already batted for more than 4 hours, scoring a skilful 68 runs and ensuring that India had a sizeable lead of 268.

West Indies faced a daunting target, but they fought hard till the end. Sreesanth initiated the demolition sending back both openers Gayle and Ganga with just 27 runs on the board. When Munaf caught Lara plumb in front for just 11, it looked like game over for the hosts but Sarwan, Bravo and keeper Ramdin gave them some hope with their aggressive batting. Ramdin played an absolute blinder, even lofting Kumble for a six into the stands. The crowd cheered him, as he tried to pull off a miracle. But it was not to be, as the great Anil Kumble took the final wicket to seal the victory, and with it, the series win for India.

It was a historic moment for India, who had not won a series in the Caribbean since 1971 and against a worthy opposition outside the subcontinent since 1986. Rahul 'The Wall' Dravid was the player of the match and the player of the series for his superb batting and leadership. His series aggregate of 496 runs in 4 tests may dwarf against the 774 runs that Sunny G amassed in 5 tests in 1971, but it was no less central to the final outcome.

Thus, India ended their tour of the Caribbean on a high note, making up for their unexpected failure in the one-day series. The players returned home with a positive mindset, and looked forward to a month and a half of rest before their next assignment - a short tour to neighbouring Sri Lanka for an ODI tri-series (with South Africa as the third side), where they hoped to bounce back from their setback against West Indies and regain their winning form in the shorter format.

21

First Signs of Trouble

Their plans got a huge shot in arms as Sachin Tendulkar was declared fit following a five-month surgery-and-rehab related layoff. The great one warmed up by scoring 3 tons for an English club side Lashings, and replaced Uthappa in the squad. Dinesh Mongia also came back, after shining as an all-rounder for Leicestershire. He took VRV Singh's place. The squad trained in Bangalore with other fringe players, and tested the fitness of some injured ones like Balaji, Nehra and Murali Kartik. From there, they flew off to an undisclosed location for three days of team bonding.

The Proteas were already there in Sri Lanka for a test series and India were supposed to join the two teams for the tri-series christened the Unitech Cup, but a bomb blast in Colombo killed 7 and injured 17 just after the test series, following which, after two days of deliberation, South Africa eventually decided to pull out of the Unitech cup. Thus, a tournament billed as a clash between three of the top contenders for next year's World Cup never really got underway. Indian team, however, in a gesture of solidarity towards a neighbour, stayed on for a three-match bilateral one-day series, which too had to be called off finally, due to excessive rains.

These back-to-back cancellations left the Indian team with only one tournament to prepare for the upcoming Champions Trophy in October. It was the DLF Cup in Malaysia, a tri-series involving Australia and West Indies as the other two teams. It was a chance for India to test their skills against two of the best teams in the world. The selectors did not make any changes to the squad that had returned without playing from Sri Lanka.

Thus, India finally played their first international match in almost 75 days and it was a match that showcased the brilliance of Sachin Tendulkar, but also the misfortune of India. The great one scored a magnificent century, his 40th in ODIs, in his first proper outing since recovering from elbow and shoulder injuries. He defied a tricky pitch - where a dent caused by a roller made the ball keep low, specially to right-handers, leading to the downfall of lesser mortals like Dravid and Sehwag - and smashed 13 fours and 5 sixes in his unbeaten 141 off 148 balls. This was the second time he had carried his bat through a one-day inning, first being the 186 against Kiwis in Hyderabad, 1999. He was dropped early on by the Windies wicketkeeper Carlton Baugh, but made them pay for their mistake; with sterling support from left-handers Irfan Pathan and Suresh Raina. He said later that it was a "special" hundred for him, as he had to overcome many challenges.

But fate was cruel to him, and his hundred proved to be futile once again, as West Indies chased down a revised target, thanks to Duckworth/Lewis method. They had made a blistering start, with southpaws Gayle and Lara hitting the wayward Indian bowlers all over the park. They reached 141 for 2 in 20 overs when rain stopped play. They had just completed the minimum number of overs required for a result and were declared winners by 29 runs by D/L method, completing their fifth successive win against India. It was a cruel twist of fate for the Indian team, who had scored 309 for 5 in their 50 overs. Tendulkar was named the player of the match for his superb innings, but he would have preferred a victory for his team.

India's second match in the tourney was against Australia and it was a rain-affected thriller that ended in a no-result. Australia won the toss and chose to bat first, hoping to put up a big score on a good batting pitch. They got off to a solid start, thanks to Shane Watson's aggressive innings at the top of the order. He played some crisp shots and took advantage of the fielding restrictions. Michael Clarke also chipped in with a fluent half-century, rotating the strike and finding the gaps in the middle overs. The lower order tried to add some vital runs, but India kept them in check with some tight bowling and fielding. Australia was all out for 244 in 49.2 overs, a decent but not daunting score. Munaf was the most successful of the bowlers with 3 wickets but it was Harbhajan who tightened the noose in the middle overs and chipped in with a couple wickets as did Agarkar.

India's chase was interrupted by rain twice, changing the dynamics of the game. The first shower reduced their target to 170 in 29 overs, making it a run-a-ball affair. The second shower came after Australia's latest pace sensation Mitchell Johnson had unleashed a devastating spell of fast bowling that rocked India's top order. He dismissed Dravid and Pathan off consecutive deliveries, both caught behind by Haddin. He then followed it up with a couple more wickets in his next over, removing Tendulkar and Yuvraj with balls that bounced and seamed away from them. India were reduced to 35 for 5 in 7 overs, and looked in deep, deep trouble.

But then the rain came again, and this time it did not stop. The match was abandoned as a no-result, much to the relief of India and the frustration of Australia. Johnson's heroics went in vain, as he finished with figures of 4 for 11 in 4 overs. He was awarded the player of the match for his sensational spell that almost won the game for Australia.

Still looking for their first win, India faced a tough challenge in their third match of the tournament, as they took on West Indies, who had just pulled off a stunning upset over Australia and booked their place in the final. India had to win this match to keep their hopes alive, but they had a poor record against West Indies in recent times. They had lost five consecutive matches to them since May, when they had won the first match of the five-match ODI series. India had to overcome their past failures and their current pressure to beat West Indies and stay in the hunt for the final.

The match was a strange and dramatic affair that ended in a narrow win for India. India batted first on a difficult pitch, where the ball bounced and seamed unpredictably. They lost wickets regularly, as Smith bowled with pace and accuracy to reduce them to 38 for 4 that soon became 78 for 6. Only Tendulkar looked at ease, as he played some sublime strokes and held the innings together with a highly skilful 65 which turned out to be the highest score of the match. He was unlucky to be run out by a freak deflection, after adding a valuable partnership with Harbhajan, who batted with courage and skill to contribute an invaluable 37. India managed to score 162 before being bundled out in the 40th over, a low but not indefensible total on this wicket.

West Indies had a bizarre strategy, as they played only one fit bowler and sent Lara in at number 9. They started well, as Chanderpaul and Morton put on a solid opening stand of 44. But then Harbhajan spun his magic, as he took three crucial wickets in the middle and turned the match in India's favour. Lara came in at 8 down, when the match was almost lost but almost pulled off a miracle with a counter attacking 40. But it was not enough, as

Harbhajan got Baugh out with a sharp turner, and Collymore was trapped plumb in front by a very impressive Sreesanth. Windies fell short by 16 runs, and India celebrated a thrilling win. Indian pace quartet all bowled well sharing 7 wickets between them and Sreesanth was especially impressive, clocking 145+mph regularly, but Harbhajan, with 3 for 35, was the pick of the bowlers and was named the player of the match for his all-round show.

Some experts raised doubts about West Indies' motives and strategies, suggesting they might have deliberately made such odd choices to avoid facing Australia in the final.

It was a do-or-die match for both India and Australia, as they faced each other in the virtual semifinal of the tournament. Australia won the toss and elected to bat first, but soon ran into trouble, as the Indians bowled and fielded out of their skins. Harbhajan again spun a web in the middle overs giving away just 24 runs in his 10 overs while also taking the wicket of the dangerous Hussey. Only Hayden showed the requisite skill to score a patient 54 before he was run out by a splendid throw from RP Singh. The rest of the batsmen struggled to cope with the bounce and seam, and only a late flourish from the two Brads - Hogg and Haddin - took them to 213, a below-par score. For India, Agarkar and RP took 2 wickets apiece while Harbhajan, Munaf and Mongia chipped in with a wicket each.

India's chase started with a controversy, as Tendulkar was given out caught behind off McGrath without anyone appealing, but the umpire changed his decision after seeing his reaction. Ponting was furious, but it did not matter much, as Tendulkar fell in the next over to Lee, who bowled with searing pace and accuracy. India lost wickets at regular intervals, as Stuart Clark and Hogg also bowled superbly. Mongia showed some resistance, but he failed to shepherd the tail in the later stages. Before that, Raina and Dhoni had briefly threatened to take India home, but they both fell to rash shots, leaving too much for the tail. Lee came back to finish off the innings, taking 3 more wickets to add to those of the two openers and ensuring Australia's place in the final. India fell short by 18 runs, and rued their poor batting performance. It was a match that showcased Australia's bowling prowess and India's batting frailty. Brett Lee won the player of the match for his brilliant 5-fer.

India's failure to reach the final sparked a strong criticism from Ravi Shastri, who was regarded as the voice of Indian cricket and a straight-shooter. He was the first expert to openly slam Greg Chappell's high-handedness and constant experimentation with the batting order, which he felt had disrupted the team's balance and confidence. He also questioned Dravid's leadership style, saying he should assert himself and call the shots instead of the coach, who wielded too much influence and interference in the team's affairs. Yuvraj Singh missing a couple of matches due to poor health also didn't help.

Whatever be the case, India had a dismal start to the new season, after having a spectacular previous one. This was a throwback to 2004, when they had a similar slump after a brilliant season, which then worsened as the season progressed. The bowling unit was still doing it's job but it was the batting that was letting the team down. The batsmen had to up their game quickly for their next assignment, the prestigious Champions Trophy at home next month, to avoid repeating the same fate.

The squad for the Champions Trophy had already been announced. The selectors had to trim the 15-man squad that played in the Malaysia tri-series to 14. They dropped Sreesanth, who was perhaps too expensive with the ball, and brought in RP Singh, who had impressed with his pace and swing for India A. They also continued to ignore Anil Kumble and Zaheer Khan, who were experienced and proven performers, but were perhaps out of favour with coach Chappell.

Champions Trophy 2006

Hosts India were clubbed with Australia, West Indies and England in Group A, and had to wait for 23 days after their last match to start their campaign, against England at the Sawai Man Singh stadium in Jaipur. Captain Dravid won the toss and decided to field first, hoping to exploit the helpful conditions for his seamers. His decision paid off, as Pathan and Munaf, both from Baroda and mentored by coach Mehdi Sheikh, bowled with pace and swing to rip through England's top order. They reduced England to 55 for 5 in 20 overs, with no batsman reaching double figures. The spinners Powar and Harbhajan then took over, and spun circles around the lower order. Collingwood tried his best to rally the tail but England were bundled out for a paltry 125 in 37 overs, with Munaf and Powar taking 3 wickets each, and Pathan and Harbhajan taking 2 and 1 respectively. The most encouraging sign for India was Irfan's return to form, as he bowled like his old self, with pace and accuracy.

India's chase started with a bang, as Harmison's first over went for 20 runs, with Tendulkar hitting him for 4 boundaries. Harmison did get Sehwag's wicket in the same over though. This was the fifth time in a row that Sehwag had failed to cross 10 while opening the inning. Tendulkar continued to dominate the bowling, scoring 35 off 32 balls with 5 fours, before he was trapped lbw by Harmison. India lost a few more wickets, as England tried to fight back, but the target was too small to defend. Yuvraj played a sensible hand of 27 not out and took India home in the 30th over with 4 wickets in hand. Munaf Patel won his first player of the match award in ODIs.

Next, India had to face a team that had been their nemesis in recent times, West Indies, and that too, after a long gap of 11 days. The players enjoyed the break, as they got to celebrate Diwali with their families. But Dravid was unhappy with the scheduling of the tournament, and he made his feelings known. He felt that the long gaps disrupted the momentum and rhythm of the team, and that it was unfair to have such an uneven distribution of matches.

India took on Windies in a crucial match, as both teams wanted to qualify for the semifinals. West Indies had the confidence of beating Australia in a thrilling match a few days back, where Lara had played a terrific innings. Brimming with that confidence, Lara won the toss and decided to field first, hoping to restrict India to a low score. His new ball bowlers, Bradshaw and Taylor, bowled with discipline and accuracy, and kept the Indian top-order in check. Dravid and Yuvraj tried to rebuild the innings, but they both fell in the same over, leaving India in trouble. Dhoni signalled a return to form with a very timely knock of 51, with 2 huge sixes, but it was not enough to lift India to a competitive total. They finished with 223 for 9 in 50 overs, with Bradshaw taking 3 wickets and the increasingly impressive Jerome Taylor taking 2.

West Indies chased down the target with ease, as their man-in-form Gayle gave them a customary flying start and Chanderpaul also played a solid knock of 51. Sarwan and Morton also batted sensibly, and took West Indies close to victory. India tried to fight back with some late wickets, including Lara and Sarwan, but it was too late. Marlon Samuels hit the winning runs with 2 balls to spare, and West Indies celebrated their place in the semifinals. Dravid's fears were not unwarranted as India looked rusty after a long break for Diwali, and paid the price for their poor batting and fielding. Chanderpaul was awarded the man of the match for his anchoring innings.

Ravi Shastri, writing for cricinfo, rightly blamed India's tactics and playing XI selection for the loss, saying that India committed a blunder by going in with 4 seamers in Indian conditions. He also termed team management's stubbornness in persisting with Irfan at one-down, foolhardy. The flamboyant former all-rounder, regarded by many (including Sachin Tendulkar) as arguably the best captains India never had, suggested that India should include Gautam Gambhir as a reserve opener, who could provide stability and aggression at the top. He also recommended that Raina should be promoted up the order to make the most of his talent. And finally, he urged Dilip Vengsarkar, the newly-appointed chairman of selectors, to step in and be more involved in the playing XI selections. He said that Vengsarkar should assert his authority and experience, and not let the coach and the captain have their way. He hoped that India would learn from their mistakes and improve their performance in the next match.

Next match, however, was a do-or-die affair against world champions Australia, with the winner qualifying for the semifinals. India chose to bat first on a typical Mohali pitch, where the ball came on nicely to the bat. But they faced a tough challenge from Australia's all-pace bowling attack, which was fast, accurate and relentless. Sehwag scored a restrained half-century and Dravid scored a fluent one, but neither of them could press on to convert it into a big one. McGrath got the better of Tendulkar again in a big game, and the other bowlers also chipped in with wickets. India ended up with 249 for 8 in 50 overs, a decent but not daunting score.

Australia chased down the target with ease, as they batted superbly on a pitch that suited their game. They started with a bang, as Gilchrist and Watson, who opened as an experiment, smashed India's wayward new ball bowlers Pathan and Munaf Patel. Watson scored a brilliant 50, and Ponting also scored a fluent half-century. Damien Martyn anchored the innings with an artistic 73 not out, and took Australia home with 26 balls to spare. India's bowlers, with the sole exception of Sreesanth who took the wickets of Gilchrist and Ponting, were treated with disdain, as Australia knocked them out of the tournament for the second time within a month. Martyn was awarded the man of the match for his masterful innings.

From thereon, Australia proceeded to beat their trans-Tasman rivals New Zealand in the semi-final and West Indies in a one-sided final to lift the Champions Trophy, the only ICC trophy that they had not won before. It was a clear message from the world champions that they were still the team to beat in the upcoming World Cup, despite the challenge from contenders like number 2 ranked Proteas and Brian Lara's West Indies, who had impressed with their resurgence.

India, on the other hand, had now completely squandered the momentum that they had so painstakingly built in the previous season, to go from being the hottest contenders to a team full of confusion and chaos. The upcoming away tour to South Africa beginning in three weeks' time was their chance to get their house in order before the World cup.

Dilip Vengsarkar, the new chairman of selectors, was a former Indian captain and a great batsman who had dominated the mid-80s, to the extent that between 1985-88, he was regarded as the best batsman in the world, ahead of greats like Viv, Border, Miandad, Gower and our own Sunny G. If Gavaskar was the Tendulkar of the Indian team of the 80s, Vengsarkar was the Rahul Dravid i.e. a close second. Suffice to say, 'Colonel', as he was fondly known, had the stature to stand up to Chappell or anyone else, as he had a lot of experience and authority.

The selection committee, led by Vengsarkar, had a meeting with the coach and the captain to discuss the recent failures of the team. They decided not to make drastic changes to the squad, but they did make three important changes. They dropped RP Singh and Ramesh Powar, who had not performed well in the tournament, and brought back two experienced players. Zaheer Khan, who had taken 78 wickets in 16 games for Worcestershire, earned a comeback after 8 months. Anil Kumble, who had not played one-dayers for more than a year, also earned a recall. He had not been a regular in the one-day team for a long time, but his experience and quality would be useful in guiding the young and inexperienced bowling attack.

The third change was a bit perplexing, as Venugopal Rao was dropped and Waseem Jaffer was included in the ODI squad. Venkatapathy Raju, the only other new member of the selection committee, hinted to the media that this might be the last chance for Kaif and Raina. He said that if they did not perform well in the upcoming series, the selectors might have to recall the experienced duo of Sourav Ganguly and VVS Laxman for the upcoming World Cup.

22

Losing the Plot

The Indians had a rude awakening at Benoni, where they faced a formidable Rest of South Africa team in their only practice match before the one-day series. They were stunned by a 37-run loss, as their batting was shattered by a fiery spell from a young tearaway fast bowler named Dale Steyn. He claimed a fifer and left the Indians in disarray. It was a shaky start for the tour for the Indians.

The one-day series was supposed to kick off at Wanderers in Johannesburg, but the fans were left disappointed as the rain played spoilsport. Not a single ball was bowled and the match had to be called off. It was a damp squib of a start for the ODI leg of the tour. Now, the series was reduced to a 4-match affair.

The one-day series finally got underway with the second match at Durban. Protean skipper Graeme Smith won the toss and chose to bat first, but it turned out to be a bad decision as he was dismissed for just 1 by Zaheer Khan, who struck in the very first over on his return to the national side. The mighty Jacques Kallis joined the action in the second over and stayed till the end, scoring a typically unhurried hundred - his 14th in ODIs but his first against India. He played cautiously on a pitch that favoured the seamers, avoiding any risky shots, and faced 160 balls. He got good support from the young and abundantly gifted AB de Villiers, who made a quick 41, and helped South Africa reach a decent 248 for 8 in their 50 overs. The Indian seamers bowled well and took two wickets each, but Harbhajan struggled to adjust to the bouncy track.

The Indian chase got off to a terrible start as Jaffer, who replaced Sehwag who had a sore back, was bowled for a duck on his debut. Kaif also failed to make use of his opportunity at number 3. Tendulkar and Dravid tried to rebuild, but they fell in quick succession, leaving the rest of the batsmen clueless against the bounce and movement. They were all out for a humiliating 91 in just 30 overs, losing by a massive 157 runs. The eccentric Andre Nel was the pick of the Proteas' bowlers, taking 4 for 13 in 8 overs, but Kallis also chipped in with 3 wickets for just 3 runs in a 25-ball spell. He was the obvious choice for the player of the match award.

Smith won the toss and decided to bat first again in the next match played at Capetown, but the move backfired spectacularly as they were reduced to 76 for 6 by the Indian bowlers. Zaheer Khan was the star of the show, bowling a superb spell of 7-4-9-3 and removing Smith and Kallis on consecutive balls. It looked like India had the match in their grasp, but they let it slip away as Justin Kemp staged a remarkable comeback. Kemp, who was dropped by Tendulkar when he was on 9, played sensibly at first and then launched a stunning assault in the last 10 overs. He smashed 7 sixes and 6 fours in his unbeaten 100, which came off just 89 balls. He added 60 runs with Pollock and a record-breaking 138 runs with Andrew Hall for the eighth wicket, taking South Africa to a formidable 274 for 7. The Indian bowlers, who had bowled so well earlier, lost the plot and bowled short-pitched deliveries that Kemp dispatched with ease. Zaheer was the only one who finished with respectable figures of 3 for 42. Kemp & co. showed no mercy to the rest of the bowlers, except for Anil Kumble who made a comeback and bowled economically, conceding only 28 runs in his 10 overs without taking any wicket.

India's chase never got going as they lost wickets at regular intervals. Pollock and Hall ripped through the top order, with Pollock dismissing Sehwag for a duck in the first over. Only Dravid and Dhoni showed some fight, scoring contrasting half-centuries. Dravid made a steady 63 off 107 balls, while Dhoni hit a frenetic 50 off 46 balls with four sixes. But their efforts were not enough as India were bowled out for 168 in the 42nd over, losing by a huge margin of 106 runs. Kemp was the deserved player of the match for his back-to-the-walls century.

The tour was off to a disastrous start for India, as they lost three consecutive matches by huge margins. This triggered a massive uproar among the restless fans back home, who demanded accountability and action. The anti-Chappell faction in the Indian Parliament also joined the chorus, calling for his removal as the coach. They were not alone, as

Shashank Manohar, BCCI vice-president, also proposed to link the players' match fee to their performance. As if things were not bad enough, India also lost their captain Rahul Dravid to an injury, which ruled him out of the rest of the limited-overs fixtures on the tour.

Next match followed a similar course to the previous one: South Africa won their third toss in a row but struggled at the start, losing Smith (to Zaheer Khan for the third match running, for the grand total of one run) and Bosman to Sreesanth for ducks, then recovered to a reasonable total, thanks mainly to Herschelle Gibbs who came to the rescue with a gritty innings, batting till the end and scoring 93 not out. He got some support from Kallis, who made a quick 49, and Pollock, who added some late fireworks with 37 with 2 sixes, helping South Africa to reach 243 for 8 in their 50 overs. Kumble with 2 wickets for 42 runs, justified his inclusion over the off-colour Harbhajan as the lone spinner. Zaheer and Sreesanth took a wicket apiece and bowled well at the start and end respectively while part-timers Sachin and Sehwag too chipped in with a wicket each.

India had a challenging task of chasing 244, but they failed miserably against the relentless South African pace attack. With Dravid missing due to a finger injury and Sehwag woefully out of form, India needed Tendulkar to fire - but he was again dismissed by the crafty Shaun Pollock for a single, and India's hopes faded with him. Rest of the Indian batsmen had no answer to the bounce and movement of the South African bowlers, as they edged and slashed their way to their doom. Dhoni and Karthik, who was picked as a specialist batsman based on his net form, both fell at third man, while the rest of the batsmen fell cheaply. Only Pathan showed some heart with a fighting unbeaten 47, but it was not enough as India were bowled out for 163 in 38.1 overs, losing by 80 runs, another huge margin. All-rounder Kemp claimed 3 wickets while Pollock and Ntini took a couple each. Kallis and Nel too chipped in with a wicket apiece but it was Gibbs who was rightly adjudged the player of the match for his wonderfully restrained knock.

The situation back home worsened as angry fans of a regional party attacked the house of Mohammad Kaif, who had performed poorly in the matches. The coach Greg Chappell also faced a backlash from the federal minister of women and child development Renuka Chaudhary, who threatened to take action against him for his remarks. Chappell had said that politicians "were paid to talk and criticise" and had no clue about cricket.

The Lone Bright Spot

In such a pressure-cooker situation, what the Indian team desperately needed was a win to calm the storm and restore some confidence. The only T20 international that was oddly placed before the fifth and final ODI gave them a chance to do that. T20 cricket was a new and exciting format that was the brainchild of Stuart Robertson, a marketing executive of the England and Wales Cricket Board (ECB). He wanted to make cricket more appealing to a wider demographic by eliminating the dull middle overs of the 50-over game. The rules were similar to the longer versions, but each team had only 20 overs to bat and four overs per bowler. There were also restrictions on the fielders' positions to encourage the batsmen to hit big shots and score high runs. This format was first played in England's domestic competition and was not meant for international cricket, but it soon became popular and was adopted by other boards as well. The ICC gave it official status in late 2005 and scheduled the first T20 World Cup in September 2007. The first T20 international was played on 17 February 2005 between Australia and New Zealand, which Australia won. India, however, was initially reluctant to play T20 internationals at first, because they thought it would devalue the 50-over game. But they later agreed to play it, and the upcoming T20 international against South Africa was going to be their debut in this format. It was a tough time to try something new.

South Africa had the advantage of winning the toss and batting first, but soon found themselves in deep trouble as the Indian bowlers unleashed a fiery spell on a damp pitch that swung and seamed, to restrict South Africa to a modest 126. Zaheer Khan was the star of the show, bowling a superb spell of 4-0-15-2, which equalled the record for the most economical four overs in T20 internationals. He was well supported by Agarkar and Tendulkar, who used their variations and guile to keep the batsmen in check.

Sehwag, spurred on by the added responsibility of captaincy, set the tone for the chase with a blazing 34 off 19 balls. However, India lost some quick wickets and needed some stability in the middle order. Thankfully, the two Dineshs - Mongia and Karthik played sensibly and kept the scoreboard ticking. Karthik, who was picked as a specialist batsman based on his net form, proved his worth with a brilliant knock of 31 not out off 28 balls. He finished the game in style, hitting off-spinner Peterson for a huge six over midwicket in the last over. He then cut the next ball through point to seal India's first win of the tour in nearly 3 weeks since they arrived in the Southern Cape, with a ball to spare. The win was a welcome consolation for the team after their earlier humiliations. Dinesh Karthik made history by becoming the first Indian player to win the player of the match award in this new and thrilling format, that was to alter the geography and economics of the sport in the very near future.

It was back to the same old story as Smith won his fifth toss in a row but decided to put India in, for a change, in the fifth and final match of the series played at Centurion. India's batsmen once again struggled to cope with the pace and swing of South Africa's bowlers on a lively pitch. Sehwag and Laxman fell cheaply (Laxman for a duck) while Tendulkar survived a torrid start to rediscover some semblance of form and score a fighting 55 off 97 balls, his 74th fifty plus score in ODIs but first in the previous 7 innings, playing some sublime strokes against the spinners and the seamers. He found some support from Dinesh Mongia, who played a dour knock of 41, and Dhoni, who unleashed some powerful hits and frustrated Nel with his aggressive 44 off 49 balls with 2 sixes, to end the series as India's highest run-getter. However, India could only manage 200, which was well below par on a flat track. Ntini was the most successful bowler with 3 for 32 while Pollock was the most miserly with 2 for just 17 runs in 10 overs, 4 of which were maiden. Kemp, Kallis and Nel also chipped in with a wicket or two.

South Africa made a mockery of India's total of 200, as they chased it down with ease and style in just 31.2 overs. Smith and de Villiers put on a masterclass of batting, smashing the Indian bowlers all over the park with power and grace. Smith overcame his nemesis Zaheer Khan, who had dismissed him cheaply in the previous matches, and scored a fluent 79 off 85 balls. He hit 3 sixes and 7 fours, and was especially harsh on Sreesanth, who was all over the place. AB de Villiers, opening for the first time, was even more impressive, scoring an unbeaten 92 off 89 balls, his highest score in ODIs. He played some exquisite shots on both sides of the wicket, driving, cutting and pulling with ease. He was dropped by Kaif when he was on 9, but that was the only blemish in his innings. The Indian bowlers had no answer to the onslaught, as they leaked runs at more than 7 per over. Sehwag's defensive field placements also did not help their cause. Smith fell in the 26th over, trying to hit another six, but by then South Africa were almost home. Pollock came in at No.3 and finished the game with de Villiers, who hit the winning runs with a boundary through point. It was a comprehensive win for South Africa, who wrapped up the series 4-0.

The series was kind of a second coming for the great Shaun Pollock, who walked away with both the player of the match as well as series, for his staggering 18 wickets and precious 87 runs in 4 matches. This splendid performance helped him climb to the top of the ICC ODI rankings for both bowlers and all-rounders.

The 4-0 drubbing was the first whitewash that India had suffered in a bilateral series since the one in Sri Lanka in 1997-98 where they were trounced 3-0. Clearly, India had a lot of soul-searching to do before heading into the test series that was 12 days away.

23

Return of the Old Guard

The message was clear. The young guns had let the team down and it was time to fall back on experience. The selection committee, led by the Colonel, brought back former captain Sourav Ganguly in the test squad, replacing the injured Yuvraj, who was taking longer than expected to recover. Ganguly had not set the domestic scene on fire, but he had other factors in his favour. He had just captained Bengal to a thrilling win over Punjab, the first match of their memorable 2006/07 Ranji Trophy campaign. He scored 6 and 43 and took five wickets in the low-scoring nail-biter. Sharad Pawar, the BCCI chief at that time, had a chat with Vengsarkar before the selection committee met to pick the side for the test series. The selectors chose Sourav in the squad, citing the team's poor batting in white-ball cricket, and his experience in South African conditions. In another major change, Laxman replaced Sehwag as vice-captain.

Sourav made a strong impression as soon as he landed in South Africa. He showed his commitment by joining the practice session straight from the airport, ignoring jet lag. He also played a vital innings of 83 to rescue the team from trouble in the only 4-day practice game at Potcheferstein. He partnered with Irfan Pathan, who scored a brilliant hundred and an unbeaten 40 in the match, but still missed out on the playing XI for the first test, due to his bowling losing its sting. The team beat a formidable Rest of South Africa side, thanks to Ganguly, Pathan and the bowlers' efforts.

Following the game, the seniors, fondly known as the 'Fab5' - Captain Dravid, Sachin, Sourav, Kumble and VVS - had a heart-to-heart, where they decided to let bygones be bygones and plan and prepare ahead for the first test. They were determined to put up a better, more united show in the test series.

Dravid returned to lead the side in the first test in Johannesburg and made a daring decision to bat first on a green and damp pitch which nearly cost them dearly. The pitch was fiery, and the South African bowlers were ruthless. India lost their openers cheaply but Dravid and Tendulkar showed their class and character, as they added 71 runs for the third wicket on the first day. It was a priceless partnership, more valuable than many of their hundred-run stands. Still, Pollock, Steyn, Kallis, Ntini and Nel made the ball bounce and swing, and India ended day1 at 156 for 5. Selectors had brought back Ganguly after a long exile, and he repaid the faith with a gutsy half-century in challenging conditions next morning. India were bowled out for 249, but it was a fighting score on that track.

Then came Sreesanth's magic spell, as he swung the ball both ways and ripped through the South African batting. He took 5 wickets for 40 runs, and reduced them to 84 all out. Earlier in the day, he had also given a memorable reply to Nel's sledging, by hitting him for a six and dancing in celebration. India secured a vital lead of 165 runs, and they never let it slip. The pitch was still tricky in the second innings and the great Shaun Pollock made history by becoming the first South African - and 10th overall - to take 400 test wickets when he dismissed Dravid and Tendulkar in quick succession. India was in trouble but the newly appointed vice-captain VVS Laxman again showed his class with an invaluable 73 that set South Africa a daunting 402 to win. Ashwell Prince fought hard with a 97, but the Indian bowlers were too good for the rest of the batsmen. Zaheer, Sreesanth and Kumble shared 9 wickets as South Africa folded for 278.

It was a historic moment for India, as they won their first test on South African soil. Sreesanth won the player of the match for his match tally of 8 wickets. Coach Chappell also praised Ganguly's comeback, saying that he had transformed himself as a batter and had much to offer to Indian cricket still.

Ganguly kept his form in the tour game against KwaZulu-Natal Invitation XI, but the hosts came back with a vengeance in the second test at Durban. Ashwell Prince scored a ton and Gibbs and Boucher chipped in with important fifties as South Africa posted 328 in their first inning. Sreesanth followed his heroics in the first test with another 4-wicket haul.

He was well supported by Kumble who picked 3 wickets. India, in response, could only manage 240, with Laxman and Tendulkar scoring fighting fifties.

South Africa batted well in their second innings as well, with Smith and Pollock hitting fifties to declare at 265 for 8. Sreesanth once again was the pick of the Indian bowlers with another 4 wickets. India faced a tough target of 354, and Ntini ripped through their batting line-up with a decisive 5-wicket haul. Dhoni tried his best to resist with a defiant 47 but India were all out for 179, losing the match by 174 runs. Makhaya Ntini was named the player of the match for his match haul of 8 wickets.

2007

The third and final test at Capetown was a thrilling series decider, as India and South Africa were tied at 1-1. India won the toss and chose to bat first, hoping to make a big score on a good pitch. They got off to a superb start, as Wasim Jaffer and Dinesh Karthik, who replaced the ill and injured Dhoni and opened the innings, put on a splendid 153-run stand. Jaffer scored a composed 116, his second test hundred, while Karthik continued to impressed with his fluent 63 that showcased his versatility. They set the platform for the middle order, as Tendulkar scored a steady 64, Sehwag smashed a quick 40 at No.7, and Ganguly added some late fireworks with a 75-ball 66. India reached 414, with Pollock and left-arm spinner with the strangest of bowling action, Paul Adams taking 4 wickets each for South Africa.

South Africa's response was a measured mix of attack and defence. Their daring captain Graeme Smith started with a bang, hooking his nemesis Zaheer's first ball for a six that flew off the top edge. Smith kept his aggressive approach, scoring 94 runs with daring shots and sweeps. He had to deal with the spin of Kumble, who troubled him from the rough outside off stump. Hashim Amla was equally adventurous, but also lucky, as he survived some close calls. The ever-reliable Kallis and Boucher steadied the ship with sensible half-centuries, taking South Africa close to India's total. Kumble was the star for India, taking 4 wickets with his guile and variations. Sreesanth also chipped in with a couple wickets, carrying on his good form in the series.

India had a slender lead of 41 runs, but they seemed unsure how to use it. They tried to be aggressive by sending Sehwag back to open the innings, but he fell in the first over, slashing at a wide ball. Jaffer was out soon after, caught off a nasty bouncer from Ntini. India were in trouble at 6 for 2, and had to focus on saving the match and the series.

South Africa sensed an opportunity, and bowled with discipline and intensity. Dale Steyn, playing his first test of the series, was the best bowler on view, taking four wickets with his pace and swing. Dravid and Tendulkar tried to resist, but they played too cautiously, scoring 47 and 14 respectively. Ganguly was in a hurry to get to the crease, due to a confusion over the batting order, but he showed some fight with a 46 that made him India's highest run-getter in the series. However, his dismissal triggered a collapse, and India were bowled out for 169.

South Africa had a target of 211 to win the match and the series. They chased it down with 5 wickets to spare in the final session of the fifth day, thanks to some solid, assertive batting from Smith, Amla and the leading run-scorer of the series, Ashwell Prince. Zaheer bowled his heart out taking 4 of the 5 wickets to fall. He dismissed Smith once more, but not before he had made his second half-century of the test that decided the series.

It was a remarkable comeback from South Africa, who had lost the first match by 123 runs. Two South African heroes, who led their team to a glorious victory, received the match and the series awards. Graeme Smith, the current captain, was adjudged player of the match for his twin fifties while the man he succeeded as South Africa's captain, the evergreen Shaun Pollock walked away with the player of the series honour for his 187 runs and 13 wickets in the three-match series.

India were left to rue their missed chances and poor batting in the second innings to miss out on what could have been a momentous maiden series win on South African soil. It was a bitter-sweet tour for India, as they lost both series, but won their first-ever T20 international. They also achieved their first ever test victory in South Africa. In the end, the Indian team returned home with some fond memories, but also some major disappointments.

24

Reset

India had two home ODI series against West Indies and Sri Lanka before the World Cup in two months. It was their last chance to fix their problems and prepare for the big event. The selectors announced the squad for the first two ODIs against West Indies and the 30 probables for the World Cup. They dropped Sehwag and Irfan Pathan, who were struggling with their form. Sehwag was sent back to Delhi to work on his batting, while Irfan Pathan lost his place to Joginder Sharma, an allrounder from Haryana. Kaif and Mongia were dropped while Raina managed to hold onto his spot because Yuvraj was still not a hundred percent. Tendulkar was appointed the vice-captain in Sehwag's absence but the biggest headline was Sourav Ganguly's expected return to the ODI team after his impressive comeback in tests. Also back were Gautam Gambhir and Robin Uthappa. Kumble was rested for the first couple of matches, while Laxman was again left out for his poor running and fielding, bringing an end to his limited-overs career.

It was a run-fest in Nagpur, where hosts India took on West Indies - a side that had been a thorn in their flesh in recent times - in the thrilling series opener. But most of India were deprived of the live action, as a broadcasting feud kept them from the screen. They could not see Ganguly's glorious return, as he dazzled with 98 runs, playing with vintage flair and finesse. He was denied a hundred by a run-out, but he had set the tone with Gambhir, who also made a superb fifty. They added 144 runs for the opening stand in about 25 overs, laying a solid platform for the rest of the batsmen to build upon. Sachin, coming in at one-down, could not capitalise on his start, but Dhoni and Dravid compensated with their explosive fifties. Dhoni blasted 62 not-out off just 42 balls with 3 fours and 4 sixes while captain Dravid blazed his way to an unbeaten 54 off just 35 balls with 4 fours and 3 sixes. Together, they smashed 119 runs in the last 12 overs, and propelled India to a massive 338 for 3 in 50 overs.

West Indies did not give up easily, as the prolific opening pair of Gayle and Chanderpaul launched a fierce assault on the Indian bowlers. Chanderpaul was unstoppable, as he smashed 149 not out off 136 balls, hitting 16 fours and 4 sixes. He shared a crucial partnership with skipper Lara, who played a delightful cameo studded with two glorious sixes. West Indies needed 100 runs off the last 10 overs, with 7 wickets in hand. But then Tendulkar struck a decisive blow, as he outsmarted Lara and got him stumped. That turned the tide in India's favour, as they managed to restrict West Indies to 324 for 8. India won by 14 runs, in a match that saw 662 runs scored, the highest for any ODI in India. Chanderpaul won the player of the match award for his brilliant knock, but he could not prevent India from taking a 1-0 lead in the series.

The second match at Cuttack was marred by a security breach, as an angry fan tried to attack Indian coach Greg Chappell while alighting from the team bus. Gautam Gambhir, the young opener, stepped in to stop him and prevent any harm. The fan, who was later arrested, confessed that he was upset with Chappell for not picking any player from Orissa in the national team. The incident raised concerns over the safety of the players and the staff for the Cuttack match.

It was a low-scoring affair in Cuttack, on an underprepared pitch unsuitable for an international match. The match was broadcasted with a seven-minute delay, after a resolution of the TV row. But the viewers did not miss much, as both teams struggled to score runs. India batted first and lost early wickets, including Ganguly and Tendulkar, who was out for a duck. They were in deep trouble at 90 for 7, but Karthik rescued them with a spirited half-century. He added 62 runs for the eighth wicket with Agarkar, who also contributed a vital 40. India reached 189, thanks to their efforts. Daren Powell was the pick of the West Indian bowlers, taking 4 wickets. Bradshaw and Bravo also continued their recent wicket-taking form against India with a couple wickets each.

West Indies were without Lara, who had a sore knee, but Chanderpaul again stood out, as he tried to hold the innings together with a characteristic patient knock this time. He did not get much support from the other batsmen, except for Bravo, who made 31. They had a useful partnership, but it was broken by Ramesh Powar, who bowled superbly and took 3 wickets in his first outing in 3 months. Maestro Sachin also took 2 wickets with his unique brand of spin, and kept the pressure on West Indies. Chanderpaul batted till the end, but he could not take his team over the line. West Indies fell short by 20 runs, and India took an unassailable 2-0 lead in the series. Dinesh Karthik was the player of the match for his brilliant 63 off 87 balls. He had shown his amazing skills in 3 different situations in the last month and a half, each time in a different format of the game. This was a testament to his adaptability and versatility.

It was a thrilling encounter in Chennai, where West Indies kept their hopes alive in the third ODI of the series. Lara came back to lead his team, and he decided to field first after winning the toss. India rested some of their key players, but they still got off to a flying start, thanks to Uthappa's blistering 70 off 41 balls, that virtually sealed his spot for the World Cup, but India lost their way towards the end, losing 7 wickets for 36 runs. Bravo was once again the star with the ball, taking 4 wickets in the death overs. India were bowled out for 268, which was not enough on a flat Chepauk wicket.

West Indies chased down the target with ease, as Marlon Samuels played a stunning innings of 98 not out off 95 balls. He showed his class and power, hitting 10 fours and 4 sixes. He had a match-winning partnership of 127 with the great Brian Lara, who also played a sublime knock of 83 off 87 balls. The Prince of Trinidad gave yet another demonstration of his absolute mastery of the spin bowling, dancing down the track and lofting the Indian spinners with grace. West Indies won by 6 wickets and more than 6 overs to spare, and reduced the series deficit to 2-1. Samuels was the player of the match for his brilliant batting display.

The fourth and final match of the series was a one-sided affair in Vadodara, where India thrashed West Indies like never before. Lara made a strange decision to field first after winning the toss, and India made him pay with a massive total of 341 for 3. Robin Uthappa got them off to a flyer, hitting 3 fours and 2 sixes in his 17-ball 28, and then former and current captains Ganguly and Dravid added 101 runs for the second wicket, both scoring solid fifties. Tendulkar, batting at number 4 at the behest of the coach, then took over as he smashed a brilliant 100 not-out off 76 balls, reaching his century with the last ball of the innings. He was well supported by MS Dhoni, who blasted an unbeaten 40 off 20 balls in typically belligerent fashion with 3 huge sixes. India scored 134 runs in the last 13 overs, and left West Indies shell-shocked. Gayle was the only bowler who escaped the carnage, taking 1 for 46 in 9 overs.

West Indies had no answer to India's huge score, as they collapsed to 181 all out. Gayle failed again with the bat, and none of the top-order batsmen could make an impact. Lara's final ODI inning on Indian soil ended in a freakish run-out, as Pathan deflected a catch onto the stumps. Samuels and Ramdin tried to salvage some pride with a partnership of 65 runs, but it was inadequate. India's spinners ran through the tail, and wrapped up the match in 41.4 overs. Agarkar and Kumble took 2 wickets each, while Zaheer, Pathan, Harbhajan and Yuvraj took 1 each. India won by 160 runs, their biggest victory by runs against West Indies. Sachin Tendulkar won the player of the match for his first century in a winning cause in 4 years. Player of the series award also went to him for his 191 runs and 3 wickets in the series.

It was a morale boosting win for the Indian team before the world cup, as they had managed to vanquish the adversary that had caused them a lot of grief in the previous season. Two of their legends - Sourav Ganguly and Anil Kumble - were back in the mix, and the other mainstays like Sachin, Dravid and Dhoni had also regained their form just in time which was a good sign.

The team had one final challenge before the world cup - a four-match ODI series against another old rival Sri Lanka, a side that was currently ranked ahead of India in the ICC rankings. It was the last opportunity for the Indian team to fine-tune their preparations and strategies before flying to the Caribbean for the biggest cricketing extravaganza. India being in the same group as Sri Lanka in the World Cup added to the interest in the series.

Rahul Dravid, the captain, stood up for Virender Sehwag and Irfan Pathan, who were struggling with their form, fitness and confidence. He persuaded the selectors to give them another chance, and they were recalled to the squad, replacing Raina and Ramesh Powar, who had to miss out. Robin Uthappa and Dinesh Karthik also earned their spots with their sparkling performances in the recent matches. The fast-bowling department was manned by the experienced Agarkar, Zaheer Khan, Sreesanth and Munaf Patel besides Irfan Pathan while Kumble and Harbhajan were the two vastly experienced spinners. Unless something unexpected happened, this was likely to be the same squad that India would be taking to the world cup.

The highly anticipated series opener was a wash out, as heavy rain at the Eden Gardens stopped the play only an hour into the match. Dravid had chosen to bowl first, hoping to exploit the fresh pitch but Sri Lanka managed to get to 102 for 3 in 18.2 overs before the game had to be stopped. Jayasuriya was on fire, smashing 63 off 61 balls, with 9 boundaries and a six. He punished Sreesanth and Zaheer who were expensive. Munaf Patel was the only bowler who impressed, taking 2 wickets with his accuracy. The rain did not relent, and the ground was too soggy to continue. The match had to be called off, to the disappointment of a hundred thousand fans who had gathered to watch their 'Maharaj' back in action in national colours.

It was a close contest in Rajkot, where Sri Lanka showed why they were the acknowledged masters of the slow choke, edging India out in a nail-biting finish. India had won the toss and opted to bowl first, and they managed to get rid of the Lankan top-order including the dangerous Jayasuriya cheaply but couldn't stop the brilliant Sangakkara from scoring a fabulous century, his sixth in ODIs. He scored 110 off 106 balls, with 11 fours and 4 sixes, and rescued Sri Lanka from a shaky 58 for 4, thanks to an excellent century stand with Dilshan, who made a brisk 56. Munaf Patel was once again the best bowler for India, taking 4 wickets, including 2 in 2 balls at the end. Sreesanth also came back strongly after the pasting he received in the previous game, taking 2 for 39 in his 10 overs. Bhajji and Sachin also chipped in with a wicket each. Kumble however was expensive and wicketless. Sri Lanka finished with 257 for 8 in their 50 overs.

India had a poor start to their chase, as they lost Uthappa and Dravid early to the much-improved Maharoof, who bowled with discipline and swing. But the old firm of Ganguly and Tendulkar steadied the innings with a hundred-run partnership, both scoring fifties. Ganguly made a steady 62 off 82 balls, while Tendulkar scored a breezy 54 off 61 balls, with 9 boundaries. He showed that he had adjusted to his new role at number 4. Jayasuriya slowed down the run-rate with his spin in the middle overs, and India needed 24 runs off the last 5 overs, with 5 wickets in hand. But they could not finish the job, as Malinga bowled superbly in the death overs, giving away only 5 runs and taking out Karthik for 31. Dhoni was the last hope for India, as he needed 6 runs off the last 2 balls. He tried to hit Jayasuriya over cover, but Maharoof took a brilliant catch on the boundary, despite the risk of colliding with Tharanga. Dhoni was out for 48, and India lost by 5 runs. His opposite number, Kumara Sangakkara was the player of the match for his match-winning hundred.

Sehwag made the cut for the World Cup as Dravid fought for him once more. With Yuvraj and Pathan, who had been sidelined due to injuries, fully recovered and ready for action, the selectors decided to play it safe and named the same 15 players from the Rajkot match as India's squad for the Caribbean crusade.

It was a do-or-die game for India as they faced Sri Lanka in the third match at Goa. They needed a win to keep the series alive, and they got it thanks to a sensational spell from Zaheer Khan. He unleashed his fury on the Sri Lankan batsmen, and sent back 3 of them in his first 3 overs, including the explosive Jayasuriya and the classy Sangakkara. He returned to complete a 5-wicket haul, his first in ODIs, and kept Sri Lanka to a modest 230 for 8, which they managed, thanks to a couple of 40s by Atapattu and Dilshan and a 66 not-out by Russel Arnold.

India had their own troubles in the chase as they lost 3 big guns - Sehwag, Tendulkar and a fit-again but rusty Yuvraj - early on. Ganguly fought hard for his 48, but his fall left India in a precarious position at 94 for 4. But then came the rescue act from skipper Dravid and Dhoni, who showed their skill and temperament in a crucial partnership of 133 runs. Along the way, Dravid became the sixth player to go past 10,000 ODI runs, enroute his 77th half-century in this format; while Dhoni played an uncharacteristically restrained knock of 67 not out. Dravid got run-out for 66 but Dhoni ensured there was no repeat of the previous match's mistake, taking India over the line with 21 balls to spare, and levelled the series 1-1. Zaheer Khan was the undisputed star of the show, and deservedly bagged the player of the match award.

It was a fitting climax to the series as India and Sri Lanka faced each other in the rain-affected fourth and final ODI at Vizag. India won the toss and curiously chose to field first on perhaps the best batting wicket of the series. Their seamers did not disappoint, however, as they reduced Sri Lanka to 56 for 4 with some superb bowling. However, Chamara Silva played a gem of an innings, scoring his maiden ODI century in 14 matches spread over a chequered 7-year career. He stitched together 3 useful partnerships with Dilshan, Arnold and Maharoof, who all chipped in with 20s. He took Sri Lanka to a respectable 259 for 7 in 47 overs. Zaheer and Agarkar shared 4 wickets, while Sreesanth, Sehwag and Ganguly took a wicket each. Ganguly broke his long wicket drought of 45 matches with his military-medium pace.

India's chase got off to a flying start, thanks to Uthappa's blistering 52 from 37 balls. He smashed 9 fours and a six, and gave India the early momentum. Ganguly retired hurt with leg cramps, but Sehwag showed some semblance of form and scored 46. Karthik, sent in at number 4 as Sachin was rested for this match, fell cheaply but Yuvraj Singh joined forces with Ganguly, who came back to bat. They put on an unbeaten 145-run stand, their second century partnership, and took India to a convincing victory. Yuvraj showed sublime form, scoring 95 not out from 83 balls. He finished the match with a flurry of boundaries in Maharoof's over. India won by 7 wickets with 6 overs to spare, and clinched the series 2-1. Chamara Silva was the Man of the Match for his brilliant hundred, while Ganguly was the Man of the Series for his 168 runs and a wicket.

Yes, Sri Lanka were without their two ace bowlers, Vaas and Muralitharan, in this series. But it was still commendable the way Dravid & co. came back from being one match down in what was effectively a three-match series against a better ranked opposition. The team looked to have overcome most of the challenges that had plagued them just before the big event. Ganguly was in the midst of a fairytale comeback with 4 fifties and a 48 in 6 innings since his return. Uthappa played some explosive innings at the top. Sachin and Dravid were reliable as ever. Dhoni found his mojo that had catapulted him to the top-ranked ODI batsman in the ICC rankings in the previous season. Karthik impressed with his skills and versatility. On the bowling front, Zaheer Khan made a triumphant return to spearhead the pace attack, with the experienced Agarkar and Sreesanth, who had improved by leaps and bounds. If Pathan could regain his spark, India would have a formidable seam attack. Harbhajan had been doing a stellar job with his off-spin in the middle overs and there was Kumble too, if needed. But the most reassuring and relieving thing was that Sehwag and Yuvraj seemed to have regained their form, before flying to the Caribbean.

25

Catastrophe

The 2007 ICC Cricket World Cup was the biggest event in cricket, held for the first time in the West Indies from March 13 to April 28. It featured 16 teams playing 51 matches, 3 less than the previous edition.

Before the tournament, the teams played some warm-up matches to get acclimatized to the West Indian conditions. The teams were divided into four groups of four, and the top two teams from each group advanced to the "Super 8" stage. In this stage, each team played against the other six teams that qualified, and also carried forward their result against the team from their group. The best four teams in this stage reached the semi-finals, where they competed for a spot in the final and a chance to be crowned the world champion.

India, ranked fifth in the world at that point in time, was in Group B with sixth-ranked Sri Lanka, ninth-ranked Bangladesh and 16th-ranked Bermuda. It seemed like an easy group for India.

India and Bangladesh faced each other in their first group stage match, after both teams had won their warm-up games convincingly. Only Australia and Pakistan were the other teams that had managed the same. This alone should have warned India that Bangladesh was not going to be an easy opponent. But still, not one cricket pundit could have foreseen what was to follow in that match.

Dravid won the toss and decided to bat first, but it was clear that India had not done their homework coming into this match. The pitch at Queen's Park Oval was slow and tricky, as Jayasuriya and Tharanga showed in their struggle against Bermuda. But Sehwag and Uthappa did not change their game plan. They played reckless shots and paid the price. Sachin Tendulkar fell to an armer from little known off-spinner Abdur Razzak that spun back sharply and beat him in flight and turn. Rahul Dravid was unlucky to be given out lbw to Mohammed Rafique, as the ball seemed to be missing the stumps.

India's innings was in trouble as they had lost 4 wickets with just 72 runs on the scoreboard at the halfway stage in the innings. Ganguly and Yuvraj came to the rescue with a vital 85-run partnership for the fifth wicket. They played with skill and flair, but they also gave away their wickets after doing the hard work. Ganguly scored 66 off 129 balls, while Yuvraj made 47 off 58 balls. Yuvi's wicket triggered a spectacular collapse as India lost 5 wickets for just 2 runs in a matter of minutes. Dhoni, Agarkar and Harbhajan were all out for ducks, as they lost their nerves and played silly shots. Only an invaluable late partnership of 32 runs between number 10 and 11, Zaheer and Munaf took them close to 200, but they were still bowled out for 191 in 49.3 overs. Bangladesh's bowlers were superb, with their spearhead Mashrafe Mortaza leading the way with 4 wickets and spinners Rafique and Razzak taking 3 each. They choked India's batsmen with their accuracy and discipline, and gave their team a great chance to win.

Bangladesh pulled off a stunning run-chase, powered by three teenagers who played with no fear and plenty of skill. Tamim Iqbal, the 17 years old opener, lit up the match with a fiery 51 off 53 balls, hammering Zaheer Khan for a massive six over midwicket. He brushed off a vicious blow on the neck and went after the Indian bowlers with panache, taking apart India's spearhead Zaheer Khan with special ferocity. He found able allies in fellow lefty Shakib al Hasan and young keeper-batsman Mushfiqur Rahim, who forged an 84-run stand for the sixth wicket and took Bangladesh to the verge of victory. The precociously talented Shakib scored a classy 53 off 86 balls, while Mushfiqur made a calm 56 off 107 balls. They hit some graceful shots and ran hard between the wickets. Mushfiqur clinched the historic win - only their second against India in 15 meetings - with a sublime cover drive in the penultimate over.

India's bowling and fielding were dismal, except for Munaf Patel's opening spell. They spilled 2 sitters and 2 half-chances and also fluffed a run-out chance. It was a stark contrast to Bangladesh who bowled and fielded out of their collective skins.

It was one of, if not the biggest upset ever in the history of the world cup. The Bangla tigers emulated their historic upset over Pakistan in the 1999 World Cup, showing their improvement after losing all their matches in South Africa 4 years ago where India were runners-up. Overall, it was their third win in World Cups, having also beaten Scotland in 1999.

For Indian team, the loss was nothing short of a nightmare. They had expected to dominate group B with ease, but their plans were completely derailed by this stunning upset. They were now on the verge of crashing out of the World Cup, just like their bitter rivals Pakistan.

The Indian media was ruthless in their criticism. They tore into the team for the lacklustre performance and timidness, questioning everything from the team selection to the game plan to the captaincy.

The fans were furious too. They had trusted their heroes to breeze through the group stage and contend for the glory. Instead, they witnessed them collapse under pressure and lose to a team that had barely troubled them before. They felt cheated and angry and unleashed their wrath on the players, the coach, and the captain. They pelted stones at Mahendra Singh Dhoni's new, under-construction house in Ranchi and set fire to effigies of players in Jaipur and Varanasi. They staged protests against the coach and captain in Kolkata with placards saying, "Go Back Chappell" and "Go Back Dravid."

Some people found some consolation in the exit of arch-rivals Pakistan at the hands of Ireland, their second defeat in as many matches. But that was a small comfort in a big disappointment. Indian team had suffered one of their worst defeats in World Cup history. And they had no one to blame but themselves.

The players knew this and were really disappointed. They knew they had no margin for error in their remaining matches. They knew they had to find a way to bounce back and salvage their pride.

But the biggest shock of the World Cup was yet to happen.

Hours after Pakistan had crashed out of the world cup after losing to Ireland, their coach, Bob Woolmer was found dead in his hotel room in Jamaica on 18 March. His body was found lying naked on his back with his legs spread apart in the early hours of 18th March in the bathroom of room number 374, on the 12th floor of the Jamaica Pegasus hotel. Initially, it seemed like he died of a heart attack, while some suggested suicide. However, the fact that there could be foul play involved was not totally taken out of consideration. However, on June 7, 2007, it was declared that Woolmer had died of natural causes, and the case was hastily shut after consultation with a South African strangulation expert.

Bob Woolmer was a cricketing legend who left his mark as both a player and a coach. Born in Kanpur, India, in 1948, he moved to England at a young age and honed his skills at Kent. He was a versatile batting all-rounder, who could also bowl medium pace and off-spin. He earned the honour of being one of the Wisden cricketers of the year in 1976. Woolmer later became one of the most successful coaches in the history of the game, guiding South Africa and Pakistan to new heights. His sudden and mysterious death sent shockwaves through the cricketing world and cast a shadow over the World Cup.

Indian team had a lot to cope with in the 48 hours since their shock defeat at the hands of Bangladesh, but to their credit, managed to put all that behind and came out hard against debutants Bermuda in their second match, which took place shortly after the Bob Woolmer tragedy.

Put in to bat in gloomy conditions, the second wicket pair set the tone with a sensible approach, building a solid foundation for the later onslaught, after Uthappa had to depart early to a catch of a lifetime by 125 kgs Dwayne Laverock. Sehwag rediscovered his touch with a blazing 114 off 87 balls, while Ganguly anchored the innings with a steady 89, his seventh fifty since returning. They added 202 for the second wicket, keeping the scoreboard ticking and punishing the bad balls.

The real fireworks, however, came from the middle order. Tendulkar, batting at an unfamiliar No.6 position, showed his class and versatility with a stunning 57 off just 29 balls. He mixed finesse and brute force, hitting 6 fours and 4 sixes in his cameo. Yuvraj was even more destructive, smashing 83 off 46 balls with 7 towering sixes. Dhoni also chipped in with a quickfire 29 as India piled up a mammoth 413 for 5, the highest total in World Cup history.

The Indian bowlers completed the task with ease, making sure that their win was more emphatic than Sri Lanka's against the same opponents. The batsmen had no answer to lone spinner Anil Kumble's spin wizardry, as he troubled them with his accuracy and variations picking 3 for 38. The rest of the wickets were taken by Ajit Agarkar and his fellow pacers, as poor Bermuda were crushed by the biggest ever one-day victory margin of 257 runs. Virender Sehwag was adjudged the player of the match for his tone-setting century, his first in 2 years and eighth overall in ODIs.

The team ticked all the boxes they needed to tick in this match. However, Sri Lanka's resounding 198-run victory over Bangladesh a couple of days later meant that they still needed to defeat a formidable Sri Lankan side convincingly in their third and final group game in to be in contention if 3 teams were to tie on points.

India started the match on a high note, as Rahul Dravid won the toss and decided to bowl first. He was rewarded by his quicks, who struck early and removed the dangerous Sri Lankan top order. Zaheer and Agarkar bowled with pace and swing, dismissing Jayasuriya and Jayawardene for low scores. Ganguly joined the party, taking the prized scalp of Sangakkara, who edged a catch to Dhoni. Sri Lanka were in trouble at 92 for 3 in the 23rd over. The 22 years old opener Tharanga held one end and played a mature knock of 64 to take his side to 133 before being castled by Tendulkar. However, they recovered through a resilient partnership between the in-form Chamara Silva and Dilshan. Silva played a gritty innings, scoring singles and finding fours with his improvisation to score 59 off 68 balls - his third World Cup fifty in a row. His clever shots behind the wicket frustrated the bowlers. Dilshan was more aggressive, making space and hitting the ball through the off side. They both got out in quick succession, but Arnold and Vaas added 38 runs in 23 balls, taking Sri Lanka to a respectable 254 for 6.

India's bowlers did a commendable job, keeping the runs in check and taking crucial wickets. Zaheer was the pick of the lot, taking 2 for 49 in his 10 while Agarkar and Munaf also bowled well and took a wicket each. Harbhajan had an off-day but Tendulkar and Ganguly more than made up for it chipping in with a key wicket each.

India's chase of 255 against Sri Lanka was a disaster from the start. They lost their top order cheaply, as Vaas, Malinga and Fernando bowled with pace and accuracy. Vaas showed his class taking a brilliant reflex catch to dismiss Uthappa and followed it with the huge wicket of the in-form Ganguly, who succumbed to a rare loose shot. But the key moment of the chase came when Dilhara Fernando cleaned up Sachin Tendulkar for a duck with a peach of a delivery in the very next over.

Skipper Dravid and Sehwag tried to put up a fight, but Sehwag's wicket was a huge blow. He was batting with confidence and flair, but failed to capitalise on his start falling prey to Murali's wizardry.

Dravid witnessed a nightmare unfold in front of his eyes. Yuvraj's run-out showed India's panic and confusion. Dhoni's clueless slash off Murali, which resulted in his dismissal for a duck, his second in this World Cup, left Dravid morose and helpless. He saw his partners come and go, as the required run-rate climbed higher and higher. Dravid had no choice but to take some risks. He unleashed his fury on Malinga, hitting him for 4 consecutive fours. But it was never going to be enough. He eventually succumbed to a shot of a defeated man after scoring a valiant 60. The Wall looked shattered as he walked back, knowing fully well that his captaincy stint shall forever be tainted and judged by this one disaster. Dilshan finished off the innings by taking the last wicket, as India were bowled out for 185 in the 44th over. Sri Lanka won by 59 runs and qualified for the next round. Big match player Muralitharan was the undisputed player of the match for his 3 wickets and 2 superb catches.

It was one of, if not the darkest day for Indian cricket. The unthinkable had happened: The team that had reached the final of the previous World Cup, the team that boasted of some of the greatest batsmen of all time, the team that had millions of passionate fans across the globe, had been knocked out of the world cup in the opening round itself.

Like any true leader and in keeping with his character, Dravid took the entire responsibility and blame for the fiasco upon himself, but the Indian media showed no mercy whatsoever. They lambasted the team for their poor performance and lack of fighting spirit. Politicians, including railway minister Lalu Prasad Yadav mocked and ridiculed the players for their failure, claiming even they would have batted better than the Men in Blue.

Former greats like Gavaskar and Kapil Dev tore into the team for their pathetic performance and lack of courage. They questioned the selection, the strategy, the leadership and called for heads to roll and careers to end.

The fans and supporters were stunned and heartbroken. They felt betrayed and angry and vented their frustration on the players, the coach, and the captain, demanding accountability and change.

The players themselves were shell-shocked and dejected. They knew they had let their country and themselves down. They were shattered and ashamed. They hid themselves in their hotel rooms for two days, mourning the worst disaster of their careers and bracing themselves for the fury of their fans and critics back home. Some of the seniors, like Sachin, even contemplated hanging up their boots for good.

Team India slipped back home in the wee hours of Wednesday night, weary and numb from the shock, but still couldn't escape the media hounding.

Some of the more outraged fans too reacted with violence and vandalism, targetting the homes of some of the players, like Dravid, Sachin, Dhoni and Agarkar, who had to be guarded by extra security. They burned posters of Indian players and staged mock funerals for Indian cricket in various cities, like Indore, Allahabad and Varanasi and threw rocks at a restaurant owned by Zaheer Khan in Pune.

26

Aftermath

A day later, the great Anil Kumble announced his retirement from the format while expressing his wish to continue in tests. Kumble, 36, ended his ODI career with 337 wickets at 30.89 in 271 matches. He had many memorable performances in the format, but his best was the stunning 6 for 12 he took in the Hero Cup final at the Eden Gardens in 1993. His last game was against Bermuda at the World Cup, where he took 3 for 38 in India's massive 257-run win. He finished his ODI career with a wicket on the last ball he bowled. His exploits in the shorter format often get overshadowed by his heroics in the longer format, but he was a genuine match winner for India in ODIs too, at least till October 2000 when a serious rotator cuff injury made him lose his place as the team's first-choice spinner to Harbhajan Singh. That notwithstanding, Anil 'The G.O.A.T' Kumble, still, to this day, remains India's highest wicket-taker in ODIs.

The BCCI president Sharad Pawar and his cronies had first vowed to punish the team for their dismal showing. "Our team has betrayed me and the nation and we will take some harsh steps" Pawar said grimly. But he soon backtracked, thanks to the wise counsel of former captains Ajit Wadekar, Bedi and Kapil Dev who asked him to be more rational. But the damage was done. Pawar had already inflamed the passions of a furious crowd that demanded the players and the coach to face the music.

The BCCI president set up a review committee and called for a meeting on April 6th. The next day, the working committee of the board would meet to discuss the report of the review committee. The working committee meeting had the BCCI's office-bearers and seven former captains, including Sunil Gavaskar, Kapil Dev, Ravi Shastri and S Venkatraghavan.

Meanwhile, the seething rift within the team was out in the open now. Team was in deep turmoil and split into two factions: the seniors' faction, which had Sachin, Sourav, Kumble, Sehwag, Harbhajan, Zaheer, who all agreed that Chappell and his methods were the cause of the disaster; and the Chappell's faction, which had only himself and his support staff, and a few youngsters like Irfan and Sreesanth. He also had some powerful allies in the board.

Rahul Dravid, who was caught in the crossfire between the two warring factions for no fault of his own, retreated with his wife and young son to a beach in Kerala, refusing to be drawn into the drama that was unfolding in the corridors of power in Indian cricket.

Greg Chappell, on his part, had already made up his mind to quit as India's coach after his troubles with some senior players, his negative image among the Indian fans, and Bob Woolmer's tragic death. But Greg being Greg, he was not going to leave quietly without a parting shot. He would present a damning report to the review committee in Mumbai on April 6, explaining why India flopped at the World Cup. The media speculated that the report contained some pretty scathing observations on some senior players like Sourav Ganguly, Sehwag, Harbhajan and even Sachin Tendulkar, who had developed serious differences with the coach over his batting position of late.

The simmering tensions reached a boiling point two days before the review committee meeting when Sachin Tendulkar - who usually stays away from controversial topics - gave an interview to the Times of India in which he made some sharp remarks about Chappell. "We know that we played poorly and, as a team, we take full responsibility for that", Tendulkar said. "But what hurt me the most is if the coach has questioned my attitude, after giving my heart and soul for Indian cricket for 17 years."

Within hours of that interview being published, Chappell announced his decision to not seek an extension of his contract and tendered his resignation as Indian coach after 22 tumultuous months at the helm.

Chappell's stint as India's coach had its highs and lows. It included a record-breaking streak of India winning 17 ODIs while chasing, and a historic test series win in the West Indies. It also saw several young players, like Sreesanth and Dinesh Karthik, making their mark in the national team.

But it also had more than it's fair share of controversy, which seemed to stem from his tough and uncompromising attitude.

Greg Chappell's stint with Indian cricket has been a subject of much analysis, discussion and debate ever since it ended and it still remains a hot topic to this day. But perhaps, the best way to sum it up was said by the eminent Sharda Ugra: 'Chappell was one of those maestros who could perform like no other but were unable to communicate their craft'.

27

Operation Rebuild

In the wake of Chappell's resignation, BCCI's 2-day review exercise was supposed to be a routine affair but it turned out to be anything but. The working committee issued some tough measures, aimed at disciplining some of the game's biggest - and, in the board's eyes, rebellious - stars, while giving a ringing endorsement to Rahul Dravid, naming him as the captain for the next three tours to Bangladesh, Ireland and England.

Sachin Tendulkar, the most revered of all, meanwhile, received a showcase notice for airing his grievances in public. So did Yuvraj Singh, who openly backed Sachin's stand.

To make it clear, the board reposed its faith in the 'youth-centric policy' advocated by Dravid and Chappell, asking the selectors to pick a "young side" for the Bangladesh tour. Moreover, they also accepted Dravid's suggestion and appointed specialists to fill the gap left by Chappell; Robin Singh as fielding coach and Venkatesh Prasad as bowling coach. While BCCI's trusted crisis man Ravi Shastri was the unanimous choice for the position of interim coach that he preferred to be called 'cricket manager' while the board went about the process of appointing a new head coach.

Two weeks later, BCCI's senior selection committee led by Vengsarkar met for two hours and announced the squads for the Bangladesh tour. The ODI squad had no Sachin Tendulkar and Sourav Ganguly, who were rested by the selectors. They also axed Virender Sehwag from the test squad, in a bold move after the World Cup fiasco. The selectors picked two newcomers, Bengal batsman Manoj Tiwary (ODIs) and Baroda spinner Rajesh Pawar (Tests), and recalled some familiar faces, like Dinesh Mongia, RP Singh, Gautam Gambhir and Piyush Chawla.

The chief selector, Dilip Vengsarkar, said that Tendulkar and Ganguly were given a break as part of the new 'rotation policy', keeping in mind the busy schedule ahead for India who had to play around 45 ODIs in the next year. He also made it clear that Harbhajan Singh, Ajit Agarkar and Irfan Pathan, who were missing from both squads, had been sacked. While Pathan and Harbhajan deserved it, Agarkar seemed to have got a raw deal as he had been one of the more consistent bowlers in the previous 6-8 months.

The tour got off to a thrilling start with the ODI series opener played at the new Sher-E-Bangla stadium in Mirpur. Bangladesh won the toss and batted first in a rain-curtailed 47-over match. Openers Javed Omar who top-scored with 80 and Tamim got off to a slow but steady start, before Shakib al Hasan held firm with a solid fifty in the middle overs and Mohammad Ashraful accelerated in the later stages to take them to 250 for 7 in 47 overs, which in these hot, humid and sappy conditions seemed like a handful. India's seamers were ineffective with Zaheer also going for a lot of runs, but their spinners - offie Ramesh Powar and part-timers Dinesh Mongia and Sehwag - bowled well and picked up 6 wickets amongst them. India's fielding continued to be sloppy though.

The Delhi duo of Sehwag and Gambhir got India off to a flyer in their chase but were both back in the hut by the end of the seventh over with 66 runs on the scoreboard. Yuvraj batting at 4, too, fell for just 1 but skipper Dravid took the score past 100 in company of Dhoni who was sent in at one down. Just as Dravid seemed to have got his eye in, Shakib had him hole out to midwicket for 22.

When Mongia too failed to stay long India were in trouble at 144 for 5, needing 107 from 113 balls, staring at the prospect of a third loss in four games against Bangladesh. But MS Dhoni, who was suffering from cramps and batting with a runner (Yuvi), curbed his natural game to play a heroic innings of 91 not out and found a perfect partner in Dinesh Karthik, who scored a tenacious 58 not out. The duo batted sensibly cutting out any risk and added an unbeaten 107-run stand to take India home with 6 balls to spare. Bangladesh's captain Habibul Bashar made it easy for them by spreading the field as India won by 5 wickets. MS Dhoni was named the player of the match for his brilliant knock under challenging conditions.

India batted first after winning the toss and put up an improved show in the scorching heat in the second match which was reduced to 49 overs a side due to early-morning drizzle. They ran hard and found the gaps, but also got some lucky breaks as Bangladesh spilled as many as 4 catches. Gautam Gambhir was the star of the innings, scoring a patient hundred despite suffering from cramps. He used his feet well against the spinners and kept the scoreboard ticking. He got some support from Dhoni (36) and Dravid (42 not out), who also batted sensibly. Bangladesh fought back towards the end, but India still managed to post a decent total of 284 for 8.

Bangladesh's chase got off to a terrible start. Tamim Iqbal, their explosive opener, was run out by a confusion with Javed Omar. Zaheer Khan then struck twice in 2 overs, removing the dangerous Shakib Al Hasan and the experienced Bashar. Bangladesh were reeling at 60 for 3 in the 13th over.

They tried to fight back through Aftab Ahmed, who scored a brisk 40 off 41 balls. He hit some powerful shots, but he fell to the spin of Powar. The star of the show, however, was the 19 years old debutant leg-spinner Piyush Chawla. He bamboozled the Bangladesh batsmen with his variations, taking 3 wickets, including that of the dangerous Ashraful.

Bangladesh never looked like chasing down the target, even when Mashrafe Mortaza smashed 4 sixes in a row off Dinesh Mongia in a 26-run over. It was an effort in vain. Bangladesh could only manage 238 for 9 in their 49 overs, losing the match by 46 runs and the series by 2-0. Gautam Gambhir was declared the player of the match for his second ODI hundred, which gave him an edge over the other two openers in the squad, Robin Uthappa and the struggling Sehwag.

The series ended on a damp and disappointing note, as the third and final ODI of the series, which was scheduled to be played at Chittagong, was washed out by rain without a ball being bowled. It was a sad farewell for Bangladesh captain Habibul Bashar, who was playing his last home match, and their coach Dav Whatmore, who was stepping down after the series.

The first of the two tests was set to be played at the same venue in a few days, and as expected the weather played spoilsport in that one too. It started as a thunderbolt, however, as Mortaza delivered a dream ball to Jaffer, who left it alone and saw his off stump flying. It was a stunning start for Bangladesh, who had lost the toss and were asked to bowl first on a flat pitch and the first of 2 ducks for Jaffer, whose wife watched in dismay among the spectators. Skipper Dravid and the other opener Karthik steadied India, but it was the returning pair of Tendulkar and Ganguly who stole the show. Both had been "rested" from the one-day squad, and both hit centuries to prove a point. Tendulkar ended his longest drought of test hundreds, while Ganguly played with flair and aggression.

India declared at 378 for 7 after rain washed out the third day, and Bangladesh crumbled. RP Singh removed both openers in one over, and only Rajin Saleh showed some fight. Kumble was ill, but India did not need him. Bangladesh were 7 down for 122, when Mortaza launched a counter-attack. He smashed 3 sixes and four boundaries in his 79, and added a record 77 with Shahadat for the ninth wicket. They saved the follow-on, and India's hopes of a win.

Dravid batted again, but not for long. He flicked Shahadat elegantly, only to see Rajin take a stunning catch. The next day, Dravid again tried to make a game of it with another sporting declaration, but it was too late. Player of the match Mashrafe Mortaza's heroics in the first innings and the rain had ensured a draw.

Munaf Patel broke down again in the middle of a tour, as he had done in South Africa last year. Unlike the two other players on the injured list - Manoj Tiwary and Sreesanth - Munaf had a history of being brittle and now there were serious questions over his cricketing future.

Team management, meanwhile, called up young Delhi pacer Ishant Sharma as a replacement for Munaf before the second test. Ishant had an impressive first-class season for Delhi, taking 29 wickets in 6 matches. He was 18 years old and had a lot of potential.

Venue for the second and final test of the series was the new Shere-E-Bangla stadium, Mirpur. Bangladesh's captain Habibul Bashar made a surprising decision to bowl first on a batsman-friendly pitch. The local media slammed his choice, which he defended as "a team decision". It backfired spectacularly, as India's top 4 batsmen all scored centuries, a feat never achieved before in test cricket.

India's openers, Wasim Jaffer and Dinesh Karthik, laid a solid foundation for a huge total, putting on 175 runs for the first wicket. It was their second century stand in three tests. Jaffer bounced back in style, scoring 138 after getting a pair in his previous outings. Karthik registered his maiden test hundred, making 129 with flair and finesse. Both had to retire hurt due to the extreme heat, but not before being part of a rare and bizarre opening stand of 408 with Dravid and Tendulkar. Dravid notched up his 24th test hundred with the innings of the match, scoring a fluent 129 in 203 balls that had 15 fours and a six. Tendulkar's ton, in contrast, was rather subdued and contained just 8 fours and a six in his 122. It was his 37th Test hundred overall, and second consecutive this series.

Bangladesh's bowlers had no answers, as they too wilted under the heat and humidity. Left arm spinner Rafique finally broke through on the second morning, but Karthik came back to complete his century. The heat also affected the Bangladesh fielders, who had to leave the field several times. Mashud also gave up his wicketkeeping duties to Shakib. India declared at 610 for 3, leaving Bangladesh with a mountain to climb.

Bangladesh's innings was a contrast of batting collapse and a late counter-attack, as they lost 4 wickets for just 7 runs by the third over. Zaheer Khan and RP Singh bowled with pace and swing, dismissing Omar, Habibul, Nafees and Ashraful in quick succession. Omar became the first batsman to be dismissed off the first ball of both innings, and also bagged a king pair. Rajin Saleh and Shakib Al Hasan showed some resistance, but they fell to Kumble and Zaheer respectively. Bangladesh were forced to follow on before lunch, trailing by 492 runs.

Bangladesh's second innings was more spirited, but still not enough to avoid an innings defeat. They lost Omar again to the first ball, this time caught behind off Zaheer. Nafees and Habibul continued their poor form, falling cheaply to RP Singh and Kumble. Ashraful then launched a stunning assault on the Indian bowlers, scoring the fastest Test fifty by minutes - 27 - and by balls - 26. He hit 10 fours and 3 sixes in his 67 off 41 balls, before he flicked Kumble to Tendulkar at short midwicket. He added 81 runs with Rajin in just 9 overs, but it was a futile endeavour. Mortaza also played a cameo of 70 off 68 balls, hitting 8 fours and 3 sixes, but he could only delay the inevitable. Bangladesh were bowled out for 253 in the 48th over, losing by an innings and 239 runs, making it the biggest victory margin for India in tests. The adjudicators did the right thing to award the player of the match to a bowler - Zaheer Khan - for his 7 wickets - including a fifer in the first inning - and 2 catches. Sachin Tendulkar was the player of the series for his 2 centuries.

India's ODI and test series victories over Bangladesh may not have been very meaningful in terms of rankings, but they were gratifying in terms of payback. It was Bangladesh who sparked India's World Cup disaster by defeating them in the first match, and it was crucial for India to get even. Jaffer and Karthik consolidated their cases further, especially Karthik who also performed well in the ODIs. But more than any individual achievement, the biggest positive of the tour was the restoration of team spirit and camaraderie among the players. For that, a lot of credit must go to Ravi Shastri, the interim coach and Indian cricket's man for all seasons.

28

A European Odyssey

India made some bold changes to their test and one-day squads for the tour of Ireland and England, which started later that month. They dropped Sehwag and Harbhajan Singh, who had been struggling with form, and Munaf Patel, who had fitness issues. Irfan Pathan also missed out, despite working on his bowling action at a camp in Mysore. They picked a new face in Ranadeb Bose, a fast bowler from Bengal, who joined Zaheer Khan, Sreesanth and Ishant Sharma in the pace attack. He was the lone newcomer who made the cut for both squads, while Rohit Sharma, the 20-year-old prodigy from Mumbai, accompanied him as the only other new face in the ODI squad.

Sachin Tendulkar and Sourav Ganguly returned to the one-day side, after being rested for the previous series against Bangladesh. Tendulkar was also chosen as Dravid's second-in-command for the test series in England, but the most astonishing highlight of the whole selection was the elevation of MS Dhoni to limited overs vice captaincy. Gautam Gambhir clinched his spot in both teams as a backup opener and India also retained the very promising Piyush Chawla and the very impressive Ramesh Powar. The changes were aimed at revitalising India's one-day fortunes, after their dismal performance in the World Cup.

Meanwhile, BCCI's search for a permanent coach had hit a roadblock as Graham Ford - the former South African coach who was working as the director of cricket at Kent - rejected their offer to be India's next head coach. This put the Indian team in a fix, as Ravi Shastri had already refused to continue in his position as interim coach, choosing to focus on his more lucrative commentary career. The team needed someone to guide them for the gruelling tour of Ireland and England. They found their saviour in Chandu Borde, another former great of Indian cricket, who took up the challenge of being the interim coach-cum-manager. Borde, 72, had served India with distinction in various roles, first as a player for over a decade from 1958 to 1969, during which he even led India for one test. Then he also served as a selector twice, from 1982 to 1984 and in the tumultuous period of 1999 to 2002. He had also been a successful team manager twice, from 1984 to 1986 and on the tough West Indies tour of 1989.

India started their long tour of Ireland and England with a convincing win over Ireland in a rain-affected one-off ODI at Belfast. It was a morale-boosting victory for India, who were looking forward to the tougher challenge of South Africa in the next 3 matches.

India's bowlers set up the win, as they skittled out Ireland for 193 in 50 overs. Sreesanth and RP Singh exploited the swing-friendly conditions, sharing 5 wickets between them. The returning Ajit Agarkar also chipped in with a wicket, but it was Piyush Chawla, the young leg-spinner, who ended up as the pick of Indian bowlers, bamboozling the Irish middle order with 3 wickets. Only Niall O'Brien showed some fight and class, scoring a gritty 52.

Rain interrupted play at the halfway point, reducing India's target to 171 in 39 overs. India lost Tendulkar in the first over, but Gambhir and Ganguly made light work of the chase. They added 163 runs for the second wicket, playing some glorious strokes. Player of the match Gambhir scored 80 off 89 balls, while Ganguly scored 98 off 88 balls. They took India to the brink of victory, before both fell in quick succession. India won by 9 wickets with 13 overs to spare.

Up next on the tour itinerary was the 3-match bilateral one-day series against number 2 ranked South Africa to be played at Stormont, Belfast for the Future Cup. But a virus swept through the Indian camp, leaving many players sick and unfit in the run-up to the first match. As many as 5 of them missed the final training session, including Dhoni, who was the first to catch the bug and had to sit out the Ireland game. Dravid was also feeling unwell. India had to call in reinforcements from the Ranji Trophy and even Rakesh Patel from the nearby Liverpool Leagues. The Indian camp even tried to get the game postponed, but it was too late. India had to scramble to find 11 healthy players for the series opener.

Tendulkar and Dravid battled hard against a hostile South African pace attack on a tricky pitch, but their eleventh century partnership was not enough to lift India to a huge total. Tendulkar, who looked set for a century, was run out for 99 in a cruel twist of fate - (this being the first instance in his long and illustrious international career that he had missed a hundred by just 1 run; and the 11th time he had got out in the 'nervous nineties', the most for any cricketer) - and his dismissal triggered a collapse in the final overs. Dravid, who played a measured knock of 74, also fell soon after, and India lost their momentum. South African bowlers, led by Kallis, tightened the screws and restricted India to 242, leaving them with a tough task to defend, especially in the absence of a fifth specialist bowling option due to the virus menace.

South Africa chased down 242 with a calm and composed unbeaten half-century from the Ice Cool Jacques Kallis, who was leading the side in this tournament in the absence of regular captain Graeme Smith who was out injured. The Proteas started well with a 56-run opening stand, but India fought back with their spinners, who took 4 quick wickets. Piyush Chawla was once again the pick of the bowlers, with 3 wickets, including the dangerous Herschelle Gibbs. However, Kallis led from the front, holding his nerve and guiding the lower order through the tricky chase. He played some classy shots and ran hard between the wickets, keeping South Africa ahead of the required rate. He finished the game with a boundary in the final over, sealing a 4-wicket win for his team to go 1-0 up in the series and received the player of the match award for his all-round excellence.

This latest win extended South Africa's winning streak over India in ODIs to 5 matches in a row. India needed to break the jinx and win the next match to keep their hopes alive in the series. But they faced a tough challenge, as Sreesanth and Gambhir also joined the list of players who were down with the virus, forcing them to miss the second match at the same venue. India got some fresh blood in the form of Ishant and Ranadeb Bose, and Ishant made his debut straight away. Dravid put South Africa in to bat and his seamers Zak and RP rewarded his decision by reducing South Africa to 7 for 2 and then 46 for 3 by the 14th over. But South Africa fought back with a solid, career-best 82 from opener Morne Van Wyk and handy knocks from Boucher (55) and Duminy (40), reaching 226 for 5 at the end. Yuvraj was the most successful of Indian bowlers, taking 3 wickets with his cunning left-arm spin, while Ishant bowled well but had no luck on debut. Rest of the spinners Chawla, Powar and Tendulkar also kept things tight but failed to get a wicket.

Chasing a tricky target of 227, the old firm of Sachin Tendulkar and Sourav Ganguly rolled back the years with a magnificent 134-run opening stand, reclaiming their record of most century partnerships with this being their 17th three-figure association in this format. Tendulkar, who also became the first batsman to cross 15,000 runs in one-day internationals along the way, lit up the stadium with a breathtaking knock of 93, smashing the South African bowlers all over the park. He hit Ntini, Langeveldt and Nel for boundaries with panache, and blasted Tshabalala's off-spin for a six and a four in a row. But he fell in the nineties for the second game running, as he chopped one on to his stumps off the same bowler. Ganguly too played yet another solid knock of 42, justifying the lavish pre-match praise he received from the South African coach Mickey Arthur. India lost their way after their dismissal, losing Dravid and Dhoni in quick succession to go from being 134 for 0 to 142 for 4 in a matter of 5 overs. But Yuvraj Singh and Dinesh Karthik came to the rescue with a rollicking, unbeaten 85-run partnership for the fifth wicket, showing their temperament and finishing skills. Yuvi remained unbeaten on 49, while Karthik's tireless running fetched him an undefeated 32, as they steered India home with 5 balls to spare, clinching a 5-wicket victory to level the series at one-all. Tendulkar was named the player of the match for his scintillating knock.

Dravid won the toss for the third time in a row and decided to bowl first in the series decider, which was reduced to 31 overs per side due to rain. Agarkar, who had recovered from the flu, and Ganguly, who used his guile, exploited the pitch and conditions to their advantage and rattled South Africa's top order, leaving them at 28 for 4 in 13 overs. Gibbs and Kemp staged a recovery with a 99-run stand for the fifth wicket, but Zaheer Khan broke it with a perfect yorker that knocked out Gibbs' stump. Tendulkar also chipped in with 2 wickets in the only over he bowled, which was also the last over of the innings, as South Africa finished on 148 for 7 in 31 overs. Agarkar, Ganguly and Tendulkar took 2 wickets each, while Zaheer Khan took one.

In reply, India too had a disastrous start, losing their top 3 for just 38 runs in 9 overs, as Ntini bowled a sensational spell. But captain Dravid and Yuvraj revived the innings, taking them past 100, before Dravid was run out in an unfortunate manner for 36. Yuvraj did not let that affect his rhythm at the crease and once again displayed his cool temperament and wide range of strokes to take India home in the company of MS Dhoni with 4 balls to spare to clinch the series 2-1. Yuvraj Singh won the player of the match award for his unbeaten 61, while Tendulkar walked away with the player of the series award for his 200 runs and 2 wickets.

Winning the Future cup in Ireland was a remarkable feat in many senses, as it came against the second-ranked team in the world, in conditions more favourable to them and after losing the first game. This was India's first series-win outside the subcontinent since 2002, when they beat England in the Natwest trophy. Yuvraj Singh, who played a vital role in both triumphs, earned high praise from his captain Dravid, who rated him "as one of the best one-day players in the world at the moment without a doubt." This victory was a great boost for India's morale and a huge step in their recovery from the World Cup debacle. The most splendid highlight of the series was the return to vintage form of their icon, Sachin Tendulkar. He may have missed two centuries by a whisker, but his twin 90s were a proof that he still possessed the charm, the flair and the skill to dazzle like the sun on his day.

Next, India and Pakistan, who had not played each other since April 2006, were supposed to play a one-off game for the 'Friendship Cup' at Glasgow, as part of the 60th anniversary celebrations of independence for both countries. India were in high spirits having just beaten South Africa in the Future cup, while Pakistan had not played since their series against Sri Lanka at Abu Dhabi in May. However, the 10000 odd fans who had bought tickets for the game were left disappointed, as the match was washed out by the rain that had been plaguing the United Kingdom for the past 10 days. The match could not start even after a delayed inspection at 2.00pm, as the ground conditions were too wet and slushy for even a 20-overs-a-side game. The match was eventually abandoned without a ball being bowled.

With that, India moved over to UK and started the English-leg of their tour with a couple of 4-day warm-up games against Sussex and England Lions. The batsmen got some valuable practice in both games, scoring runs in the first innings. However, the bowlers struggled to finish off the matches, as they could not take the last wicket of Sussex and allowed England Lions to pile up a huge total. Both games ended in draws, leaving India with some questions about their bowling ahead of the first test. Another cause of concern was Dhoni's decline behind the stumps. Never a natural wicketkeeper, he had shown remarkable improvement in the previous season thanks mainly to his hard work but the fumbles had reappeared in the alien conditions of UK.

The series kicked off with a nail-biting test at Lords, where rain and swing made batting a challenge. England chose to bat first and dominated the first day, as Strauss and Cook smashed the erratic Indian bowlers. But the second day brought a biblical downpour that flooded the ground and threatened to wash out the game. The ground staff worked wonders to resume play, but the pitch had changed. India struck back with some stunning wickets, including Ganguly's first test wicket in 18 months and Kumble's double strike. Strauss missed his hundred by a whisker, and Dravid took his 150th catch in tests. Pietersen was given a lifeline by a controversial umpiring decision, but he wasted it soon after. England collapsed from 268 for 4 to 298 all out. Sreesanth with 3 for 67 was the most successful of Indian bowlers. Zak and RP also chipped in with a couple wickets each.

India fared no better in their first innings, with only Jaffer resisting with a solid 58 as Anderson bowled superbly to take 5 wickets. He produced a gem of a delivery to dismiss Ganguly, who was beaten by late swing. India lost their last 6 wickets for 46 runs, and conceded a 97-run lead. England lost 2 early wickets in their second innings, but Pietersen came to the rescue with an absolute masterpiece of a century. He was shaky at the start, but grew in confidence and fluency. He added 119 runs with wicketkeeper Prior, and reached his ninth test hundred with a flurry of boundaries. He was the last man out for 134, as England set India a target of 380 in 4 sessions. RP 'Swing' showed some flashes of brilliance and earned his maiden test five-for.

The final inning was a tense and dramatic affair, as India chased a daunting target of 380 in fading light. England struck early, removing Jaffer and Dravid, and then celebrated wildly when Panesar trapped Tendulkar lbw for just 16. Panesar's jubilant dance was a sight to behold, as he sprinted towards the boundary with his arms and legs flailing. India were in trouble at 137 for 3 at stumps on day4.

The next day, Lord's was spared from the rain that soaked the rest of the country. India lost Karthik and Ganguly in quick succession, both well-set, but an under-pressure Laxman and Dhoni resisted. Dhoni, in particular, played some unconventional shots and survived some close calls, as he frustrated England. After lunch, the light deteriorated further, and Vaughan wasted time with his field settings and frequent light-meter checks. England finally showed some urgency when they took the ninth wicket, and switched to spin only. In the gloom, Panesar appealed for an lbw against Sreesanth, but Bucknor turned him down. Then, just before tea, the umpires offered light to the batsmen, who accepted it gratefully. India had escaped with a draw by the skin of their teeth, with MS Dhoni returning unconquered on 76 off 159 balls. This uncharacteristic match-saving effort further strengthened his growing case as a future India captain.

Kevin Pietersen was named the player of the match for his exceptional century in the second innings.

The second test at Trentbridge started with Rahul Dravid winning a crucial toss and opting to bowl first on a damp pitch. Zaheer Khan struck twice in his second over, removing Strauss and Vaughan with some fine swing bowling. Tendulkar took both catches at first slip, sending back the two batsmen who had tormented India at Lord's. Zaheer and RP Singh bowled superbly from both ends, swinging the ball both ways and troubling the England batsmen with their angles. Pietersen was the only one who resisted, but he fell for 41 to a brilliant catch by Dhoni. England collapsed from 94 for 3 to 198 all out, with Zaheer taking 4 wickets and Kumble 3.

India replied strongly with their openers, Karthik and Jaffer, who defied the England bowlers with some luck and skill. They survived some close calls and edged boundaries, but also played some confident strokes. They added 147 runs for the first wicket, their third century opening stand in 5 tests so far and the first for India in England since 1979. No other Indian pair who opened in at least 5 tests had a better average than their 88.50. They both missed their hundreds, but set the platform for India's famed batting trinity of Dravid, Sachin and Ganguly, all three of whom made valuable contributions, despite some poor umpiring decisions. Dravid made a solid

37, Ganguly a fluent 79 while Tendulkar became the third batsman after Border and Lara to go past 11,000 Test runs, but fell short of his hundred by just 9 runs when he got a dubious call off Paul Collingwood's gentle medium pace. Ganguly too was wrongly given out caught behind by umpire Simon Taufel, who had a rare off day. India took a massive lead of 283 runs, thanks to their openers and middle order.

Late on the third evening in India's innings, something pivotal happened. Zaheer Khan, the number 9, walked out to bat and noticed jelly beans on the pitch. He was furious and gestured with his bat at Pietersen, who denied any involvement. Ian Bell, fielding at short-leg, was suspected, but never caught. English media dubbed it the "Jellybeangate" and English captain Vaughan apologised later. But the damage was done, as Zaheer was fired up to bowl his best in England's second innings, and inspired his team-mates with his aggression.

(India also misbehaved, mainly Sreesanth, who bowled a beamer at Pietersen and a bouncer at Collingwood from the crease. He didn't apologize for either of these actions, and shoulder-barged Vaughan too. Dravid scolded him, and the ICC fined him 50%)

England faced a daunting task of saving the match, as they had to bat for 2 days on a deteriorating pitch. They started well, as they survived the last session of the third day without losing a wicket. But the fourth day brought trouble, as a fired up Zaheer Khan found some swing and dismissed Cook early. Strauss and Vaughan fought hard, but luck deserted them. Vaughan was bowled by a freak delivery that bounced off his thigh pad and rolled onto his stumps. He had batted brilliantly for his 124, but his dismissal triggered a collapse. Bell and Prior fell cheaply, and England lost their last 7 wickets for 68 runs. Zaheer was the hero, taking 5 wickets and bowling with rare skill and passion.

India needed only 73 runs to win, and their openers again gave them a solid start. Tremlett bowled with pace and bounce, and took 3 wickets, including Tendulkar who was caught at leg gully. But the captain and his predecessor ensured India reached their target comfortably, and celebrated their historic win.

It was only their fifth victory in England in 47 Tests and 75 years. Zaheer Khan was named the Man of the match for his outstanding performance with the ball. He took 9 wickets in the match, and swung the game in India's favour.

The team enjoyed a break after 2 hard-fought Tests, and had 8 days to prepare for the final one. They faced Sri Lanka A, who had a successful tour of England, losing only 1 game out of 7. Dravid & co. utilised this opportunity to work on their perennial problem of losing an away test right after winning one. This poor trend began in 2001 at Harare, and continued in many places like Kandy, Port-of-Spain, Adelaide, Multan, Johannesburg and even Mumbai. They hoped to avoid the Trent Bridge-Oval scenario.

The three-day game ended in a draw but India left with some positives, such as their captain Dravid's return to form, Ranadeb Bose's 5-wicket haul and Jaffer and Gambhir's twin fifties, which saved the match in the second innings.

On the eve of the third test, the selectors announced the teams for the 7-match bilateral one-day series to follow, and the upcoming inaugural Twenty20 world cup that was to be played in South Africa next. The one-day squad against England was the same as the one that won the Future cup, except for Munaf replacing Ishant Sharma.

India had barely tasted Twenty20 cricket, playing just one T20I against South Africa. The big three opted out of the Twenty20 World Cup, at Dravid's behest. The selectors blended old and young blood, recalling Harbhajan, Sehwag and Irfan to join Dhoni, Yuvraj and Agarkar. They also picked some fresh faces like Chawla, Joginder, Yusuf Pathan and Rohit Sharma. The biggest headache was to choose a captain for this highly experimental unit. Chairman of selectors Dilip Vengsarkar, who travelled with the team in UK, after a lot of brainstorming and feedback from the likes of Sachin and Ravi Shastri - who managed the team in Bangladesh - took a bold gamble on MS Dhoni as the skipper of this youthful squad in this novel format. Yuvraj Singh was named his deputy. Lalchand Rajput, former Mumbai player and India's U-19 coach was named the team manager for the world event and would take over from Chandu Borde, who was in charge of the team on the ongoing tour of England. Many players in the squad had been under Rajput's guidance in the U-19s, so the decision made sense.

India went in to third and final test at the Oval leading by 1-0 and needing just a draw to win the series. Lady luck smiled on Rahul Dravid again as he won another vital toss and decided to bat first on a belter of a wicket. All that India's famed batting line-up needed to do now was to bat for 2 days and seal the series. They did just that, and amassed the highest ever score in India-England tests, smashing many records in the process. Jaffer fell after scoring a brisk 35 but Karthik (91) and Dravid (55) gave them a solid foundation adding 127 runs for the second wicket. England's bowlers tried hard, but James Anderson was the only one who looked threatening. Matt Prior had a nightmare behind the stumps, conceding 35 byes and dropping a couple of catches. Ganguly looked in fine touch, but he was robbed of a big one by umpire Ian Howell of South Africa, who made a series of 'Howellers' in this match. Tendulkar and Laxman posted half-centuries, but Tendulkar struggled to score freely and took 5 hours for his 82.

India's lower order then batted England out of the match and the series by adding a whopping 247 runs for the last 4 wickets. Dhoni celebrated his ascension to T20 captaincy with a blistering knock of 92, hitting 9 boundaries and 4 sixes. He was caught in the deep, trying to reach his hundred with another six. The real scene stealer, however, was the evergreen Anil Kumble who scored his maiden test century at the age of 36 years 297 days. He was the last man standing, unbeaten on 110. He had waited for 118 tests to achieve this feat, the longest ever in test history. India finished their first inning at 664. Strauss was dismissed before stumps on day2, making it even worse for England.

England had a slim hope of saving the match, as the pitch was still good for batting. They batted well, with Collingwood making 62 and Bell playing fluently for 63. But they could not cope with India's bowling, especially Zaheer Khan, who took another 4-fer. England were bowled out for 345, and, in a much-debated decision, Dravid chose not to enforce the follow-on. He wanted to bat England out of the game, but his decision almost backfired when India lost 3 quick wickets, including Tendulkar for just 1. Dravid played an excruciatingly slow innings of 12 from 96 balls, while Ganguly scored a breezy 57. Dravid declared at 180 for 6, setting England a target of 500.

England had no chance of winning, and only tried to survive. They batted well on the final day, with Pietersen scoring a brave century and Bell continuing his good form with 67. They added 144 runs for the fourth wicket, and frustrated India's bowlers. India needed 5 wickets in the last session, but they could not break through, in the absence of a second spinner. England held on for a draw, but India clinched the series 1-0. It was a historic achievement for India, who had not won a series in England since 1986 when Kapil's Devils reigned supreme over Gatting's England. Kumble was the player of the match for his century and 4 wickets while Zaheer Khan and James Anderson shared the player of the series honour for their excellent bowling.

The significance of this victory can not be overstated. It was not merely the first home-series defeat for England's Ashes-winning captain Michael Vaughan, but also marked only the second time England had lost a series at home in the 21st century, after the 2001 Ashes debacle.

But more than anything else, it was a cherished dream come true moment for India's 'Golden Generation' - Sachin Tendulkar, Anil Kumble, Sourav Ganguly, Rahul Dravid and VVS Laxman - who might not have another opportunity to play in England.

Next, India faced Scotland for the first time in an ODI at Glasgow, a month before their T20 World Cup opener against the same opponents. With that in mind, team management rested the senior players and gave a chance to the youngsters, who did not disappoint. Dravid's decision to bowl first paid off as his pace attack rattled the Scottish top order. Agarkar, RP Singh and Munaf Patel, who returned from a back injury, shared 4 wickets among them. Scotland recovered from 40 for 4 thanks to a gritty partnership between Hamilton and McCallum, who scored 44 and 41 respectively. They took Scotland to 203 before rain intervened and revised India's target to 209.

India's chase was smooth and steady, as Uthappa and Gambhir put on a 104-run opening stand. Uthappa, playing his first ODI since the World Cup, started slowly but then accelerated with some crisp strokes. He made 55 before falling to Wright's inswinger. Karthik did not last long, but Gambhir held one end with a determined 50. He was supported by Yuvraj, who smashed a brisk 38, and Dravid, who received a warm welcome from the crowd in his old stomping ground (he had played for Scotland in the county circuit in 2003). India reached the target in the 40th over with 8 wickets in hand.

Rain ruined the warm-up game between India and England Lions at Northampton, where the hosts scored 296 for 8, thanks to a couple of big partnerships. Luke Wright, touted as England's next batting hope, smashed 75 and Joe Denly made 67. India were 32 for no loss, with Ganguly hitting 3 classy fours, when the rain came and washed out the game.

The 7-match ODI series got underway with the first match at Southampton. Dravid opted to bowl first but soon rued his decision as his pacers, especially Agarkar, struggled to trouble the England openers with the white Kookaburra ball. Cook and Bell batted superbly and scored their maiden ODI hundreds, adding a record 178 runs in 31 overs. Bell was the star of the show, hitting 126 off 118 balls with 16 fours and a six. He even outshone Pietersen, who came in after Cook fell for 102, and powered England to a huge 288 in their 50 overs. Zaheer and RP were the only bowlers to take a wicket each.

India's batting was a stark contrast to England's, as they collapsed to 34 for 4 by the end of the twelfth over courtesy a brilliant opening spell by James Anderson. Flintoff, playing his first game for England after a long injury lay-off, bowled with pace and hostility, and removed Dhoni with a bouncer. Dravid tried to hold the innings together with a patient 46 but his innings was cut short by a clever stumping by Prior, who was quick to whip off the bails. After his departure, none of the other Indian batsmen could lend adequate support to Karthik who fought till the very end with a plucky 44 not-out off 45 balls. India were bundled out for 184 in the last over, giving England a massive 104-run win and a 1-0 lead in the 7-match series. Ian Bell won the player of the match for his wonderful hundred.

India came back strongly in the second match at Bristol, where the batsmen had a field day on a flat pitch with short boundaries. The 16,000-strong crowd witnessed a run-fest, with 11 sixes and 73 fours flying off the bat. India, who won the toss and opted to bat, piled up their highest ODI total against England - 329 for 7. Tendulkar and Dravid were the architects of the innings, scoring magnificent nineties despite suffering from flu-like symptoms. They were hardly troubled by the English bowlers, who lacked variety and penetration. England's decision to leave out Panesar and play an extra seamer in Chris Tremlett proved costly, as he went for 73 runs in his 10 overs. Tendulkar played a masterful innings, scoring 99 runs off just 112 balls with one six and 15 fours. He was unlucky to miss out on a deserved hundred by a single run for the second time on this tour, as he was wrongly given out by the umpire. Dravid matched him with a classy knock of 92 not out off only 63 balls, hitting a six and 11 fours. He showed his best form in a long time, with elegant strokes all around the ground.

England had a daunting target to chase, but they were given a lifeline by India's sloppy fielding. India dropped 5 catches in the first 19 overs, allowing the England batsmen to get off to a good start. However, they could not capitalise on their chances, as they lost wickets at regular intervals. Spinners Chawla and Powar turned the tide in India's favour, taking 4 wickets between them and putting pressure on the middle order. Dmitri Mascarenhas gave England some hope with a stunning fifty that included 5 sixes, but he fell in the penultimate over with 31 still needed. Stuart Broad tried his best with 21 off 13 balls, but India held their nerve and clinched a narrow win to level the series 1-1. Rahul Dravid was adjudged the player of the match for his captain's knock.

Dravid chose to bowl first in the third ODI at Birmingham, but was again let down by their seamers and fielders. They allowed Cook and Prior to get England off to a strong start with a 76-run opening stand in 13 overs. They both fell in quick succession, but Bell took charge at his home ground. He played a superb knock of 79 off 89 balls, his third fifty in a row in the series, and forged a vital 75-run partnership with Collingwood. He also displayed his brilliance in the field, taking two catches and a run-out, and highlighting the gap in fielding quality between the two teams. Chawla bamboozled Pietersen for the second game running but England still finished with a strong 281 for 8, with some late fireworks by their captain Collingwood and Owais Shah, who made up for Flintoff's absence with some big hits. RP Singh picked up 3 lucky wickets at the death, but Ramesh Powar was the most impressive bowler for India, taking 2 for 45 with his accurate off-spin.

Chasing 282, India lost Tendulkar and Karthik early - Karthik for a duck and Tendulkar, to James Anderson for the fifth time on this tour alone - but Ganguly and Dravid added 76 for the second wicket. The crowd, mostly

Indian fans, cheered them on, hoping for a repeat of Bristol. But Tremlett struck twice in two overs, removing both the batsmen. The pitch was slow and the bowling was tight, and India could not keep up with the required rate. Anderson bowled superbly, taking 3 for 32, while Collingwood chipped in with 2 wickets with his medium pace in the middle overs. Yuvraj's run-out for 45 was the final nail in the coffin for India. They were bowled out for 239 in the 48th over, giving England a 42-run win and a 2-1 lead in the seven-match series.

India had a poor outing with the bat in the fourth ODI at Manchester, as they were restricted to 212 by a disciplined England bowling and fielding performance. The new-ball duo of Anderson and Broad swung and seamed the ball with great skill and precision, showing glimpses of their future greatness. They ran through the famed Indian batting line-up snatching 7 wickets in a brilliant spell of fast bowling. The supporting cast of Flintoff, Panesar etc too did not allow the Indian batsmen to play their shots, and kept them under pressure throughout. Tendulkar grafted hard for his 55 off 86 balls, but threw away his wicket to Pietersen's part-time after doing all the hard work. Yuvraj Singh took his time to settle down, reaching his fifty off 90 balls, but then accelerated to make 71 off 104 balls. Tailenders Zaheer Khan and Piyush Chawla added some valuable runs at the end as India finished with 212 on the scoreboard.

England had a tough time chasing a modest target of 213, as India showed a rare intensity and fire in the field. Seemingly inspired by Shahrukh Khan's 'Chak De', Indian bowlers and fielders put pressure on the England batsmen right from the start. Agarkar, back in the playing eleven, led the attack with renewed passion bowling with pace and swing, and taking 3 wickets. India also held on to their catches and appealed with gusto. England were in a spot of bother at 114 for 7, when two youngsters came to their aid. Ravi Bopara, who had earlier run out his captain, and Stuart Broad, who had taken a career-best 4 for 51, displayed remarkable composure and skill. They added an unbeaten 99-run stand, playing sensibly and hitting timely boundaries. Broad had a close shave on 45, when he was given not out for a lbw appeal against Chawla. The 21 years old made India pay for it, batting like his father, former English international Chris Broad, who was watching nervously from the stands. He scored 45 not out off 49 balls, while Bopara made 43 not out off 60 balls. They took England home with two overs to spare, giving them a 3-1 lead in the series. Broad, the baby faced assassin, was named the player of the match for his all round brilliance.

It was a do-or-die match for India at Leeds, where England chose to field first. But they soon regretted their decision, as India's most prolific opening pair, Sachin Tendulkar and Sourav Ganguly, put on a masterclass of batting. Sachin was majestic, playing with elegance and aggression, while Sourav was dependable, playing with flair and confidence. They set the tone for the innings with a 116-run opening stand, that lit up the gloomy Headingley with their sparkling display, reminiscent of their heroics in that famous test at this very ground five years ago. Sachin departed for a blistering 71 off 59 balls, studded with 13 boundaries, in the 20th over, and Sourav followed him for a compact 59 off 79 balls, laced with 7 boundaries and 2 glorious sixes, leaving India at 150 for 2 in the 27th over.

The momentum was carried forward by Yuvraj Singh, who reached the milestone of 5,000 one-day runs, during his flamboyant 72 off 57 balls, that had 10 fours and 2 sixes. He was well supported by Gautam Gambhir, who showed intestinal fortitude despite a broken thumb with a tenacious 51 off 66. Captain and his deputy provided the finishing blitz as India amassed 324 for 6, their highest total against England in England.

England's chase started badly when they lost Cook early to Agarkar, but Matt Prior and the in-form Ian Bell kept them in the hunt with brisk forties. Then Ganguly struck with his gentle seamers, taking 2 key wickets in successive overs. He was backed by Dhoni, who was brilliant behind the stumps, stumping Prior and catching Pietersen and Bell. Zaheer Khan also bowled a beauty to dismiss Pietersen. Dhoni was involved in all the first 5 wickets and set a new Indian record of 6 dismissals, the first by an Indian and the eighth overall. Only Collingwood showed some heart, scoring a defiant 91 not out from 71 balls, but it wasn't to be. England's target was revised twice due to rain interruptions, but they still fell short by 38 runs, as India reduced the series deficit to 3-2. Sourav Ganguly was declared the player of the match for his all-round performance.

The teams moved to London for the final 2 matches of the long and tiring tour, with the series on the line. England chose to bat first at the Oval, but lost their openers early. Bell and Pietersen rebuilt the innings, but Bell missed what would have been his fourth fifty of the series by just 1 run and skipper Collingwood was run out in the next over, leaving England at 83 for 4 in the 18th over. Pietersen adapted his game to play cautiously as the situation demanded, but he too was run out for 53 off 82 balls.

England were in trouble at 137 for 5 in the 31st over, when debutant Luke Wright and Owais Shah changed the game. Wright smashed a 38-ball fifty, and Shah scored his maiden international hundred in a blaze of boundaries. The climax came when Dmitri Mascarenhas thumped Yuvraj for 5 sixes in a row in the final over, a feat only matched by Gibbs and Afridi at this level. England ended with a massive 316 for 6, thanks to some atrocious bowling by Yuvraj and Agarkar. Only Zaheer and Chawla escaped the onslaught while taking a wicket each.

India faced a daunting target of 317, but the phenomenal Sachin Tendulkar rose to the occasion and played his most uninhibited innings of the tour, before cramps slowed him down. He played with freedom and flair, hitting 16 fours and a six in his 94 off 81 balls. He was in agony as he walked back for 94, falling in the nineties for the fifth time on this tour and had to be assisted up the stairs by his teammates, but he had given his team a fighting chance and left a lasting impression with his trailblazing innings.

Broad's sledging at the other end riled up Ganguly and the elder statesman showed him 'who's your Dada' with his bat. He smashed a rapid 53 and helped Tendulkar put on 150 in 23 overs; the 21st and final century partnership between *the* most prolific opening pair in one-day internationals. Gautam Gambhir also contributed with a valuable 47 at one-down but England fought back with regular wickets, leaving India needing 42 from the last four overs. Uthappa, playing in an unfamiliar position of a finisher, and Dhoni took the game to the wire, smashing Anderson for 28 runs in 47th and 49th overs. With 10 needed in the final over, Uthappa kept his cool and creamed back-to-back boundaries to take India to the series-levelling victory, with 2 balls to spare.

It was a nail-biting finish to one of the more memorable one-dayers in recent memory, and even the usually stoic Dravid could not contain his excitement as he ran out to celebrate with his team. Tendulkar was rightly named the player of the match for his virtuoso performance.

With the series level at 3-3, the stage was set for a thrilling finale. Indian captain made a surprising decision to bat first on a gloomy morning at Lords, and paid the price for it. England's bowlers were relentless, bowling with pace and accuracy, and giving nothing away. Anderson troubled Ganguly with his short balls, and dismissed him and Gambhir in quick succession. Flintoff, playing on a steroid injection, was even more hostile claiming the prized scalps of Dravid and Tendulkar; Dravid for a duck and Tendulkar for 30, both caught behind by Prior. Tendulkar's dismissal was controversial, as he seemed to miss the ball by a whisker, but umpire Aleem Dar raised his finger. Mascarenhas was the most economical bowler though, bowling a straight line and varying his pace. He took 3 wickets for just 23 runs in his 10 overs, putting the brakes on India's scoring. Dhoni tried to salvage the innings, but he was shackled by the situation. He reached a half-century, but was the last man out for 50 off 72 balls. India were bowled out for a paltry 187 in the 48th over, giving England a huge advantage in the series decider.

England had a modest target of 188 to chase but they got off to a shaky start, as RP Singh struck twice in his first over. He dismissed both the openers, Wright and Prior, who were playing in place of Cook. India had a chance to put pressure on England, but they let it slip away. Bell was in the form of his life, and he anchored the innings with his fluent strokes. He was unlucky to be run out by a bad call from Pietersen, who made up for his mistake with his best knock of the series. KP played with aggression and confidence, and he found a reliable partner in Collingwood, who was his usual unruffled self. They took England closer to the finish line, and skipper Collingwood sealed the victory with a boundary in the 43rd over. It was a historic win for England, as they clinched their first one-day series at home since 2004, by a narrow margin of 4-3.

Kevin Pietersen was named the player of the match for his match-winning 71 not out, while Ian Bell was awarded the player of the series for his consistent run-scoring throughout the series, adding to his burgeoning reputation as someone who was equally adept in both formats of the game.

It was a fair result, as India's sloppy fielding finally came back to haunt them in the series decider. They had been dropping catches left and right throughout the series, and it was a miracle that they were still in the hunt till the end. But their flaws were exposed in the final match, and they paid the price for it.

Be that as it may, the tour was still a memorable one for Indian cricket as Dravid & co. achieved a historic feat and displayed some thrilling cricket throughout. The Wall, despite dealing with limited resources and injury concerns, can take pride in his leadership. He steered his side to a rare test series win in England after 21 years and showed promising signs of a revival in the one-dayers as well, winning 7 out of 12, including the prestigious Future Cup triumph over South Africa. He would have been thrilled by the way India bounced back from the humiliating defeat at Old Trafford and levelled the series going into the final match.

Section 4

THE CLIMAX

29

A New Dawn

Thus, after a gruelling but satisfying tour of 77 days, the young guns hopped on the flight to South Africa for the first-ever Twenty20 world cup, while the trinity of Sachin, Sourav and Rahul headed back home. Four days later, they were invited to add some star power to the grand launch event of the 'Indian Premier League', a new and ambitious T20 league in India. They were joined by some other international cricketers of repute, such as Anil Kumble, Glenn McGrath and Stephen Fleming. The event was also attended by BCCI President Sharad Pawar, ICC Chairman Malcolm Speed and heads of many national cricket boards. Former Indian captains like Tiger Pataudi, Chandu Borde, Krishnamachari Srikkanth and Dilip Vengsarkar, former BCCI presidents Raj Singh Dungarpur, Indrajit Singh Bindra and Ranbir Singh Mahendra were also present on the occasion. It was a glittering occasion, marking the beginning of a new era in Indian cricket.

The Indian Premier League or 'the IPL' was the brainchild of Lalit Modi, a loyal aide of the BCCI President Sharad Pawar. Modi originally envisioned it as a 50-overs tournament in 1996, but it was put on hold. It resurfaced only when the Zee group headed by Subhash Chandra started the 'Indian Cricket League', a rival T20 event that had everything the IPL had, except the most important thing: the official approval from the cricket authorities, the BCCI and ICC, who dubbed it a 'rebel' league.

The IPL was to be a professional Twenty20 cricket league in India, based on the franchise model of some popular sports leagues in the USA, such as the NBA, MLS and NFL. The first season of the IPL was set to take place in April-May, 2008, with a huge prize money of $3 million, making it the most lucrative domestic cricket tournament already. The eight teams would play 14 matches each, seven at home and seven away, against every other team. The top four teams would qualify for the semifinals, and the winners would face each other in the final. The IPL was governed by a council of former Indian captains and BCCI officials, with Lalit Modi as its Chairman and Commissioner.

The IPL got the approval and backing of all the members of the ICC, the global cricket body. The cricket boards of India, Australia, England and South Africa also teamed up to launch a 'Champions T20 League', similar to the 'Champions League' in Football. This league would feature the top two teams from each country's domestic T20 tournaments.

This marked the beginning of the end for the ICL, which folded up by 2009 after only two seasons plagued by unprofessionalism, scandals and low-quality cricket.

The very next day, Rahul Dravid tendered his resignation from the post of the Indian captain in his typical understated manner, sans any fanfare or drama. He said he wanted to focus on his game, and give the chance to a new leader.

Dravid's resignation from captaincy came as a shock to many, as he had just guided India to a glorious series win in England, their first in 21 years. He had been India's captain for 2 years, winning 8 Tests and 42 ODIs, and his run included that world-record 17 wins in chasing in ODIs and important away test series victories in West Indies, Bangladesh and England. As captain, he averaged 51 in tests and 44 in ODIs (though his test form did take a slight dip towards the end of his tenure). He faced many trials and tribulations, both on and off the field, but always led with honour, dignity and grace. The only blot on his otherwise stellar record was the world cup disaster, where his team could not deliver on the hopes of a billion fans. But like the ideal 'Man' in Rudyard Kipling's immortal poem 'If' - who saw the things he devoted his life to, shattered, Rahul Dravid stooped and rebuilt them with worn-out tools, without ever breathing a word about his loss. And in doing so, left behind a resilient team that had overcome that tragic setback, for his successor(s) to carry on.

He stepped down as one of India's most successful captains, but also one of its most unappreciated.

History should be kinder to his captaincy tenure, and acknowledge his sacrifices for Indian cricket[4].

A Rollercoaster Start

That evening, India's largely new-look team had a dismal start to their campaign as their first game of the ICC World T20 was washed out by steady rain in Durban. Scotland's skipper Ryan Watson opted to bowl first at Kingsmead, but the players never got a chance to take the field as the rain returned before the match could begin. Both teams shared a point each which meant that India needed to avoid a big loss to Pakistan on Friday to qualify for the Super Eights while Scotland crashed out, having lost their opening match to Pakistan.

India had to face their arch rival in their first real match of the T20 World Cup, as their opening game was washed out by rain. India had played only one T20I before, against South Africa. India had been the most hesitant to embrace T20 cricket, with BCCI being the last board to agree to join the inaugural world event, after losing a vote in the ICC meeting in 2006. But once they agreed, they launched a new domestic T20 competition in April-May 2007, named after the flamboyant batsman of yore, Syed Mushtaq Ali. Tamilnadu, led by Dinesh Karthik, won the first edition by beating Punjab in the final. Some of the players like Yuvraj, Dhoni, Dinesh Mongia etc showed their skills in the new format with some good knocks, but it was the prodigiously talented Rohit Sharma from Mumbai who stole the show with a 45-ball 101.

Pakistan, like India, had a new team and a new captain, Shoaib Malik. *Jumma* began on an auspicious note for the Men in green as Malik called it right and put India in on a damp wicket. Mohammad Asif, who had been involved in an ugly physical spat with Shoaib Akhtar earlier in the

---

4. **Update-** History has indeed been kinder to The Wall. When I wrote the above line in mid-2023, it was just a hopeful sentiment. However, by the time this book went to print, Rahul Sharad Dravid had achieved his lifelong dream of winning a World cup trophy, if not as a player then as the coach of the recently crowned T20 World cup winning Indian team. And in a fitting twist of poetic justice, this triumph occurred on the same Caribbean soil, where he had to endure one of his lowest moments. Rahul Dravid's heroic journey is a testament to the fact that nice guys too can, and do finish first.

tournament, bowled like a dream, reminding everyone of the great Glenn McGrath. He made the ball talk in the gloomy weather, and tormented the Indian batsmen with his seam and swing. He caught Gambhir off his own bowling, bowled Sehwag with an inside edge, and did the same to Karthik after he had hit two beautiful boundaries.

Robin Uthappa was the only one who defied, as he hit some classy shots. He flicked one off his pads for four, and drove one over the infield off Gul. But he had no support, as Yuvraj lobbed a dolly to mid-off. India were gasping at 36 for 4.

Uthappa and Dhoni tried to rebuild the innings after Asif finished his spell. Uthappa hit Arafat for a couple of sixes, but both of them found it hard to score against Sohail Tanvir, who had a unique bowling action like Mike Proctor.

Afridi came on to bowl, but Uthappa kept attacking him with cuts and drives. He reached his 50, but then rain stopped play. When play resumed, he edged one to the keeper off Tanvir. Pathan joined Dhoni and had a mini-battle with Afridi. He smashed him for 2 sixes over midwicket, but Afridi got him out with a faster ball that hit his leg stump.

Dhoni hit Arafat for a four and a six, but Pakistan came back strongly, as Tanvir and Gul removed Dhoni and the tail. India managed to reach 141 for 9. It was a modest total, but it proved just enough in the end.

Pakistan found the chase tough as India's young guns bowled and fielded with great intensity. RP Singh nailed Nazir with a yorker. Sreesanth and Agarkar choked the runs, and Agarkar snared Butt with an edge. Pathan then bowled a magical over, running out Akmal and castling Younis to leave Pakistan gasping at 65 for 4.

Skipper Malik and Misbah steadied the ship with some clever singles and big hits. But just then, Malik lost his cool and skied Pathan to Harbhajan. Afridi came too late and left too soon, giving a catch to Karthik off Bhajji. But Misbah kept fighting. The 33-year old, who was a controversial pick for Pakistan, made a superb 53 off 35, smashing Harbhajan, Agarkar and Sreesanth for sixes, and brought Pakistan within touching distance in the last 3 overs. He needed 1 run from 2 balls, but Sreesanth denied him with a dot and a short ball. Misbah tried to steal a single, but Yuvraj's throw was too good. It was a tie, and a bowl-out was needed to decide the winner.

The 'bowl-out' was a unique way to decide the winner of the tied match. It involved 5 bowlers from each team aiming at an unguarded set of stumps. The team that hit the stumps more times would win the match. India, who had been practising bowl-outs in the nets, picked Sehwag, Harbhajan, Uthappa, Sreesanth and Pathan as their bowlers. Pakistan, who were clueless about the rules, chose Yasir Arafat, Umar Gul, Shahid Afridi, Mohammad Asif and Shoaib Malik on the fly. India won the toss and decided to bowl first.

The bowl-out turned out to be a one-sided affair, as India hit the stumps 3 times out of 5, while Pakistan missed all their attempts. Arafat and Gul came close, while Afridi, Asif and Malik were nowhere near. Sehwag, Harbhajan and Uthappa were on target for India, while Sreesanth and Pathan missed by a hair. India celebrated their thrilling victory with unbridled joy, while Pakistan were left stunned by their poor performance and lack of preparation.

India faced New Zealand in their first Super-Eights match. Dhoni chose to bowl first on a tricky pitch. New Zealand had a roller-coaster innings, as they switched between attack and defence, depending on the bowlers and the situation. Brendon McCullum started with a flurry of boundaries, hitting Sreesanth and RP Singh for 4 fours in 2 overs. But Dhoni brought in Pathan and Agarkar, who bowled with discipline in their first spell and brought down the scoring rate. Harbhajan spun his magic, getting Fulton and McCullum with his variations. Fulton was trapped leg-before by a quicker one, while McCullum slog-swept a floater to long-on to be dismissed for 45 off 31 balls. Ross Taylor and Scott Styris also fell soon, leaving New Zealand in a mess at 81 for 6.

But the mercurial Craig McMillan (44 off 23) and all-rounder Oram (35 off 15) changed the game with a stunning counter-attack, hitting 6 sixes and 4 fours in 3 overs. They targeted Yuvraj, Sreesanth and Agarkar, who had no answer to their power-hitting. Oram hit 2 sixes over long-on, while McMillan hit one over long-off and one over long-on off Sreesanth. Vettori too chipped in with 3 boundaries off 5 balls in the final over to take his side to 190. Harbhajan Singh was the best bowler for India, bamboozling the bowlers with his off-spinners, doosras and faster ones to pick 2 for 24 in his 4 overs. RP Singh also took 2 wickets for 29 runs, while Sreesanth, Agarkar and Yuvraj leaked a lot of runs.

India had a dream start to their chase of 191, as Delhi boys Sehwag and Gambhir went berserk. They punished Mark Gillespie, Bond and Jeetan Patel for boundaries, with Sehwag's sixer over cover being the highlight. They sprinted to 76 in 6 overs, and looked set to win the game.

But Vettori spoiled India's party with an absolute masterclass of left-arm spin. The Kiwi skipper bowled with guile and skill outwitting Uthappa and Gambhir with his variations, and dented their chase. Yuvraj, Dhoni and Pathan also succumbed to the pressure, and India collapsed. Vettori took 2 more wickets in the 17th over, and sealed the game for New Zealand. India lost by 10 runs, despite their fiery start. Daniel Vettori was named the player of the match for his all-round excellence.

The loss again put India's campaign on the backfoot, as their remaining 2 matches in the Super-Eights stage had virtually become must wins if they wished to qualify for the semi-finals. To make matters worse, their next opponent was England who, despite their poor form in this tournament, had the most exposure to this format.

30

Magic

With their backs against the wall, India chose to bat first at Kingsmead against England in their next Super-Eight clash. They unleashed their fury on the hapless English bowlers, who were clueless against the onslaught of Sehwag, Gambhir and Yuvraj. The openers set the tone with a fiery partnership, ripping apart the English attack with daring strokes. Sehwag was given a lifeline on 41, and he made them regret it with a barrage of boundaries that took him to a 38-ball fifty. Gambhir kept pace with him, reaching his own fifty - his second successive in the tournament - in 2 fewer balls. The dashing Delhi duo once again showcased the undeniable chemistry they shared, adding 136 - the second-highest opening-partnership in Twenty20 internationals - in less than 15 overs.

But the real carnage came when Yuvraj walked in at the fall of Uthappa's wicket in the 17th over. Right away he had a heated exchange with Flintoff, and then vented his anger on Broad, who bore the brunt of his wrath in the penultimate over. Yuvraj did a Gary Sobers, smashing 6 sixes in an over and sending the ball into orbit with each swing of his bat.

The first shot was a booming rocket that flew over the midwicket boundary and almost landed outside the stadium, and the second was a flick that sailed over the square-leg fence. After a graceful loft over the extra cover region and another smash over the point boundary off a dreadful full-toss, you could sense the thrill and anticipation in the air.

English skipper Collingwood and Broad had a chat, but it proved futile, as a majestic sweep over the midwicket fence was followed by another monstrous hit over the long-on boundary. Six balls, six sixes, 36 runs, and complete annihilation for the shell-shocked English team that had already been knocked out of the tournament. The crowd went berserk as the Indian vice-captain created history, becoming the first batsman to achieve the feat in Twenty20 cricket and the fourth in all cricket. He reached his fifty in a record 12 balls and finished with 58 off 16 balls, as India posted a mammoth 218 for 4.

To England's credit, they put up a brave fight in their chase of 219, but could not overcome another excellent performance by Indian bowlers and fielders. Vikram Solanki and Darren Maddy launched a fierce assault, slicing and hooking the ball with force, while Joginder Sharma was denied 2 wickets on debut by sloppy fielding. Kevin Pietersen joined the fray and blasted a few shots over the fence, but his spectacular dismissal by Harbhajan off his own bowling turned the tide decisively in India's favour. Shah and Collingwood tried to revive the innings with some lusty blows, but a brilliant over from RP Singh sealed their fate, as they both fell in quick succession. Flintoff was left with too much to do, and India celebrated a memorable victory by 18 runs and an unforgettable rampage by player of the match Yuvraj Singh.

Less than 24 hours later, Men in Blue faced an even tougher hurdle when they took on the hosts South Africa - the only team with a perfect record in the tournament - in a must-win game. They were dealt a further blow when last night's hero Yuvraj Singh, had to sit out due to tendonitis.

India's captain MS Dhoni chose to bat first in another highest-stakes encounter at Kingsmead against the hosts. But they faced a tough test from local legend Shaun Pollock, who bowled a brilliant opening spell on his home turf. Gambhir attacked from the start, but he got a reprieve when Philander dropped him. Pollock got his reward on his home soil, getting rid of Gambhir and Karthik in no time. Sehwag also departed soon after, caught behind off Ntini, and India were in a mess at 33 for 3.

Uthappa and Rohit Sharma attempted to rescue the innings, but Uthappa survived a dropped catch by Philander before succumbing to Morne Morkel. Rohit Sharma, on the other hand, displayed his talent and flair, hitting some elegant shots through the covers and over the midwicket. The 20-years old, who had made his debut just the previous night and was playing his maiden T20I inning, teamed up with his captain courageous and they built a superb 85-run partnership that shifted the balance of the match.

Rohit Sharma impressed as much with his temperament, as with his dazzling strokeplay, ending the innings with a humongous six over square leg off a Van der Wath full-toss. He remained unbeaten on a brilliant 50 off 40 balls, living up to the hype his name created in the domestic scene back home. Dhoni (45 off 33) was also aggressive, hitting Albie Morkel over long-on with a tennis forehand, and getting a fortunate six over the keeper. Morne Morkel also gave away a massive six over midwicket as he bowled a no-ball, and India finished with a flourish, scoring 56 in the last 5 overs. They reached 153 for 5, and gave themselves a fighting chance in the match. Shaun Pollock with 2 wickets for just 17 runs was the stand out bowler for the Proteas.

South Africa's chase of 154 began with a flurry of runs, as Sreesanth sprayed 4 wides and a boundary in his first over. But that was the only moment of joy for the hosts, as RP Singh ripped through their top order with his lethal swing and disconcerting bounce. He sent back Gibbs and Smith in quick succession, leaving them stunned. Sreesanth then joined the fun, as he nailed de Villiers plumb in front with a delivery that would have hit the middle stump. Kemp and Boucher tried to steady the ship, but they were clueless against the movement in the air and off the pitch. Kemp was run out by a spectacular throw from Rohit Sharma that reminded everyone of the great Jonty Rhodes, and Pollock was bowled by an absolute peach of a delivery from RP Singh, who seemed simply unplayable on this particular day. South Africa were in shambles at 31 for 5.

Boucher and Albie Morkel attempted to rescue the innings, but the asking rate was soaring. Morkel drove Joginder Sharma and Pathan for fours, but the Indian bowlers were mostly accurate and disciplined. Harbhajan Singh leaked 15 runs in his first over, as Boucher hit 3 fours. Morkel also hit a monstrous six off Joginder Sharma, but they still needed 12 runs per over.

The pressure got to them, as Sreesanth came back and bowled Boucher with an inside edge. South Africa then gave up on winning, and aimed for 126 to qualify for the semi-finals. Philander and van der Wath both fell in vain, stumped by Dinesh Karthik - who had taken over from Dhoni behind the stumps after Dhoni suffered some back pain early in the innings - off the Turbanator, but the *coup de grace* came when RP Singh delivered an inch-perfect yorker to finish off Morkel's resistance at 36. The dreaded 'C' word returned to haunt South Africa as India won by 10 runs and booked their semi-final berth against Australia. RP Singh deservedly walked away with the player of the match honour for his dream spell of 4 overs 13 runs and 4 wickets. Sreesanth and Harbhajan also chipped in with a couple wickets each while a resurgent Irfan and Joginder Sharma too kept things tight in the middle overs.

Not a single expert gave this bunch of rag-tag greenhorns any chance before the tournament began, but they surprised everyone with two huge back-to-back wins in the space of 24 hours. Dhoni's boys made all the pundits, and their next opponents, the mighty Aussies, sit up, take notice and reconsider their opinions about the threat this Indian team presented.

Australia had a roller-coaster ride to the semi-final. Coming off a break, the world champions in tests and ODIs had a terrible start here in this new format, losing shockingly to Zimbabwe and then to Pakistan. But they bounced back, winning their next 3 games, including a 10-wicket demolition of Sri Lanka in their last Super-eights game that sealed their semi-final spot and indicated that they were peaking at the right time yet again.

The main architect of that revival was their bowling, with Stuart Clark emerging as the bowler of the tournament so far, with 12 wickets in 5 games at an average of less than 9 and economy of 5.34. Lee and Bracken supported him well. On the batting front, Matthew Hayden was the leading run-scorer of the tourney thus far, with Gilchrist as his partner-in-crime. However, the openers' dominance meant that their middle order had little chance to bat long. Also, the injury that kept their inspirational captain Ricky Ponting out of the Sri Lanka match had still not healed enough for him to be able to take the field in the semis.

India had one more major advantage over Australia going into their semi-final clash. They had played 4 of their 5 matches - even the rained-out game against Scotland - in Kingsmead, Durban, the city boasting of highest number of expat Indians, making the Men in Blue feel right at home.

Thus, the stage was set for another chapter in the hottest rivalry of the decade, as India and Australia locked horns in a blockbuster semi-final to determine who would qualify for the grand finale against Pakistan, who had already booked their berth courtesy of a clinical win against the Kiwis earlier in the day.

MS Dhoni's good run with the coin toss continued and he elected to bat first, hoping to put up a big score on the board. India got off to a steady start, scoring 30 in the first 5 overs, but then lost Sehwag and Gambhir to the fiery Mitchell Johnson in quick succession. They were 41 for 2 at the end of the eighth over, and needed a partnership to revive their innings.

That's when Robin Uthappa and Yuvraj came to the rescue, with Uthappa playing a solid knock of 34 off 28 balls with 3 booming sixes, and Yuvraj going medieval on the Australian bowlers. Back from the injury that kept him out from the previous match, Yuvraj was in absolute beast mode, as he smote 5 fours and 5 sixes in his 30-ball 70, including 3 sixes in a row off Symonds. The final impetus to the inning was provided by captain himself MS Dhoni, who hammered 36 off 18 balls with 4 boundaries and a six, as India posted a formidable total of 188 for 5 in 20 overs.

Australia had a daunting task ahead of them, as they had to chase down 189 at a rate of 9.45 runs per over. They began well, as Gilchrist and Hayden put on 36 runs in 5 overs. But Sreesanth got India the breakthrough, as he clean-bowled the stand-in captain Gilchrist with a beautiful seam delivery. Brad Hodge and Haydos then tried to rebuild the innings, but they were kept in check by Pathan, who also got rid of Hodge for just 11. Hayden was the only batsman who looked comfortable against the Indian attack, as he scored 62 off 47 balls with 4 fours and 4 sixes. But he too couldn't last beyond the 15th over, as Sreesanth cleaned him up with a deadly yorker.

Australia needed 55 runs off the last 5 overs, with Symonds and Hussey at the crease. They tried to accelerate, hitting 22 runs in 12 balls, but Pathan got his payback when he bowled Symonds with a stunning swinging delivery. Clarke came in to join Hussey, but the two Michaels were no match for the pressure and the precision of the Indian bowlers, especially the Turbanator Harbhajan, who spun circles around them and bowled Clarke with a lovely *doosra*. With 22 runs needed off the final over, Joginder Sharma showcased good temperament, bowling a superb over, striking twice and removing Lee and the dangerous Mr. Cricket as Australia finished at 173 for 7 in 20 overs, falling short by 15 runs.

The whole of India rejoiced as their young and unfancied team eliminated the mighty Australia - who had never tasted defeat in a semi-final before - to set up a mouth-watering summit clash with arch rivals Pakistan. It was another remarkable performance by Dhoni's boys who again demonstrated their bravery and talent in a high-octane encounter.

31

Ecstacy, at Last!

Pakistan too had a splendid run to the final, except for that minor blip against India in the first round, where they lost via a bowl-out. They bounced back from that disappointment and beat Sri Lanka, Australia, Bangladesh and New Zealand to make it to the final. Their bowling was their forte, as always, but their batting and fielding also rose to the occasion. Shahid Afridi was the leading candidate for player of the tournament and Shoaib Malik, the Pakistani skipper, guided his young and raw team commendably, just as Dhoni had done for India.

It was a 'Clash of the Titans', as cricketing Gods conspired to finally grant the dream final that every true cricket fan had hoped, wished and fantasized for since the advent of the World Cups. India and Pakistan faced each other in the inaugural Twenty20 World Cup Grand Finale at Wanderers on 24 September 2007. The stakes were as high as could be, the emotions were intense, and the drama was unforgettable.

India had a setback right before the toss, as the explosive Virender Sehwag was ruled out with a groin injury. He had to be replaced with debutant Yusuf Pathan, the elder brother of Irfan, who had a massive responsibility to fill Sehwag's shoes. Dhoni kept his midas touch with the coin toss and stuck to the time-tested formula of batting first in a high-pressure match. Yusuf gave India a flying start, clubbing a six and a four, but his untempered aggression cost him his wicket. He was dismissed by Mohammad Asif for 15 off 8 balls. Robin Uthappa also departed early. India were in trouble at 40/2 in the sixth over, and the young team felt the heat.

But Gautam Gambhir, the top-scorer of the tournament, displayed his class and big-match temperament. He crafted a gritty knock of 75 off 54 balls, holding the innings together and keeping the scoreboard moving. He found a willing ally in Yuvraj Singh and the pair added 63 runs for the third wicket, before Yuvraj fell prey to a sensational second spell by Umar Gul, who bowled him with a yorker. Gul then struck again, knocking over Dhoni's stumps with another yorker. Gambhir tried to break the shackles, and a colossal six that crashed into the scoreboard at midwicket had the Indian fans cheering, but Gul had the last laugh. A flick-paddle went awry and landed in the hands of Asif at short fine leg, ending Gambhir's superb innings, which was studded with 8 fours and 2 sixes.

The scoreboard now read: India 130 for 5 after 18 overs. Enter the 'Hitman' Rohit Sharma, who, in the company of Irfan Pathan, unleashed a late onslaught, plundering 27 invaluable runs in the last 2 overs to boost India's total to a somewhat fighting 157 for 5. The 20-years old remained unbeaten on a 16-ball 30; a cameo whose significance in the context of the game cannot be overstated.

Pakistan had a daunting task ahead of them, chasing 158 in a high-pressure final. The talented Imran Nazir stepped up to the challenge, blasting 33 off 14 balls, including 4 fours and 2 sixes. He took Sreesanth to the cleaners, scoring 21 runs in his second over.

But India fought back, as RP Singh struck twice in his first 2 overs, removing Mohammad Hafeez for 1 and Kamran Akmal for a duck. Imran's brilliance at the other end was cut short by a terrific piece of fielding from Robin Uthappa, who ran him out with a direct-hit. Pakistan were reduced to 53-3 in the sixth over, and the momentum shifted in India's favour.

Pakistan tried to rebuild, reaching 65-3 in the ninth over, when disaster struck again. Irfan Pathan delivered a double blow, dismissing Younis Khan and Shoaib Malik in the same over. He also got rid of Shahid Afridi, the hero of the semi-final, for a first-ball duck. Pakistan were in tatters at 76 for 6 but Misbah found an unlikely ally in Yasir Arafat, who helped him take his side past 100. Pathan, however, struck again, shattering Arafat's stumps for 15 and giving India another crucial breakthrough.

Pakistan looked doomed when they slumped to 104-7 after 16 overs, but Misbah-ul-Haq had other ideas. He revived Pakistan's hopes with a stunning assault of 43 off 38 balls. The valiant Misbah and his lower-order allies plundered 19 runs off Harbhajan Singh's 17th over, 13 off Sreesanth's

18th and 7 off an excellent 19th over bowled by India's bowler of the tournament, RP Singh, leaving just 13 to win from the last over.

Joginder Sharma, a rather quirky choice by India's maverick captain to bowl the all-important final over, started with a wide and then conceded a massive six to Misbah, who brought the target down to 6 from 4 balls.

The third ball was the moment of truth. Misbah tried to play a scoop shot over short fine-leg, but he mistimed it. The ball soared into the sky, and Sreesanth, who was positioned there, kept his cool and grabbed a simple but all-important catch amidst the noise and the pressure. It was an epic end to perhaps the most thrilling finals in the history of the game, as Pakistan's jinx of never beating India in a World Cup or world championship game remained intact. The players rushed to Sreesanth, who was mobbed by his teammates in ecstasy, as India had triumphed by a mere 5 runs to be crowned the first ever Twenty20 World Champions.

It was sweet redemption for Irfan Pathan, who was rightfully adjudged the player of the final for his game-changing spell of 3 for 16, while Shahid Afridi walked away with the player of the tournament award despite falling for a golden duck in the final.

A jubilant Mahendra Singh Dhoni lifted the trophy, and the crowd erupted in joy. It was a historic moment for Indian cricket, a moment that would be etched in the memories of millions of fans. It was a moment of glory, a moment of pride, but more than anything else, it was a moment of redemption, as a side that had been knocked out of a world cup barely six months back, was now crowned World Champions after a long and arduous wait of 24 years.

It was a collective effort by the young Indian team, who had many heroes in their ranks. This world cup witnessed the rise of Gautam Gambhir, who was the backbone of the Indian batting and the highest run-scorer of the tournament, scoring 227 runs in 7 innings, including a magnificent 75 in the final. Virender Sehwag made a smashing comeback to the Indian colours, scoring 68 against England in a must-win game and giving India flying starts with his aggressive batting in many games. Yuvraj Singh set the tournament on fire with his explosive hitting, tonking 6 sixes in an over off Stuart Broad, a first in T20 history. He also scored the fastest fifty in

T20 history, off just 12 balls and came close to repeating the feats in the semi-final against Australia. Rohit Sharma emerged as the brightest young star of the tournament and displayed his talent and temperament to end up as India's second highest run-scorer of the tourney, scoring a match-winning fifty against South Africa and a crucial cameo in the final against Pakistan that made all the difference in the end. Irfan Pathan redeemed himself as an all-rounder, scoring 100 runs and taking 10 wickets, including the 3 he took in the final that earned him the player of the final. Harbhajan Singh too showcased his class as a spinner, weaving magic in the middle overs and choking the run flow while also picking up crucial wickets, including 2 against Australia in the semi-final. Sreesanth was the erratic but effective bowler, who delivered some absolute jaffas, such as the ones that dismissed Gilchrist and Hayden in the semi-final. RP 'Swing' was the leading wicket-taker for India and a close-second overall, taking 12 wickets in the tournament and filling in the shoes of Zaheer Khan admirably.

Team manager Lalchand Rajput deserved credit for the way he managed the young and inexperienced bunch. Bowling coach Venkatesh Prasad and fielding coach Robin Singh too did an admirable job, with fielding in particular showing extraordinary transformation compared to the horrors seen on the previous England tour, underlining the fact that young legs matter.

And last but not the least, the captain, Mahendra Singh Dhoni. Leading any side for the first time in his life, Dhoni emerged not only as a captain but as a maestro orchestrating a symphony of cricketing brilliance. His calm demeanour belied the roaring tempest of pressure, providing a steadying anchor for a team navigating uncharted waters. Dhoni's tactical acumen was a beacon, a guiding light that led his men through the stormiest of matches with precision and grace. His decisions were like strokes of a master painter, each one adding depth and dimension to the canvas of victory. But it was in the crucible of crisis that Dhoni truly shone, his unflinching resolve turning adversity into opportunity. Whether with the bat in hand or with a word of encouragement, he infused his team with a belief that transcended the boundaries of the field. Dhoni was not just a captain; he was a leader who conjured a mosaic of trust, unity and unyielding determination. His influence was the bedrock upon which the triumph of the Twenty20 World Cup was built, etching his name forever in the annals of cricketing legend.

Dhoni's youth brigade earned a whopping $490,000 as the champions of the World Twenty20, while the BCCI rewarded them with an extra $2 million for their splendid performance.

Back home, the reception for the victorious team was nothing short of a grand carnival. Thousands of fans lined the streets, waving flags, cheering, and chanting the names of their cricketing heroes at an open bus parade that was organized in honour of the champions. The victorious players were welcomed as national icons, their faces adorning billboards and newspapers. Dhoni's leadership and composure under pressure became an inspiration for millions, and his iconic 'helicopter' shot became synonymous with his name. The celebrations transcended boundaries of age, gender, region and religion uniting a diverse nation in a shared moment of sporting glory. Former players and cricketing legends, too, joined in the chorus of congratulations. They recognized the historic significance of this victory and praised the young Indian squad for their determination, skill, and sportsmanship. Greats like Kapil Dev and Sunil Gavaskar, who had once brought World Cup glory to India in 1983, expressed their heartfelt joy at witnessing a new generation of cricketers carrying forward the legacy of Indian cricket on the global stage.

Epilogue

As the final pages of this chronicle draw to a close, one cannot help but reflect on the incredible journey that Indian cricket had undertaken in the span of these seven years. From the darkest days of the match-fixing scandal, where the very soul of the sport was called into question, to the euphoric redemption in the form of the Twenty20 World Cup triumph, this tale is one of resilience, determination, and unwavering belief.

The heroes of this saga, both on and off the field, demonstrated that the spirit of cricket is indomitable. They showed that with integrity, discipline, and an unbreakable bond of camaraderie, a team can rise from the ashes to achieve the seemingly impossible. Through the visionary leadership of stalwarts like Sourav Ganguly, Rahul Dravid, and the astute captaincy of Mahendra Singh Dhoni, Indian cricket not only reclaimed its lost glory but also set new benchmarks for excellence.

The journey was marked by countless moments of brilliance, by the blood, sweat and tears of players who wore the blue jersey with pride. From the immortal Sachin Tendulkar to the 'once-in-a-generation' Yuvraj, each player contributed to the grand collage that is Indian cricket. They carried the hopes and dreams of a nation on their shoulders, and in doing so, became forever etched in the hearts of millions.

In the hearts of every Indian cricket lover, the flame of aspiration burned brighter than ever. The echoes of the 1983 World Cup victory and the Twenty20 World Cup triumph of 2007 serve as a constant reminder that the Men in Blue are capable of achieving the extraordinary. With a blend of seasoned veterans and young, fearless talent, the future held boundless potential.

As we turn the page to a new chapter, the promise of the future shone brightly. The dawn of 'Mission 2011' loomed on the horizon, a challenge that this team, forged in the crucible of adversity, seemed more than ready to embrace. The legacy of the past shall serve as a foundation upon which greater triumphs shall be built. The scars of the match-fixing era were now mere footnotes in a story of resurgence, a testament to the power of redemption and the unwavering spirit of a cricket-crazy nation.

As the final words of this chronicle settle on the page, they resonate with a promise, a declaration of intent. **Mission 2011** was well and truly on. The journey continues, the challenges await, but the spirit of Indian cricket, unyielding and resolute, shall carry forth the legacy, painting new chapters of glory on the canvas of the sport we all hold dear.

The saga endures, and the best, one dared to believe, was yet to come.

THE END

In the Pipeline

Book 2 of 'The Century of India' Trilogy: **Reign of Gold – The Decade of Dominance** (*tentative* title)

Recounting the events that took place post the historic high of the 2007 T20 World Cup triumph till the sad exit following a brilliant campaign in the 2015 ODI World Cup, Book 2 delves into a transformative, and arguably **the most successful era** in Indian cricket.

Witness the statesman-like leadership of Anil Kumble as he steers a team in transition through the infamous 'Monkeygate' row in Australia, setting the stage for a new era under the charismatic MS Dhoni. Relive the electrifying moments as Dhoni's fresh-faced squad clinches India's **first-ever VB Series win in Australia** and embarks on an unforgettable journey; first, clinching the **number one ranking in test cricket** for the first time in history & then ascending to the pinnacle of ODI cricket with **the 2011 World Cup victory**, powered by new heroes like Yuvraj and Gambhir.

But the road to glory is paved with challenges. From the emotional farewells of legends like Sourav Ganguly and Anil Kumble to the dazzling debut of the **Indian Premier League**, the narrative captures the pulsating heartbeat of Indian cricket. Feel the highs and lows as the team faces humiliating whitewashes abroad, only to bounce back with a resounding **Champions Trophy win in 2013**. As more stalwarts from the 'Golden Generation' like Tendulkar, Dravid, Laxman, Sehwag, Yuvraj, Harbhajan and Zaheer fade away, new superstars like Virat Kohli, Ravichandran Ashwin, and Rohit Sharma rise to the occasion, heralding a new dawn for Indian cricket.

Get ready to journey through this riveting saga of passion, resilience, and transformation as Indian cricket scales new heights and faces fresh challenges. **Book 2** promises to be an even more epic tale of triumphs and trials, setting the stage for an exhilarating future.

Coming out in Summer 2025!

Acknowledgement/In Gratitude

While my name is on the cover, this book wouldn't exist without the support of so many amazing individuals. First and foremost, I would like to offer my sincerest thanks:

- To the most important woman in my life, **Maa**: your unshakeable belief in me, even when everyone had given up on me, including myself, has been a source of incredible strength. You are the one true love of my life, and being your first-born has been the greatest blessing I could ever ask for.

- To **Ashish**, for being the best younger brother anyone could ever have. Thank you for everything man! I just want you to know that you are the only one I have got in this world. So, please take good care of yourself, because I need you by my side for the next 40 years as well. (Yeah, I am selfish like that)

- To **Gunjan**, whom I affectionately refer to as my *Bahu*: thank you for always being patient and respectful, even though I may not be the most conventional or ideal elder brother-in-law. Your constant support, enthusiasm, and wonderful ideas for the book's marketing and publicity are also deeply appreciated.

- To the second most important woman in my life, for being a profound influence on my life for the past almost thirty years (and counting). Our time together, though brief, was filled with an intensity, depth and 'magic' that remains unforgettable. Some people we just have to learn to love from a distance, but you will always hold a cherished place in my heart.

- To my extended family on both sides, paternal and maternal. I owe much of my understanding of English to the genes I seem to have inherited from my respected grandfather, **Shri Vishwambhar Singh Srivastava**, retired Professor of English in Pokhrayan. I bow down to thee, grand sire!

- To my *Nana ji*, **Shri Suresh Kumar Srivastava**: you have been a true father figure, someone I have always looked up to and shall forever worship. If I can be half the person you are, I will consider my life a success.

- To my *Nanihal*: you are the best *Nanihal* anyone could ever hope for. Thank you for always being there for us, through thick and thin.

- To my alma mater, **Sacred Heart Inter College, Sitapur**: thank you for being the best school ever. I am especially grateful to my favourite teachers—starting with the Head-Mistress Treeza, Miss Deepti, the late Mrs Amita Sinha, Mrs Aarti Mishra, and Miss Rekha—for nurturing and shaping a shy and introverted child into a confident and joyful teenager with their gentle love and support.

- To **Amit Jindal**, my brother-from-another-mother, and the entire Jindal clan: thank you for being my biggest cheerleader and a true pillar of support through all my ups and downs (and, as you know, there have been more downs than ups).

- To my other **close mates** over the years, whom I affectionately refer to as my *Bhailog*—Sachin Srivastava, Piyush Chandok, Mani Sareen, Apurva Saxena, and Sumit Kumar—thank you for being my *Jigris* at various stages of my life and for your lasting brotherhood.

Also, to every single member of the legendary **GreenShields XI**. Those were the most magical years ever!

- To my **special female friends**, whom I affectionately group together as my *Sakhis* or *darling log*—especially Vartika, Yogita, Priyanka, Neelam, Shuchi, Geetanjali, Shaifali, Mansi, the late Shweta, Shivangi, Rachna, Nidhi, Shivani, Reetika, Garima, Pooja, Aarti, Neetu, Azmi, Mehwish, Deepti, Shruti, Tarishi, Shambhavi, Anupriya and Richa—thank you for always being so sporting and supportive over the years. Your continued affection and goodwill have truly enriched my life.

➢ To some **truly remarkable people** whom I've had the honour of befriending on Facebook and hope to meet in person someday: Mr. Rajiv Tyagi, whom I fondly address as my Gurudev, whose recommendation led me to choose Notion Press for this book; Darshan Mondkar; Nitin Joshi; Mohit Kumar; Abhishek Asthana, better known as @GabbbarSingh on Twitter; Mr. Atanu Banerjee; the eminent Ranjana Sengupta & Team A Suitable Agency, for their kindness; Dr Shivani Salil; the visionary Sahana Ahmed; Miss Sarvapriya Sangwan; the great Anil Yadav & Krishna Kalpit; Mr. Shailendra Pratap Singh (Retired IPS, UP Police); Miss Shruti Gautam; Sushobhit (whom I no longer interact with but still hold in the highest of regards as a writer); the Pride of Sitapur, Vaibhav Raj Gupta (of the 'Gullak' fame); Rumika Joshi, Abhishek AJ & Kanwaljeet Singh. Thank you all for inspiring me to attempt this in some way or another.

➢ A special shout-out to my Orkut Cricket Community (**OCC**) brethren: Masud Vorajee, Vibhore Singh, Kuldip Nair, Pratik Tatikola, Anil KV, the unforgettable Ravi M, Alex Thomas, Imran Mirza, Mahak Vyas, Vibhor Daga, Keshav Bapat, Aamir Ismail, Faraz Zaidi, Vishal Vasavada, Subhradip Saha, Nilesh Kulkarni, Dhananjay Shettigar, Arjun Sinha, Pratik R, Saurabh Mathur, Anil Kumar, Abhishek Vora, Aditya Pandit, Parameswaran Subramanian, Sree Kirakodu and Siddharth Chhaya. Thank you all for being such an integral part of my cricket journey.

➢ To **ESPNcricinfo & YouTube**, for being the primary and most valuable resources in the writing of this book.

➢ To **Notion Press Publishing** and their wonderful production team, especially Abhinesh Rolla, Puja Chand Deupa, and my wonderful Publishing Manager Joshua Nethan, for turning my manuscript into a beautifully designed book.

➢ To each and every member of the '**Class of 2000**,' for being the heart and soul of this book and serving as the main cast of this narrative. You all are true icons and role models, who have given us countless memorable moments and, more importantly, restored the faith of millions of fans in Indian cricket after it's darkest period.

And last, but by no means the least,

➤ To the wonderful game of **Cricket**: thank you for still being my one true source of solace, even after all these years!

About The Author

Sudeept Shrivastav is a seasoned explorer of both code and cricket, and an avid pursuer of the profound power of words. At 42, he revels in the journey of a happily unmarried life based out of Pune, where his heart beats to the rhythm of leather on willow, his soul finds solace in the world of storytelling, and his spirit soars on two wheels.

While he may bear the mantle of a (reluctant) software engineer by vocation, his true calling has always been that of a Seeker, exploring the unexplored and finding the extraordinary in the ordinary, often while riding a Steel Horse; & a connoisseur of cricket, unearthing the untold stories that echo within the hallowed grounds of the sport.

Beyond writing, cricket, and riding, Sudeept is deeply passionate about social causes. He goes by just his first name, a protest against the casteism prevalent in Indian society. He also organized a free ration and lunch packets drive during the first lockdown, with the help of some friends, to support migrant labourers in need. Additionally, he is a registered eye and organ donor—few gestures that quietly enrich his life and reflect his values.

Sudeept aspires to take up writing full-time, fuelled by a relentless passion to craft narratives that resonate and leave an indelible mark on readers' hearts. His debut book captures the essence of his journey, blending his love for cricket with his talent for storytelling.

www.ingramcontent.com/pod-product-compliance
Lightning Source LLC
Chambersburg PA
CBHW051129130726
47988CB00005B/1769